LOVE IN ACTION
THE SOCIOLOGY OF
SEX

Dr. Fernando Henriques M.A.

Lecturer in Social Anthropology, Leeds University

Love in Action

THE SOCIOLOGY OF SEX

★

Illustrated

NEW YORK

E. P. DUTTON & CO., INC.

1960

CONTENTS

LIST OF PLATES

LIST OF PLATES

ILLUSTRATIONS IN THE TEXT

LOVE IN ACTION
THE SOCIOLOGY OF
SEX

CHAPTER I

Preparation for Sexual Life

To discuss sexual behaviour as a manifestation of social life it is necessary to divide human society into categories. We can make certain simple divisions. On the one hand there is a majority of human societies that are characterised by a primitive or simple technology; on the other hand our own, or Western, type of society that possesses an advanced technology. In between there are societies progressing from one stage to the other. Unfortunately the term 'primitive' carries overtones of inferiority. For the ordinary person the word conjures up a brutish, confused existence in squalor and filth. We hope to make it clear that this is far from the truth. A simple technology, such as that of the Australian Aborigines, does not necessarily imply a simple social structure, or one which is in any way inferior to our own. In fact these aborigines possess a highly complex system of social relationships.

Another way of distinguishing the main categories of societies is to speak of one division as pre-literate, that is those peoples whose languages remain purely oral. But whatever term is used (and there are many), primitive, simple, pre-literate, or savage, one should remember that it is not an emotional description but merely a useful method of distinguishing one group from another. Connected with the picture of the inferior 'primitive' in many people's minds is the idea that such societies represent stages on the way, or evolution, or development through which we in our society have already passed. They are, as it were, cases of arrested development. This, of course, is nonsense. All contemporary human societies are separated from their origins by the same time interval. Each has followed its particular line of development or evolution. There is not one line of development: there are many.

In analysing the sexual and social behaviour of man, we must dispense with the emotional and concentrate on the facts.

All individuals pass through phases of development from birth to death. These phases, depending upon the society, are either marked by elaborate rites and ceremonies, or emphasised in a moderate way, or are partially ignored. For example, no people allows death to pass unnoticed—it is a time of crisis for those related to the dead person and, at the simple level, for the society at large. Again marriage in a majority of societies is regarded as an event of major importance. It creates new social bonds and is the precursor of a new family. It must be marked in an appropriate way. A minority of societies at both the simple and advanced levels distinguish the occasion in an elementary way. Our own is partially of this kind. The individual may marry with great public demonstration, or he may observe the simple requirements of the law before a registrar, unnoticed by all.

Of these phases of development adolescence is as much a time of crisis as death or marriage. Amongst the simple peoples this is generally recognised in relation to boys, and less so in relation to girls. The French sociologist, A. van Gennep,([1]) called these phases of development *rites de passage*, that is literally, rites of passage from one stage to another in life. It is clear that in small-scale society such events must be of paramount importance. It is less so in the case of so-called advanced peoples. In a large scale-society, such as our own, we are no longer bound together by ties of blood and clan. Our wider relationships are characterised by the impersonal and anonymous. Interests and loyalties are bound up with our jobs and homes, and with a remote 'State.' Puberty rites and initiation ceremonies, characteristic at the simple level, would be meaningless and out of place in our kind of society. Nevertheless, the fact that we very largely deny the existence of a social status for adolescence does not mean that it is not a time of crisis for those involved. That there is need of some recognition from the society, formal or otherwise, is clear if contemporary youth cults are studied. The 'zoot' suit movement of the thirties and forties in the United States, the English Teddy Boys and their Russian equivalents, and, perhaps in a slightly different category, the 'Beat Generation' of the American West Coast, are all manifestations of the youth's bewilderment and anxiety at his in-between status of neither boy nor man. That more youth clubs and 'Outward Bound' schools may be the answer is debatable.

If the western world looks upon male adolescence as a kind of disease out of which the boy will grow, the simple societies do not. To them adolescence is a time when the boy must be prepared for life as a man. He must be trained to fulfil his proper role as a full member of the society. This means he must not only acquire the skills necessary for survival and learn the duties and obligations that will rest upon him, but he must also be prepared for sexual life, for he is to be a husband and father. To carry out these aims there are initiation and puberty rites, which naturally vary greatly from society to society. Basically, however, they are concerned to give the boy knowledge and security regarding his approaching adult status. Secret lore may be imparted; there may be rigorous tests of skill and endurance; wounds may be inflicted. Van Gennep demonstrated that there were always three stages in rites of passage: separation, transition, and incorporation. This is very clearly brought out in the puberty rites of many societies. In a number of cases initiation is closely linked to age-grade associations. These are groups, composed of individuals of similar age, which may have important social and ritual functions. The existence of such associations often entails a successive series of initiations as the individual progresses from grade to grade. This is the case amongst the Murngin tribes of Australia.[2]

An example of what may be regarded as fairly typical of puberty rites in general exists amongst the Kipsigis. The Kipsigis are an African Negro people living in Kenya, east of Lake Victoria. The great Tumdo ceremony is an extremely important event. It consists according to Peristiany of four main elements.

'(1) Circumcision, without which no marriage or sexual relations (for the boys) can be established with other members of the tribe.

'(2) Initiation into the secret rituals of the tribe. This is one of the strongest links uniting not only the Kipsigis, but all the Nilo-Hamitic tribes of Kenya.

'(3) Teaching in tribal custom received at the hands of the Motirenik (sponsors) and the elders; also infliction of bodily pain to harden the physical endurance of the youngsters.

'(4) A *rite de passage* separating childhood from adult membership of the tribe.' (3)

There are six main ceremonies dealing with such things as circumcision, purification, and instruction in tribal lore. The Tumdo in fact applies to the first initiation a boy goes through. But 'At every stage of his existence the Kipsigis must perform a certain ceremony or be initiated into some special duties related to his age. . . .' (4)

An initiation ceremony can take place at any time, except during the rainy season. The age of an initiate varies between fourteen and eighteen years. The number of boys for a particular ceremony will number five to ten. An old man (he is called pamango, father) is chosen to be the mentor of the boys. They live with him for a period and he feeds them. He receives a payment of a female animal from the boys' fathers. One month before the circumcision rite the boys visit their fathers' relatives and their mothers' brother. The pamango then organizes the boys to build a hut (menjit) near his house in the bush. On the day of the ceremony everyone is dressed up and painted, the women are garlanded. Displays of dancing and singing are given in front of their parents' houses. These preliminaries terminate comparatively near to the menjit initiation hut. The evening is now given over to the adults. Round a large fire the warriors sing and dance. As the time goes on restraints are loosened and married women dispense their favours where they please.

At dawn the boys are conducted by their sponsors to the hut of an old man where they are stripped. A corridor of sticks has previously been made in the hut. The whole passage is covered with stinging nettles. Both the sponsors have only the minimum of clothing. One leads the way into the corridor, the boys follow, the other sponsor brings up the rear. This passage of the stinging nettles is repeated four times. At no time must the boys utter cries of pain. The elders sit round the hut waiting to laugh if this happens. The ritual is clearly a test of the boys' endurance, and the Kipsigis say it stops the flow of blood after circumcision.

After the ordeal of the nettles the boys are taken one by one into the darkest corner of the hut. A sponsor tells the boy that under some monkey skins is a terrible being with a gigantic penis. Then follows a most extraordinary colloquy in which the boy is questioned as to whether he has copulated with a woman. If he admits to this the woman has to be purified by proxy (as she is unknown) in a special ceremony, otherwise she will remain barren and unclean. 'The motiryot (sponsor) will now threaten the boy that, if he does not reveal his sexual life at once, the "thing" beneath the skins will come that very same night while he sleeps and perform sodomy on him; "his penis is so huge that you will surely die". The man who is hidden beneath the skins begins now to move, uttering ferocious grunts of "Moo-moo", hence his name of Arap Mogoss. The boy is by now thoroughly terrified. The motiryot takes him apart and asks him the same question in private, and if his answer is still negative, he leads him back to the heap of skins. There behind Arap Mogoss's back and the skins covering him, hide two more men, one with a squeaky feminine voice and the other holding a stick in a narrow hole where water has previously been introduced. If the boy denies copulation, the feminine voice issues from the skin, saying: "Only last night you were sleeping with me; do not deny it. You were holding my legs so fast that you nearly broke them; do not deny it," and so on giving more and more details about the boy's physique and the alleged intercourse, while the other man, by rotating the stick in the wet hole, produces a sound imitating that of coitus. The boy is then flattered by the motiryot "You are a clever boy; you can surely tell us what this is"; and if he does his lies may be found out. . . .' [5]

After this if the boy persists in his denial he is told that he may slap Arap Mogoss, but if he tries to do so he is led away. The boys are now led to the fire and informed that the circumcision knife is in the fire. They are told if they rush through the fire they will come out circumcised. Again, if they attempt this they are prevented. A further ordeal now occurs. A boy is led to a stool covered with nettles. His head is covered and he is told to sit down. Naturally the pain makes him jump up, but the performance has to be repeated four times. Another ordeal is over.

Now the circumcision is about to take place. The boys are taken before the 'Elder of the Ceremony' who marks the foreskin of each to indicate where the incision will be made. The boys now sit down. Behind each is a man of his father's generation. Opposite sits their father or an elder brother who generally places a stick in the ground and tells the boy to look at it or he will be beaten by it. It may happen that the 'Elder of Ceremony' is too old to operate and his function is taken over by a skilled man. The operation consists of cutting off the marked part of the foreskin, but not all the skin is trimmed off. A slit is made in the remaining skin and the penis is pulled through, the skin being fastened on either side by a thorn. This will fall out when the wound is healed.

Throughout the ordeals and the operation not the slightest cry or indication of pain by the initiate must be given. In fact very few do succumb to the pain. A boy will wear an amulet or bracelet given him by his girl friend. If he has proved his manhood satisfactorily she will treasure it always. On the other hand if he has cried out he has to throw the amulet into the bush. But there are more serious consequences than that. When the initiation is completed he will be known as a coward and be humiliated and ostracized, and in the end may be forced to move away from the village.

Curiously enough after circumcision the boy is regarded as being even more unclean than before. Now he cannot touch food or sacred things with his hands but use only his mouth or leaves.

At suitable intervals the other ceremonies, marked by meticulous detail of rites, take their course until after more than six months the boy is finally declared fully initiated. From this time on he may copulate with or marry any of those girls with whom it is permissible to do so.

The Kipsigis also have initiation ceremonies for girls which are very similar to the male rites, with some obvious differences. Clitoridectomy, that is the removal of the clitoris, takes the place of circumcision. Again, a girl may admit to having a lover in her songs when she asks the other girls to have nothing to do with him.

'. . . When the girls are due to retire, the old women form a circle round the hut and, addressing the men, sing the following song, "Let us refuse him who has no erection this night" the meaning being that the men will now have to abstain from intercourse with their sweethearts, who will be kept secluded in the hut. . . .'(6)

'What is the purpose of initiation? To sharpen the endurance of the initiate, to make good warriors out of men, and to teach women to love and care for their husband's cattle. To teach men that they are part of a complicated organisation, family, clan, pursuit, and age-set, to each of which they must show obedience.'

'Do the initiation ceremonies really fulfil their purpose? . . .'(7) The answer according to Peristiany seems to be that they do. It appears that the boys take as long as six months to recover from their dreadful experience. They seem for a long time to be completely at a loss, incapable of talking intelligently about anything. But when they do recover they are quite normal. They have shared an unique experience—they belong to a group, and they have started to be men.

This type of induction into society is extremely widespread amongst the pre-literate peoples. Examples from North America, Australia and New Guinea all bear out the implications of the Kipsigis ceremonies—manhood must be tested, instruction must be given. To be a man it is necessary to be able to survive physical pain. This belief must be seen against the background of life in the simple society. Survival of the individual and his family may depend upon his qualities of endurance and his skills. Thus the pattern of pain in initiation is repeated in society after society at this level. For example, flagellation with whips, thistles, or branches is a constant motif in the initiation rites of North American Indians. Catlin gives numerous examples of terrifying ordeals to which Indian boys were subject which are only equalled by the tortures of concentration camps.(8) In South America a favourite test was the handling of virulent ants by the initiate. He might, as amongst the Macuri Indians of Guiana, be sewn up in a hammock with ants.(9) All to be endured without a cry!

The same picture of cruelty and endurance is exemplified by African societies as well as those of Central Asia and Melanesia. The practice is so widespread that it would suggest that it fulfils the same need in each case—to demonstrate your ability physically and mentally to be a man.

Another feature which is characteristic of initiation is the seclusion of the initiate from his fellows. This was shown in the case of the Kipsigis where the boys are taken from their families for the whole period of initiation. In many North American Indian tribes there is a preliminary period of seclusion before the ordeals when the boy will have to wander in the prairie by himself for several days without food. After initiation the individual is restored to his society complete with his new status.

In European society there are few instances of initiation in the sense we have described. It appears that the admission of the Spartan boy to manhood was conducted in a most severe manner. At a later period in Europe the nearest approximation to initiation is that of the training and vigil of the would-be knight. But this applied only to a very small section of the people.

From the evidence it appears that initiation ceremonies are confined to the less advanced peoples. In general the emphasis is on male initiation. Where girls are initiated it is usually as a necessary preliminary to marriage, as for example among the Bánaro of New Guinea. An exceptional society is that of the Shasta, a Californian Indian tribe. These people have no initiation rites for men, only for girls.[10]

Male circumcision, which as we saw is an integral part of Kipsigi initiation, is an extremely widespread phenomenon. It appears to form part of the preliminaries to be gone through before the boy is deemed capable of sexual intercourse and marriage. What might be called the classical form, that is the excision of the prepuce, seems to be almost entirely confined to the Semitic peoples, the Jews and the Arabs, and to peoples influenced by them. It is, of course, the form favoured by contemporary Europe and America. The reasons for its current vogue in our midst is not due to our anxiety for boys to fulfil their sexual function, but solely on grounds of supposed hygiene. In Britain there is royal example to be followed. It is said that when a prominent infant male member of the royal family was to be circumcised, notable surgeons were passed over, on grounds of inexperience of the operation, in favour of an old Jewish rabbi who had been responsible for thousands of such cases.

Among some Arabs a particularly revolting form of circumcision called Al-salkh is practised. The penis is stripped of skin in its entire length, and all the hairy skin surrounding it is cut away. The operation is performed in the presence of the boy's father and his intended bride. Burton states that if the boy cried out the father would at once kill him, and that a fifth of the boys die as a result of the operation.[11] It is also said that the girl, if the boy shows the pain he is suffering, will shout out that he is a woman and she will have nothing more to do with him.

Simple excision of the prepuce together with slitting (sub-incision) the penis along the urethra is found among a number of Australian peoples. It is only after the second operation that the boys are ready for marriage. According to one report it also has a practical use. For these subincised men act as sexual partners to boys who have not yet been initiated and who are forbidden to copulate with women. They may even form quite durable unions.[12]

The Australian operation has been described as follows '. . . At a certain signal the novice is laid upon his back, the assistant of the operation grasps the foreskin and pulls it out as far as possible, whereupon the operator with a quick movement severs it with a small stone knife. The blood from the wound is allowed to flow into a shield, and, in a dazed condition, the Wurtya is taken back to his brake where he receives the congratulations of the men, who inform him that he is now a proper man. . . . Meanwhile the youth stands over a dampened fire the smoke of which is supposed to be efficacious in healing the wound. . . .'[13] After the boy has re-covered from this operation preparations are made for the second and major rite. '. . . Upon a certain day before dawn everything is ready. The novice is not told what is about to happen to him. When he arrives at the ceremonial ground he is told to lie down flat upon a living table formed by two initiated men; as soon as he is in position another man sits down astride his body and grasping the Arakurta's (initiate) penis puts it on the stretch; the operator then quickly approaches, and with a stone knife lays open the perile portion of the urethra. This operation over, the Arakurta is now regarded as having passed to the stage of an Atua-kurka, or initiated man. The blood from the wound is allowed to flow into a shield, which is then emptied into a fire. . . . If the wound be painful the initiate puts some glowing pieces of charcoal into the ashes and then urinates upon them, the steam thus arising from the fire is said to ease the pain. Until the wound is healed the Atua-kurka must lie upon his back, otherwise it is believed his penis will grow crooked. . . . It often happens that at the conclusion of the Arilta operation, other initiated men, who are present and who have already been

operated upon on some previous occasion, will voluntarily offer to
undergo a second and third operation. In such cases the old incision
is enlarged. . . .'(14)

In our view it is quite terrifying and revolting but apparently to
the Australian something which gives prestige and should be
experienced more than once!

A method of circumcision more widely practised than the
Australian one is to make a slit over the foreskin. This often leaves

Fig. 1. A type of male infibulation

scars or cicatrices which may be highly prized. This method is
found all over Polynesia and in many Melanesian areas in the
Pacific, as well as in Malaya. It also occurs in Africa amongst the
Masai and Kikuyu tribes which have been subject to Moslem–Arab
influence and have adopted the Semitic mode of excision of the
prepuce.

A somewhat peculiar variant of circumcision occurs in certain
tribes of Indonesia and Papua, such as the Kiwai, Bisasya, and

Bataks. This is the actual boring of a hole through the penis by a sharp piece of wood. Objects are then inserted in the penis. In copulation the effect is to produce lacerations in the vagina of the woman who is said to enjoy the voluptuous sensations so produced![15]

The mildest kind of male circumcision appears to have occurred in the Americas. In Indian tribes of South America, for example, the commonest form consisted of making a small slit or incision of the prepuce. Elsewhere scarification was usual.

It is difficult to reconcile the various views about male circumcision which have been expressed from time to time. The rationalization amongst ourselves that it is a sanitary measure has little to recommend it. What is quite clear is that in the majority of cases where it occurs it serves to demonstrate that the boy has been reborn physically and socially into a new status, that of a man. The sexual organ is the means of generation, the means whereby he demonstrates his manhood. After circumcision he can now enter full sexual life.

Whereas male circumcision can be shown to have a highly symbolic function it appears that female cirumcision is possibly of a much more practical nature. In many instances it is really a form of artificial defloration. For example, the Arunta women in Australia have performed on them what is called 'cutting the vulva'. Which in fact very often means that not only is the hymen cut but the clitoris itself may be amputated, as well as pieces of the labia minora.[16] Similarly in some tribes of the Amazon basin and Northern Peru a girl is subjected to this operation after she has been intoxicated. What follows is indicative of the essentially sexual implications of female circumcision. A penis made from clay of the supposed dimensions of the sexual organ of her prospective husband is inserted in the vagina. This completes the ceremony and she is ready to be wed.[17]

Circumcision of girls is common in many parts of Negro Africa. It generally includes excision of part of the labia minora and clitoris but not penetration of the hymen.[18] This seems to be an indigenous practice, but it is also typical of Arab societies in the north. It is not mentioned in the Koran but some Muslim authorities, while not enjoining it, recommend it. On the other hand the Ethiopian Jews regard it as essential. Some Indian peoples have the same custom but it is by no means widespread in India. Similarly in Malaya and Indonesia a minority of tribes insist upon female circumcision.

There seems to be no evidence that European societies have ever practised female circumcision. The advice given by a Greek doctor, in classical times, that women in Greece should be circumcised, does not seem to have been adopted.[19]

There is no evidence that the Greeks practised male circumcision either. Strabo (XVII, 284) writes of circumcision as an Egyptian and Jewish custom. The Greeks did, however, have a method of infibulation for males whereby the foreskin was drawn forward over the end of the penis and securely tied. This was done as a protection against possible damage in gymnastic exercises. The Romans, from whom the word is derived, used a fibula (stitching needle) inserted through the prepuce to prevent copulation.[20]

Regarding the age at which circumcision is performed on girls in different societies a table is given in H. Ploss and M. & P. Bartels's monumental work, *Woman* (English edition, 1935, edited by E. J. Dingwall, vol. 1, p. 346).

As we have said, female circumcision is connected with defloration. In the same way defloration forms part of a complexus of custom of which the other components are infibulation, that is the closing of the sexual orifice, and defibulation. These practices are dependent in great part on the attitude of the peoples concerned towards virginity and sexual purity in woman.

Societies throughout the world appear to be divided into those with a deep regard for virginity and pre-nuptial chastity, those with a vaguely restrictive attitude, and those that permit and approve pre-marital sex relations. Various estimates have been made as to the proportion in the latter category. For pre-literate peoples in selected samples the figures have varied from 40 to 70 per cent.[21] It would seem that in such cultures there is probably a majority that approve, either openly or otherwise, of pre-marital sexual activity. We shall discuss such societies later on.

There is no Western type of society that openly approves such sex relations. To do so would be in direct contradiction of the Christian sexual ethic. It is possible to place our society in a special category, as some writers have done.[22] It is perhaps more accurate to place it in the second category of vague restriction. From the earliest days of Christianity there has been an ambivalent attitude towards sex relations outside of, and before marriage. This ambivalence has been illustrated in the behaviour of all classes. Some peasant European groups in Holland, Austria, Germany, Switzerland, Norway, Portugal, and Italy have, in defiance of the Church's teaching, indulged in pre-marital sex relations, respectability and ecclesiastical approval being attained after pregnancy and marriage.[23]

Upper-class amours and liaisons are of course notorious throughout European history. The extraordinary phenomenon of romantic love and chivalry with its accompaniment of seduction, adultery and illicit love is indicative of the same ambivalence.

Today in Britain and America statistical evidence shows the same conflict between publicly expressed ideas regarding sexual behaviour and actual practice. The Victorian obsession with female virginity seems to have very largely disappeared. It was at its peak when men were discreetly permitted to keep a mistress or frequent a brothel, but had to marry a virgin. Contemporary evidence from the United States indicates the change in attitude.

' . . . The data shows that 3 per cent of the females in the total sample (5940), irrespective of the age at which they had married, had had coital experience by fifteen years of age, 20 per cent had had it between the ages of sixteen and twenty years, and 35 per cent had it between twenty-one and twenty-five years of age. In the next twenty years something over 40 per cent of the unmarried females were having some pre-marital coitus. . . .'[24]

Figures from other European societies are comparable to those from the U.S.A. In Australia, out of a sample of one hundred European girls who married between seventeen and twenty-three, 20 per cent had had sexual experience, and of those married after thirty, 70 per cent.[25] For Britain Comfort states, 'The practice of one or both types of pre-marital intercourse is extremely widespread in our own society. In 1938, 40 per cent of girls marrying under twenty, 30 per cent marrying at twenty, and 20 per cent marrying at twenty-one were pregnant at the time of marriage, and these figures represent only that proportion of cases in which conception took place. They could probably be doubled to cover all forms of pre-marital experience in coitus.[26]

It seems as if a progressive shift is taking place in attitudes. In our society the prize of the virgin in marriage is giving way to sexual enjoyment on the part of both sexes before marriage. The churches are fighting a desperate rearguard action to maintain what are called 'moral standards'. They are in fact bound to lose, for the type of sexual freedom now in vogue shows no signs of diminishing in strength. It will be interesting to see what adaptations, or concessions, the churches are prepared to make in face of this remarkable revolution.

'. . . Virginity at marriage will be close to the vanishing point for males born after 1930, and for females born after 1940 . . . intercourse with future spouse before marriage will become universal by 1950 or 1955. . . .'[27]

The dichotomy between public affirmation of pre-nuptial sexual purity for women and current social behaviour produces conflict which is perhaps in part responsible for the type of aberrant adolescent behaviour already mentioned. But it is possible for apparent reconciliation between the two to take place. This is seen in the West Indies. The predominantly detribalised Negro population does not accept the standards set by a minority of the population in relation to sexual ethics. Nevertheless the Christian denominations flourish side by side with the highest illegitimacy rate in the world. As we have tried to show elsewhere the use of the ordinary sense of illegitimacy in this context is meaningless. Sexual unions outside of marriage have become the norm.[28]

A much greater public tolerance of pre-marital sexual activity exists in contemporary Sweden than in Britain. The result is the highest illegitimacy rate in Europe (over 12 per cent in 1939). This is in obvious conflict with the teaching of the Lutheran Church (the state church of the country) in this matter, which is nevertheless well supported. There are other contradictions in Swedish society, such as the attitude towards alcohol and homosexuality, which we cannot discuss here.[29]

Coincident with the regard for virginity in Europe there developed methods of deceiving the husband on his wedding-night, or hoodwinking the client of the brothel. These varied from surreptitious staining of the bridal sheets to the insertion of minute breakable containers in the vagina which would puncture on contact and send forth the desired colouring matter. Tiny blood-soaked sponges were also placed in the vagina. A former Persian practice was for a surgeon to put a few stitches in the labia prior to the wedding night.[30] The burden of remaining a virgin but enjoying intercourse is well illustrated by a story attributed to Cervantes, *La tia fingida*.

The aunt (tia) of the story is the perfect pander and prepares her niece well for her part. The niece, however, protests at the suffering the constant restoration of virginity imposes upon her. '. . . I will not be tortured by your hand again, however much you may offer

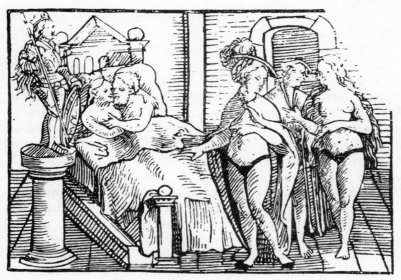

Fig. 2. Women wearing mediaeval chastity belts

me. Three flowers have I already given away; just as many as your ladyship has sold, and three times have I gone through unbearable pain. Am I then made of brass? Has my flesh no feeling? Do you know of no better way of doing it than sewing it with a needle like a torn dress? By the holiness of my mother, whom I have never known, I will not undergo it again. Let me now, Aunt, keep the gleanings in my vineyard for, in many cases, the gleaning tastes better than the first crop. If, however, you have determined to sell my garden pure and intact, then seek another milder way of closing the portal, for you must not imagine that my flesh will again approach a locking with silk twist and needle.' The aunt replies with great experience. 'You silly, there is nothing on this earth to be compared with needles and flesh-coloured twisted silk: all else is trumpery. Sumac and ground glass are of little use, leeches less, myrrh is of no use at all, neither is sea onion, nor pigeon's crop, nor any other loathsome and disgusting mixture that one has—for nowadays no man is such a ninny. If he pays the least attention to what he is doing, he at once perceives the use of counterfeit coin. Long live my thimble and needle; long live at the same time, thy patience and endurance. . . .'[31]

The appetite and obsession for virgins as brides, and as inmates of brothels in Europe, continued to the end of the nineteenth century.

The pre-literate societies, in this category of lip service to female virginity, vary considerably in their attitudes. For example, the Yakut of Siberia seem to favour a variant of the European chastity belt. Pubescent girls were condemned to wear a pair of thick leather breeches, well fastened both day and night: a most effective means of protection.[32] A fairly typical pattern in a considerable number of societies is 'you can do what you like so long as we don't know about it'. This is found in several North American Indian tribes such as the Kiowa Apache, Kickapoo, the Klamath and Seminole; in African societies such as the Azande, Chagga and Yako, as well as in the Pacific among the Orokaiva and the Alorese. The Andamanese in the Indian Ocean also have this semi-tolerant attitude.

In such societies adolescents indulge in numerous affairs which are theoretically hidden from the parents. Flagrant behaviour, however, will lead to punishment. Pregnancy is generally followed by an arranged marriage. In the majority of instances the type of intercourse for these young people is either coitus interruptus or interfemoral (between the thighs). In addition there are various contraceptive expedients in use, varying from pads to medicines, and abortifacients.

The rule seems to be in many of these primitive societies in this category, as well as in those that prohibit such activity altogether, that restrictitions are applied much more to girls than to boys. It may be forbidden to boys before initiation, as we saw in the case of the Kipsigis and the Australian Aborigines, but after initiation the world is open. It is very similar to the attitude of European society which looks on a young man's sexual adventures as sowing his wild oats, but is liable to condemn utterly the unmarried mother. The girl may not be so severely dealt with as in Europe, but she is liable to meet with disapproval.

In the first category of societies, those that place restrictions on pre-marital sexual activity, differing attitudes can be discerned. One section, the largest, insists, or attempts to insist, on chastity for girls prior to puberty but relaxes prohibitions after the first menses. The Ashanti of West Africa, the Siberian Chuckchee, the Ao of Assam, and the Lamba and Swazi of Central Africa come within this group. The same rules apply to boys in these and other societies. The rationalisation here being that until you have become *socially* a man or a woman, which is what initiation makes you, sexual intercourse is dangerous and unhealthy.

Another group of societies in this category continues to prohibit intercourse after puberty until marriage. The attitude of such peoples as the American Indian Arapaho, Cheyenne, and Papago, is somewhat similar to that of the contemporary Americans and British who try to insist on virginity in the nubile girl but forgive the young man his sexual transgressions.

To achieve this aim of preventing adolescent sexual activity different methods are adopted—the variation is considerable. The most obvious way is to prohibit sexual play of any kind by the young child. The Ashanti boy is gravely warned by his father not to masturbate. The Kwoma carry the warning a stage further by beating the penis of any boy seen with an erection. Various punishments are enforced but clearly it is almost impossible to prevent manifestations of sexual play unless the children are constantly watched.

The sexual talk of adults is another danger which must be guarded against. Accurate sex information can be withheld as successfully as it was in our own society until recently. For example, amongst the Chagga of Tanganyika the gooseberry bush and stork interpretations of childbirth are very popular. While, of course, children will play their secret sexual games and see animals copulating there is also the danger of the literal example of adults. In the crowded living and sleeping conditions of primitive life this constitutes a serious problem. As in overcrowded working-class homes in Europe and America, all the parent can do is to wait until the children are presumed asleep, and then copulate.

With the young man or young girl, as distinct from the child, the

problem of control is much greater. Segregation in separate sleeping quarters, typical of many societies, does not necessarily provide
a solution as there are so many opportunities for clandestine meetings. Supervision by adults is subject to the same disadvantage, it
cannot be enforced continuously. An unique solution to the whole
problem is provided by a tribe in British Guiana, the Wapisiana. If
a couple sleep together they automatically become married without
more ado.

Unfortunately not all societies have remained content with an
ideal of virginity safeguarded by somewhat ineffective means. A
group of societies in North-East and Central Africa (Galla, Somali,
Danakil, some Beduin groups, Harari) practise what is known as
infibulation, that is the sewing up of the vulva. This is the only
absolutely effective method of preserving female virginity. In
order to produce infibulation it is necessary for the labia to be cut or
excised; the raw tissue then forms a congealed scar so blocking the
vulva, or in some instances the flesh is sewn together. Either a small
opening is left for menstruation and the passage of urine or this is
made after the infibulation has taken place. Amongst the Somali
clitoridectomy, that is the excision of the clitoris, is practised in
conjunction with infibulation, but this is not so for all the peoples
mentioned. Infibulation is generally performed between the ages of
five and eight years.

F. Peney gives the following account of Sudanese infibulation.
A feast is prepared to which female friends and relations are invited.
Prior to this the child has been put in charge of the woman who is to
perform the operation. ' . . . When the hour comes, the child is
laid on a bed and held down and in position by the assembled
women, while the matron, kneeling between the patient's thighs,
begins by slicing off the tip of the clitoris and the edges of the inner
lips, then the razor shears along the rims of the outer lips, removing
a ribbon of flesh about two inches wide. It lasts between four and
five minutes. In order to drown the shrieks of the girl, the assembled
guests and kin raise the loudest and shrillest din conceivable until
the process is over. Then, when the flowing blood has been
staunched, the girl is laid flat on her back, her legs extended and tied
firmly together so that she cannot walk, otherwise the desired
effect would not be produced. Before leaving the girl to the healing
process of nature, the matron introduces a hollow cylinder of

wood, about as thick as a goose's feather, into the lower portion of
the vagina, between the bleeding edges of the wound, and this is
kept in place until the scar is completely formed, for purposes of
menstruation and micturition. This tiny orifice is all that remains of
the vaginal outlet. . . .'[33]

There is no question that this type of female circumcision is most
effective in its practical aspects—the protection of virginity, but
there may be other sociological reasons for its existence as Nadel
suggests. '. . . Female circumcision never appears by itself in the
Nuba Mountains: it accompanies or succeeds the adoption of
juvenile male circumcision. It thus comes to impress the conception
of a balance of the sexes . . . that female life should parallel male
life, and a *rite de passage* of the women duplicate one of the men.
Indeed, where female circumcision appears, this conception of
balance is deeply rooted in the social structure. . . .'[34]

In other words female circumcision is the equivalent of male
circumcision: the one marks the onset of manhood, the other
emphasises the importance of virginity and the future fulfilment of
women in the consummation of marriage.

But it remains a horrible and painful operation for the girls
concerned. An interesting point is that whereas female circumcision is in almost all instances performed at an early age there is
one apparent exception. The Dilling, a tribe in the Nuba Mountains of Kordofan in the Sudan, do not perform clitoridectomy on
young girls, but on women when they are about to have their first
child. The Dilling say 'We circumcise only women who have lain
with men.'[35] The explanation is that the clitoridectomy has the
meaning of a second defloration, which symbolises an intensifica-
tion of the status of woman as a wife.

Infibulation is generally so successful that for intercourse to take
place at the socially approved time—marriage—another operation
is required. Peney, whom we have already quoted, describes the
process of defibulation thus: '. . . When the Nubian marries she
has recourse to the wise woman, in order to have her vulva prepared and enlarged, for the infibulated aperture is far too small and
too inelastic—because of the scars of connective tissue which sur-
round it on every side—to admit even the roughest and most
merciless husband. So the expert matron intervenes and makes a
longitudinal slash, and intercourse takes place; but first the matron

introduces a fresh tube or cylinder of wood or vegetable fibre far
bulkier than the first, into the vagina, to the distance of three or
four inches. This remains *in situ* for a fortnight until the new
wound has healed and scarred when its presence becomes unnecessary.

'Nor is this all. If the woman conceives—and she generally does
—she is again put through the ordeal of the knife; for the same
rigid circlet of scars that locked the vulva against copulation from
the outside is equally a barrier against the dilation of that part thro'
which the baby emerges. So what will not stretch must be slashed
open with wide and deep strokes. Often the child at the moment of
passing the genital cleft is grievously injured. . . . '[36]

Other tribes in the same area insert a model of the husband's
penis instead of the tube mentioned above. The operation may be
performed frequently as the husband may demand partial infibulation again after the birth of the child.

Infibulation and its associated practices do have important
symbolic meaning, but they remain essentially cruel and revolting
processes. Apart from the element of cruelty there are serious
consequences at the birth of children to such women as Peney
points out.

Pharaonic circumcision or infibulation was prohibited by a law
of the Sudan Government in 1947. Sunna circumcision or clitoridectomy was the only type to be permitted henceforth. Unfortunately this has not proved successful as only the pharaonic type is
acceptable to the majority of Sudanese. The solution is difficult and
probably lies in the development of education, the substitution
of a form of circumcision less painful but giving the same
safeguard of chastity, and the performance of the operation under
anesthetic.[37]

Female virginity may be safeguarded by seclusion or more
practical means in those societies which value virgin brides. But
while the hymen is the prize of the lucky bridegroom he may be
compelled to surrender it to another. Custom may demand that
defloration is performed by a substitute of the husband, by manual
manipulation by someone other than the husband, by an operation,
and so on. Superficially this would appear to be a highly irrational
custom. To appreciate it, it is necessary to understand the implications of marriage in the primitive world. As we shall see later

marriage may be connected with prestige, childbearing, and economic transactions, but it also remains a spiritual matter. Van Gennep has pointed out that the husband's surrender of his right to deflower his bride may be the effect of the desire to retain sexual purity on the threshold of the sacred world of marriage.[38] Another interpretation might be that there is spiritual danger attaching to initial sexual union, and this should be avoided by the bridegroom. A more cynical and practical view is that defloration is never a very satisfactory process and is best left to others.

The magical or spiritual element is exhibited very strongly by those people who impose a period of continence immediately after the wedding. The period of continence can be as long as a month, or more as was the case amongst the North American Thligit. Generally speaking, however, it varies from a day to a week. A week was the interval laid down for Egyptians,[39] three days for the Warrawunga of Australia,[40] and one night for the people of Luzon in the Philippines. To attain the desired end of non-consummation various devices are used. The most usual is for a child or old woman to sleep between the couple. The abstention from intercourse is in a sense part of the ritual of marriage. This is clearly brought out in the following account of a wedding night amongst the Bahutu of Ruanda in East Africa. '. . . During the night the young wife goes veiled to the house of her husband which he has built in the domain of the parental dwelling. At the first light of dawn she must return to the parents-in-law. The whole night through the husband and wife struggle fiercely, often even on three or four following nights. The wife slashes and scratches the husband; the partition walls are torn down, even the house pillars, and everything is done without speaking a word. The parents, of course, hear the noise, but they say nothing, for it is the custom. After a month (with poor people about ten days) the wife definitely moves into the husband's house. That gives the opportunity for the "unveiling". This ceremony is accompanied by a general carousal and the "time of fear" concludes in the natural way. . . .'[41]

Public defloration, in which several individuals participate, is somewhat rare. The name given to this custom is the Nasamonian rite, from the people (Nasamonians of Cyrenaica) who are first reported to have practised it. '. . . When a Nasamonian marries it is the custom for the bride on the first night to lie with all the guests in turn, and each, when he has intercourse with her, gives her some present which he has brought with him. . . .[42] The same usage was current amongst the ancient inhabitants of the Balearic Islands. '. . . They have a strange custom at their weddings; for on the wedding night the oldest friends and guests lie first with the bride, then the others in the order of their ages. The bridegroom is the last man who is admitted to that honour. . . .'[43]

There is better evidence for the so-called Nasamonian rites than from these classical and perhaps apocryphal sources. Spencer and Gillen have described the rite in great detail as it exists among the tribes of Central Australia. According to the Australian system of social classifications and relationships, a girl at puberty is in a special relationship with a group of males of whom her future husband is one. Prior to marriage the hymen is perforated with a bone knife or with her finger by a woman designated for this purpose. Then each of the men standing in this special relationship with the girl have intercourse with her in turn.

This type of ritual defloration occurs in parts of Central and South America, the Marquesas Islands, as well as in New Guinea.[44] The number of societies concerned, however, is quite small, so that it can be regarded as a comparatively rare phenomenon. The Nasamonian rite must not be interpreted as an orgiastic festival. In all the instances cited the proceedings are conducted with appropriate ceremony. It is quite definitely the transference of the responsibility and danger of the initial sexual act from the bridegroom to a particular group of people.

What is far more common is for the responsibility to be undertaken by an individual. The Todas, an aboriginal Indian tribe, invite a stranger to function in this respect. ' . . . Certain ceremonies are performed shortly before the girl reaches the age of puberty. . . . Fourteen or fifteen days later a man of strong physique, who may belong to either division and to any clan, except that of the girl, comes and stays in the village for one night and has intercourse with the girl. This must take place before puberty, and it seemed there were few things regarded as more disgraceful than that this ceremony should be delayed till after this period. It might be a subject of reproach and abuse for the remainder of the woman's life, and it was even said that men might refuse to marry her if this ceremony had not been performed at the proper time. . . .'[45]

Nothing could be further from the Victorian apotheosis of virginity.

The employment of a stranger, as in the Todas's case, is found amongst some Central African tribes. This was apparently also the case, at the time of their discovery, in the Philippine Islands, where some men made defloration into a profession.[46]

In other instances friends of the bridegroom are employed for this purpose. Perhaps the most curious of reported instances of this kind are those in which the father of the bride deflowers her. Such reports are to be treated with caution in face of the almost universal prohibition of father-daughter incest. It has been suggested that this occurred in the seventeenth century in Ceylon, amongst the Sakai people of Malaya, and in the Eastern Moluccas. But the authorities are not to be relied upon.

Defloration can of course be performed by the use of a finger or a toe, or by means of an instrument. Where a female performs the operation one of these means is used. For example, in the Peru of the conquistadors a marriageable girl was brought into a public place and in full view of the assembled crowd her mother broke her hymen with her own hand thus demonstrating the value of the girl to potential suitors.[47] A similar practice prevailed amongst the Kamchadal of Siberia, but it was done in private. Among a people of Baluchistan, the Jatt, an old woman carried out the operation with a razor just prior to intercourse between the girl and her newly married husband. Obviously a most painful process.[48]

Where the husband does not enlist the aid of outsiders to assist him, and does not wish to deflower his wife in the normal way, he resorts to other means. He may use a stick as in some tribes of Central Australia; or, perhaps, what is more common, his forefinger, as in Samoa. Apparently digital defloration was reported in Egypt in the 1930's as quite a common practice. The husband deflowered his bride with his forefinger covered by a muslin handkerchief. He then presented it to her parents, and subsequently exhibited the bloodstained handkerchief at the wedding feast for the edification of the guests.[49]

Another element enters into the situation when defloration takes place by a priest, god or king. Not only is the responsibility, with its attendant dangers, taken from the husband, but the bride is sanctified or made holy by the act.

The priest or ruler is invoked for this purpose in widely differing cultures. The custom occurs in India, the Canary Islands, Papua, Morocco, Greenland, America, North America, and Indo-China. But it is possibly in Malabar in India that the custom was most widespread. We have to rely here not on sound anthropological evidence, but travellers' tales. One established authority, the Abbé Dubois, who wrote in the early nineteenth century, makes no mention of such practices. On the other hand various explorers in the seventeenth and eighteenth centuries, such as Alexander, Verhoeven, Sir Thomas Herbert, Hamilton, wrote such accounts as the following: ' . . . When the Samorin marries, he must not cohabit with his bride till the Nasabourie or chief priest has enjoyed her, and, if he pleases, he may have three nights of her company, because the first fruits of her nuptials must be an oblation to the god she worships: and some of the nobles are so complaisant as to allow the clergy the same tribute; but the common people cannot have that compliment paid to them, but are forced to supply the priests' places themselves. . . .' [50]

The role of the Nambutiri Brahmin, usurping the husband's right, has Vedic precedent, but it does not give authority to a priest to act in this way, only the gods. The Vedic marriage service stated that ' . . . Soma has her first, next she is received by Gandhara, the third to have her is Agni, fourthly she belongs to the man born of mortals. . . .' [51] On the bridal night a staff representing the god was placed between the married couple. That night was passed in self-denial. [52]

In the north of India this function is undertaken by the ruler. Amongst the Bhutanese and the Hunza of the North-West Frontier the local chieftain had the right to deflower the newly married bride. The same custom prevailed amongst some tribes of Senegal, where it is said the king had this right, as in Adamawa in Northern Nigeria. But in most cases, for example the aborigines of the West Indies, our knowledge is based on hearsay evidence rather than authentic accounts such as we have in the case of male and female circumcision. That being so we can accept the hypothesis of the fear of the bridegroom being transferred to an outsider, for the evidence is considerable. On the other hand, although the sacredness of priest and king is well recognised (see Sir James Frazer's *The Golden Bough*), the evidence for the use of either as the instrument of defloration is weak.

The Romans, an essentially practical people, held the belief that a statue of the appropriate god could very well perform the function of defloration. Brides were placed on the gigantic phallus of a Priapus or Tutunus, and, perhaps painfully, the operation was accomplished. The same act when performed by married women was held to promote fertility. It should be remembered, however, that these reports come from a hostile source, Christian writers.[53]

It has been maintained by a number of writers that the *jus primae noctis*, the right to take the maidenhead of a virgin prior to her marriage, existed in Europe amongst feudal chiefs and leaders. One writer, as recently as 1953, suggested that ' . . . the best authorities now accept that it existed. . . .'[54] This does not quite appear to be the case. Belief in a *droit de seigneur* has a romantic fascination conjured up by pictures of peasant girls torn from their marriage beds by lustful mediaeval barons. Unfortunately there is a singular lack of any definite evidence in the form of law books, charters, etc. This was pointed out by Dr K. Schmidt in his '*Jus primae noctis*' published in 1881. Confusion arose on account of the existence of a fine payable in feudal times to the lord of the manor when a vassal's daughter got married. This was regarded as a payment made in place of the lord's right to sleep with the bride. A more sensible interpretation is that the lord was entitled to service from the girl. On marriage, she might, following her husband, leave the estate. Thus the fine was recompense for loss of services. A similar argument was made out that the fines exacted on newly married couples by the Bishop of Amiens in the fourteenth century were of the same type as the *droit de seigneur*. In fact ecclesiastical law had decreed at one time that the newly wed should refrain from intercourse on the first three nights after marriage. In time this had been commuted by a money payment which gave a dispensation.

The Irish evidence regarding the kings of Ireland contained in the MS. *The Book of Leinster* dating from the middle of the twelfth century is quite specific. It tells how Conchobar, the King of Ulster, slept with all the marriageable girls in his kingdom. This incredible feat is on the same plane as giants and the slaying of thousands in battle.

The argument that anthropological material supports the view that the *jus primae noctis* in Europe is an attenuated form of what is found in non-European societies is without foundation. As we have said, strictly speaking there is little accurate information regarding the *droit de seigniur*.[54]

So far we have discussed the practices obtaining in societies which have restrictions on pre-marital intercourse. In the following chapter we shall describe some societies in which this type of sexual activity is socially approved.

REFERENCES AND NOTES

1. A. van Gennep, *Les Rites de Passage*, Paris 1909.
2. L. Warner, *A Black Civilisation*, Revised Edition, N.Y. 1958, pp. 130–131.
3. J. G. Peristiany, *The Social Institutions of the Kipsigis*, London 1939, p. 6.
4. *ibid*, p. 7.
5. *ibid*, p. 11.
6. *ibid*, p. 25.
7. *ibid*, p. 26.
8. G. Catlin, *Manners and Customs of the N. American Indians*, London 1866, Vol. I, pp. 169 *et seq.*
9. E. Im. Thurn, *Among the Indians of Guiana*, London 1883, p. 221.
10. R. B. Dixon, *Shasta Puberty Ceremonies for Girls, in Primitive Heritage*, ed. by M. Mead and N. Calas, London 1954, pp. 175–179.
11. W. R. Burton, *Personal Narrative of a Pilgrimage to El-Medinah and Mecca*, London, 1885–6, Vol. III, pp. 80 *et seq.*
12. H. K. Laatsch in *Proceedings of the Australasian Association for the Advancement of Science*, Adelaide 1907, pp. 581, *et seq.*
13. M. F. Ashley-Montagu, *Coming into Being among the Australian Aborigines*, London 1937, p. 42.
14. *ibid*, p. 43. See also W. B. Spencer and F. J. Gillen, *The Native Tribes of Central Australia*, London 1899, pp. 251 *et seq.*
15. This is discussed at greater length in the Chapter on Lovemaking.
16. W. B. Spencer and F. J. Gillen, *Northern Tribes of Central Australia* London 1904, pp. 133 *et seq.*

17. F. de Castelneau, *Expedition dans les parties centrales de l'Amérique du sud*, Paris 1850-9, Vol. IV, p. 379.

18. See G. St. Orde Brown, 'Circumcision Ceremonies among the Awimbe', *Man*, Vol. XIII, 1913, pp. 139 *et seq.*; and 'Circumcision Ceremonies of the Chuka', *Man*, Vol. XV, 1915, pp. 66 *et seq.* A. C. Hollis, *The Masai*, London 1905, p. 299, and *The Nandi*, London 1909, p. 299.

18. C. W. Hobley, *Bantu Beliefs and Magic*, London 1922, p. 85; and 'British East Africa', J.R.A.I., Vol. XXV, 1903, p. 351.

19. *Paulus Aegineata*, Vol. VII, p. 70.

20. H. Licht, *Sexual Life in Ancient Greece*, London 1932, pp. 512-13.

21. L. T. Hobhouse, G. C. Wheeler and M. Ginsberg in *The Material Culture and Social Insts. of the Simpler Peoples*, London 1915, p. 167, state 50 per cent of 120 societies approve of pre-nuptial intercourse.

   C. S. Ford in *A Comparative Study of Human Reproduction*, New Haven 1945, p. 100, says 40 per cent are openly permissive.

   In a sample of 158 societies 70 per cent were permissive in this respect according to G. P. Murdock in his 'The Social Regulation of Sexual Behaviour' in *Psycho-sexual Development in Health and Disease*, N.Y. 1949, pp. 256-66. Murdock estimates *loc. cit.* that less than 5 per cent of peoples totally prohibit extra-marital sex activity.

22. A. C. Kinsey and others, *Sexual Behaviour in the Human Female*, London 1953, p. 285.

   C. S. Ford and F. A. Beach, *Patterns of Sexual Behaviour*, London 1952, p. 185.

23. See for example H. Harvard, *La Hollande Pittoresque*, Paris 1878, p. 219.

24. A. C. Kinsey and others, *Sexual Behaviour in the Human Female*, London 1953, p. 288.

25. L. A. Fink, 'Premarital experience of girls in Sydney', *Inter. Journal of Sociology*, Vol. IV, 1950, pp. 33-5.

26. A. Comfort, *Sexual Behaviour in Society*, London 1950, p. 90.

27. Lewis M. Terman, *Psychologic Factors in Marital Happiness*, N.Y. 1938, p. 323.

28. F. Henriques, *Family and Colour in Jamaica*, London 1953, p. 84 *et seq*, and *Jamaica*, London 1957, pp. 185 *et seq*.

29. For a survey of Swedish pre-marital sexual patterns see A. Myrdal's *Nation and Family*, London 1945, pp. 42–47.

30. See H. H. Ploss, M. & P. Bartels, *Woman*, London 1935, pp. 46–47, for a review of these devices.

31. M. de Cervantes, *Obras Completas*, Madrid 1863–4, Tome 8, pp. 277–8.

32. C. M. Czaplicka, *Aboriginal Siberia*, Oxford 1914, p. 108.

33. F. Peney, 'Études sur l'Ethnologie, etc., des races de Soudan', *Bulletin de la Société de Géographie*, Paris 1859, Series IV, Vol. XVII, pp. 338 *et seq.*

34. S. F. Nadel, *The Nuba*, Oxford 1947, p. 478.

35. Nadel, *op cit*, p. 438.

36. F. Peney, *op cit*, p. 338.

37. M. Helber, 'Female Circumcision', *Journal of the Medical Women's Federation*, April 1951, pp. 24–27.

38. A. van Gennep, *Les Rites de Passage*, Paris 1909, p. 242.

39. E. W. Lane, *An Account of the Manners and Customs of the Modern Egyptians*, London 1871, Vol. II, p. 273.

40. W. B. Spencer and F. J. Gillen, *The Northern Tribes of Central Australia*, London 1904, p. 138.

41. P. Schumacher, 'Die Ehe in Ruanda', *Anthropos*, 1910, Bd. V, pp. 870–906.

42. Herodotus, *Historiae*, Bk. 9, p. 172, Rawlinson Trans., London 1875.

43. Didorus Siculus, *Bibliotheca Historica*, Vol. XIV, 4, p. 25.

44. C. G. Seligman, *The Melanesians of British New Guinea*, Camb. 1910, p. 473.

45. W. H. R. Rivers, *The Todas*, London 1906, p. 503.

46. A. de Morga, *Philippine Islands*, etc., London 1868, pp. 304 *et seq.*

47. G. de la Vega, *1st Part of the Royal Commentaries of the Yncas*, translated by C. R. Markham, London 1869–71, Vol. I, p. 59.

48. D. Bray, 'Census of India', 1911, Vol. IV (*Baluchistan Report*).

49. A. B. Clot-Bey, *Aperçu général sur l'Egypte*, Paris 1840, Vol. II, p. 44.

50. A. Hamilton, 'New Account of the East Indies', in *Pinkerton Collection of Voyages*, Vol. VIII, p. 324, London 1811.

51. *Rig-Veda*, Vol. II, p. 537, Prague 1876–88.

52. The Grihya-Sûtras (iii) 8.8 *et seq*, *The Sacred Books of the East*, Vol. XXX, p. 267, translated by H. Oldenberg, Oxford 1886 and 1892.

53. St. Augustine, *De Civitate Dei*, VI, 9, 3, and VII, 24, 2.
54. G. Rattray Taylor, *Sex in History*, London 1953, p. 31.
55. For a review of the available evidence see E. Westermarck, *History of Human Marriage*, London 1921, Vol. I, Ch. V, pp. 166–200.

CHAPTER II

Pre-Marital Sexual Behaviour

In MANY of those societies which approve of adolescent sexual activity matters are not left to chance. There are special institutions that provide, as it were, facilities for the young people to meet and spend time together. These vary from the highly organised communal dormitory (ghotul) of the Muria aboriginal Indian tribe, to the casual visiting of girls' houses by boys among some groups in the Philippines. But, and this is an important point, in a great range of human societies all over the world there are what are called village dormitories—separate buildings for boys and unmarried men and, less frequently, for unmarried girls. These dormitories can be divided into two types. There are those that aim at the segregation of the male youth and are devoted to masculine pursuits such as war, magic, and hunting; and there are those that encourage adolescent sexual liaisons.

The function of the first type has been summed up in this way. 'The men's house is usually the largest building in a tribal settlement. It belongs in common to the villagers; it serves as council chamber and town hall, as a guest house for strangers, and as a sleeping resort of the men. Here the more precious belongings of the community, such as trophies taken in war or in the chase, and religious emblems of curious sorts are preserved. Within its precincts, women and children, and men not fully initiated members of the tribe, seldom or never enter. . . . '[1]

The purpose of such club houses varies from society to society. The place it occupies in one New Guinea tribe, the Iatmul, is observed by Bateson. 'The ceremonial house is a splendid building, as much as a hundred and twenty feet in length, with towering gables at the ends. Inside the building there is a long vista from end to end down the series of supporting posts, as in the nave of a darkened church; and the resemblance to a church is carried further in the native attitudes towards the building. There is a series of taboos on any sort of desecration. The earth floor must not be scratched nor the woodwork damaged. A man should not walk right through the building and out at the other end; he should turn aside and pass out of one of the side entrances. To walk right through the building is felt to be an expression of overweening pride—as if a man should lay claim to the whole building as his personal property.

'But the analogy between the ceremonial house and church must not be pushed too far, for many reasons: the ceremonial house serves not only as a place of ritual but also as a club-house where men meet and gossip and as an assembly room where they debate and brawl. Further, the ceremonial house does not stand to the natives as a symbol of their devotion, but rather as a symbol of their pride in head-hunting. Where we think of a church as sacred and cool, they think of a ceremonial house as "hot", imbued with heat by the violence and killing which were necessary for its building and consecration. . . . '[2]

This type of club-house is common throughout New Guinea and Melanesia.

In many African examples the emphasis seems to be much more on the training and initiation of the young men, rather than on providing a social club or meeting house, as in the case of the Iatmul. This is so for the Bawenda. The 'tondo', or men's house, is in fact a school for boys, who are initiated there. A similar emphasis is found in the 'habits' of the Brazilian Bororo to which boys were admitted at six or seven. They were allowed to visit their parents only at infrequent intervals. It sounds very much like our own boarding schools with perhaps one or two significant differences. In the evening the local chief would visit the boys and enthral them with tales of war and adventure.

The second type of club or dormitory, that encourages youthful sexual activity, is equally widespread. In different forms it is found in a number of societies in Melanesia, Polynesia, India, Africa, Malaya, and the Philippines.

Sexual initiation is one of the functions of the 'Imeium', or youths' house, in the New Hebrides. 'All villages have special houses where all unmarried circumcised males live, and to this house comes at special seasons a girl known as the "Iowhanan" whose special task it is to initiate the boys into the mysteries of sex. No man can contract a marriage who has not been initiated by the Iowhanan, and a man may not be betrothed until he has been touched by her. There is no special ceremonial act in the touching and it is admitted that it is generally the prelude to connexion with the woman. There is no payment made to the woman for this service, but the village or tribe that furnishes her receives compensation. She is painted in a special manner as a sign of her profession and wears turtle-shell earrings and other ornaments, while a shorter skirt distinguishes her from other women. After a circumcision ceremony, the Iowhanan is sent to live in the bachelors' house with the unmarried men. . . . The youths make use of the Iowhanan while she is living with them, but when she is absent a period of abstinence prevails. After her services are no longer required she returns to her village and later makes a good marriage, for there seems to be no ill feeling against her. . . .'[3]

Amongst the Igorot of Luzon in the Philippines there are girls' houses which are called 'olag'. The boys have their own separate dormitory. A girl will steal something belonging to a boy during the day and at night he has to come and retrieve it. Fulfilment awaits him there.[4] Temporary visitation, where the girl stays for a time in the 'house', is found in the Pelew Islands in the East Indies. This is also true of the African Nandi. The unmarried Nandi warriors sleep in groups in separate huts. Unmarried girls visit them and stay with them for varying periods. When the warriors are absent the girls look after the huts.[5]

Missionaries were the first people to report on what they were inclined to term orgiastic living conditions in the Pacific Islands.

One wrote, 'The Devil has founded here seminaries of debauchery.'[6] Another said that the clubs were 'a gross epicurism'.[7] These 'seminaries of debauchery' were here, as elsewhere, remarkably well organised.

The 'manyatta' of the Masai of East Africa is an extremely good instance of sexual freedom being granted to youth in a socially approved way. The Masai are divided into age-grades. While serving as members of the various classes of the age-grades the boys live in special villages away from the rest of the people. These villages are called manyatta. Elder women with their children, in particular the various sisters, also live there—the women to look after the huts, the girls to act as lovers. The manyatta is made up of several huts which are built and lived in by the warriors' mothers or some other married relative. For a girl to be present in the manyatta her brother or brothers must also be there. There is no physical division inside a hut. The mother and her young children occupy one end, at the other the warriors and the girl friends sleep together. The boys do not sleep in their own mothers' hut. Several boys and girls sleep on one large bed. 'No girl may sleep with a man except she is absolutely nude, but on the other hand although she may not refuse to sleep with a man, she is not necessarily expected to allow him full sexual intercourse, and in fact often does not do so. . . . Besides the casual day-to-day lovers described above a girl has very often a more permanent lover in her "manyatta" chosen from the ranks of those who have been her casual lovers. . . .' This choice is made publicly and may eventually be followed by marriage. Such permanent arrangements, however, may be affected by the fact that the girl has already been betrothed to another in childhood, which is customary. If she does not wish to marry her betrothed but prefers her 'choice' then she generally manages to become pregnant by the latter and all is well. But in practice most girls do marry their fiancés rather than their lovers.[8] The Masai 'manyatta' is clearly more institutionalised than the 'olag' of the Igorot. A stage further in this process, where the dormitory has become a fully accepted institution of the people, is represented by the 'bukumatula' of the Trobriand Islands.

The Trobrianders allow the sexual impulse almost entire free play prior to marriage. Thus there are childish romances with a strong sexual element as well as fugitive affairs amongst the young adolescents. But '. . . . it is obvious that the lasting liaisons of youths and adult girls require some special institution, more definitely established, more physically comfortable, and at the same time having the approval of custom.

'To meet this need, tribal custom and etiquette offer accommodation and privacy in the form of the "bukumatula", the bachelors' and unmarried girls' house of which mention has already been made. In this a limited number of couples, some two, three, or four, live for longer or shorter periods together in a temporary community. It also and incidentally offers shelter for younger couples if they want amorous privacy for an hour or two. . . .'(9)

These 'bukumatula' are situated in the inner ring of huts in the Trobriand village amongst yam houses, which have religious significance, and the houses of the chief and his kinsmen. Inside one of these huts all the usual furnishings except for bunks with mat coverings are missing. The inmates keep their belongings in the households with which they are associated in the day time. The general impression is one of bareness. Ownership of the hut is vested in the group of boys who use it, but one of them is the titular owner. Each boy owns the bunk which he uses. If a couple breaks up it is usually the girl who goes to another bunk, to another boy.

There is no promiscuity within the bukumatula—in fact the emphasis is much more the other way. A very strict code is in force and to abuse it by trying to sleep with a girl not your own is, as the Trobrianders say, 'like adultery with a friend's wife'. There is no atmosphere of sexual orgies, and to exhibit voyeurism would be disgraceful. Copulation is performed when others are asleep in such a way 'as not to wake up the other people in the bukumatula.'

The core of the relationship developed in the bukumatula is that the couples are attracted to each other sexually and can part at will. There are no rights, duties, and obligations concerned as there are in marriage. Meals are taken apart in the parents' houses. There is no question of a joint home or household. Couples may or may not perpetuate the relationship by marriage, but this is irrelevant. The bukumatula is for love and sexual enjoyment. For an unmarried girl to have a meal with a boy friend is, in Trobriand eyes, as Malinowski points out, the equivalent of spending the weekend with him in our society.

'The institution of the bukumatula is, therefore, characterised by: (1) individual appropriation, the partners of each couple belonging exclusively to one another; (2) strict decorum and absence of any orgiastic or lascivious display; (3) the lack of any legally binding element; (4) the exclusion of any other community of interest between a pair, save that of sexual cohabitation.'[10]

The Trobriand bukumatula represents the middle stage in the institutionalisation of pre-nuptial intercourse. We have to look to India for the most developed form.

Forms of visiting between boys' and girls' houses; or communal dormitories, are found amongst the aboriginal Indian peoples, such as the Nagas of Assam; the Bhotias of Almona; the Santals of Bihar; the Uraon, Munda, Birhor, Kharia, Juang, Konds, and Bhuiya of Orissa where it is extremely well developed; the Muthuvan, Mannan, and Paluyan of Travancore; and the Hill Maria of Bastar, where it is vestigial.

Curiously enough it is also in Bastar State in the Central Provinces of India that the most highly organised type of communal dormitory is found, amongst the Muria. The Muria term this the 'ghotul'.

Whatever may have been the situation in the past, the contemporary ghotul combines two very different functions. It serves both as the village guest house for visiting officials, and as the communal dormitory. It is sometimes said by the Muria that this is a useful arrangement as the guest house has to be well kept and there is always youthful labour on hand to do this. One result of the combination is that most ghotuls have large airy buildings which serve both purposes admirably. The typical ghotul will stand in the middle of the village inside a spacious compound surrounded by wooden stakes. There will be a large central house with a deep verandah, perhaps more than one open hut, and a number of small sheds. This plan will vary according to the particular village, its size and surroundings. The inside of the ghotul is generally decorated with paintings and carvings. These in many instances have a sexual connotation, or are actual reproductions of the sexual organs, and so on. For example there may be a wooden vagina carved on the central pillar of the house, or a drawing of a boy with an enormous penis and a girl in his arms. Furnishings are simple in the extreme. There are no beds and only a few wooden headrests.

This then is the physical setting of the ghotul. The dormitory is organised on a basis of discipline and recreation. Two types can be distinguished. The first, the Jodidar, has the rule that once a boy and girl have paired off, they are in a sense 'married'. 'Divorce' is permitted, but unfaithfulness is punished. In the second type no boy can claim the undivided possession of any one girl. If a boy sleeps with the same girl for more than three days he is punished. In all other matters the two ghotuls are identical. The two types are found co-existing throughout Muria territory. The first type appears to have been the older classical model. Today the majority of ghotuls have adopted the more permissive rule.

In the Jodidar the 'marriage' of the young people is in fact a permanent matter. When the couple have achieved maturity in the ghotul a special marriage ceremony may be performed. The permanency of this relationship in the ghotul may cause emotional distress when the partners leave and go out into the world and marry in the ordinary way. But the majority seem to accept the situation without too much disturbance. A minority, however, do elope with their ghotul partners and make regular marriages. Ordinary marriage is governed by a whole series of complicated financial arrangements and relationships amongst families.

The second type of ghotul is 'sometimes called the "mundi-badalna" because in it you change from girl to girl just as you change your rings from finger to finger.'[11] The atmosphere is quite different from the jodidar. The whole emphasis is upon impermanence in sexual relations. No one can regard the other as his property in any way. Your companion is for three nights only. If afterwards you betray jealousy, by word or gesture, punishment awaits you. The advocates of the mundi-badalna say that a lasting attachment to one girl is not a good preparation for marriage to someone else. 'Too much love before marriage will mean too little after it.' Another important aspect from the Muria point of view is their belief that a constant change of partners prevents pregnancy. Only complete absorption in the girl mentally and physically will ensure pregnancy. This view is not borne out by a comparison of pregnancy figures for the two types of ghotul.[12] But it must not be assumed there is a kind of general promiscuity in the mundi-badalna. In practice either the allocation of partners is made by the head boy or girl, or a boy tends to consort with a small group (3) of girls. The average ghotul has only about 20 members. 'A remarkable thing about these arrangements is that they interfere with the normal course of sexual selection. The beautiful girl and the ugly or even deformed girl has exactly the same sexual opportunity, exactly the same sexual privilege. So with the boys. . . .'[13] Both boys and girls must abide by the rules of the ghotul.

Apart from these two types of ghotul there is a third category. In these the girls attend every evening but will only pass the night there infrequently.

A boy is known as a 'chelik', and a girl as a 'motiari'. Children first begin to attend the ghotul when they are six or seven though this varies. They are not at this stage full members. This comes later when they are given their ghotul names, of which they are very proud, and admitted to full membership. There is a hierarchy of names and gradings at the head of which is the 'Diwan' of the boys and the 'Belosa' of the girls. These are in charge of the ghotul. To each individual falls a particular task in the ghotul, such as cleaning, the maintenance of discipline, entertainment, and so on.

The unnamed ones, the young of both sexes, have to perform all the menial tasks. Their position is very much like that of fags at an English public school (private). Naming and full membership means they have become prefects and can claim privileges. The children are instructed by the older ones in how to behave, in dancing and ghotul games. Theoretically everyone passes through the hierarchy in time. The Diwan and Belosa are chosen by the others not by voting but by approval: frequently office goes to the seconds-in-command who assist the Diwan and Belosa.

The ghotul comes alive only in the evening. During the day it is deserted, the girls are working at home and the boys in the fields. After supper at home the boys begin to arrive. 'They come one by one carrying their sleeping mats and perhaps their drums. The little boys bring their daily "tribute" of wood, "clock in" by showing it to the official responsible and throw it in a corner. The elder boys gather round the fire; one takes a half-smoked leaf pipe from his turban and ignites it by placing a bit of glowing wood in the cup, another plays a few notes on his flute, a third spreads his mat and lies down. . . . Gradually all the boys assemble. . . .'[14] The girls, who have probably been gossiping at someone's house nearby, arrive altogether in a rush. Some sit with the boys, others lie down by themselves, others start singing. Perhaps a dance will start spontaneously and the older children all join in. The younger ones will play exciting games amongst themselves. Later there will be stories told, songs to be sung, riddles asked and so on. These give place to discussions of expeditions to be planned, or possibly a disciplinary trial. Perhaps they will merely sit around the fire and talk. There is no compulsion for group activity for the motiari and chelik may split up in twos all over the compound.

When this part of the evening is over a different type of activity begins. What might be called a period of salutation now commences. The junior boys go round saluting each of the senior boys in a specified way. Next the girls do the same. The ceremony is called 'Joharni'. This is followed by the distribution of tobacco and leaf pipes to the boys, by the girl whose duty it is. The tobacco is taken from the store to which all have contributed.

The girls now arrange among themselves how the very important ritual of combing the boys' hair and massaging their bodies should be done. This appears to be quite arbitrary. It does not mean that the motiari who massages a boy will spend the night with him. Nearly the whole of the body is massaged, and not only by the hands. 'But this is not the end of the comb's work. The motiari now uses it to titillate the skin of the arms and back. She rubs the points of the comb very gently to and fro, up and down, over the back, and then when she has massaged that, takes each arm in turn and runs the comb up and down. . . . '(15)

The combing and massaging is the preliminary to going to bed: 'It is now fairly late and boys and girls prepare for bed. In fine weather they may scatter about the compound and in the various huts; when it is cold or wet they seem to prefer crowding into the main ghotul building. The little boys and girls lie down in a long row, two boys, then a girl, a boy, two girls, and so on. Boys without partners—and there are often fewer girls than boys—lie down two and two on their little mats.

'Those who have permanent or temporary partners lie down with them, side by side, facing each other in each other's arms on the sleeping mat. They often have to lie very close together; sometimes two boys have one girl between them; many of the couples actually touch each other. In the big ghotul real lovers and those who intend to have sexual intercourse may go and sleep in the smaller huts in the compound. . . . '[16] Before dawn the Belosa awakens the girls who slip away: 'A girl should be hard at work husking or grinding corn before her parents are up.' The boys depart a little later, they too have their duties to go to. To remain after the village is at work would be to invite disgrace.

There are order and discipline both in the evening and in the morning. But there is a great deal of discipline in the ghotul altogether. From the first the very young children are told 'you must come every day, or you will be punished.' The background to the code of the ghotul, as it is with the tribe, is the necessity for preserving unity. To act pre-eminently as an individual is to destroy that unity. Thus, actions which are considered anti-social are to be condemned and punished.

The most serious offence a member can commit is to repeat what has occurred inside the ghotul to the outside world. This is to betray the solidarity of the group. Expulsion is the penalty. Apologies and fines may expiate the offence and permit re-admission. Quarrelling is almost as serious and disrupting. This is quelled by threats of expulsion, actual expulsion, or fines. Cleanliness of the body and house is the rule. Omissions by those responsible for keeping the ghotul clean may result in dirt or ashes being poured over them. No one may urinate within the building, if he does he is punished. Spitting is allowed, but to break wind is a serious offence. In one case the offender had to go to each boy in turn and say, 'Johor, maharaj, I have farted.' But to counteract this abasement there is a rule that others may not laugh excessively at the offender. A menstruating girl who attends the ghotul, which is forbidden, must provide liquor and a sacrifice to Lingo Pen, the tutelary god. Members who fail to attend the ghotul regularly are punished. Girls who do not co-operate, not only by neglecting the duties allocated to them but by being unresponsive and moody, are fined. On the other hand it is a breach of the code for a boy to force a girl against her will. The boy who is unco-operative is also regarded as an offender. Possessiveness and jealousy meet with strong disapproval. If a boy transgresses the rule that he must not sleep more than three nights with one girl, or if he commits 'adultery', that is sleeps with a girl who is assigned to someone who is absent, punishment will follow. All must comport themselves modestly and obey the rules.

The two most extreme penalties are expulsion and refusal of the ghotul members to attend one's wedding. This last is a very severe penalty for it means that the wedding will have no music or dancing, for it is the young people who provide both on such occasions. To the Muria, for whom dancing and music are so important, it is a dire punishment. Less severe are fines and a variety of ingenious punishments. These vary from filling the vagina of a dirty or neglectful girl with ashes to numerous cruel exercises such as standing on one leg for a long time, pushing and pulling the victim about by everyone, and having one's hands tied together to the roof. But there is never any corporal punishment in our sense of the term.

It can be seen that membership of the ghotul implies undertaking to fulfil the rules and regulations. The ghotul is conducted with discipline.

The time for leaving the ghotul is when one is married in the outside world. For a girl this is automatic. Once she is married she can never come back. There may be a final ceremony at which she massages every chelik for the last time. For a boy, marriage does not automatically exclude him. He continues as a member for some time, until in fact he can pay for a feast for everyone. It is generally a period of three to four months after his wedding that a chelik gives his feast and says farewell.

'Now you are a married man, come no more to the ghotul and mix no more in the dance and song of the children. Look after your own house and property. Eat and live and have many children of your own.'(17)

Various reasons are given by the Muria for the existence of the ghotul. Their reasoning has to be seen against the background of tribal life with its essentially public existence. According to Elwin (*The Muria and their Ghotul*) parents are quite open about it. 'One of the reasons often given by Muria to explain the existence of the ghotul is that "it is sinful for the parents to sleep in the presence of their children." "As soon as a child understands what it (that is, sexual intercourse) is, we send it to the ghotul." "The reason for the ghotul," said the headman of Jhakri, is that it is sinful to sleep before a daughter or a son. They must never see the parents sleeping on one mat, either by day or night. Suppose a girl comes home late at night for some reason and finds her parents holding each other on the mat, they are very angry and abuse her saying, "Haven't you got a ghotul to live in? Why do you want to come here?" '(18)

Granted the conditions of village life this seems very reasonable —in fact it is the only way that parents will get privacy at night. But very little children are also sent, just to get them out of the way as the Muria say. It means that the father and mother do not have to care for them in the evening, and know they are safe and happy. Such children do not, of course, have proper membership of the ghotul and in a sense form a community of their own within it. But they are looked after and begin to learn how to behave through watching the others.

The significance of the ghotul is not only in the field of sexuality, important as that is. The child at an early age is exposed to a series of relationships which are wider and more complex than those of the house. The ghotul teaches him to live with his fellows. The head boy and girl of the ghotul become parent substitutes and their orders and punishments are more feared than those at home. What the dormitory really becomes for the child is a school of manners, a society of his own, and in time an introduction to and a fulfilment of sexual life. In other words it fills what is a remarkable gap in western society—a community of adolescents and near-adolescents who are free to behave as they wish, who enjoy sexual freedom without a sense of guilt and who invent their own discipline. The results are seen in adult Muria society which is curiously free from the tensions and inhibitions characteristic of so many peoples.(19)

The Muria convention is that parents do not know what goes on in the ghotul. The fact is they know most of what happens, but it is considered improper to admit this. As we saw, the children are forbidden to speak of their activities to people outside and there are punishments for the transgressors. Psychologically the convention strengthens the faith of the children in their own world of the ghotul. In face of the evidence provided by the ghotul there is little doubt that it functions effectively and fulfils a definite need, a need which is by no means confined to Muria society. But there is one problem which is of some importance. If girls become pregnant while in the ghotul, what happens?

In the ordinary course of events the Muria child is betrothed. This can happen either before puberty or later. After a period of years marriage follows. These arrangements do not interfere with membership of the ghotul. Marriage and betrothals are arranged according to clan affiliations to suit the interest of families and the couple concerned. The attachments of the ghotul do not enter into this. There are no severe punishments in the ghotul for those guilty of clan incest, the attitude here seems to be essentially permissive, for such behaviour would not be tolerated outside. Betrothed couples, that is couples who have been betrothed outside the ghotul, are free to choose partners as they wish. Adult writs clearly do not run here. But if a girl becomes pregnant the matter may assume serious proportions.

Pregnancy, as a result of what is considered clan incest outside the ghotul, is severely censured. In such a case there is punishment both inside and outside the ghotul. The boy will have to pay a heavy fine or may even be expelled from the tribe. On the other hand the elders of the village may merely fine him lightly and arrange for the girl to be married as quickly as possible to her proper fiancé. This is the procedure in the case of ordinary pregnancy where incest is not involved: a fine is payable and the girl married to her legitimate betrothed. The legal husband is ordinarily quite willing to accept the paternity of the child. Difficulties only arise in either type of pregnancy when the ghotul couple wish to marry each other and thus perpetuate the relationship. Some of these cases have tragic consequences, but they are comparatively few. When incest is absent from the picture and the ghotul couple insists on marriage they are dissuaded, for it means adjustment of complicated financial arrangements arising out of child betrothal. But if the couple still insist, the matter can be arranged. What should be realised is that the Muria attitude in respect of pre-marital pregnancy is entirely different from our own. It is summed up by their saying: 'Even an elephant with four legs sometimes stumbles', or 'What can you do to one who has missed the road?' Their tolerance is in part based on their free admission of the importance of sex in life. This is not to say that there are not difficult financial arrangements to be made in such cases and temporary disgrace for both boy and girl. But it is not the kind of permanent disgrace current in the West. In our own case it might be suggested that our intolerance of pre-marital conception is due to our guilt feelings about sexual behaviour in general.

It must not be thought that pregnancy is an extremely frequent problem in the ghotul. 'Out of 2,000 cases, eighty men admitted to having made their ghotul partners pregnant, and in the 220 ghotul I examined, I found a history of 327 pregnant girls.'[20] This gives a rate of 4 per cent. In relation to the amount of sexual activity it suggests that the Muria women are relatively infertile. Surprisingly enough it is only at this stage of their lives that this is so. In normal adult married life they are as fertile as any comparable group who do not possess the ghotul.

How in fact do the Muria manage to avoid pregnancy? In the first place they believe that they are under the protection of the gods, Lingo Pen and the Earth Mother. At her first menses a girl as she bathes prays to the Nahandi Karyong (Bathing Maiden), 'So long as I live in the ghotul, see that my blood flows by the moon, and that I do not conceive. If you grant my desire I will make you an offering at my wedding.'[21] Such beliefs are backed up by definite precautions. According to the Muria the most favourable time for conception is just after menstruation hence they abstain for as much as a week after the period. There is a very strong belief that frequent changes of partners inhibits conception, which is expressed in the rule of the modern ghotul that partners must change after three days. This belief has clearly accelerated the change from the classical type of ghotul that demands a constant relationship Allied to this frequency of change is the idea of spacing cop ulation so that the boy only copulates once or twice a week with the same girl. This is controlled by those in charge of the ghotul.

Various herbs are reputed to have contraceptive powers, such as white garlic or a type of creeper called 'bamen'. These are eaten after an appropriate ritual. It is difficult to judge how efficacious they are. If these fail recourse may be had to abortifacients of a similar kind. They sometimes work.

Recourse to the supernatural and dubious herbs are not sufficient to explain the low rate of 4 per cent quoted. Avoidance immediately after the menses may have some effect, just as belief in the powers of the gods may give a psychological security which militates against conception. But the Muria case is not exceptional, for similar phenomena of pre-nuptial sterility have been reported among several peoples of New Guinea (Massim, Wogeo), the

Philippines and the Trobriand Islands.[22] Malinowski summed it
up when he wrote: 'Can there be any psychological law which
makes conception less likely when women begin their sexual life
young, lead it indefatiguably, and mix their lovers freely? This, of
course, cannot be answered here, as it is a purely biological question; but some such solution of the difficulty seems to me the only
one, unless I have missed some very important ethnological
clue. . . . '[23]

Spacing the copulatory act has scientific backing. 'Undoubtedly
there are human matings in which a single act of coitus, or at most
coitus repeated at intervals throughout one menstrual month,
would infallibly produce conception, but there are exceptions.
Most couples who succeed in reproducing do so in spite of certain
imperfections in the conceptive mechanism . . . most people are
relatively and not absolutely fertile. . . . '[24]

General scientific opinion seems to indicate that there is a period
of relative sterility in adolescents so that pre-nuptial sexual activity
will be comparatively free from pregnancy. This would obviously
explain why such institutions as the ghotul can flourish as well as
unorganised forms of pre-nuptial sexual freedom.

'It seems probable that in the human female and in the mammals
which have thus far been studied, there is generally an interval of
anything up to five years or more between Menarche (the first
menses) and the ability to procreate, during which the female is
functionally sterile and unable to reproduce. . . . '[25]

Western ethical considerations apart, it certainly appears as if the
Murias have to a great extent solved the problem of adolescent sex.
The possibility of creating a similar institution in our own society
raises such enormous problems, not only of religion but also of
tradition, and the dissimilarity of social context is so great that it
would seem unthinkable. On the other hand the problems of the
back street abortionist, the unmarried mother with her deprived
child, and the furtive, unhealthy background of adolescent sexual
behaviour in our midst, should make us think. Despite the realities
of the situation few attempts have been made to advocate publicly
some form of permissible adolescent sexual activity. A notable
example was the American Judge B. B. Lindsey's proposals in the
twenties for a type of companionate marriage which would have a
term set to it.[26] But with the exception of the Scandinavian

countries the West has refused to think constructively regarding this problem.

The opposing point of view, that what is required is a return to the golden age of chastity, of which incidentally there appears to be surprisingly little evidence in any historical period, is very forcibly put, both by doctors and clerics. Medical and psychiatric opinion seems to be divided over the question whether such sexual experience is beneficial. The various grounds for and against pre-marital coitus are admirably set out by Kinsey.[27] These range on the side of chastity from the view that abstinence develops will power to the danger of pregnancy; and on the side from training for marriage to the satisfaction of a psychological need for a sexual outlet. There is little doubt that the opposition between the ideal, professed standards of sexual morality of the society and the actual sexual behaviour of adolescents produces an undesirable type of conflict in the individual. It is thus difficult to agree with such views as those expressed by Dr A. Torrie: 'My own experience is that many immature and insecure persons seek in sexual relations a solution for their psychological conflicts and that the mature man or woman who has no sense of guilt or shame about normal sexual wishes or dreams can remain chaste without being neurotic...'[28] Apart from other considerations it would seem that 'the mature man or woman' only constitutes a very small minority in our midst. Torrie bases his arguments in favour of pre-nuptial chastity on the evidence provided by J. D. Unwin's book *Sex and Culture*. This when it appeared in 1934 received severe criticism from anthropologists for its misleading use of statistical material. Unwin's main thesis is that societies which have limited sexual opportunity outside of marriage have proved virile and civilised while those whose sexual opportunities are not so limited have been degenerate and barbaric. Or, put another way, the state of culture in a society is governed by the limitations on sexual freedom imposed. An amazing thesis but unfortunately not supported by the evidence adduced for this purpose.[29]

The attitude of the Christian Church of England is well put by the Bishop of Rochester in an article entitled 'The Church and Sex' which appeared in 1954.[30] His argument is one of sublimation. Men and women can fulfil their sex instinct in a variety of creative ways. This is undoubtedly true for some individuals but

certainly not for all. In any event it would appear to apply only to
the 'mature' person mentioned above rather than the adolescent
who is not yet aware of his powers, creative or otherwise. The
Bishop goes on to say: ' . . . This truth (sublimation), which
experience confirms, would be more widely recognised, and continence much less difficult, if the modern media of popular education and of conditioning adolescent imagination—the press, drama,
advertisements, and the like—were not sex-obsessed and did not go
out to stimulate lust, and immature sexual satisfaction. . . . '[31]
Such a statement could be criticised in many ways. For example, at
what stage is the individual to be regarded as ready for the performance of his sexual functions? At thirty-five for a man, as it is on
average in Eire? How in fact is this to be decided? The argument
reminds us of the married colonial official happily ensconced with
his wife telling his new unmarried subordinate to 'leave the native
women alone'. It is advice which only those who are, through
circumstances, above desire can give. This problem of chastity and
creativity is dramatically presented by Alberto Moravia in his novel
Conjugal Love.

The further argument maintained by the Bishop of Rochester
that pre-marital intercourse hinders a satisfactory relationship after
marriage is rebutted by the evidence Kinsey produces that the
intensive American 'petting' habits, which halt just short of coitus,
do not inhibit full sexual relationship in subsequent marriage.[32]
The Christian apologist should not attempt to rationalise his position but take his stand squarely on the ground that sex outside of
marriage is sinful. For those who are religious this is quite sufficient;
for those who are not, rationalisations will make no appeal. In
any event this is not an academic question we are faced with. The
fact is that, in the face of overt standards of sexual morality in the
West, adolescents are demonstrating in a very real way their
willingness to subscribe to a different ethic which allows them
sexual freedom.

The gulf between scientific opinion and the views of the
'Establishment' on such matters was clearly shown by the controversy concerning the British Medical Association booklet *Getting
Married* in March of this year. The opinions expressed, in our
view, were forthright and sensible. For example, Dr Eustace Chesser
in his article 'Is Chastity Outmoded?' stated: 'Pre-marital sexual

intercourse, despite the fact that it is a limited relationship, can also be more than ordinarily pleasant. By the kind permission of society we are allowed to close our chastity when married. All too often events prove this is to be too little and too late. . . . ' Or those of Dr Roger Pilkington, the geneticist, who begins his section with the question 'So you're a bride, and you are pregnant, too ?', and proceeds to state that one woman in eight is pregnant at marriage, 'We all know the baby is a "mistake", but surely it is a mistake which is understandable.'

In the same week in which it was published the B.M.A. withdrew the booklet. The chairman of the Association, Dr Wand, said that this was due to internal criticism in the B.M.A. It is significant that condemnation also came from ecclesiastical quarters. The *Church Times* wrote: 'If the British Medical Association wishes to convince the country that there is no longer any connexion between medical and Christian morality, it is certainly going the right way about it.' (*The Times*, March 6th, 1959.) Some of the authors and the editor of *Getting Married* protested publicly at the action of the B.M.A., and two of them resigned from the Association. Clearly criticism was to be expected but in view of the fact that the B.M.A. cannot normally be regarded as being in the vanguard of the fight for sexual freedom how the booklet came to be published by them at all is the real mystery.

In this connection it is worth noting that while pre-marital intercourse is not forbidden by law in Britain it is illegal in thirty-five of the States in the U.S.A. [33] To protest at the moral degeneracy of the young, as so many critics do, is not to alleviate the conflict inside the adolescent. More positive action is called for. That is why we feel a consideration of the behaviour, in this respect, of societies other than our own may help to clarify our thinking.

All societies, as we have seen, are presented with this problem of how to canalise and control the awakening sex drive of the young. The solutions adopted depend upon the social and cultural factors which exist in a particular society. Vague judgments of a moral kind regarding these solutions do not help our understanding of them. They can only be understood in their context as part of a functioning whole which we call society.

In the next chapter we shall deal with a somewhat different aspect of man's sexual activity—modesty.

REFERENCES AND NOTES

1. Hutton Webster, *Primitive Secret Societies*, 2nd Ed., N.Y. 1932, pp. 1–2.
2. G. Bateson, *Naven*, 2nd Ed., California 1958, pp. 123–4.
3. C. B. Humphreys, *The Southern New Hebrides*, Camb. 1926, p. 45.
4. R. F. Barton, 'The Igorots Today', *Asia*, June 1941.
5. A. C. Hollis, *The Nandi*, Oxford, 1909.
6. Father Le Gobien, *Histoire des Isles Marianes*, Paris 1700. pp. 61–2.
7. H. Freycinet, *Voyage autour du monde par ordre du roi*, Paris 1825–39, pp. 369–70.
8. L. S. B. Leakey, 'Some Notes on the Masai of Kenya Colony', J.R.A.I., Vol. LX, 1930, and A. C. Hollis, *The Masai*, Oxford 1905, pp. 122 and 310–11.
9. B. Malinowski, *The Sexual Life of Savages*, London 1932, p. 60.
10. For this and other quotations in the text regarding the bukumatula see B. Malinowski, *op. cit.* pp. 62–4.
11. V. Elwin, *The Muria and their Ghotul*, Oxford 1947, p. 343.
12. *ibid.*, p. 344.
13. *ibid.*, p. 347.
14. *ibid.*, p. 372.
15. *ibid.*, p. 376.
16. *ibid.*, pp. 378–9.
17. *ibid.*, p. 369.
18. *ibid.*, p. 322.
19. Cf. The people of Dobu and Manus Islands in the Pacific where jealousy, hatred, and witchcraft are rampant. See R. Fortune, *The Sorcerers of Dobu*, London 1932, and Margaret Mead, *Growing Up in New Guinea*, N.Y. 1939.
20. Elwin, *op. cit.*, p. 461.
21. *ibid.*, p. 462.
22. See C. G. Seligman, *The Melanesians of British New Guinea*, Camb. 1910, p. 500.

    H. I. Hogbin, 'The Native Culture of Wogeo', *Oceania*, Vol. V, 1935, pp. 320 *et seq.*

    R. F. Barton, *Philippine Pagans*, London, 1938, p.11.

    B. Malinowski, *The Sexual Life of Savages*, London 1932, pp. 161 *et seq.*
23. Malinowski, *op.cit.*, p. 168.

24. S. R. Meaker, *Human Sterility*, London 1934, p. 41.

25. K. T. Chan and J. M. Wright, 'Gynaecological Notes: Canton Hospital', *China Medical Journal* 1925, pp. 684–7.

For various opinions on the subject see:

M. F. Ashley-Montagu, 'Adolescent Sterility', *The Quarterly Review of Sterility*, Vol. XIV, 1939, pp. 13–34, 192–219.

S. Zuckerman, 'The Physiology of Fertility in Man and Monkey', *The Eugenics Review*, Vol. XXVIII, 1936, p. 39.

C. B. Hartman, 'On the Relative Sterility of the Adolescent Organism', *Science*, Vol. LXXIV, 1931, pp. 226–7.

26. B. B. Lindsey and W. Evans, *The Companionate Marriage*, London 1928.

27. A. C. Kinsey and others, *Sexual Behaviour in the Human Female*, London 1953, pp. 307–10.

28. A. Torrie, 'Pre-Marital Chastity', in *The Practitioner*, No. 1030, Vol. 172, April 1954, pp. 415–19.

29. See G. H. Morant, 'Cultural Anthropology and Statistics', *Man*, 1935, Sect. 35, also A. J. Kobber, 'New Ways of presenting an old idea: The Statistical Method in Social Anthropology', J.R.A.I., Vol. LXXXII, Part II, 1952, pp. 134–5.

30. Bishop of Rochester, 'The Church and Sex', *The Practitioner, op. cit.*, pp. 350–54.

31. *ibid.*, pp. 350–51.

32. Kinsey, *op. cit.*, pp. 261–5.

33. Torrie, *op. cit.*, p. 415.

CHAPTER III

Modesty

SEXUAL modesty can be defined as an inhibitory mechanism which controls the desire for sexual display on the part of man. As an aspect of the natural human sexual drive, display has as its corollary —modesty. Both can be regarded as innate in the sense that the tendency towards the exercise of the one or the other is part of the ordinary biological endowment of man. But in fact, as Flugel has suggested, display and modesty are opposed to each other and complete simultaneous satisfaction would appear to be impossible.[1] For the individual the way out of the dilemma is the development of coyness. Coyness is a partial solution to the problem as it manages to combine both display and modesty. It is by no means confined to man as the courtship activities of many animals demonstrate. The male pursues the female, she retreating in a frenzy of modesty. But if he appears to lose interest she will turn and display herself in order to excite him to the chase again. The function of coyness in man appears to be very similar.

If sexual modesty be considered as innate, its manifestation, on the other hand, is entirely dependent upon factors external to the biological sex drive. That is, factors which are essentially social or cultural control the particular forms which sexual modesty will take in any given society.

Although clothing provides an excellent means of demonstrating modest behaviour it need not necessarily do so. The habitat of the Greenland Eskimo forces them to adopt extremely thick and heavy skin clothing for both sexes alike. Inside their huts or igloos, however, all clothing is removed and placed outside to air. Men and women remain naked even though strangers may be present. This lack of modesty, if so it can be termed, extends to the performance of the excretory functions '. . . They do not blush to sit down and ease themselves in the presence of others. Every family has a urine tub placed before the entry, in which they make water.'[2] In public assemblies indoors the same rule of discarding clothing is observed. It is clear that for the Eskimo the appropriate occasion for wearing clothes is in the open air. The convention has been established that to wear clothes inside a building is improper. Nudity does not appear to create a tendency for licentious behaviour amongst the Eskimo. Although they sleep naked several in a bed together for warmth and practise sexual hospitality, that is the loan of one's wife or daughter to a stranger or relative, their behaviour is, generally speaking, essentially decorous.

The Eskimo are possibly unique amongst the simpler peoples in having this abrupt conventionalised transition from heavy clothing to complete nudity.

Amongst advanced societies the Japanese and Finns are nearest to the Eskimo in their disregard for clothing in mixed groups. But in both cases the communal nudity has a ritualistic aspect.

The Japanese public bath, equivalent to the European Turkish Bath, is patronised by everyone. The following nineteenth century account creates the scene vividly. ' . . . In the public baths they are rather sparing with the hot water. Each bather gets only a small jar full, and, crouched down on the tiled floor, he washes then pours over himself what is left; the water then runs outside by means of a channel in the middle of the floor. Finally everybody has a last scalding in an enormous tub filled with hot water which is for the common use. Many bathers use the same water after one another, just as the same bathroom serves for all, so that men, women, and children of all ages are to be seen scambling about in the most wonderful mixture. Even the presence of strangers does not disturb their peace of mind. . . .'[3] Understandably things are better ordered today but the practice is still the same. As in the case of the Eskimo there does not appear to be any overt display or licentiousness. What is perhaps curious is that the traditional Japanese dress for women is so designed that the actual form of the body is entirely concealed, this being effectively achieved by means of the 'obi', or girdle, which forms a gigantic bundle over the buttocks.

The Sauna, or Finnish steam bath, is very largely a family affair in which the members of the family have a steam bath by pouring water over hot stones, and thereafter beating each other with birch twigs. This is followed by a roll in the snow or a plunge into an icy stream. The occasion hardly calls for behaviour other than that connected with hygiene. No doubt sexual pleasure could be extracted from the Sauna by the confirmed sado-masochist, but not by the ordinary individual.[4]

Both these examples take place on specialised, almost ritual, occasions and are concerned with washing the body. In this they are quite distinct from the Eskimo custom in which transition from clothing to nudity is of daily occurrence and has no element of ritualism. But the Finns and the Japanese are instances in developed societies of the same abrupt communal transition from heavy clothing to complete nudity irrespective of sex.

In mediaeval Europe public mixed bathing in the nude was by no means confined to Scandinavia. It appears to have been associated with the practice of sleeping in bed without clothes, which persisted until the eighteenth century. This latter custom is exemplified by the German mediaeval poem of Parsifal. Parsifal is received at the palace of the Holy Grail in the following manner

> 'Youths very nimble
> Remove his shoes, his legs are bare.
> Many sprang to aid him,
> Also did his garments doff
> Many a lad of gentle birth.
> Now entered by the door
> Four maidens pure
> Who should look
> If all be well
> And soft the bed . . .

Parsifal, the nimble man
Under cover quickly sprang.
Thus they spake: Thou shalt wake
For our pleasures yet a while.
In his haste he had himself
Quite beneath the bed concealed,
His face alone their glances meeting
Eye to eye in high delight
Ere they had received his greeting.'

In another passage a queen turns to Parsifal for assistance. 'Alone in his bedchamber at night, not with the desire that makes a maiden unexpectedly a woman in one night, but for help and counsel. She robed herself in state in a white silk shift and a cloak of samite. Her trouble impelled her to go. She knelt down by his bed, but he would not suffer that and offered her his place. She asked him to honour her virtue and not touch her limbs. He promised solemnly and she then hid in his bed while she told him her plight. He heard her and freed her town whereupon she gave herself to him.[5]

It appears that Wagner in appropriating the Parsifal theme was somewhat selective in his approach in that he avoided the overtly sexual versions of the legend. The version of the poem we have quoted suggests that the absence of night clothes at least facilitated immodest behaviour. The second passage indicates from the queen's point of view that fornication was a reasonable reward for the knight who had restored to her her city.

Literary evidence of this kind is supported by woodcuts of the period depicting everyday scenes, such as a woman clad only in a nightcap pouring the contents of a chamber pot on men who are serenading her, or ladies receiving visitors while still in bed, the upper portion of their bodies being quite naked. These and similar subjects are quite common. In Tudor times in England it was customary, as it was in the eighteenth century in France, for the nobility to receive friends and suitors while seated on a night commode. Ideas of modesty in terms of the bed and bedroom were clearly broader than they are today.

This freedom of the bedroom obtruded into public life. Sermons of the fourteenth and fifteenth centuries contain many references to what might be termed immodest behaviour. For example a fifteenth century text of Guiler von Kaiserberg states that the 'Third sin is to have a desire to grasp the bare skin, or touch women or maidens on the breast. For there are many so inclined that they think they cannot talk to a woman without touching her on the breasts; that is a great indecency.' Others inveigh against the kissing and grasping of the sexual parts of women in public.

That this danger is still with us in Britain is shown by the following extract from the London *Times* of April 25th, 1958. It is headed

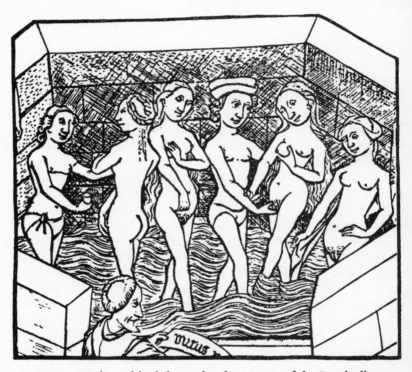

Fig. 3. Mediaeval bath house by the Master of the Bandrolls

' "Wild Weddings" in the Isles. Elders Condemn Dancing and Drunkenness', and continues: 'The Outer Isles Presbytery of the Free Presbyterian Church of Scotland have passed a resolution viewing with grief and alarm "wild" festivities after marriage within their bounds. At a meeting at Stornoway, Isle of Lewis, they condemned the practice of drunkenness and dancing at wedding celebrations. . . . The Presbytery have asked their people to comply with the following regulations in connexion with marriage certificates: That old and young enjoy themselves without having recourse to drunkenness, "which destroys any feeling of shame, stupifies the senses, shamefully degrades men and women, and gives rise to filthy jesting and gestures." That they do not have recourse to promiscuous dancing, "so well fitted to inflame and set ablaze unholy and unclean passions." . . . '

In almost all societies the celebration of weddings provides the occasion for behaviour varying from the slightly immodest to the openly lewd. A marriage is in fact regarded as a licensed, privileged occasion on which conduct normally condemned is permissible. From time to time the guardians of morality may be disturbed and show their disquiet in the manner quoted above, that is by public exhortation.

But the public bath house of the fifteenth century, depicted by Breughel and the illustrators of manuscripts, cannot claim the immunity of a privileged occasion. They became bordellos as well as bathing places. One account states, '. . . The public bath houses of the town, also, where men and women, maidens and youths, monks and nuns bathe together quite naked, certainly could not promote chastity. . . . Early in the morning the baths were most frequented. He who was not bathing paid visits to his acquaintances who were bathing. From the galleries which ran round the baths he could speak to the bathers and see them eat and play at the floating tables. Beautiful maidens begged for alms and he threw coins to them, to catch which they spread out their garments, thus displaying voluptuous charms. . . . '(6)

The mediaeval evidence suggests that general concealment of the body tends to encourage the development of clandestine or sem - clandestine immodesty. The criterion of modesty being, of course, that which prevailed at the time. In European societies conceptions of modesty, in terms of dress and behaviour have changed perpetually. Today the normal sobriety and concealment in the clothing of men is offset by the socially sanctioned semi-nudity of women. Nevertheless convention operates so as to demand that where the minimum of clothing is worn publicly it shall be confined to a quasi-ritualistic occasion—the bathing beach. The evolution from the bathing bloomers of the nineties to the bikini has been dramatic in its effect. But it could be debated whether for the average nineteenth century European male the sight of a woman's ankle once in a while was not more sexually stimulating than the constant display of semi-nude women on the seashore is for the men of today. In this connection it is noticeable that Britain each year sees publicity departments of seaside resorts torn by internal disputes as to whether landscape, or the scantily clad charms of a

Fig. 4. 'They became bordellos as well as bathing places'

nubile girl on a poster has more appeal to the potential visitor. Railway stations throughout the country bear witness to the state of the battle. This is an excellent example of the contemporary ambivalence of attitude towards modesty.

There is considerable evidence from savage societies, as well as from present-day nudist camps, to indicate that the free display of the body in time inhibits sexual interest. For those who fulminate against contemporary immodesty in America and Europe the answer would seem to be the open advocacy of public nudity on all possible occasions.

But the problem for our type of society with regard to standards of modesty cannot be solved in the happy mediaeval manner of nakedness in bed and bath house. The British and the American world is compounded of bikinis, striptease, static nude shows, advertisement for female underwear, the pin-up girl, the 'cleavage' and the sweater cults, the lubricous movie poster, and so on. All these contribute to a general atmosphere of salaciousness in which former conventions of modesty and immodesty seem to have largely disappeared.

Despite this there is a remarkable restraint exercised in relation to action in public. The restraint appears to be of the same order as that which controls the appropriateness of clothing for the occasion. Beach wear, in Britain at any rate, can only be tolerated by the sea or its immediate confines. Elsewhere the scantiness of the costume would be held to be indecent and thus a criminal offence. The logic here is that the clothing is not in itself improper, but the setting in which it is worn can make it so. This is indeed a logical advance on the Middle Ages. For this reason the current advertisements in Britain for a certain type of central heating, depicting a family in ordinary domestic surroundings but clad in underwear and beach-wear, must have caused more disquiet to the average citizen than all the other elements of suggestiveness mentioned above.

The European approach to the problem of modesty and display is governed very largely by what can be described as the preservation of public decency. This varies considerably from age to age. Anomalies do, of course, occur. The severity of Victorian female dress is broken by the deliberate and alarming provocativeness of the bustle. The free display of the bosom in the seventeenth and eighteenth centuries is creeping back today in the form of 'cleavage' dresses. Ideas of public decency are governed by Judeo-Christian thought on the subject. This places the emphasis on the sexual aspects of modesty, and attempts to control any overt signs of sexual activity. With what success we can judge for ourselves.

The so-called savage comes to the problem with his mind unencumbered with conceptions of the obscene culled from the early Fathers of Christianity. Nevertheless he has definite ideas of what constitutes public decency. For example, the Ona women of Tierra del Fuego at the southern tip of South America are naked except for an animal skin thrown over the shoulder. However they always sit down so as to effectively conceal the genitals. On the other hand there may be complete disregard of the sexual organs as is shown by the male Suk and Nandi of the Sudan. The men are elaborately clothed but leave the sexual region prominently exposed. But such disregard of the genitals is somewhat rare: for what is of great importance to the savage is the possibility of magic being directed against this most vital part of the anatomy.

All the openings of the body are regarded as being particularly defenceless against magic. There is also the widespread belief that the soul or spirit may escape, or be drawn out, or evil influences enter through such openings. Thus it is fairly common practice amongst a great number of peoples for the ears, mouth, nose, anus, vagina, and penis to be guarded by some object, design, or material having the power to ward off evil magic. North American Indians, many tribes in Indonesia, Australian Aborigines, the Hindu peoples of India all possess examples of this type of magical protection of the orifices of the body.

Of these orifices the most important are the sexual openings. These are regarded as being exposed to a constant series of dangers. For a woman there is always the danger that she may be impregnated from a distance by a variety of agencies ranging from evil spirits to lightning. In India the belief was common that not only were women liable to be sexually assaulted by spirits or demons, but that the attacks might be so frequent that they might die from supernatural ardours. Similar beliefs were held by many South American Indian tribes, and by the Eskimo.

For men the ever-present hazard is the occurrence of impotence, which is widely believed to be of supernatural origin. For example, the Shilluk of the Sudan maintain that the evil eye can render a man impotent. Similarly the male inhabitants of the New Hebrides carefully guard their penises against witchcraft.

Thus for both men and women it is of prime importance that the sexual organs should be protected. Pure concealment is not in itself necessarily the best means to achieve this end. In fact devices used for this purpose vary enormously in size, design, and efficacy. Amongst Hindus in the past according to the Abbé Dubois, '. . . Even the private parts of the children have their own particular decorations. Little girls wear a gold or silver shield or cod-piece on which is graven some indecent picture; while a boy's ornament, also of gold or silver, is an exact copy of that member which it is meant to decorate. . . . '[7] A fairly common practice is for women who wear little or no clothing, as amongst some Nilotic tribes, to have a string of cowrie shells, a belt of some material, or a bunch of leaves, as is the custom in some tribes in the north of Ghana, suspended either above the buttocks, or passing between the legs and attached to a waist belt. Protection by such means does not always extend to children. The Acholi of the Upper Nile allow their unmarried girls to go naked except for bracelets and anklets of beads. Married women on the other hand have to wear a tiny apron made of bead chains. The reasoning here is that virgins have a natural protection which is lost after marriage.

The guarding of the sexual organs of both men and women by means of amulets, etc., by peoples who are otherwise almost entirely nude, does not necessarily lead to immodest behaviour. Obviously it draws attention to the sexual region but the purpose is not overtly to stimulate attraction but very definitely to ward off evil. At the same time the covered area of an otherwise naked body must act as a sexual stimulant. Such peoples have combined symbolic or actual concealment as a barrier against magic with erotic display. It is possible that in such societies, where the body is familiar in all its aspects, the decoration of the vulva or penis may have an aesthetic-titillatory function in addition to the protective power.

In many instances tattooing serves the same purpose of providing a symbolic covering. Examples can be drawn from peoples of the Congo, such as the Mangbettu and the Basonge; the Tupi Indians of Brazil; and Polynesian tribes. In all these cases women are either tattooed or painted in the pubic region. A skirt or garment may be

worn over the marks but their efficacy against evil spirits resides in
the actual marking of the skin. A striking instance of this type of
protection comes from Ponape in the Caroline Islands in the Pacific
where the most intricate and elaborate designs were woven around
the vulva. In most Polynesian societies a prospective bridegroom
had the right to demand a view of the tattooing before marriage, to
see whether his wife-to-be was adequately defended.

The European belief that clothing and modesty go hand in hand
is simply not borne out by the facts. There are some interesting
accounts which demonstrate this. A Portuguese, writing early in
the sixteenth century about Brazil, states: ' . . . All of them goe
naked, as well men as women, and have no kind of apparell, and are
nothing ashamed; rather it seemeth that they are in a state of
innocencies touching this behalf. . . . Now alreadie some doe
weare apparell, but esteem it so little that they wear it rather for
fashion than for honesties sake, and because they are commanded to
weare it; as it is well seene by some that sometimes come abroad
with certaine garments no further than the navell without any
other thing, or otheres onely a cap on their heads and leave the
other garments at home. . . . '(8)

Christian missionaries, perhaps unconsciously more concerned
for themselves than for the people, felt impelled to inculcate what
amounted to an alien sense of modesty. The Jesuits in South
America had this problem. The Indians when given clothes would
tear them up to make scarves and turbans. When asked about it they
answered they were ashamed to be seen wearing clothes on their
bodies. Early missionaries in Australia had the same difficulty. But
the attitude has been modified. In Northern Ghana, where many of
the women habitually go bare breasted, we were surprised to see
them in and around a Roman Catholic monastery. We questioned
the Fathers on this point. To our surprise they said they had been
worried at the start of the mission, and had thought of forbidding
female converts to remain uncovered. They had however reached
the conclusion that it would be better to let example (there is a
convent of nuns nearby) provide the incentive. This is a surprisingly
refreshing attitude in complete contrast to the earlier missionaries
who regarded the concealment of the body of the savage as the
prime work of the Lord's labourers.

The European is necessarily bound by his clothes, and finds it difficult to conceive of people who do not associate licentious behaviour with nudity or semi-nudity. In fact, as we have tried to show, modesty is determined not only by the intrinsic function of the devices which people adopt for such purposes but also by the meanings which are placed in the devices. In other words the state of mind of the individual is as important as the material that he uses to create a modest effect.

In many societies at the pre-literate level women's sexual organs are not only to be guarded against magic, they are themselves sources of evil directed against men. Two factors may possibly operate here. One is the debilitating effect of the sexual act on man —the experience has given great pleasure but the feeling of lassitude indicates that it is weakening and so dangerous. The other is the occurrence of menstruation, which from a male point of view is an alarming phenomenon. The latter has been advanced by many sociologists, notably Emile Durkheim,[9] as fundamental in the development of female sexual coverings, and hence a basic source of female bodily modesty.

In practically all societies the menstruating woman is subject to tabus of various kinds. These cover a wide range of behaviour. One of the most common forms of tabu is avoidance of the woman in this state. This frequently involves her segregation from the community. It may be carried out by providing a special hut or place where the woman has to stay until her period is over. This is characteristic of the Eskimo and all North American Indian tribes. Among the Tlingit Indians of British Columbia a girl at her first menses was confined in an isolated hut. No one was allowed to approach the hut except her female relatives who supplied her with pre-masticated food. She could not lie down but had to support herself on logs. Her head was covered with a mat and her face smeared with charcoal. She had to take every precaution not to expose herself to the sun. The girl was regarded essentially as an object of dread and fear from whom evil was emanating.

The menstruous woman was a source not only of evil magic but also of physical ill. The Canadian Beaver Indians believed that to walk on the same path as such a woman caused people to develop sores on the legs. In many societies after her first menses a girl was subjected to an elaborate process of disinfection. An extreme example is that of the Guarani Indians of South America. The girl was sewn up in a hammock in the same fashion as a corpse, a tiny open-ing being left for her to breathe through. The hammock was then suspended over a smoking fire for several days, and in this way was the girl purified. The Araucanian Indians of Chile believe that such is the evil residing in a menstruous woman that her presence at a sick bed is sufficient to ensure death for the invalid.

The segregation and avoidance pattern is also found amongst the aboriginal tribes of India. The Gonds of Central India build special huts out of sight of the village where the women are confined at this time. Food for them is left outside. Women are regarded as being essentially impure during the menses and are capable of bringing tremendous evil upon anyone who looks at them. In South India it was the general practice after the menstrual period for women to go through the most elaborate purification rites before they were judged fit for ordinary society again.

Similar attitudes towards menstruation are common in African societies. Breach of the segregation tabu by a Kikuyu entailed destruction of the hut which she had polluted. The tabu was not so strong amongst the Baila of Rhodesia. Here avoidance in a special hut was not insisted upon but the woman was forbidden to sit in other people's company, had to sleep on the floor, and on no account was allowed to cook her husband's food.

Polynesia exhibits the same pattern. Tongan society demanded isolation and elaborate ceremonial purification rites. In Tahiti the woman herself was tabu but she was allowed to remain in the family hut. The Maoris regarded the menstruating woman as unclean and she was isolated for a period.

The Australian Aborigines had great horror of women during their menses. Some tribes in Queensland had the practice of bury-ing a menstruating girl up to her waist in the sand. A thorn bush fence was then built round her. She was fed by her mother, and given a stick so that she might scratch herself as she had to avoid touching her own body.

An exception to the almost universal tabu regarding the men-struating woman is provided by the Akamba of East Africa. Part of the general avoidance pattern is that sexual relations are abso-lutely forbidden at this time. But the Akamba apparently obliged a husband to copulate with his wife on the night her menses began. This was done in the belief that the woman was much more likely to conceive at that time. Such a practice appears to be quite exceptional.

The evidence from a vast majority of human societies suggests that woman becomes unclean, evil, and dangerous with unfailing regularity every month. A corollary of this is the equally wide-spread belief that the time of childbirth is also a dangerous crisis when contamination of others may take place.

But fear of menstruation is by no means confined to those societies we call savage. Ancient Persia, classical Greece and India show the same insistence on danger. The Zoroastrian sacred books are quite explicit. ' . . . For a fiend so violent is that fiend of menstruation, that, where another fiend does not smite anything with a look, it smites with a look. . . . '[10] A Persian woman was confined to a special apartment in her house. No fires were allowed while her period lasted. After the menses were over all her clothing had to be destroyed, and she was purified by being washed in bull's urine. Violation of these tabus by a man resulted in his being punished by a public flogging.[11]

The Hindu Laws of Manu lay down that a man becomes impure if he touches ' . . . a menstruating woman, an outcast, a woman in childbed, or a corpse. . . . ' And that ' . . . The wisdom, the energy, the strength, the sight, and the vitality of a man who approaches a woman covered with menstrual excretions utterly perish. . . . '[12]

Euripides in his *Iphigenia in Tauris*[13] equates the impurity of a menstruous woman with that of a corpse. Although not as ex-plicitly formulated as the Hindu conception there is little doubt that amongst the Greeks the menstruating woman was someone to be avoided.

The expression in Pliny of Roman beliefs concerning the same theme remains the basis of much contemporary European folklore on this topic. Such ideas as that a menstruous woman could not make butter or cream, that she would turn wine in vats, that flower and fruit trees wither at her touch, and so on, are common at the present day in Europe. An amusing example from the late nine-teenth century in England is provided by the British Medical Journal (Vol. I, p. 324, 1878). A doctor wrote to the effect that ' . . . It was a very prevalent belief amongst females, both rich and poor, that in curing hams women should not rub the legs of pork with the brine pickle at the time they are menstruating. . . . ' Other letters from medical gentlemen supported this view, some writers being amazed that its authenticity should be questioned. '. . . None but an Australian black would deny it. . . . '(14) The savage's inherent fear of woman's periodicity has become transformed into terms of her nuisance value with regard to cooking and growing things.

If it is granted that in savage society the female sexual region is one which possesses a great potential for evil, and the evidence is very strong, it is reasonable to assume with Durkheim that here is the main source of female sexual modesty. Here, in fact, is the region which must be guarded and hidden either actually or symbolically. Therefore it becomes the pivot upon which woman's modesty will tend to revolve. She will not wish to break the tabus involved, for the penalties are severe. The basis of her attitude is concerned more with magic than sexual modesty. Clothes in this connection are irrelevant, as we have seen. The tabus are just as severe in cases where the people are almost nude as when they are fully clad. Sexual morality has little connection with modesty or indeed with the lack or presence of clothes. The savage is primarily concerned with the magical powers possessed by the female sexual organs, and the harm that may come to them, so that modesty is inseparable from magic.

The modesty revolving round the sexual region is equally well marked amongst men, for similar reasons. The covering may be merely symbolic or indeed non-existent, or of grotesque size as in the case of the people of the New Hebrides where the penis is wrapped in yards of cloth forming a giant bundle. But whatever is done with the penis as regards concealment, it is not to be touched or stared at. To do so would be bad manners, immodest and dangerous.

For the savage the basis of modesty is a magical or supernatural one. A look, a gesture, a touch, may let loose the forces of magic. So modesty guards him against such dangers.

In considering our own type of society it is clear that sexual modesty has lost its magical basis and is primarily concerned with sexual behaviour. Clothes, as the body is normally completely covered, play a very important part in determining modest behaviour. The gradual revealing of a woman's body in a strip-tease is held to represent lubricous behaviour. But this is far re-

moved from the sixteenth century Arab belief that if a woman
meeting a lion in the desert were to expose her body the lion would
lower his eyes and run away. [15] In that context magic still operated.
The nineteenth century saw the last remnants of this type of belief.
Goethe wrote of his experience of seeing a naked woman for the
first time that it was like the sight of a fearful and unknown mon-
ster. [16] Flaubert in his autobiography says: ' . . . The first time I
saw the breasts of a woman entirely unclothed I nearly fainted.
. . . ' [17] Perhaps these are exceptional cases concerning unduly
sensitive writers, but there is no question that clothes in our society
have promoted ideas of modesty connected with sex which are
quite alien to the savage, secure in his elemental world of magic and
the supernatural.

Although the basis of modesty may be different in Europe from
what it is in savage society, in both cases the sentiment of offended
modesty is concerned with the breaking of a tabu. It was suggested
at the beginning of this chapter that modesty was the counterpart of
display, and both were part of the natural sexual drive of man and
to that extent were innate. As the child's sexual drive develops so
will modesty and display. The forms they take will be dependent
upon the values and beliefs current in a particular society at a given
time. In the great majority of human societies magic and fear are
associated with the sexual region of the body and amongst these
peoples modesty tends to have a magical basis. By contrast, in
other societies, such as our own, which have as it were become
secularised, and where sex is no longer associated with magic, conventions and tabus of modesty are primarily concerned with not
altogether successful attempts to conceal the body as a source of the
lewd. The process of socialisation or indoctrination in any society
results in the individual accepting the majority of conventions as
being of the natural order of things; especially if they are emotionally loaded as are those connected with modesty.

For the savage, breach of the tabu is visited by frightful punishment which may be both spiritual and material. Not only does he
become impure, he may also suffer banishment. His beliefs are such
that a breach in private has the same effect upon him as public
commission: if he has sinned, whether seen or unseen, his punishment will be the same. Whereas for the contemporary American or
Briton, no longer confronted with hell fire as a reward for sin in

general (the equivalent of a breach of the savage's tabu), or lewdness in particular, the way is open for the titillating experience of
breaking the tabus of sexual modesty. There is still an inheritance of
guilt left with us from the days of belief to make the experience
enjoyable.

Christian religious orders and sects may command their members not to look at their own or other individuals' bodies in the
mistaken idea that the nude body is the source of lubricity. The fact
remains that in our kind of society it is the manipulation of clothing,
of which the striptease act is the finest flower, that is the source of
lasciviousness. A curious element in this attitude is the empasis upon
woman as the promoter of lewdness in dress. (Male homosexuals
come into a rather special category.) The mediaeval codpiece and
points are isolated examples of the European male's attempt to
attract attention to his body and emphasise his sexual characteristics. It could be argued that the wearing of a rapier in the seventeenth and eighteenth centuries was a type of sexual symbolism
designed for the same purpose. But compared with the extravagance and suggestiveness of women's clothes in the same periods
male efforts are very puny. One explanation of this may be the
effect of Patristic literature and thought on Christian ideas in such
matters. The Holy Fathers represent a definite break with pagan
ideas regarding sex, woman, and the human body. To criticise, one
might say they were obsessed with the thought of woman as a
vessel of evil. From St. Paul's somewhat mild injunction 'It is
better to marry than to burn' to Clement of Alexandria's 'Every
woman ought to be filled with shame at the thought that she is a
woman',[18] the first centuries of Christian life are filled with
exhortations to the virgin life and for the relegation of sexual
activity, and woman, to the outer darkness. Filtered through the
churches these doctrines have had a profound effect on the relationship between men and women, not only in the past but at the
present time.

The emphasis in our society on the inherent dangers of the naked
body as the source of immodesty creates a danger. Not a danger in
the sense that such attitudes promote socially undesirable sexual or
quasi-sexual activity, the incidence of such behaviour appears to
have been fairly constant throughout European history, but rather
in extending our condemnatory attitude to peoples whose ethical

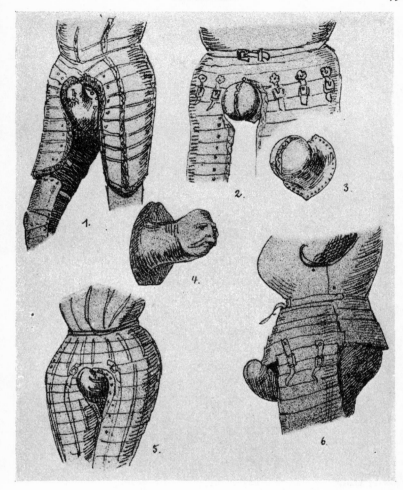

Fig. 5. Sixteenth century codpieces in armour

outlook is, as we have tried to show, entirely different in conception and sentiment. This is to fall into the stupid error of parochialism, of judging the world by the standards of your own market place.

In the sphere of modesty the two worlds of the savage and our own are apart. Each has its own terrors and fears. The savage dare not break his tabu as the consequences are too terrible to contemplate. For us, in our sophistication, sexual immodesty of an extreme kind, such as exhibitionism, although it may end in disaster produces erotic thrills which may be unique.

Arthur Schnitzler in his novel *Fräulein Else* illustrates this precise point. The heroine is importuned by an elderly pervert to exhibit herself to him naked. In return he will help her father's failing finances. Else at first refuses then, instead of revealing herself in private, which was all the situation demanded, she does so publicly in an hotel, and commits suicide.

'. . . His eyes say to me: Come. His eyes say: I want to see you naked. Well you swine, I am naked. What more do you want? Send the telegram off . . . at once. Thrills run over my skin. The lady goes on playing. . . . Delicious thrills run over my skin. How wonderful it is to be naked. The lady goes on playing, she doesn't know what's happening. Nobody knows. Nobody sees me yet. Scamp, scamp. Here I stand naked. Dorsday opens his eyes wide. At last he believes. The scamp gets up. His eyes are glowing. . . .'[19]

Such refinement may well be beyond the competence of the savage.

REFERENCES AND NOTES

1. J. C. Flugel, *The Psychology of Clothes*, London 1930, pp. 19–21.
2. H. Egede, *A Description of Greenland*, London 1818, p. 127 *et seq.*
3. W. Heine, *Reise um die Erde nach Japan*, Leipzig 1856, Vol. II, p. 34.
4. Londoners can now (1958) conduct the experiment themselves as a Sauna bath, complete with birch twigs but with a shower in place of the icy stream, is available at Finland House in the West End.
5. Parsifal quoted by H. H. Ploss and M. & P. Bartels, *Woman*, ed. E. J. Dingwall, London 1935, Vol. II, pp. 10–11.
6. *Op. cit.* Ploss & Bartels, p. 8.
7. A. Dubois, *Hindu Manners, Customs, and Ceremonies*, 3rd edition, reprinted London 1947, p. 333.
8. 'A Treatise of Brazil', in *Purchas His Pilgrimes*, Glasgow 1905–7, Vol. XVI, pp. 4222 *et seq.*
9. Durkheim, 'La prohibition de l'Inceste et ses Origines', *L'Année Sociologique*, Paris 1898, Vol. I, pp. 44 *et seq.*
10. *The Sacred Books of the East*, ed. F. Max Muller, Oxford 1879–1910, Vol. V, p. 27.

11. *Zend-Avesta, Sacred Books of the East, op. cit.*, Vol. IV, pp. 185–8.

12. *The Laws of Manu, Sacred Books of the East, op. cit.*, Vol. XXV, p. 18.

13. *Iphigenia in Tauris*, translated by Gilbert Murray, London 1911, pp. 330 *et seq*.

14. *British Medical Journal*, 1878, Vol. II, p. 654.

15. G. Leo Africanus, 'Descrittore del l'Africa', in G. B. Ramusio, *Navigationi et Viaggi*, Venice 1554, Vol. I, Fol. 100.

16. W. Goethe, *Briefs aus der Schweiz*, Cotta 1885, *Werke*, Vol. IV, p. 469.

17. F. Flaubert, 'Memoires d'un fou', *Oeuvres de Jeunesse Inédites*, Paris 1910, p. 521.

18. *Paedogogus*, ii, 2 in J. P. Migne, *Patrolgiae Cursus Completus Series Graeca*, Paris 1857, Vol. VIII, col. 395.

19. A. Schnitzler, *Fräulein Else*, translated by F. H. Lyon, London, N.D., pp. 124–5.

CHAPTER IV

Love and Love Magic

IF WE define love as a prolonged and mutual attachment both sexual and spiritual between two people, we find that it is sometimes considered as primarily a European phenomenon. Romantic love in Europe appears to have been unknown prior to the appearance in late eleventh century France of the troubadors and trouvères. That is not to say that attachments of this kind did not exist between individuals before that time, but that it was not accepted and formalised as a popular conception. For example, the emphasis in the Norse Sagas is almost entirely on heroic deeds and adventure. Heroines are formidable women who would not be guilty of lukewarm, feminine passions—they are admired for male qualities. This is in marked contrast to the essential erotic element in Provençal poetry of the following centuries.

The overwhelming emphasis on sexuality and sexual passion which is characteristic of the pagan literatures of Europe, particularly the Irish, is not evidence for the existence of romantic notions of love. For example the picture which emerges from Celtic Literature is of a society devoted to sexual pursuits but paying very little regard to the relationships between individuals. The incident in the *Feast of Bricriu* when the hero Cuchulain and his followers, who are being entertained by the King of Ulster, are offered fifty women each for their sexual needs—the number includes the Queen and her daughter—can be regarded as typical of Celtic ideas of love.[1]

The essential refinement with which the troubadours cloaked adulterous love is indicative of the climate of the times. One of the most remarkable features of the rise of romantic love was that the same period was characterised by extremely barbaric, brutal and disgusting practices by both men and women. Sexuality might very well be the theme of magnificent poetry but at the same time '. . . To judge from contemporary poems and romances, the first thought of every knight on finding a lady unprotected and alone was to do her violence. . . . '[2] There are numerous instances of this kind of behaviour both in prose and poetry. The *Lai de Graelent*, by Marie de France, tells how a gentle and perfect knight meets a damsel alone in the forest. He brutally assaults and rapes her. However he is forgiven for underneath it all he is fundamentally courteous and honourable.[3] The contradiction is quite extraordinary. It is seen again in the instructions given to the good knight Sir Perceval by his mother. '. . . If thou see a fair woman, pay thy court to her, whether she will or no; for thus wilt thou render thyself a better and more esteemed man than thou wast before. . . . '[4] The argument is well put by Chrétien de Troyes. A knight finding a damsel alone must offer her no harm but if another knight accompanies her, and he defeats him in combat, the lady is his to do with as he wishes.[5] The distinction is subtle but real. The adulation of fighting was on a level with love. No reasonable woman would refuse a conquering knight. To take her by force, as in Marie de France's poem, was really not quite the thing to do.

Different interpretations can be made of this early literature of romantic love. One view, which we are inclined to support, is that the essential lawlessness and brutality of the period was overlaid by a film of idealisation of the feminine which was at times acted out in reality, at other times grossly disregarded. Another is that the knights and troubadours constituted a kind of island of culture and gentility in a sea of barbarism—that in fact the two worlds were not connected. This we find difficult to accept in the face of the evidence.

Vernon Lee suggests in *Euphorion* a picture of a Provençal court.[6] The court consists of all those with any pretensions to nobility from the greatest lord to the lowliest page. These, as opposed to the brutal peasantry without, were united in their service to the wife of the great lord, and her ladies. The atmosphere is redolent of dedication and service; the realities of mediaeval life elsewhere—the burning and sacking of castles, the rape of women, the torture of peasants—are far removed. To pretend that there were not strong elements of graciousness, even of spirituality, in some Provençal courts would be untrue, but at the same time to discount the barbaric elements both within the court and outside in the teeming world is unrealistic.

It is true that Provence at that time enjoyed comparative peace compared with the condition of the rest of Europe. It is very probable that cessation from perpetual warfare and forays enabled the noble poets to develop and embellish this extraordinary manifestation of the human spirit. This would explain the transposing of ordinary knight service into service to a lady. Instead of preoccupation with war the lord could now afford amatory adventures. It does not explain, however, the startling invention of the courts of love with their exacting interpretation of minute points of courtly behaviour in what seems direct imitation of scholastic theological disputes. Lovers were bound by the rules of 'cortesia', patience and moderation—that is restraint. The real problem is to discover the realities of the situation. In the literature there is a metaphysical and allegorical aspect together with an appreciation of the grossest sensuality. The precepts of behaviour we have quoted have to be set against the exacting fealty to one's lady demanded by the courts of love and exemplified in Chrestien de Troyes's *Lancelot* (Lines 5641 *et seq.*) The obscenity of the earliest troubadours, Count William of Poitou, for example, is unbelievable. The vast majority of his notable successors such as Arnaud Daniel and Bertram de Born are equally at pains to show that it is physical not spiritual possession which they desire. There is a very real contradiction here for in the *Lancelot* of de Troyes there are numerous references to abstractions such as Love and Reason on an altogether different plane from sensuality. There are many other examples. The blending of sensual love, service to womankind, allegory and ambition is a strange one. But whatever interpretation is used the fact remains that the concept of courtly love invented by the troubadours in Provence was the starting point for all the subsequent European manifestations of romantic love. In this connection it is interesting to see that the eighteenth-century French nobility prided itself on its gentility and courtesy but at the same time was notorious for its licentiousness. [7]

Going back to our definition of love as an exclusive sensual attachment in conjunction with emotions of a spiritual kind, it has been suggested that this is a concept which is alien to so-called savage peoples. The evidence here is extremely conflicting.

Apropos West African peoples, Mary Kingsley wrote: 'Affection, with the savage, is not so deeply linked with sex; but the love between mother and child, man and man, brother and sister, woman and woman, is deep, pure and true. . . . '[8] This view can be compared with that of Margaret Mead who found that the Samoans were reduced to laughter at the story of Romeo and Juliet. Such behaviour to them was inconceivable. 'Romantic love as it occurs in our civilisation, inextricably bound up with ideas of monogamy, exclusiveness, jealousy, and undeviating fidelity, does not occur in Samoa. . . . '[9] Lewis Morgan, one of the pioneers of anthropology, came to the conclusion that love was unknown to the North American Indians. [10] There is evidence of a similar kind from various parts of Africa, New Zealand, New Guinea, and South America.

The argument here is based on the assumption that in most primitive societies there are few barriers in the way of sexual gratification. There may, as we have seen, be formalised pre-nuptial sexual relationships. The result is that the intense romantic passion characteristic of Europe cannot develop satisfactorily. Put in another way it is the restraints of conventions and ideas which have promoted love in the European sense. This sounds extremely plausible. But there are loopholes both in the evidence and the hypothesis.

One real error may spring from the apparent dislike of many peoples for exhibiting their feelings. This particularly applies to relationships between the sexes. The lack of demonstration noticed by the observer need not necessarily be an indication of the true state of affairs. The anthropologist in England might easily form the impression from observation of the public behaviour of married

couples that love in any sense was minimal. To argue further that
the incidence of arranged marriages is so high in primitive society
that it indicates an absence of romantic feeling is beside the point.
Arranged marriages occur in all societies including our own, it is
only the degree of arrangement which varies. The dictation of class,
background, wealth and interests can be as powerful determinants
in bringing marriages about in our type of society as parental
considerations of cattle and finance in primitive communities.

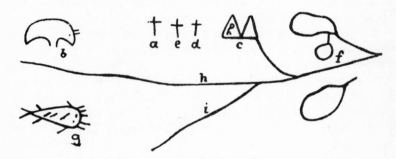

Fig. 6. An American Indian love letter

The positive evidence for the existence of romantic passion in the
simple peoples is considerable.

In a great number of societies, the Dyaks of Borneo, North
American Indians, Siberian tribes, Tibet, peoples of New Guinea,
the Maoris, and many African groups, elopement as a method of
achieving marriage is used. In a minority of instances elopement is a
formalised affair to which the parents concerned are privy. But in
ordinary circumstances it is reasonable to assume that individuals
elope because of their desire to overcome obstacles in the way of
their marriage. That they will act in this way would appear to be
proof of a romantic attachment in the European sense.

Suicide for reasons of love is found in all types of societies. It has
been reported of the Pima Indians of North America, of the
Tahitians, of the inhabitants of the New Hebrides, of the Fijians,
and of some Australian Aborigines[11]. It appears from this type
of evidence that exclusive passionate attachments do exist amongst
the less advanced peoples of the world.

There remains the hypothesis that the prevalence in savage

societies of arranged marriages in conjunction with pre-nuptial sexual activity is not conducive to the development of romantic love; whereas the inhibitions and barriers towards intercourse between the sexes have, in Europe, provided a fruitful ground for the growth of such sentiments. The facts seem to be at variance with this. Arranged marriages appear always to have existed in Europe side by side with the exercise of free choice. In primitive society it is undoubtedly true that the individual's choice is circumscribed by rules and regulations of a fearsome magnitude. His choice, if it is a choice, may be narrowed down to a very small group of women. On the other hand it is comparable to the tendency in Britain for various social groups, such as 'county' families, to marry within the group with unfailing regularity, as a reading of the engagement columns of newspapers show. Theoretically the arranged marriage and similar restrictions could promote romantic feelings as much in the primitive world as in Europe.

Pre-nuptial sexual licence indicative of sexual freedom is presumed to coarsen the feelings of the sexes for each other—sexual access being so easy. But is this really so? Verrier Elwin in his exhaustive study of the sexual life of an Indian aboriginal tribe[12] has shown, with a wealth of evidence, that this kind of sexual licence is productive of the most tender feelings between the sexes, evinced not only in behaviour but in their erotic literature. In Europe, as we shall see, many peasant courtship practices ultimately lead to sexual intercourse before marriage. In addition there has been a steady growth in this type of behaviour throughout Europe and the English-speaking world. Western society, in conjunction with its increasing tolerance of sexual activity before marriage, maintains its belief in romantic love on the most gigantic scale, fostered by films, television, radio, and literature.

In our view romantic love may vary in its incidence and intensity according to the society considered, but it exists wherever men and women meet each other.

Love, considered as a manifestation among advanced non-European peoples, is seen to be as romantic in conception as it is in the West. Yet some critics have condemned what they call the gross animal desire which colours oriental love.[13] This is to ignore the essential basis of romantic love, which is after all an expression of sexual passion however it may be disguised or concealed. To compare, for example, the *Song of Solomon* with a love poem of Donne illustrates two aspects of the same type of feeling. Close comparison reveals that perhaps they are not so far apart as may first appear, even though separated by centuries and profound cultural differences. The lines from the Song of Solomon 'Thou has ravished my heart, my sister, my spouse; Thou has ravished my heart with one of thine eyes' are not so removed from the sentiment of Donne's 'And we were mutual Elements to us, And made of one another. My body then doth less involve . . .' (*The Dissolution*). Other comparisons could be made between the English Metaphysical poets and the Persian mystics. Both use a vocabulary which, if not directly sexual, has sexual overtones. It is not our task here to trace the connection between the use of language and sexual repression, but much mystical poetry could be profitably analysed from this viewpoint. It has been suggested that the choice of sexual imagery by European and Oriental mystics is an obvious one, for sex is a natural appetite and therefore can legitimately be used to express the love of God. In this connection it is as well to remember that St. Bernard of Clairvaux evolved the concept of Divine Love during the same period as the troubadours were extolling adulterous love.

The whole problem of the courtly love of the troubadours, and its relation to the heretical doctrines of the Cathari, as well as mystical poetry with its erotic context and overtones, is extremely complicated. The contemporary Christian attitude is very forcibly put by Denis de Rougemont in his *Passion and Society* (London 1956, pp. 58–136). Sexual love can be repressed, distorted, refined, or sublimated, but its origin and basis must not be forgotten.

If oriental erotic poetry is taken at its face value as a straightforward address to the senses it would seem to indicate strong sentiments of romantic love in the cultures which have fostered its development. For example, the feelings expressed in the *Chauraspanchasika* of the eleventh century Sanskrit poet Bilhana are of the same order as those of the English Romantics, such as Byron, in the nineteenth century. The Persian poets Hafiz and Sa'di, who speak so eloquently of love, have their European parallels. The same is true of Arabic poetry—there is a complete rejoicing in the freedom of the senses. It would be exaggeration to speak of gross sensuality unless Schiller, Heine, Byron and Shelley were to be equally accused.

Lines such as Byron's 'She walks in beauty, like the night Of cloud-
less climes and starry skies;' can be set against 'Watch in your garden
low, from place to place, Seeking, the disappointed zephyr goes;
A rose he dreams of, lovely as thy face', from one of Hafiz's odes.

The Tuareg of North Africa with their institution of the 'A'hal',
or poetical evenings, can be held to exemplify the importance
attached to the romantic in many oriental peoples. '. . . The art of
poetical composition is in the nature of a polite accomplishment,
common to all, and enjoyed by all, and the love of poetry and song
is one of the most characteristic and striking features of Tuareg
social life. . . . [14] The a'hal is similar in many ways to its
mediaeval Provençal equivalent, to which it is frequently compared. An a'hal is conducted by a woman renowned for her beauty
and ability to improvise poetry or songs. The young of both sexes
provide the audience. Tuareg women are famous for their freedom
of behaviour as compared with other Arab nations. Witty conversation, story telling, songs and the recital of poetry are an
integral part of the procedure of the a'hal. The a'hal is by no means
undisciplined but governed according to a highly formalised etiquette. This formality is reflected in the special clothing which it is
incumbent upon members to wear. [15] Women are as competent
as men in composing poems. As with the troubadours, Tuareg
poetry is full of love and war. The following is a poem addressed
by a woman to her lover

> 'Shall I compare thee to a white mehari, to a camel of Termai?
> To a herd of Kita antelopes? To the fringe of Jerba's red scarf?
> To grapes which have just ripened?
> In a valley where alongside of them ripens the date?
> Arrûnen is the thread on which have been strung the pearls of my
>   necklace.
> He is the cord on which are hung the talismans of my heart.
> He is my life.' [16]

The a'hal is an unique phenomenon, not only amongst the Arab
peoples, but in the world as a whole. The persistence for centuries
of a profound interest in the making of poetry and music by ordinary people rather than by the specialist is extraordinary. There is
little doubt that the expression of erotic sentiments by the Tuareg
is of the same order as in Europe.

In Indian, Persian and Arab stories and legends there is as strong a romantic element as in their European equivalents. The Indian Ramayana is as evocative of sensual and tender sentiments as the Tristan legends. Chinese and Japanese literature of this kind follows a similar pattern. Our assumption here is that human love has an essentially sexual basis. It would follow that passionate attachments between individuals occur in all societies. The particular forms they take are dictated by the particular culture. Romantic obsession may be characterised, as amongst the ancient Greeks, as a form of mania, or regarded with pity and horror as in parts of Polynesia, but it occurs everywhere. There may be naked sensuality, as shown in some Indian sculpture, or the restrained voluptuousness of some European art. The particular variant with which we are familiar, namely that of Europe, has possibly had more effort, money, and care lavished on it than any other. Hence the tendency for it to become a kind of Everest in the Himalayas of sexual passion. Some comment on the more recent European scene is perhaps not out of place here.

Contemporary romanticism can be interpreted in terms of money. The phenomenal amount, running into millions, spent by women in Britain and America in an effort to achieve the un-achievable, that is romantic beauty, is remarkable testimony to the hidden finances of romance. Forms of entertainment such as films, plays, television, radio, as well as some literature, portray individual sexual passions. This both tries to satisfy an insatiable demand and is extremely profitable. The process is circular. The romantic tradition is already established and these forms serve to satisfy an existing appetite. At the same time the perpetual depicting of romance stimulates the appetite for more.

The origins of this marriage of sexuality and money lie in the last century. In the nineteenth century we can see a curious dualism in the behaviour of the middle classes. Outwardly it is an era of the large bourgeois family and family virtues. Love is, or should be, marital. However, discreetly, the men have recourse to erotic pursuits outside the home. Because of convention they could not treat their mistresses as Greek *hetairae*, theirs were hole-and-corner affairs. One very peculiar phenomenon was the carrying of the idea of the virgin-wife into the brothel. At one time the demand for virgins in English brothels was so excessive that to maintain the supply various devices to simulate virginity were employed. This traffic was exposed by G. W. T. Stead in the *Pall Mall Gazette* in 1885 (July 6th, 7th, 8th, and 10th). The idealisation of the woman was even sought in the arms of paid performers. It should be remembered that for 'decent' women to show even a slight interest in sexual performance or enjoyment was thought degrading. For sexual pleasure men sought prostitutes and courtesans. For the unmarried man economy could be achieved by sharing a kept woman, as was the case of the author of *Erewhon*, Samuel Butler, before his marriage. The entire tissue of relationships between men and women was shot through with contradiction after contradiction between overt belief and hidden practice. And yet this was the age of romantic poets, the gay nineties, and later of Ouida and Amanda Ros. The dualism is very real: on the one hand the respectable family seething with virtue; on the other the gross debaucheries of the brothel, and in between the strange mixture of ethereal love and spiritual sensuality of Ouida and her kind. The near-rapes on tiger-skin rugs of that charming authoress no doubt delighted a whole generation of adolescent readers. Yet her writing shows the same hypocritical evasion of the truth of sexual passion which is typical of the whole Victorian-Edwardian atmosphere.[17]

Pornography, or the attempt to excite deliberately the sexual appetite either in words, or visually, has always existed. In the contemporary Western world there is apparently a legitimate use of words of a sexual connotation or meaning providing the context is appropriate. The test of the appropriate is difficult. The use of sexual imagery, as in the famous lines of Somerset Maugham's *Rain* which liken the outlines of the hills of Dakota to a woman's breasts, is permissible, at any rate by the law in Britain. But descriptions of the sex act unalloyed by any literary diversions, as in Henry Miller's *Tropic of Capricorn* or in *Lady Chatterley's Lover* are not. In such cases the whole is banned for the offensive parts or an expurgated version is published. When books such as those of Aretino, or the notorious pornographic novel *Fanny Hill* are considered it is clear that the primary object of the authors is to produce sexual excitement. Curiously enough, the public display in advertisements of the nude or semi-nude female figure although held offensive by a minority is legally perfectly proper. This is on a level with the curious attitude towards nudity on the stage. Static nudity is permissible. Nudity with movement is pornography of the worst kind and cannot be permitted. But books which treat of sex as a natural function are regarded as dangerous and if extreme enough are banned, unless the mantle of the classical past falls upon them.

On the other hand the dissemination of sexual information in the form of manuals or encyclopedias presents no difficulties. Through the use of technical language and a laboured style they can hardly be regarded as aphrodisiac. But change the language to that of the everyday and even the fact of their respectable origin will not prevent prohibition.

Europeans' definitions of love seem to vary with their epoch. We have mentioned that the Greeks thought of love as a form of madness. Victims were to be pitied and condoled—there was no remedy for the disease except distraction through the Arts. This is an attitude which is expressed by Theocritus in his *Idylls*. There is in much of Greek poetry an exquisite refinement of thought and feeling with regard to love. This is far less evident in Roman poetry. The Romans tended to treat of love as a practical expression of sensuality. 'They marry without love and love without respect and refinement.' (Tacitus.) The writings of Ovid illustrate the essentially down-to-earth conception of Roman love.

The seventeenth-century European had little in common with Greek sentiments. Montaigne wrote ' . . . Love is nothing else but the thirst of enjoying the object desired; or Venus any other thing than the pleasure of discharging one's vessels. . . . ' A sensible if somewhat cynical point of view. Another down-to-earth view is that of La Rochefoucauld: 'Love is difficult to define. It may be said that, spiritually, it is passion for dominion; intellectually, it is sympathy; and physically, it is only a deep and subtle longing to possess its object, after sharing many secrets.' By the nineteenth century, however, romanticism has swept all before it. We have Balzac's lyrical conception: 'Love, as we instinctively feel, is the most melodious of harmonies. Woman is a delicious instrument of pleasure. . . .' Or Stendhal's ' . . . To love is to enjoy seeing, touching, and sensing with all the senses, a closely as possible, a lovable object which loves in return. . . . ' To which Tolstoy's view in the *Kreuzter Sonata* is an admirable if jaundiced corrective. ' . . . in theory love is something ideal, elevated, whereas in practice it is

abominable, swinish, a thing of which it is abominable and a shame
to think or speak. . . . ' The conception of the effect of love is
movingly conveyed by Kierkegaard: 'It is said that love blinds; it
does more than it, it deafens, it paralyses; for the man who suffers
from it closes up like the mimosa plant, and no pick-lock can open
it; the more violent one is, the more firmly does it close.'

Contemporary or near-contemporary views are totally different
in feeling. When not scientific or almost clinical in tone they
express a quasi-mystical note. The latter appears in the psychiatrist

Fig. 7. A mediaeval conception of love

Erich Fromm's statement: 'Erotic love, if it is love, has one premise: that I love from the essence of my being, and experience the other person in the essence of his or her being. In essence, all human beings are identical. We are, all part of One; We are One. . . .' This is clearly not the language of ordinary folk. They express themselves about love in a very different way: ' "Yes, it happened to me at 9.45 p.m. on January 4th, 51, at a dance. A lightening of the heart, a feeling of utter joy. It's been that way ever since. Her name is Gladys, she's a nurse here." '

' "Love at first sight. We seemed to get on ever so well from the very beginning. The look in Frank's eyes—I can't describe it. I've only seen it two or three times since." "She seemed like a magnified (magnet)." "Her talk, everything about her." "It was sort of inside me—a feeling it was her." '[18]

The sublime, the practical, the commonsensical, the romantic, and the inarticulate—are all products of their age. Finally the views of the nineteenth-century German philosopher Hartmann express what is possibly a logical but isolated attitude: 'Love causes more pain than pleasure. Pleasure is only illusory. Reason would command us to avoid love, if it were not for the fatal sexual impulse—therefore it would be best to be castrated. . . .'[19] Unfortunately the facts do not support Hartmann. Castration does not necessarily destroy desire, it merely impairs the ability to achieve satisfaction.

Attraction between the sexes is not always mutual. The desire for reciprocal passion, however, is universal. A constant motif in romantic literature throughout the world is that of the rejected lover. Wonderful as are the effusions promoted by unrequited love the individual is often not content to remain in this state. He or she is driven to practical or near-practical means to achieve the object of his or her heart's desire.

'. . . For this is its power: they who drink of it together love each other with their every single sense and with their every thought, forever, in life and death. . . .'[20] The magic love potion that Tristan and Iseult drank in error is probably the most famous in the world. The effect was disastrous and helps us to understand why some peoples regard love as a kind of mania. '. . . Love pressed them hard, as thirst presses the dying stag to the stream; love dropped upon them from high heaven, as a hawk slipped after long hunger falls right upon the bird. And love will not be hidden. . . .

But in every hour and place every man could see love terrible, that rode them, and could see in these lovers their every sense overflowing like new wine working in the vat. . . . '[21] This is the desired state. If it does not occur naturally recourse must be had to artificial means. Individuals in all societies, from the simplest to the most advanced, have special methods and knowledge for preparing love-inducing preparations. Care has to be taken—secrecy is generally an important aspect of the preparation of the potion or philtre—and the 'medicine' may either have a general effect, that is on anyone who consumes it, or specific for an individual. In some instances it may be politic or necessary to reduce the artificially stimulated passion as the following example from the Solomon Islands shows. 'To make a woman love you get some leaves of the plant rarakot and powder some sisiwa (a magical substance made of powdered lava) on to them, rub the two together and smear the mixture on to a piece of tobacco which you then give to the woman you desire. Then take a little more sisiwa and make it hot over the fire. As she smokes the tobacco, and as the sisiwa gets hot, so she will become warmed towards you and the next day she will come to you. She will be hot with desire for you, and you will copulate and copulate and copulate. When you are tired of her, and want the affair to come to an end, take a little sisiwa and put it into water, her passion will then be cooled. . . . '[22] A most useful substance sisiwa. It is in fact used for all sorts of magical preparations. Love inducement is only one of its attibutes.

At the basis of the belief that love can be induced or controlled is 'contagious' and homoepathic or 'imitative' magic. In the former the dormant idea is that the feelings and emotions of an individual can be transferred to another person. Barriers of time and distance create no problems. This type of magic is exemplified by the practice in peasant Ireland, Jamaica, France, and elsewhere of a woman in labour being given some garment of her husband so that he will bear some of the pain for her. The pain is transmitted through the garment to her husband. Thus love spells may invoke the name of the person who is desired, and the spell be worked from a distance against him or her. An image of the desired individual or part of him may be made and the enchantment worked over the image.

The most outstanding examples of homoepathic or imitative

magic are in the category of renewal rites in which miming takes a prominent place. Such rites by appropriate ceremonies ensure that, for example, a particular species will continue to perpetuate itself. Such practices are typical of the Australian Aborigines. In classical China it was the function of the Emperors at the proper time of the year to perform rites which ensured the changing of the seasons. This is paralleled by the widespread custom of eating the flesh of an animal in order to assume his ferocity, or eating some part of your enemy to absorb his power. In love magic 'imitation' takes the form of making the person eat or drink a potion or food which contains ingredients of a special nature. These may consist of hairs, pieces of clothing, or anything belonging to the beloved guaranteed to inculcate the wished-for sentiments. The ceremonies may mime or simulate the desired state. Both 'contagious' and 'imitative' magic depend upon what has been called a principle of sympathy. Love magic may have different objectives. Primarily it is used to create a love which has hitherto not existed, but it is also used to perpetuate love, to find out who loves one, recapture a former lover, and, as we saw in the Solomon Islands example quoted above, to cut off an *affaire* which has gone on too long. The practitioners who dispense the magical substances for these purposes, and who create the spells, can either be witches who are connected with evil magic which disturbs relationships, or persons who produce a benign magic. This distinction between black and white magic, as it were, is made in practically all societies where magic exists. The Jamaican Obeahman is prepared to assist one in affairs of the heart. His connection in many ways is with evil—he controls evil spirits. But his counterpart, the myalman or healer, exerts a benign influence and also works love magic. In Haiti the vodun priest (Hungan) or priestess readily produces love charms and potions. But recourse can also be had to sorcerers who create a diabolical magic. Spanish peasants make the same distinction between the Sabia who has benevolent powers given her by God to cure and control human behaviour, and the Bruja or witch whose attributes and power are wholly evil.[23]

One society is so riddled with magic that every man becomes his own magician. This is the island of Dobu in the Western Pacific. The Dobuans believe that all important aspects of life are affected by magic. Love is no exception. 'Without a love charm to arouse

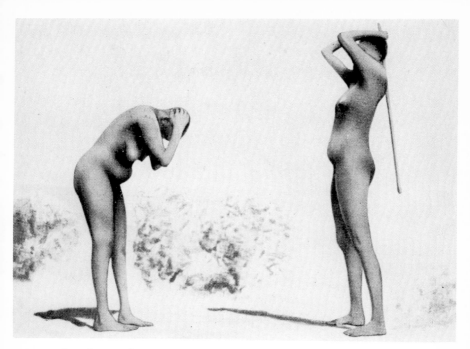

1a. Australian aboriginal women.

1b. South American Indians. After Prince zu Wied.

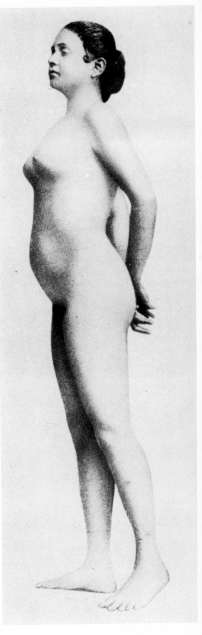

2a. Cingalese girl.   2b. Japanese girl.

3a. East African lip distortion.

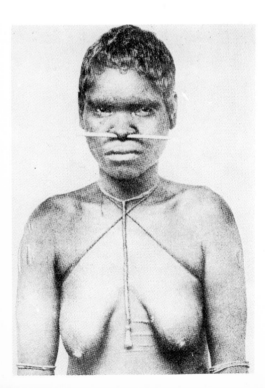

3b. North Australian
aboriginal woman with
nose decoration.

4a. Ovambo women from East Africa.

4b. Married couple from the Andaman Islands.

5a. Hottentot women with steatopygia.

5b. South African Bantu girl.

6b. East African girls.

6a. Chamacocco Indian girl, South America.

7a. Peasant courtship in the eighteenth century.

7b. Peasant love.

8a. An eighteenth century
declaration of love.

8b. The newly married.

and create desire, desire does not exist according to the native theory. Men and women mate only because men are constantly exerting magical power over women, and women over men. . . . A man without love magic is not a real man, only half a man. . . . [24] As one would expect the Dobuans have a great number of love charms. Many are the property of individuals who never reveal them. Others are of a more general nature and are employed by everyone.

One Dobuan method of inducing love is to put some of the sap of a particular tree, koiwaga, which has a fine scent, on the body. One legendary account says that koiwaga is a tree which grows near the home of the spirits of the dead. It is a single, unique tree which was once a woman. The sap is the tears of the woman weeping for her hard-hearted lover who changed her into a tree: difficult but possible for the Dobuan well versed in magic. Another version is that koiwaga is a waterfall made of the tears of the same woman.

All magic of this kind has as part of its ritual the exhortation of the individual's spirit to leave his body and to work on the spirit of the beloved.

Dobuan society is somewhat unique in its obsession with magic and the participation of the whole community in magical practices. In other societies this is generally left to the specialist.

In this field of magic amongst primitive peoples the most commonplace and the most extraordinary ingredients are used to manufacture the 'medicine' which will produce the desired effects. One ingredient which has a natural association with the result is elephant sperm, obtained just at the moment when the animal is about to copulate but is frightened by someone—a dangerous proceeding one would imagine. But the people of Central Sumatra believe that the sperm smeared on the body or clothes of the loved one is most efficacious. In Sfax in Tunis, women prepare what is called 'May Sausage'. This is made from the entrails of a lamb killed in May sprinkled with the powder of a burnt mouse. The man who eats it is immediately filled with inordinate love for the cook. A common belief is that to attract love one should smear the face or body with a natural substance such as gum. This is practised by some tribes in Eastern New Guinea. [25] More elaborate preparations and rites were in use amongst North American Indians. The medicine-man of the Chippeway Indians manufactured a highly effective love powder. It consisted of vermilion, powdered snake root (*polygala senega L.*), a little blood of a girl who was menstruating for the first time, and a piece of ginseng root. These were shaken together in a small cotton bag. With appropriate sacrifices and songs it was handed over to the love-stricken individual.[26] Sometimes simple incantation by the bereft lover is sufficient. In Ceram and the Gorang Islands in Indonesia the individual takes off his clothes, goes into a stream, sits down, and holds up his or her hands pronouncing this invocation: ' . . . In the name of the god of mercy, light of the firefly Montana, look upon me, full moon, look upon me, the blessing from where there is no God as God, the blessing of Mohammed, God's ambassador; so-and-so look upon me who slaves like the moon, look upon me full moon, look upon me star, look upon me sun, look upon me prophet Mohammed, the ambassador of God. . . . ' This concluded you blow over both hands and anoint your head with water.[27]

Love charming in a similar manner is also practised by the Australian aborigines. Amongst the Arunta tribe a highly valued shell ornament, Lonka-lonka, is charmed by singing over it in some quiet place. In his song the man asks the lightning to come into the Lonka-lonka. This done it is hung on a stick at the dancing ground until night time. The man then ties it on his belt ready for the dance. 'While he is dancing the woman whom he wishes to attract alone sees the lightning flashing on the Lonka-Lonka, and all at once her internal organs shake with emotion. If possible she will creep into his camp that night or take the earliest opportunity to run away with him. . . . '[28] Women who wish to charm men will make special fur-string necklets which they put round the man's neck. Ordinary food can also be magicked in this way with equally good results.[29]

Contemporary Jamaica puts its faith in the perfection of ingredients to produce the desired state. An Obeahman, the Jamaican specialist in magic, told the author:

' . . . Once a girl of nineteen year old came to me and told me that she see a man who say that he love her. But she say he will not agree to marry her he only want her for an "outside friend" (mistress). The girl say she would like me to help her so that the man can marry her. And I told her that if she can get a water-frog which we call spring chicken, those that live in the water, and any time she get that she can come to see me on a Wednesday morning about 10 o'clock. I told her she must catch it herself by putting a white gloves on her hand. She are going to hold it, and I told her to bring me a bottle of ingage (engage) essence with the frog when she are coming and the oil of compelance (compliance) and the oil of mur (myrrh). And so she did as I told her. And I let her make a little box, and I let she take the frog to a ants' nest, and I let she put the frog into the ants' nest, and turn down the box to cover the frog. And I told her that thirty-two day times she must go to the ants' nest and turn over the box and take up the frog and bring back to me. And when she came back the last time she came without the frog. I send her back and told her to look carefully in the ants' nest and she will see a part of the frog and "Luck". And she brought the same part to me. I put it into a white vessel and all the things she brought along with a measurement of her finger and have them well sware (sworn). And I send her back to the water where she catch the frog with a part of the things which she brought. But the bone that resemble "Luck" and the ingage essence did not go back to the water where she catch the frog. I take some of the essence and use on the bone and told her that anywhere she and the man meet she must take the bone and touch the man on his clothes. And after doing that I told her to put the bone in her pillow and the remainder of the essence is to be use when she are having a bath. And she must drop three drops into the bath pan and after she have her bath try to go to the direction where the man are. And so she did. And in eleven days' time the girl come back and told me that the man agree to give her an ingage ring.' [30]

Classical societies, however advanced, as compared with savage groups, were not averse to the use of incantations, philtres, and 'medicines' to produce symptoms of love. In the Sanskrit *Atharva Veda* there are many incantations to preserve or excite love in a man. '. . . This plant is born of honey, with honey do we dip for thee. Of honey thou art begotten, do thou make us full of honey. At the tip of my tongue may I have honey, at my tongue's root the sweetness of honey! In my power alone shall thou then be, thou shalt come up to my wish! . . . I am sweeter than honey, fuller of sweetness than licorice. Mayst thou without fail long for me alone (as a bee) for a branch full of honey. . . .' Or again '. . . I dig up this plant, of herbs the most potent, by whose power Rwal women are overcome and husbands are obtained. . . . O thou (plant) with erect leaves, lovely, do thou, urged on by the gods, full of might, drive away my rival, make mine husband mine alone. . . . I am overpowering, and thou (O plant) are completely overpowering. Having both grown full of power, let us overpower my rival! About thee (my husband) I have placed the overpowering (plant), upon thee placed the overpowering one. May thy mind run after me as a calf after a cow, as water along its course. . . . '[31]

The ancient Hindus also had recourse to the usual type of love magic: 'If a man cuts into small pieces the sprouts of the vajnasunki plant and dips them into a mixture of red arsenic and sulphur, and then dries them seven times, and applies this powder mixed with honey to his lingam, he can subjugate a woman to his will directly he has had sexual union with her, or, if by burning these very sprouts at night and looking at the smoke, he sees a golden moon behind, he will then be successful with any woman; or if he throws some of the powder of these same sprouts, mixed with the excrement of a monkey, upon a maiden, she will not be given in marriage to any body else. . . . '[32] This sounds most effective, but the last instructions are perhaps somewhat difficult to follow out. With their devotion to and assiduity in sexual matters it is not surprising that the Hindus have probably what is the most comprehensive erotic literature in the world, covering all phases of sexual love.

Greece even at the height of its civilisation was still subject to a belief in magic and witchcraft. In the Hellenistic period, due to the influence of the Near East, magical practices became exceedingly complex. Precepts were collected into books. Some of these have been preserved in papyri collections.[33] Enchantment in matters of love was commonplace. ' . . . Different methods were employed —sometimes incantation; sometimes a narcotic such as a weak infusion of hemlock (Ovid, *Amores*, III, 7, 27), to mix which in the victim's drink opportunity had to be found; and sometimes the puppet method was used, for which it was only necessary to form a wax model (Ovid, 29f; *Heroides*, 6.21) of him who was to be bewitched, and to stick a needle into the position of the liver, whereupon the man himself became impotent, for the liver (Theocritus, 30, 10; Horace, *Odes*, 1, 13, 4; 25, 13) was regarded by the ancients as the seat of sensual desire. . . . '[34]

The forms and ingredients of Greek love magic were very similar to those quoted for primitive groups.

Despite their genius for the practical and matter of fact the Romans appear to have been almost as addicted to the use of magic in matters of love as the Greeks. Lucullus, it was reputed, by using too potent a love philtre went mad and died. Lucretius committed suicide as a result of imbibing a love potion. The ordinary Roman people were almost as fond of magic as the Dobuans. Apparently sexual liaisons needed the guiding force of supernatural powers.

The Europe of the Dark and Middle Ages perpetuates this classical pattern of magical practices connected with love. There is, of course, considerable variety in the means utilised. One of the most popular, which had obvious connections with witchcraft, was the making of wax or other images of the beloved and casting spells over it. The image was melted by fire or in the sun. By sympathy the heart was supposed to be filled with the heat of love. Another typical method employed was the brewing of a special mixture which contained something belonging to the person it was wished to charm. As the mixture boiled so the person was compelled, often at the risk of their life, to rush to the side of the lover. There are many variants of this method.

Herbal mixtures and animal ingredients for making potions were also greatly favoured, as were fragments of garments worn by the individual. Mediaeval love magic appears to have survived among peasant populations in Europe up to the present day. The Eastern European gypsy's image-making is very similar to the mediaeval practice. ' . . . If a maiden wishes to compel a certain boy to love her, she forms a human magic out of the paste, with which she further mixes, if possible, hair, spittle, blood, nails, etc., of the beloved man. Then she puts his name on the image. The figure is then buried in the ground at the cross roads when the moon is waning, and the girl urinates on the place and says these words "Peter, Peter, I love thee: when thy image is rotten thou shalt run after me, my dearest, as the dog runs after the bitch !". . . '(35)

In peasant Germany animals figure in much love magic. For example, in Prussia the lover sticks a needle through two mating frogs. With this needle he then attaches the clothes of his beloved to his own for an instant. The result is to gain her love for ever.

One of the more interesting European beliefs is in the efficacy of human sweat to arouse passion. There seems to be a connection with the sweating produced in copulation. At any rate it is a common belief that a garment impregnated with one's sweat will, placed in contact with someone else, arouse desire. The handkerchief is one of the most usual articles of clothing used for this purpose. An almost unique practice in some parts of Germany is the placing of a biscuit or apple in the vulva overnight so that it becomes saturated in sweat. This is then given to the lover next day. If he eats it, passion for his lady consumes him. Amongst Czech peasants hair from the armpits is sometimes baked in little cakes, which have the power to make whoever eats them fall in love with the owner of the hair. More common is the practice in France for a man to carry a swallow's heart on his penis which ensures success with all women. In the same way the Yugoslav girl will carry a bat under her left shoulder, which makes all men fall in love with her.[36]

There is, in fact, an infinite variety in the methods which European peasants adopt in order to win a person's heart. It is probably the greatest field for the exploitation of man's credulity. It would be mistaken, however, to associate this entirely with uneducated peasants. There is considerable evidence of various kinds to suggest that contemporary Western man, secure in his technology, still seeks magical aids to make his love life prosper. On the one hand there is the popularity of fortune tellers and soothsayers in most European countries. In Britain, apart from the sporadic activities of so-called witches in Somerset and Suffolk, there is the amazing support given to newspaper accounts of what the stars foretell. On the other hand, both in Britain and the U.S.A. there are people who manufacture and operate machines which they claim can not only diagnose disease and evil influences from a drop of a customer's blood, but can effect cures and influence events by bombarding the sample of blood with 'electrical' impulses. Whereas the Ozark mountaineers in America faithfully follow the age-old tradition of making wax images of one's enemies and lovers,[37] the 'machine' inventors have developed a magic more fitted to the age of the sputnik. But the old tradition and practice is not yet exhausted in the cities of Europe. '. . . Miss "Baby" Siegfried Knudsen, a beautiful Swedish blonde, who was born in Manchester, was awarded £450 damages by a Paris court yesterday against Mme. de Tanis, a fashionable fortune teller, from whom she had "love philtres" and "magic potions". Miss Knudsen complained that Madame de Tanis had had £14,000 from her for the potions, which were designed to retain the love of Baron Jean Empair, thirty-three-year-old Belgian millionaire whom Miss Knudsen hoped to marry. Police who visited the home of Mme. de Tanis . . . found all kinds of magical apparatus, including incense, crystals, toads in bottles, and stuffed owls. Mme. de Tanis, a stout, alert-faced woman, told the examining magistrate that her clients included some of the crowned heads of Europe and many leading personalities in French society. . . . '(38)

Perhaps the very nature of love, its unpredictable characteristics, its approximation in its worst manifestations to frenzy, its uncontrollable quality, has fostered the belief in practices which claim by magical means to control it. The argument that the failure of love magic to work has been demonstrated innumerable times in countless societies so that belief in it must have been destroyed is not valid. Nearly all love magic is concerned, as we have seen, with details of concoction and spells. In cases where it does not work the blame is attributed not to the magic but to failure to carry out the instructions properly.

On the other side, as regards efficacy, there is the effect on the bewitched person of knowing that a spell has been cast on him, or that he has drunk a love philtre, and so on. Such knowledge in cases of ordinary witchcraft has been known to produce death, by the side of which falling in love is merely a simple effort.

The compelling romantic character of the love charm for all people is brought out by this Arab song. It is sung by Tunisian Arab women sitting naked before a brazier throwing magical ingredients into it. There is no room for doubt as to its effect.

> 'Coriander: bring him here mad!
> Wild carraway: bring him to me insane,
>
> Raving without a path!
> Mastic: arouse in his heart longing and sorrow!
> White chalk: prepare in his heart a restless night!

If he sits at peace, burn him!
If he should forget, remind him!
If he sits on the mat, chase him away!

———

If a maiden stands before him, turn her into a black slave.
If a man stands before him, turn him into a saucepan!
If a woman stands before him, turn her into dirt!
If a little girl stands before him, turn her into a spider.'[39]

Yet even love magic is not the only assistant to love. There are other aids which are specifics in that they are supposed to maintain or excite sexual appetite. The usual term for these is aphrodisiacs. Their main purposes appear to promote or increase sexual excitement, restore loss of virility and, as the *Kamasutra* puts it '. . . .if a man pounds the seeds or roots of the trapa bispenosa, the basurika, the tuscan jasmine, and liquorice, together with the kohirakpoli (a kind of onion) and puts the powder into milk mixed with sugar and ghee (clarified butter), and having boiled the whole mixture on a moderate fire, drinks the paste so formed, he will be able to enjoy innumerable women. . . .'[40]

There has always been in Europe widespread faith in the efficacy of an amazing range of vegetable and animal substances as sexual excitants. ' . . . Aphrodisiacs are medicaments which are said to produce an increase in the sex impulse either by control or peripheral stimulation (hyperoemia or slight irritation in uterus and vagina). Most of these things are really quite ineffectual. Thus the *radix satyri*, for example has to thank its testicle-like bulbs for the faith in its effect. The working of the sea-holly (*eryngium campestre*) could have been done by wet sponges, etc., for it was put under the man's bed clothes so that he should not forget his conjugal duty. Celery has an exciting effect; (held in that regard as a sexual stimulant in Belgium); asparagus is uretic and supposed to be exciting. Deadly nightshade (*Atropa Belladonna*), thorn apple (*datura stramonium*) and mandrake (*atrapa mandragura*) have a stronger effect. They all belong to the nightshade plants and owe their reputation to the condition of intoxication which occurs after indulgence in them. Thorn apple, like *Cannabis Indica*, or cocaine, produces an insatiable libido and orgasm in women. . . .'[41]

There are in fact drugs or near-drugs which produce a species of irritation in the sexual parts and so may lead to stimulation. The most well known is Cantharides (*Litta vesicatoria*), popularly called Spanish Fly. This is a species of coleoptera which contains cantharadin the action of which is to produce excessive irritation in the kidneys and urinal passage. This may lead to erection in the male, and itching in the vagina in the woman. It is an extremely poisonous substance. Castoreum and asafœtida can be used in the same way. Less well known are Yohimbin and Muiracitin. The former is an alkaloid made from the bark of the West African tree, Yohimbe. Its effect is to stimulate the sacral cord which leads to dilation of the blood vessels in the genital area and so to erection. It has been used for treatment in cases of impotence. Muiracitin is of Brazilian origin and has a very similar effect to Yohimbin. Not so well attested is the dust made from the hellebore which is supposed to act as a powerful irritant when applied externally.

Opium is used in India as an aphrodisiac. It diminishes sensibility and thus delays orgasm. More modern drugs such as amylnitrite have the same effect.

While the effectiveness of drugs can be tested it is not quite the same when particular food and miscellaneous substances are held to have aphrodisical qualities. Popular opinion inclines to classify rich and rare foods as possessing erotic attributes. Thus oysters, caviare, and exotic heavily spiced dishes are believed to be sexually stimulating. It is very probably true that after a good meal the individual feels more disposed towards sexual activity than after a poor one. But that particular foods are aphrodisiacs is debatable. The reputation of some plants may be due to a false association of ideas; the mandrake, for instance, notorious for its use in European witchcraft generally, probably owes its popularity to its resemblance to the human figure. This is also true of the sea-holly and the onion (held in great repute by the Greeks)—due in both cases to their resemblance to testicles. At the time of the potato's introduction to Europe it was believed to have strong aphrodisiacal properties. But this was probably due to its rarity rather than its appearance. The case for foods, vegetable and animal, as aphrodisiacs seems to be largely a question of superficial similarity to the sexual organs, and their scarcity value.[42]

Alcohol comes in a similar category to foodstuffs. Drinking

loosens the inhibitory mechanisms, so that sexual advances are more likely to be made and well received when alcohol is consumed. But alcohol is a depressant and sexual performance rather than being stimulated may actually be impaired. Nevertheless wine has for centuries been regarded as a powerful sexual stimulant. The early Church, in the person of Clement of Alexandria, expressed very strong views as to the erotic qualities of wine.[43] Chaucer writes of the defenceless state it produces.

> *Whenever I take wine I have to think*
> *Of Venus, for as cold engenders hail*
> *A lecherous mouth begets a lecherous tail*
> *A woman in her cups has no defence,*
> *As lechers know from long experience.* [44]

A very natural belief was that concerning the erotic qualities of semen. In the fourteenth century Bishop Burchard inveighed against women who swallowed their husband's semen to make themselves sexually more exciting. The penance for this was one of seven years.[45] The connection with virile powers is obvious. In the same way the eating of human or animal testicles by women is reputed to be the cause of excess of sexual feeling. This has been reported of tribes in Central Africa, of Cornish women, and others. Pliny (XXVIII, 248) states that to wear the right testicle of an ass in a bracelet increased virility. Up to the eighteenth century in Europe semen was commonly believed to have great medicinal properties and was used as a cure for all sorts of conditions.[46] This is also the case amongst some Australian aborigines. The Marquis de Sade suggests in various of his works that the practice of fellatio, that is stimulation of the penis with the lips and tongue, was popular because of women being able to swallow semen which increased their sexual excitement. John Hunter, the eighteenth-century surgeon, likened its effect in the mouth to spices.[47] Whatever their real as opposed to imagined effects decoctions and preparations from semen and the male genitals have had a wide esteem in many societies as promoters of erotic feeling.

Parts of plants or animals which bear a resemblance to the male organ are also believed to have aphrodisiacal powers when suitably prepared. For example, today there is an extensive trade in rhinoceros horns from Africa to China where it is regarded as being a powerful aphrodisiac and is appropriately expensive. It is ground into a powder and eaten. Some peoples, while attributing no specific erotic powers to plants, nevertheless have sexual ideas about them. One of the commonest of such plants is the banana. This is well illustrated by the legend of the woman who copulated with a banana, given by Miss Blackwood in *Both Sides of Buka Passage*.[48] The connection here is again quite obvious—the banana flower has an uncanny resemblance to a human penis.

With their strong belief in magic as an aid to love both the Greeks and the Romans possessed a great range of aphrodisiacs. A number of Roman recipes are given in F. Dufour's (P. Lacroix) *Histoire de la prostitution chez tous les peuples du monde*, published in Paris in 1851–4. The Greek prescriptions are extremely varied in character. Ovid pointed out that some were dangerous such as 'satyrion', a kind of orchis. Ground pepper and nettle-seed mixed together, and old wine added to pyrethron (pellitory) are all in this category. Those considered safe are onions, wild cabbage, eggs, honey and pineapples.[49]

There are a number of references in Pliny to various specifics both for sexual potency and impotence. An extremely comprehensive list is contained in papyri in the Louvre and the British Museum.[50]

It is interesting to see that Nicholas Culpeper in his *The English Physician Enlarged* attributes the same lust-making qualities to the orchis; of the onion he says, ' . . . to be used with honey and rue, increases sperm, especially the seed of them. . . . ' Of the sea holly mentioned above 'the plan is venereal and breedeth seed exceedingly, and strengthens the spirits procreative. . . . '[51]

One of the more bizarre and drastic methods of increasing male potency was attributed to the Amazons by Eustathius in his *Commentari ad Homerum* (403–9). 'The Amazons broke either a leg or an arm of the captives they took in battle, and this they did, not only to prevent their attempts at escape, or their plotting, but also, and this more especially, to render them more vigorous in the venereal conflict; for, as they themselves burnt away the right breast of their female children in order that the right arm might become stronger from receiving additional nutriment, so they imagined that, similarly, the genital member would be strengthened by the deprivation of one of the extremities, whether a leg or an arm. Hence, when reproached by the Scythians with the limping gait of her slaves, Queen Antianara replied, "the lame best perform the act of love." '

In England in the Age of Enlightenment the approach to the problem of flagging sexual appetite was perhaps more practical. John Davenport in his *Aphrodisiacs and Anti-Aphrodisiacs* (London, 1869), a book which contains some very curious information, quotes the account of a lecture given by a Dr James Graham in 1783. Graham was a follower of Cagliostro, and from time to time gave a series of what he termed sanitary lectures in London. Present with him on the rostrum was his Goddess of Health. At one time this role was fulfilled by Emma Hart later to become famous as Lady Hamilton, Nelson's beloved. The lecture in question begins with a detailed account of various aphrodisiacs. 'But, gentlemen, if all the above means and methods, which I have thus faithfully, ingenuously, and with the frankest and most unreserved liberality, recommended, fail, suffer me, with great cordiality, and assurance of success, to recommend my celestial, or medico, magnetico, musico, electrical bed, which I have, with so much study and at vast an expense, constructed, not alone to insure the removal of barrenness, when conception is at all in the nature of things possible, but likewise to improve, exalt, and invigorate the bodily, and through them, the mental faculties of the human species. . . . The Grand Celestial State Bed! then, gentlemen, which is twelve feet long by nine wide, is supported by forty pillars of brilliant glass, of great strength, and of the most exquisite workmanship. . . . The sublime, the magnificent, and, I may say, the super-celestial dome of the bed . . . is very curiously inlaid or wholly covered on the underside with brilliant plates of looking-glass, so disposed as to reflect the various attractive charms of the happy recumbent couple, in the most flattering, most agreeable and most enchanting style.

'On the top or summit of the dome, are placed, in the most loving attitudes, two exquisite figures, representing the marriage of Cupid and Psyche, with a fine figure of Hymen behind, and over them, with his torch flaming with electrical fire in one hand and, with the other, supporting a celestial crown, sparking, likewise, with the effulgent fire over a pair of real living turtle-doves, who on a little bed of roses, coo and bill under the superanimating im-pulses of the genial fire. . . . At the head of the bed, in the full centre front, appears sparkling with electrical fire, through a glory of burnished and effulgent gold, the great, first, ever-operating commandment, BE FRUITFUL, MULTIPLY AND REPLENISH THE EARTH ! Under this is a most elegant and sweet-toned organ, in the front of which is a fine landscape of moving figures on the earth, birds flying, . . . village nymphs strewing flowers before priests . . . who all entering into the temple of Hymen disappear from view . . . and the whole view is terminated . . . by a little church, the dial of which points out truly and distinctly the hour.

'In the celestial bed no feather bed is employed . . . springy hair mattresses are used . . . in order that I might have for the important purposes, the strongest and most springy hair, I procured at vast expense, the tails of English stallions, which when twisted, baked, and then untwisted and properly prepared, is elastic to the highest degree.

'But the chief elastic principle of my celestial bed is produced by artificial lodestones. About fifteen hundred pounds' weight of artificial and compound magnets are so disposed and arranged as to be continually pouring forth in an ever-flowing circle in-conceivable and irresistibly powerful tides of the magnetic effluxion, which is well known to have a very strong affinity with the electric fire.

'Such is a slight and inadequate sketch of the grand celestial bed, which, being thus completely insulated—highly saturated with the most genial floods of electrical fire—fully impregnated moreover, with the balmly vivifying effluvia of restorative balsamic medicines . . . and moreover, all the faculties of the soul being so fully ex-panded, and so highly illuminated, that it is impossible, in the nature of things, but that strong, beautiful, brilliant, nay, double-distilled children, if I may use the expression, must infallibly be begotten. . . . ' The price of this hymenal couch was £50 sterling.

It is a pity Dr Graham wasted his obvious talents on pseudo-electricity—he would have prospered in almost any business.

From what has been said it is clear that the pursuer of sexual vigour charts a somewhat dangerous course. It can be summed up by a quotation from Davenport's book (*op. cit.* p. 120) where he

points out the danger of using stinging nettles for this purpose.
'The lubricity of those unfortunates is sometimes uncontrollable;
they suffer violent priapisms, which are followed by ejaculation,
whenever a severe itching forces them to scratch themselves with a
kind of furor or madness.'

Most aphrodisiacs, like love potions, must be considered as
belonging to the kingdom of wish fulfilment rather than to the
scientific world. Persistence of belief in their efficacy is due to the
unpredictable nature of sexual love. Most of us would like to
believe in the charming episode from the 'Tale of Beauty Spot' in
the *Arabian Nights*. Before the hero of the story, Beauty-Spot, is
born his father finds that he is no longer able to satisfy his wife.
Failing to obtain sound advice from the local druggists he resorts
to a 'creature of fabulous debauch' who prepares the following
mixture. '. . . He took two ounces of Chinese cubebs, one ounce
of fat extract of Ionian hemp, one ounce of fresh caryophyle, one
ounce of red cinnamon from Serendib, ten drachms of white
Malabar cardamon, five of Indian ginger, five of white pepper, five
of pimento from the isles, one ounce of the berries of Indian star-
anise, and half an ounce of mountain thyme. These he mixed
cunningly, after having pounded and sieved them. He added pure
honey until the whole became a thick paste; then he mingled five
grains of musk and an ounce of pounded fish roe with the rest.
Finally he added a little concentrated rose-water and put all in the
bowl.

'After this work was completed, he carried the bowl to Sham-
seddin, saying: "Here is a sovereign mixture which will harden the
eggs and thicken the sap when it becomes too thin. . . . You must
eat this paste two hours before the sexual approach, but for three
days before that you must eat nothing save roast pigeons excessively
seasoned with spice, male fish with the cream complete, and lightly
fried ram's eggs. If after all that you do not pierce the very walls of
the room and get THE FOUNDATIONS OF THE HOUSE WITH CHILD,
YOU CAN CUT OFF MY BEARD and spit in my face . . . Sham-
seddin scrupulously followed Sesame's diet for three days and then
ate the paste, which he found delicious. Soon he noticed that his
blood was boiling as it had been when he was a boy and made bets
on certain matters with lads of his own age. He went to his wife and
mounted her; she met him half way and they were both astonished

with the resulting hardness, repetition, heat, jet, intensity, and thickness. That night the syndic's wife well and truly conceived. . . .[52]' That was clearly the most perfect aphrodisaic ever invented.

REFERENCES AND NOTES

1. Fled Bricrend, *The Feast of Bricriu*, translated by G. Henderson, Irish Texts Society, London 1899, pp. 69, 81.
    For a survey of the period see H. d'Arbois de Jubainville's *L'épopée celtique en Irlande*, Vol. V of *Cours de Littérature Celtique*, Paris 1892.

2. H. D. Traill and J. S. Mann, *Social England*, London 1893-7, Vol. II, p. 782.

3. Marie de France, *Poésies*, ed. B. de Roquefort, 2 vols., Paris 1820, Vol. I, p. 506.

4. *The Mabinogion*, translated by C. Guest, ed. A. Nutt, London 1904, p. 247.

5. Chrétien de Troyes and Godfrey de Laigny, *Le Roman du Chevalier de la Chorette*, ed. P. Tarbe, Rheims 1860, Vol. V, lines 1302 *et seq.*

6. 'Vernon Lee', *Euphorion*, London, Vol. II, p. 136 *et seq.*
    For differing points of view see C. S. Lewis, *The Allegory of Love*, O.U.P., 1946, Ch. I, pp. 1–44.
    A. Jeanroy, Introduction to *Anthologie des Troubadours*, Paris 1927.
    R. Briffault, *The Mothers*, London 1927, Vol. III, Chs. 28–9, pp. 376–506.
    Denis de Rougemont, *Passion and Society*, London 1956, pp. 58–136.

7. See Choderlos de Laclos, *Les Liaisons Dangereuses*, translated by R. Aldington, London, N.D.

8. M. Kingsley, *West African Studies*, London 1901, p. 42.

9. M. Mead, *Growing Up in Samoa*, London 1943, p. 88.

10. L. H. Morgan, *Systems of Consanguinity and Affinity of the Human Family*, Washington 1871, p. 207 note.

11. A. K. Kroeber, 'A Minor Record of the California Indians', University of California Publications: *American Archaeology and Ethnology*, VIII, 6.

C. Wilkes, *Narrative of U.S. Exploring Expedition* 1833–42, London 1845, Vol. IV, p. 45.

F. Speiser, *Two Years with the Natives in the Western Pacific*, London 1913, p. 235.

B. H. Thomson, *The Fijians*, London 1908, p. 241.

12. V. Elwin, *The Murias and their Ghotul*, O.U.P. 1947.

13. J. L. Burckhardt, *Notes on the Bedouins and Wahábys*, London 1830, p. 155.

14. H. M. & N. K. Chadwick, *The Growth of Literature*, Cambridge 1940, Vol. III, p. 659.

15. An excellent account of the Tuareg a'hal is given in R. Bazin, *Charles de Foucauld*, London 1923, translated by P. Keelan, cf. P. Fuchs, *The Land of Veiled Men*, London 1955, pp. 72–6.

16. Bazin, *op. cit.*, p. 278.

17. An amusing sexual history of the times is given by Cyril Pearl in his *The Girl with the Swansdown Seat*, London 1955.

18. The quotations regarding love are taken from the following in numerical order:

Essays of Montaigne, translated by Charles Cotton, London 1893, Vol. III, p. 103.

Maxims of le Rochefoucauld, translated by F. G. Stevens, Oxford 1940, 68, p. 25.

H. Balzac, *Physiologie de Mariage*, Meditation VII.

Stendhal, *On Love*, translated by G. & S. Sale, London 1957, p. 27.

L. Tolstoy, *The Kreuzter Sonata*, translated by L. Weiner, London 1942, p. 43.

S. Kierkegaard, *The Journals*, translated by A. Dru, Oxford 1938, 376, p. 27.

E. Fromm, *The Art of Loving*, London 1958, p. 55.

G. Gorer, *Explaining English Character*, London 1955, p. 88.

E. Slater and M. Woodside, *Patterns of Marriage*, London 1951, p. 101.

19. H. Hartmann, *Philosophie des Unbewussten*, Berlin 1869, p. 583.

20. J. Bedier, *The Romance of Tristan and Iseult*, translated by H. Belloc, London 1913, p. 47.

21. Bedier, *op. cit.*, pp. 55–6.

22. B. Blackwood, *Both Sides of Buka Passage*, O.U.P. 1935, p. 121.

23. J. Pitt-Rivers, *The People of the Sierra*, London 1954, pp. 190–2.

24. E. F. Fortune, *The Sorcerers of Dobu*, London 1932, p. 235.

25. P. V. Comrie, 'Anthropological Notes in New Guinea', *Journal of the Royal Anth. Institute* 1876, Vol. I, p. 109.

26. W. J. Hoffman, 'The Mide-Wivin of the Ojibwa', *7th Annual Report of the Bureau of Ethnology*, Washington 1892.

27. J. G. F. Riedel, *De sluik-en kroesharige Rassen tusschen Selebes en Papua*, s'Gravenhage 1886.

28. W. B. Spencer and F. J. Gillen, *The Native Tribes of Central Australia*, London 1899, pp. 544–5.

29. Spencer and Gillen, *op. cit.*, p. 548.

30. Fernando Henriques, *Jamaica, Land of Wood and Water*, London 1957, p. 176–7.

31. *Atharva-Veda*, translated by M. Bloomfield, Oxford 1897, Section III, 18, I, 34.

32. *Kamasutra of Vatsyayana*, Anon., English trans., Paris N.D., pp. 277–8.

33. R. Wünsch, *Aus einem grieschischen Zauber-papyrus*, Bonn 1911.

34. H. Licht, *Sexual Life in Ancient Greece*, London 1932, p. 371.

35. H. V. Wlislocki, *Volksglaube und religiöser Brauch der Zigeuner*, Munster, 1891.

36. For these similar customs see H. V. Wlislocki, *op. cit.*, and F. S. Krauss, 'Liebeszauber des Völker', *Anthropophyteia*, 1906, Bd. III, pp. 165–8.

37 V. Rudolph, *Ozark Superstitions*, N.Y. 1947, pp. 162–8.

38. London *Sunday Express*, 18 July 1937.

39. R. Narbeshuber, *Aus dem Leben de arabischen Bevölkerung in Sfax (Tunis)*, Leipzig 1907.

40. *Kamasutra, op. cit.*, p. 279.

41. E. Kohler in Halban & Seitz's *Biologie und Pathologie des Weibes*, Berlin 1924, Vol. II, pp. 242 *et seq.*
    See also M. Hirschfeld & L. Linsert, *Liebesmittel*, Berlin 1929.

42. For the range of supposed aphrodisiacal foods see P. Liebault, *Trésor des Remèdes Secrets pour les Maladies des Femmes*, 1585 pp. 104 *et seq.*

43. *Paedodogus*, Bk. II, Ch. II.

44. Chaucer, 'The Wife of Bath's Prologue', *The Canterbury Tales*, translated into Modern English by Nevill Coghill, London 1951, p. 295.

45. Bishop Burchard's *Penitential*, Ch. CLIV.
   F. W. H. Wasserschleben, *Die Bussordnungen der abendländicher Kirche*, Halle 1851, p. 660.
46. M. Schurig, *Spermatalogia*, Dresden 1730, Ch. VII, pp. 317–57.
47. John Hunter, *Essays and Observations*, London N.D., Vol. I, p. 189.
48. B. Blackwood, *op. cit.*, p. 30.
49. Ovid, *Ars Amatoria*, ii, 415.
50. *Anastasy*, British Museum, Greek pap, 1, 90. Ed. Wessely.
51. Nicholas Culpeper, *The British Herbal and Family Physician*, Halifax N.D., pp. 240–1, 130.
52. *The Book of the Thousand Nights and One Night*, translated by J. C. Mardrus, ed. by E. Powys Mathers, London 1923, pp. 148–50.

CHAPTER V

Love-making

SEXUAL feelings are undoubtedly a part of a deep instinctive drive. Unfortunately there is not necessarily a correlation between the intensity of the feeling and the ability to translate it into action, in other words there is no inborn ability which enables us to make love. This is something which has to be acquired, so that in discussing techniques of making love the variety exhibited must be regarded as essentially a product of particular cultures. The phenomenon of ignorance in matters of love is delightfully expressed in the classical story of *Daphnis and Chloe*. The protagonists are supremely in love and supremely ignorant of the means whereby to gratify their passion. They pass through a number of trials and tribulations. One passage tells of Daphnis's frustration when he tries directly to imitate nature, 'therefore he began to ask of Chloe that she would give him free leave to do with her what he listed and that she would lye naked with him, and longer too than they were wont. . . . But Chloe asking him, whether anything remain'd more than kissing, embracing, and lying together upon the ground; or what he could do by lying naked upon a naked Girle? That (quoth he) which the Rams used to do with the Ewes, and the he-Goats with the She's. . . . How Daphnis? And dost thou not see the she-Goats and the Ewes, and he-Goats and the Rams how these do their work standing, and those do suffer standing too; those leaping and those admitted them upon their backs? And yet thou askest me to lye down, and that naked. . . . Daphnis is persuaded, and laying her down, lay down with her, and lay long; but knowing nothing of that he was made to do, lifted her up, and endeavour'd to imitate the Goats. But at the first finding a mere frustration there, he sate up, and lamented to himself, that he was more unskillful than a very Tup in the practice of the mystery and the Art of love. . . . '(1)

This frightful dilemma is overcome by Daphnis receiving expert instruction from the young wife, Lycaenium, of an old neighbour. Lycaenium speaks to him in this way. . . . 'If then thou wouldst be rid of thy misery, and make an Experiment of that pleasure, and sweet Nerve which you have sought, and mist so long, come on, deliver thyself to me a Swect Schollar, and I, to gratifie the Nymphs, will be thy Mistress. At this Daphnis being a rustick Goat-herd, a Sanguin Youth, and burning in desire, could not contain himself for meer pleasure, and that Lubency that he had to be taught; but throws himself at the foot of Lycaenium, and begs of her, that she would teach him quickly that Art, by which he should be able, as he would, to do Chloe. . . . She bid him sit down as near to her as possible he could, and that he should kisse her as close and as often as he used to kisse Chloe; and while he kist her to clip him in his arms and hugg her to him, and lye down with her upon the ground. And now he was sitting, and kissing, and lay down with her; She, when she saw him itching to be at her, lifted him up from the reclination on his side, and slipping under, not without art, directed him to her Fancie, the place so long desired and sought. . . . '(2) Daphnis afterwards is greatly excited and wishes to run straight to Chloe to put his newly gained knowledge into practice but Lycaenium emphasises that matters are different with her as she is not a virgin. '. . . But if thou strive with Chloe in this list, she will squeak, and cry out, and bleed as if she were stickt. But be not thou afraid of her bleeding; but when thou hast persuaded her to thy pleasure bring her hither into this place, and although she should cry and roar, no body can hear; and if she bleed, here's a clear fountain, she may wash. . . . '(3) All this dampens Daphnis's

ardour so he reverts to his former quiet love-play. But in the end
the two are married and Daphnis is able to repeat his lesson.
'. . . But Daphnis and Chloe lying naked together, began to clip,
and kisse and twine, and strive with one another, sleeping no more
than birds of the night; and Daphnis now did the Trick that his
Mistress Lycaenium had taught him in the thicket. . . . '(4)

We have quoted the story of *Daphnis and Chloe* at some length
because it reveals a typically European attitude towards sexual
instruction. The convention for a very long period in European
history, and which still exists today, was that the bride was supposed
to be innocent in every meaning of the word. To her husband was
left the task of initiating her. That there were many exceptions is
proved by the courtship customs we quote in a later chapter, but
medical and psychiatric evidence from the nineteenth century onwards demonstrates the, at times, appalling consequences of female
ignorance encountering male clumsiness. If all husbands were of
the calibre of Jules Romains's hero in *The Body's Rapture* no doubt
there would be no problem.(5) (On his honeymoon he reveals
himself as a master of tact and sympathy.) Unfortunately few
newly-wed husbands have the experience and finesse to enable
them to behave in this way.

For people so apparently concerned with the erotic, both in the
arts and life, this admission of chance into what is in fact an extremely important aspect of life is extraordinary. (It must be admitted that the initial sex act of a couple may determine the quality
of their enduring sexual and marital relationships.) A possible
explanation of this deficiency is the presence in the different periods
of European history of a puritanical attitude towards sex. The
adulation of the female, the veneration of the virgin, Pauline conceptions of marriage, the Nonconformist conscience, have all
played their part in denying sexual knowledge to the unmarried
woman. To suggest openly that women should have instruction in
sexual techniques before marriage would meet with instant condemnation by members of the 'Establishment'.

The middle-class nineteenth-century male was supposed to have
gained his sexual knowledge from prostitutes. He would have been
ashamed to meet the sexual dexterity of his mistress or favourite
prostitute in his wife. There is obviously an important connection
here between the conception of marriage held at any time as a

relationship between two people—the kind and quality of this relationship—and attitudes towards sexual activity in general. The Greek conception of the wife as housekeeper and bearer of children, while the *hetairae* were for love and intellectual pleasure, is not entirely absent in the Victorian age.

From a male point of view this heritage of the desirability of the virgin and ignorant bride is still, despite the rapid increase of pre-nuptial sexual activity, operative in our society. The husband, other considerations apart, wishes to imagine that he is the first man in his wife's life. This no doubt feeds his ego, but is not exactly designed to promote sexual harmony for the pair. According to Kinsey's statistics over 40 per cent of males in his sample wished to marry virgins but only 23 per cent of females expressed anxiety to marry men innocent of sexual experience. These figures may be compared with those given in the British *Chesser Report*, where it is stated that 17 per cent of the single women in the total sample thought that it important that they and their future husbands should not have had pre-marital intercourse. 16 per cent thought it was fairly important. A majority, therefore (67 per cent) dismissed it as unimportant. [6] The process today is one where the female virgin is tending to disappear and 'If the drop should continue at the average rate shown for those born since 1890, virginity at marriage will be close to the vanishing point for males after 1930 and for females born after 1940. It is more likely that the rate of change will become somewhat retarded as the zero point is approached and that an occasional virgin will come to the marriage bed for a few decades beyond the date indicated by the curves. It will be of no small interest to see how long the cultural ideal of virgin marriage will survive as a moral code after its observance has passed into history. . . . '[7] But the aspect which distinguishes Western society from many others is that such sexual initiation, as we have pointed out, is of a furtive, clandestine character which does not have the open approval of society.

In contrast to this, as it were, secret acquisition of sexual knowledge, there are many simple societies where sexual activity amongst the unmarried is not only tolerated, but actively encouraged by adults. Such behaviour, as we saw in Chapter II, may be institutionalised, as it is in the Trobriands and Central India. This, of course, is not always the case, and the young may be left to their own devices with the full approval of the adult members of the society, as is the case of the Chewa of Central Africa, the people of Lesu in New Ireland, and the Easter Islanders. Clearly in all cases it is the attitudes and beliefs concerning sex which determine the type of sexual behaviour permitted and approved. Europe appears never to have got over the association of sin and sexual pleasure which has been more or less prominent in thinking about such matters since the time of the Early Christian Fathers, whereas societies whose beliefs are of a more uninhibited nature appraise such activity for what it is—the supreme sensual pleasure available to man. At times, beliefs of this kind may take strange forms. The Lepchas of Sikkim believe that a girl cannot become a woman unless she has sexual intercourse. This is paralleled in our own midst by the widespread belief that masturbation induces insanity. But however sexual knowledge is acquired such knowledge brings the development of techniques of love-making.

To most Europeans the tactile or mouth kiss is an essential aspect of love-making. While it is probably true to say that kissing forms part of the prelude to coitus in all European societies, this is by no means a universal practice.

There are several varieties of kisses in addition to those which are associated with sexual love. To the Roman categories of *osculum*, the kiss of friendship on the face or cheeks, *basium*, the kiss of affection on the lips, and *suavium*, the lovers' kiss, may be added the kiss of salutation, the kiss of homage, the religious kiss, and the olfactory or nasal kiss. Our proper concern is with the Roman *suavuim* and the nasal kiss as these are the only two forms which are specifically erotic.[8] It could be argued that the tactile sensation produced by the meeting of lips or of the placing of the lips on a specific part of the body is connected with sensual pleasure and thus basically with the erotic. But the connection is extremely tenuous. For example, it would be ridiculous to suggest that the kiss of peace, given as a symbol of amity after battle, had a sexual basis. On the other hand some writers have maintained that the maternal kiss of mother and child is the origin of the sexual kiss proper. There are more grounds for such a supposition in that the relationship between mother and suckling child may have definite sexual overtones.[9] That it is possible for the sexual kiss, in the form of a salutation, to be equivocal is seen in the rabbinical condemnation of the interchange of such kisses between the sexes except on specific occasions: it is felt they might give rise to lewd behaviour.[10] The love feasts (agape) of the early Christians came in for similar criticism from contemporary critics. Tertullian has strong views on the subject.[11] The Hindu proverb that 'A moist kiss is better than a hasty coitus' is quite meaningless to numerous peoples in the world. There are societies where this form of kiss is completely unknown. The sexual kiss is found in its most developed form in Europe, India, and a number of widely dispersed societies such as the Kwakiutl Indians of the N.W. Coast of America, and the Trobrianders. The Indo-European form of the kiss is the one which is most familiar. There are, however, several variants. In Europe and amongst Europeans in any part of the world 'simple' kissing consists of the pressing of the lips against those of the partner. Pressure may be slight at first in the preliminary stages but increased as the kiss develops. Some couples never go beyond this stage. The kiss in this form can hardly be described as arousing profound erotic feelings. The tactile sensation is pleasant but not very much more. It is a different matter with 'French' or 'deep' kissing in which the use of the tongue is paramount. The 'French' kiss probably owes its name in the English-speaking world to the same type of reasoning that made the French describe homosexuality as 'le vice anglais'. This type of kissing involves the seeking out with the tongue of the inside of the lover's mouth, the sucking of the lips and tongue, and the caressing of the inside of the lips with the tongue. A variant is the gentle and, at times, savage biting of the partner's lips and tongue. The inside of the mouth is peculiarly sensitive so that contact of this kind has a strong erotic effect. In fact the erotic stimulus may be so powerful that orgasm results without any contact in the genital area.[12]

T. Van de Velde in his *Ideal Marriage* (pp. 133–4) describes a localised French form of the deep kiss. This is the 'Maraichinage' '. . . in which the couple, sometimes for hours, mutually explore and caress the inside of each other's mouths with their tongues as profoundly as possible. . . . ' The name is derived from the Maraichins or inhabitants of the district of Pays de Mont in the Vendée in Brittany.

There are no accurate European figures as to the incidence of deep kissing, but Kinsey has provided statistics for Americans in his

study of the human female. 'Deep kissing was in the petting experience of approximately 70 per cent of the females in the sample
who had not had pre-marital coitus. The incidence, however, rose
with increased coital experience, and deep kissing was in the
histories of something between 80 and 93 per cent of those who had
had coitus before marriage. . . . '[13] Kinsey goes on to remark that
there are significant differences in the percentage with relation to
generations. For example of those born before 1900 who had no
pre-marital sexual experience only 44 per cent had experienced
kissing of this character. This indicates, if we can take such figures
as being reasonably accurate, that the use of the French kiss as a
sexual technique is increasing. But whether its use is subject to
fashion in such matters, or whether there has been a continuous
development it is almost impossible to decide in the face of the
equivocal evidence for either view.

Such evidence as exists is both literary and pictorial. The classical
lover's kiss is well attested. There are numerous references for
example in Greek and Latin poets such as Theocritus, Anacreon,
Ovid, and Catullus. But detail on which to base an opinion as to its
incidence, as we can on the evidence of Kinsey with regard to contemporary America, is lacking. Some of the wall paintings in
Pompeii show lovers kissing, but certainly not in an ecstatic manner. Far more attention is paid to details of copulation. This is also
the case in Greek vase paintings and sculptured reliefs. An obvious
reason for this is the difficulty of depicting the kiss in a manner
which conveys the action and feeling. There is little accurate information as to the kissing techniques of the pagan tribes of Europe.
But to assume from this that the kiss was unknown is perhaps too
extreme. On the other hand there is a great deal to suggest, both in
literature and art, that the sexual kiss was extremely popular in
mediaeval Europe.

The same can be said of Elizabethan England. Marlowe's famous
evocation from *Faust*: 'Sweet Helen, make me immortal with a
kiss. Her lips suck forth my soul: see, where it flies . . . ' typifies this
attitude to kissing.

The non-erotic kiss, as opposed to the sexual, became in time the
most usual form of European salutation for both sexes. In England,
however, by the end of the seventeenth century this free use of the
kiss is limited, and the emphasis is confined to sexual kissing

between lovers, and to kissing between parents and children. Congreve puts the point nicely in *The Way of the World*: 'You think you're in the country where great lubberly brothers slabber and kiss one another when they meet, like a call of Sergeants—Tis not the fashion here. . . .'[14]

In most European countries, as opposed to Britain, kissing as a salutation has persisted into our own day. The U.S.A., however, has tended to follow British practice in this respect. As in so many other ways the prudery of Victorian England appears to have affected the use of the kiss as part of sexual behaviour. This is not surprising in view of the Victorian middle class male's desire for a literally virgin and untutored bride. Practice seems to have been at variance with theory, for nineteenth century prose and poetry is redolent with the praises of the meeting of lips. Byron in the early part of the century writes:

> *A long long kiss, a kiss of youth and love.*
> *And beauty, all concentrating like rays.*
> *Into one focus kindled from above;*
> *Such kisses as belong to early days,*
> *Where heart and soul and sense in concert move,*
> *And the blood's lava, and the pulse ablaze.*
> *Each kiss a heart-quake—for a kiss's strength,*
> *I think it must be reckoned by its length.*

That must have stirred the bosom of many a virginal miss. It was doubtful if her husband ever produced such ecstasies in her. The imagination boggles at the idea of the immediate descendants of Jane Austen's heroes and heroines hurling themselves into such transports. It seems doubtful that the same rift between theory and practice was apparent in the nineteenth century France. When Flaubert wrote, ' "Yes, yes, kiss me, kiss me deep! Your kisses bring me new life!" she cried. . . .'[15] he was not expressing a remote poetic feeling, he was describing what his readers would know from experience.

By the twentieth century the importance of the sexual kiss is a commonplace in European literature. In the vast majority of modern novels dealing with love this type of kiss is part of the hero's sexual armoury.

It is in India, however, that we find the most attention paid to this aspect, as indeed to all aspects of sexual technique. Numerous Indian erotic authorities have enumerated various forms and types of the sexual kiss. Vatsyayana (*circa* 100–600 A.D.), the author of the *Kamasutra* describes three forms of kiss for the young girl: the nominal kiss, the throbbing kiss, and the touching kiss: 'When a girl only touches the mouth of her lover with her own, but does not herself do anything, it is called the "nominal kiss". When a girl, setting aside her bashfulness a little, wishes to touch the lip that is pressed into her mouth, and with that object moves her lower lip, but not the upper one, it is called the "throbbing kiss". When a girl touched her lover's lips with her tongue, and, having shut her eyes, places her hands on those of her lover, it is called the "touching kiss".'[16]

Another category consists of the straight kiss, the turned kiss, the pressed kiss, the greatly pressed kiss, the kiss of the upper lip, and the clasping kiss: 'A woman, however, only takes this kind of kiss from a man who has no moustache. And on the occasion of this kiss, if one of them touches the teeth, the tongue, and the palate of the other, with his or her tongue, it is called the "fighting of the tongue".'[17]

The lover is told all that he or she should do in the way of kissing, and, as we shall see, is instructed in every conceivable aspect of sexual technique. In this connection it is surprising to see in a recent German work dealing with sexual customs a statement that '. . . All in all, however, it must be said that Indian love technique adds nothing to what young people in other countries find out for themselves without scientific instruction. . . . '[18] The author appears to have forgotten his *Daphnis and Chloe* and to have disregarded a great deal of clinical evidence to the contrary. However strong the sexual instinct, we are not born with a knowledge of how to perform sexually. That is something of which we may acquire a deep knowledge and understanding, but it is probably true that a majority never get beyond an elementary technique. Havelock Ellis expressed similar views and quoted from a lecture of Sir James Paget on 'Sexual Hypochondriasis' to support his contention: 'Ignorance about sexual affairs seems to be a notable characteristic of the more civilised part of the human race. Among ourselves it is certain that the method of copulating needs to be taught, and that they to whom it is not taught remain quite ignorant about it.'[19]

If this were not the case there would hardly be the considerable sale in our midst of marriage manuals and the like.

The most charming Indian kiss is 'When a person kisses the reflection of the person he loves in a mirror, in water, or on a wall, it is called a "kiss of showing the intention" . . .'[20]

For some North American Indian peoples, the inhabitants of the Trobriand Islands, and those of Alor and Truk in the East Indies, the sexual kiss is more elaborate than that of the ordinary European deep kiss. The lips and tongue are sucked violently, and then, at the appropriate moment, saliva is allowed to flow from one mouth to the other. This is regarded as a normal part of sexual intercourse. In other societies, such as those of the Plains Indians (Cree, Crow, etc.) and Indians of the American South-West, the kiss approximates much more to the orthodox European form.

Although the joining of lips and mouths appears to be an obvious thing to do in the preliminaries of sexual play, there are many peoples who rely on the olfactory or nasal kiss to produce the same effect. It is true, of course, that the smell of the partner may act as a sexual stimulant, which fact has given rise to a variety of sexual fetishistic practices. But to avoid what is considered the normal mode of kissing by the European appears at first sight strange. Not only is oral kissing in these societies not practised, but it is regarded as being disgusting in the extreme. Admittedly the free mingling of saliva and so forth has little to recommend it on hygienic grounds, but if that argument is pursued the whole sex act might be condemned as unhygienic and unaesthetic. The societies in question are the Balinese, the Central Africa Thonga, the Fijians, the Manus of New Guinea, the Lepchas of Sikkim, the Tinguian of Luzon, and a few other groups. The substitute of the olfactory kiss amongst these peoples has been erroneously described in the past as 'rubbing of noses'. Its mode of operation has been well described by Covarrubias: ' . . . The love technique of the Balinese is natural and simple; kissing as we understand it, as a self-sufficient act, is unknown and the caress that substitutes for our mode of kissing consists in bringing the faces close enough to catch each other's perfume and feel the warmth of the skin, with slight movements of the head. . . .'[21]

What factors have influenced the rejection of the ordinary tactile kiss by these peoples it is impossible to say. The fact that they are

widely divergent in geographical location and culture, and surrounded by societies which do not have a similar rejection, makes
the problem even more intractable. The thesis that the sexual kiss of
Europe and India is the result of a higher form of culture not possessed by simple peoples breaks down on a consideration of the
many simple societies which have the same technique. To rebut the
argument absolutely there is the case of the Japanese. A people with
an elaborate civilisation they yet have no place in their scheme of
sexual play for the kiss. There are few references in Japanese
literature to the kiss, nor is it portrayed in drawings or paintings.
'. . . Kisses and embraces are simply unknown in Japan as tokens
of affection, if we except the solitary fact that Japanese mothers, like
mothers all over the world, lip and hug their little ones betimes.
After babyhood there is no more hugging or kisses; such actions
except in the case of infants, are held to be immodest. . . .'(22)

Whereas the kiss is a familiar European phenomenon those
customs which are concerned with implementing the work of the
penis in coitus are, so far as we know, unknown in Europe.

India and South East Asia are the chief areas in which considerable ingenuity has been displayed in embellishing the male organ.
Such embellishments do not make the penis any the more efficient
as a source of pleasure for the man but appear to be designed to
enhance the sensations experienced by the woman. The Dyaks of
Borneo perform a minor operation on the glans of the penis. A
silver needle is inserted and left until the aperture made in this way
has healed as a channel. When required various objects can be
introduced into this channel. These may be tiny metal or ivory rods,
or ingenious contrivances with tiny bristles at either end forming
brushes. The Dyaks maintain that their use gives inordinate
pleasure to women. It does seem as if women are the inspirers of
this somewhat extravagant addition to nature. '. . . The men who
have several such perforations and can wear several instruments are
specially sought after and admired by the women.'(23) Women will
sometimes indicate to their lovers the desired size of object they
should utilise for this purpose. This is done by placing a home made
cigarette of the requisite size, rolled up in a leaf in their food. Such
penis devices have various names such as 'ampallang', 'untang', and
'kampion'.

Certain refinements are noticeable in similar devices found in the

North Celebes in Indonesia. There the eyelid of a goat with the eye-lashes is tied around the corona of the glans. Somewhat cruder is the practice of binding the whole penis, except the glans, with strips of goatskin. This obviously increases the frictional powers of the erect penis, and so presumably enhances the woman's pleasure. In Sumatra the Batta tribe insert tiny stones or pieces of metal under the skin of the penis with the same object in view.[24] The men of Pegu in Burma tend to wear little balls on the top of the penis so

Fig. 8. The geskel, a little horse hair brush attached to the penis by the Araucanian Indians of the Argentine in order to increase female pleasure in the sexual act

that the vagina is distended by it during coitus. The most charming refinement is reported of Chinese roués who bind their penises with the down from birds' feathers. Interestingly enough there is a reference in Frank Harris's *Autobiography* to a similar use of feathers manipulated by the hands. The same delicacy is exhibited by the Malays of Borneo who perforate the penis and introduce a very fine brass wire which is spread out like a brush at the ends.[25] This is similar to one of the few examples from the New World. The Araucanian Indians of the Argentine attach a little brush of horse hair by threads to the penis. This is called a *geskel* and apparently is most effective.[26] Balinese women, while not favouring mechanical devices for their men, possess a number of vegetable substances

which they insert in the vagina and which supposedly enhance
sensation during coition. One of the commonest is the leaves of
the Padang-derman (*Artemisia vulgaris L.*). A resinous powder
called gopita is also used in a similar fashion.[27]

In India, according to the *Kamasutra*, additions to the penis for
the purposes of exciting women are termed 'apadravyas'. Basically
their purpose seems to be to increase the size of the organ so that it
fits the vagina (yoni). These apadravyas should be made of gold,
silver, copper, iron, ivory, buffalo's horn, wood, tin, or lead. They
'should be soft, cool, provocative of sexual vigour, and well fitted
for the intended purpose. . . .'[28] They take the form of armlets or
bracelets made to fit the man's penis and the particular vagina it is
intended to penetrate. A special variety is the Kantuka or Jalaka,
'a tube open at both ends, with a hole through it, outwardly rough
and studded with soft globules, and made to fit the size of the yoni,
and tied to the waist. . . .'[29] Apparently these devices can be used
in connection with the penis or in place of it.

But in addition to the use of apadravyas in the way described the
Kamasutra recommends types of Dyak ampallangs. Precise instructions are given for the operation. '. . . Now, when a young
man perforates his lingam (penis) he should pierce it with a sharp
instrument, and then stand in water so long as the blood continues
to flow. At night he shall engage in sexual intercourse, even with
vigour, so as to clean the hole. After this he should continue to wash
the hole with decoctions, and increase the size by putting into it
small pieces of cane . . . thus enlarging the orifice. . . . In the hole
made in the lingam a man may put apadravyas of various forms,
such as the "round", the "round on one side", "the wooden
mortar", "the flower", "the armlet", "the bone of the heron",
"the goad of the elephant", "the collection of eight balls", "the
lock of hair", "the place where four roads meet", and other things
named according to their forms and means of using them. All these
apadravyas should be rough on the outside according to their
requirements. . . .' [30]

The relative size of the penis to the vagina is of definite concern
to the author of the *Kamasutra*. The more closely they approximate
to each other the more pleasurable the union. But the methods
recommended to a man who wishes to enlarge his penis may appear
a little alarming to some readers '. . . He should rub it with the

bristles of certain insects that live in trees, and then, after rubbing it for ten nights with oils, he should again rub it with bristles as before. By continuing to do this a swelling will be gradually produced in the lingam and he should then lie on a cot, and cause his lingam to hang down through a hole in the cot. After this he should take away all the pain from the swelling by using cool decoctions. The swelling, which is called "Suka" . . . lasts for life. . . . '(31) For temporary enlargement there are prescriptions principally composed of oil expressed from a number of vegetable sources. Two of these are the garden-egg or aubergine, and the cucumber. The affinity in appearance between plant and organ need not be developed.

As a complement to the activities of the man the woman can, by the use of ointments, cause her vagina to contract or be enlarged. For the former purpose the fruit of the arteracantha longifolia or kokilaksha is used. Unfortunately the contraction lasts only for a night. But it would have been a useful addition to the European women's prescriptions for creating pseudo-virginity or artificial hymens which we have remarked on elsewhere. For enlargement of the vagina roots of the blue lotus and other plants are mixed with ghee (clarified butter) and honey. This somewhat recherché compound is rubbed into the vagina.

The use of these artificial aids is essentially more practical than the majority of magical and near-magical practices described in the last chapter. What is surprising is the relative paucity of such aids in the world at large. Perhaps one reason for their absence in Europe is that their manufacture and use require an extremely uninhibited attitude towards sexual intercourse. This, in our view, is of rare occurrence in Europe, where the individual, particularly the woman, tends to see the sex act through a curtain of romanticism. The choice of language in contemporary sex manuals is ample proof of this attitude. The woman who insists that her lover wear an ampallang cannot indulge in coyness or false modesty.

'In a state of sexual need and desire the woman's lips are firm and vibrant, the breasts are swollen, and the nipples erect. The intelligent husband cannot be deceived by these signs. If they do not exist, it is his part to provoke them by his kisses and caresses, and if, in spite of his tender and delicate excitations, the lips show no heat and the breasts no swelling, and especially if the nipples are disagreeably irritated by slight suction, he must arrest his transports and abstain from all contact with the organs of generation, for he would certainly find them in a state of exhaustion and disposed to repulsion. . . . '(32)

That quotation indicates the importance of the female breasts in love-making. The connection between the uterus and the breast is well known. But the importance of the bosom has perhaps been over-emphasised in many societies. The overdeveloped mammaries have become in the United States, Britain, and most of Western Europe the ultimate symbol of sexuality. This is evidenced in various ways—the extraordinary adulation given to film stars with prominent breasts is one example. As Sir Hartley Shawcross put it in an address to the Public Morality Council in London (reported in *The Times* of October 31st, 1958) '. . . What can one say of a society where some dumb blonde, suffering from some glandular disease causing excessive swelling of the bust, is extravagantly paid for exhibiting herself at the theatre?' The male inhabitant of these countries has been so conditioned by the continuous display on the films, on the stage, and by posters and pictures of the female breasts that his sexual response has become almost automatic. Contemporary Western man can be well described as breast-obsessed.

This is not in fact a new phenomenon. The Early Christian Fathers condemned the display of any part of the female body in no uncertain terms, but by the thirteenth century there was a strong reaction against this tabu. The breasts among upper-class women began to be displayed—rouge was applied to the nipples to make them more provocative. From this time on concealment and display fluctuate from one period to another. As conceptions of modesty vary the bosom is hidden, almost openly displayed, or half concealed. It is a fascinating history in which varied comparisons can be made. The near nudity of the bosom of the nineteenth century French 'Incroyables' can be contrasted with the almost complete concealment (for daytime wear) with the buttock-emphasis of the bustle in late nineteenth-century Britain. Today, while the nude breast is confined to the stage or inanimate representation, it remains paramount in the field of sexual symbolism, with the buttocks a very poor runner-up.(33) Within this general field there are nuances of refinement to be distinguished.

For example, Americans take a serious view of the display of 'cleavage', that is the artificial valley between the breasts, on the cinema screen—in fact such display is banned—whereas in Britain no such scruples prevail. One result of this is that British films which exhibit actresses in this way have to be modified for the American market.

Contemporary European breast worship undoubtedly stems from classical Greece. As one authority (H. Licht) puts it: 'Ancient literature and art practised a true cult of the female bosom. . . . One would have to write a special book if all the passages were to be collected in which homage is paid to the beauty of the bosom. . . . '[34] Two examples will make this clear. The first is the story of the maiden Phryne told by Athenaeus of Naucratis in his *Banquet of the Learned*.[35] Phyrne is in court being held responsible for a dreadful crime. The court is about to condemn her when her defender tears open her clothes. The dazzling sight of the beauty of her breasts is such that her judges find they cannot find her guilty. A possible parallel of a more restrained character could be found in the trials of so-called 'crimes passionels' in contemporary France where the defendants are women. So far as we are aware French defending lawyers have won their cases without recourse to the Greek expedient.

The other story is a frequently repeated episode in Greek literature (Euripides, Aristophanes and others, but not Homer), concerning Helen and Menelaus. When Menelaus regains his wife he feels that he must avenge his honour so he threatens Helen with a sword. Helen bares her bosom at the sight of which Menelaus is transported with joy and casting his sword from him takes her in his arms. The episode figures in numbers of Greek vase paintings.[36]

It would thus appear that the contemporary cult of the bosom has impeccable classical sources.

Granted the widespread pre-eminence of the female breast as the ultimate in Western sexual symbolism, some anomalies can be seen when practical aspects are considered. Kinsey has shown that the majority of virgins in his sample permitted manual caressing of their breasts by their lovers (72 per cent). This figure was increased to 95–98 per cent in the case of women who had had some pre-nuptial sexual experience.[37] Oral manipulation, however, was another matter. Only 30 per cent of women who were virgins allowed this type of caress. The percentage increased, according to the extent of pre-marital intercourse, to 87 per cent in the case of those who had had extensive experience of this kind. The highest incidence was found in the groups of female graduates where it varied from 86 to 97 per cent according to the degree of coital experience.[38] Reasons for the lack of acceptance of, for example, mouth-breast contacts, appear to be both psychological and physical. In the latter sphere it is probably true that a substantial minority of women have little or no feeling of pleasure if their breasts are manipulated. A much smaller minority are intensely sensitive in this area so that if the breast is caressed for a time they will have an orgasm. Kinsey cites the figure of 11 per cent in his sample of women who stimulated their own breasts during masturbation.

In the majority of American women who have a normal reaction to the oral stimulation of the breast psychological feelings may play an important part. It would seem among the less educated groups this type of sexual play is felt to have an element which is too overtly erotic to be tolerated. This may seem absurd in a context which in any event is sexual. But even prostitutes in Britain will often react violently to suggestions that they should step outside what they consider the bounds of sexual decency. What is permissible is clearly a relative matter. It could be argued that the American male's ideas of what is proper or appropriate in sexual relations are tied up with his unconscious attitude towards women in general and the deification of 'Mom'. The mystique of 'Mom' in the U.S. has reached enormous proportions.[39] The use of the breast which suckled you, despite its significance as a symbol of sexuality, for overt erotic purposes may create unconscious barriers. It is noticeable that the greatest incidence of oral manipulation occurs in the most highly educated group of females, college graduates. Obviously this group has less inhibitions about overtly erotic play. Male partners would tend to be of the same educational standard and thus would be less liable to succumb to the lure of 'Mom'.

In Europe, unfortunately, there are no comparable studies to those of Kinsey and his associates in the United States. While useful in many ways the *Chesser Report* does not cover so wide a field in such depth as the two Kinsey *Reports*. Such evidence as there is in the form of literature, both prose and poetry, as well as pictorial material, suggests that European men differ little in their overt attitudes from Americans with regard to the female bosom. Vital statistics are no less important to the American than to the European. It is difficult to assess the popularity of the manual and oral manipulation of the breasts as a form of erotic play. Manuals of sex instruction in Britain do not give a too prominent place to this aspect of love-making. This of course does not necessarily mean that it is not a popular practice.

Oriental erotic literature in general stresses the significance of the breast as a symbol of sexual delights. *The Song of Solomon*: 'Thy two breasts are like two young roes that are twins, which feed amongst the lilies', is probably one of the best-known examples. But there is almost as much emphasis on the other parts of the female anatomy such as the buttocks and thighs: 'Oh fair One, with thighs like the tusks of elephants', 'She walks slowly along, such is the weight of thighs and breasts. . . .' (Sanskrit poem *Kuttaimatam*.) Indian sculptural representations of the female form emphasise the breasts, buttocks, and thighs. It would seem that the Asian peoples have managed to preserve a balance, a sense of proportion, with regard to what are considered sexually exciting parts of the female body, in contrast to the breast obsession of the European.

As regards the function of the breast in love-making techniques such books as the Indian Vatsyayana's *Kamasutra* and the Persian Nefawzi's *The Perfumed Garden* contain instructions as to how the nipples and breasts should be caressed by mouth and hand. Again, in the absence of specific studies with regard to practice, there is little indication of the incidence of such techniques amongst Asian and Arabic peoples. The antithesis of those societies, such as our own, that emphasise the mammary glands as sexual symbols is represented by a number of fairly divergent pre-literate groups. The Kwakwuitl Indians of the North-West Coast of America. The Siriono Indians of Bolivia, the Kwoma and Manus of New Guinea, the Lesu of New Ireland, and the Kurtatchi of the Solomon Islands, are some of these societies in which it is reported there is no type of breast stimulation whatever. If copulation takes place in the normal face-to-face position, contact of the woman's breasts and the man's chest is inevitable. But this is not at all the same procedure as the conscious manipulation we have been discussing.

Lack of interest in this type of love-play may indicate a general antipathy towards all forms of sexual preliminaries. Energy and interest are concentrated upon the copulatory act itself. This is certainly the case amongst the Kwoma. 'After the wedding ceremony, the couple live together as man and wife, and the customs which regulate marital sexual behaviour apply to them. They never sleep in the same bed but lie alone on separate bark slabs, joining only for copulation, which is performed with a minimum of embracing and foreplay. . . . A woman supposedly takes the initiative in sexual intercourse even after marriage. It is the wife who visits the husband's bed. . . . '[41]

Another and much larger group, composed of pre-literate and some advanced non-European societies such as some North American Indians, the Trobrianders, the Marquesans, the Jamaicans, the Alorese, and the Ifugao of the Philippines, indulge in breast stimulation as a form of sexual foreplay. Amongst many of these peoples the symbolic titillation of the woman's nipples is the first step towards intercourse, an invitation. This is true of the island of Alor in the East Indies. 'Intercourse is solicited of young women by touching their breasts. A common euphemism for intercourse is "to pull a girl's breasts", since it is supposed that no woman can avoid being aroused by such a caress or would be able to resist a man who approached her in this fashion. "Our hands move about at random and touch a girl's breast. That makes her spirit fly away, and she has to sleep with a man."[42]

The author (C. du Bois) of the study from which that quotation is taken goes on to say that because of childhood experiences, and the role in Alor society which women are expected to fulfil, it is inevitable that erotic feeling should be centred in the breast. Lacking the means of display and communication that Western societies possess, the Alorese have yet managed to achieve the same result in focusing attention on the female breast. The lack of display in our sense (film, pictures, etc.) is not felt as women leave the upper part of the body bare.

The Marquesans allow their women to have a far more dominant role in sexual matters than is found in most societies. At private feasts which were of an orgiastic character the man's 'role was to excite the woman by sucking her breasts and by *cunnilingus* (oral stimulation of the female genitalia) until she was excited to a high pitch and gave the signal for intercourse. . . . '[43] Such behaviour seems to be in complete contrast to the Alorese code where the woman remains essentially passive.

Some authorities suggest that the hiding of the breasts, though making them prominent, increases their erotic significance. This is a view maintained by Kinsey who states that in tropical America, where there is a tendency for women to expose the breasts, there seems to be little or no erotic symbolism attached to them.[44]

On the other hand the opinion advanced by Ford and Beach suggests that there is no correlation between exposure of the breasts and the lack of interest in them as erotic centres.[45] It is certainly true that in a majority of societies the female bosom is displayed, and that in such communities both emphasis and disregard of the breasts as erotic centres is found. The sexual significance attached to any part of the anatomy does not depend upon its concealment or display but rather upon the ideas about them which are formulated and traditionally established. It is possible that in the West highly literate cultures have fostered ideas concerning the female breast so that its erotic qualities are inextricably bound up with conceptions of sexual modesty. An even more telling example is the late Victorian and Edwardian adulation of the female ankle. Normally hidden by the dress its sudden display was supposedly sufficient to cause violent erotic reactions in a male audience. So far as is known the ankle is not, biologically speaking, an erotic or erogeneous zone, that is an area which is sexually receptive to touch. The culture creates the sexual content, and the response. Contemporary Western man exposed to different influences and stimuli, has little interest in the ankle.

The view was advanced by Erasmus Darwin and Havelock Ellis that we are basically attracted by the breast in adult life through our infant experience of suckling, with its associated pleasure. This may very well be the basis of the widespread incidence of admiration of the female bosom and techniques of titillation associated with it. The Freudian implications are inescapable as the following quotation shows: ' . . . All these various kinds of pleasure at length become associated with the mother's breast which the infant embraces with its hands, presses with its lips, and watches with its eyes; and thus acquires more accurate ideas of the form of its mother's bosom than of the odour, flavour, and warmth which it perceives by its senses. And hence at our maturer years, when any object is presented to us which by its wavy or spiral lines bears any similitude to the form of the female bosom, whether it be found in a landscape with soft graduations of rising and descending surface, or in the forms of some antique vases, or in other works of the pencil or of the chisel, we feel a general glow of delight which seems to influence all our senses; or if the object be not too large we experience an attraction to embrace it with our lips as we did in our early infancy the bosom of our mother. . . . '(46)

In contrast to caressing of the breasts, *fellatio*, that is the oral stimulation of the penis by the woman; *cunnilingus*, that is the oral stimulation of the clitoris by the man, and the joint performance of both, which is known as *soixante-neuf*, due to the opposition of the numerals 6 and 9 (69), are far less common.

Amongst primitive peoples it seems to be largely confined to societies in Oceania, such as the Trukese. One group we have already mentioned, the Marquesans, whose domineering females demand that their lovers shall excite them by sucking their breasts and kissing their vaginas. Two societies in this group, that of Ponapé and Sansol in the Caroline Islands, have carried this particular sexual technique to elaborate lengths. In Ponapé, '. . . Very long and pendulous labia minora are considered particularly attractive in women. They are deliberately produced and cultivated from early childhood by manipulations performed by elderly men who have become impotent. These manipulations are continued until the approach of puberty. At the same time, and as part of the same training, the clitoris is not only subjected to prolonged friction, but also to suction, and a certain large kind of ant (native to the islands) is applied to this region in order that its sting may produce a brief but acute and not unpleasant stimulation. . . . The cult of sexual pleasure is correspondingly ingenious. In order to arouse their mates to the highest pitch of excitement, the men use not only their tongues but their teeth as well. . . '(47)

Matters are carried even further by the insertion of a small fish in the vagina which the man then proceeds to lick out very slowly. This is clearly a refinement of technique which is not everyday practice, and in fact is confined to sexual preliminaries before copulating with one's chief wife in order to make her pregnant. *Soixante-neuf* as a sexual technique was known to the Greeks and Romans. References in their literature tends to be denigrating. This of course is not necessarily an indication that it was not a popular practice—rather the reverse. Perhaps it should be stated here that *soixante-neuf* has always been part of homosexual relations. This of course would help to explain the ambivalent references in classical literature. It also clarifies the attitude, which we discuss below, that *soixante-neuf* is degrading and perverted. In fact, in contemporary life, it is an ordinary sexual technique for both male and female homosexuals. An analysis of the case history of an American Lesbian states, ' . . . She claims *cunnilingus*, active and passive, with her Lesbian friend constituted the source of her greatest sex pleasure. Her first experience of this kind she describes as follows: "I slid down with my head between her legs. She was lying on her back and I on my stomach. I licked her clitoris, moved my lips over the area just below as I did so, sometimes I sucked her clitoris a little while while rolling my tongue over and around it. I realised great satisfaction and happiness with this activity. I felt closer to her that way than any other, and have a great desire for it. . . .' "[48]

In Indian erotic literature a similar condemnatory attitude to that of the Greeks and Romans is found. The *Kamasutra* gives detailed instructions as to how it should be performed but castigates it as being practised by specially trained eunuchs on the one hand and by prostitutes on the other, the suggestion being that no decent man or woman would have anything to do with it.

' . . . The male servants of some men carry on the mouth congress with their masters. It is also practised by some citizens, who know each other well, among themselves. Some women of the harem, when they are amorous, do the acts of the mouth on the yonis (vaginas) of one another, and some men do the same thing with women. The way of doing this (i.e. of kissing the yoni) should be known from kissing the mouth. When a man and a woman lie down in inverted order, i.e. with the head of the one towards the feet of the other and carry on this congress, it is called the congress of a crow.

'For the sake of such things courtesans abandon men possessed of good qualities, liberal and clever, and become attached to low persons, such as slaves and elephant drivers. (Compare 'society' women and boxers amongst ourselves.) The *auparishtaka*, or mouth congress, should never be done by a learned Bramin, by a minister that carries on the business of state, or by a man of good reputation, because though the practice is allowed by the Shastras, there is no reason why it should be carried on, and it need only be practised in particular cases. . . . '[49] The classical Indian lawgivers are quite open in their condemnation of *auparishtaka*, classifying it

Fig. 9. Indian erotic sculpture from Elephanta showing mouth congress

as unnatural intercourse. It is sometimes equated in heinousness with the murder of a Brahman. The women of Bengal come in for particular criticism as being so full of inordinate desire they do with the mouth what is the business of the vulva.[50]

Despite this type of condemnation there is a wealth of evidence in pictorial and sculptural form of genital-oral contacts from ancient civilisations as those of India, Greece, Rome, Japan and Peru.

The same process of associating *soixante-neuf* with homosexuality and perversion appears to determine people's attitudes in contemporary Western society. For example, according to Kinsey only 3 per cent of women in his sample who had not experienced sexual intercourse permitted their partners to practise *cunnilingus*. This percentage rose steeply as experience of coitus increased to 46 per cent of women who had had intensive experience. With regard to *fellatio*, or oral stimulation of the male genitalia by the women, the figures are comparable, 2 per cent rising to 43 per cent. The evidence suggests that in the case of *fellatio* it is generally performed on male initiative and that few women are stimulated sexually by it. A very small minority of women may have an orgasm while stimulating the male in this way.[51] Married couples exhibited somewhat higher figures: for *cunnilingus* 54 per cent, for *fellatio* 49 per cent.[51]

These figures are surprisingly high in the face of the apparently strong sanctions against genital-oral contacts in our type of society. There are prohibitions against such practices in both Jewish and Christian codes.[52] Other factors affecting the incidence of *soixante-neuf* are undoubtedly connected with the aesthetic. Havelock Ellis illustrates the balance between repulsion and attraction with regard to it extremely well.[53] Modern manuals of sexology are ambivalent in their attitude. Van de Velde, in his famous *Ideal Marriage*, refuses to use the ordinary scientific terms we have used above on the grounds that they refer to 'pathological practices', whereas the 'genital kiss' as he terms it, is '*absolutely unobjectionable and legitimate, ethically, aesthetically and hygienically.*'[54] Van de Velde is also at pains to point out the danger 'in approaching that treacherous frontier between supreme beauty and base ugliness. . . . '[55] It is a pity that a book which has done a tremendous amount to destroy sexual inhibitions in the West should employ a form of language which is reminiscent of the 'bees and flowers' epoch in sex education.[56]

However, *pace* Dr Van de Velde, the fact remains that in most Europeans' minds the combination of homosexual and pathological associations, memories of moral and religious prohibitions, together with aesthetic considerations, acts as a deterrent against more universal adoption of this sexual technique. That there is nothing inherently 'unnatural' about such techniques is evidenced from the behaviour of apes who favour this type of contact.[57]

A further consideration is no doubt the fact that the English-American Common Law, and most of the United States legal codes, expressly forbid such contacts. Proceedings in the U.S. do not appear to be taken very frequently against offenders. Such laws are on a par with those in some states which make adultery a criminal offence. On the other hand contacts of this kind would be considered just grounds for divorce in the majority, if not all, of the states in the Union.[58] One alarming statement made by Kinsey is that several wives have murdered their husbands for insisting on mouth-genital contacts.[59]

Granted the background we have cited, the employment of *soixante-neuf* in love-making implies a considerable amount of sexual experience and *savoire faire* which is not always possessed by the individual.

The same considerations do not apply in the case of manual stimulation of the genital area. This type of erotic play has a much wider distribution than oral-genital contacts. It is found in North American Indian societies, in the Polynesian area, in Asia, as well as in Europe. It is possibly, after kissing, the most usual type of pre-coital behaviour. The stroking of the vagina by the man is, generally speaking, more common than the female caressing of the penis. In some societies there are tabus against touching the female genitalia in any way. This is true of the inhabitants of Tikopia and the island of Wogeo off the Northern Coast of New Guinea. In the case of Tikopia in the Solomon Islands the man is also not supposed to touch his own genitals, and the woman is thus apt to guide his penis into her vagina. In several societies (Dahomey, Marianas Islands in the Pacific, Crow Indians of North America) it is customary behaviour for the man to play with his partner's clitoris or labia before attempting intercourse. Such attention has led in some instances to a concentration on the labia as a source of sexual attraction. Their size is increased by massage and pulling. This occurs amongst the Hidatsa and Crow Indians, the Hottentot and Namaqua of S.W. Africa, and some peoples of Dahomey and Uganda.[60] The Crow use this kind of stimulation as a means of soliciting clandestine intercourse.

In our type of society handling of the female genitalia by men and of the penis by women can be said to be a characteristic form of sexual preliminary. Kinsey's percentage for the former is 95 per cent, for the latter 91 per cent. These figures include occasional as well as frequent use of this technique. There are variations according to the year of birth and the educational level of the individuals concerned, but this does not affect the conclusion that it is a practice common to the vast majority of people, at any rate in the U.S.A.[61]

Reasons for this popularity are not far to seek. In the first place there are no moral or religious prohibitions against it. It does not bring in the ambivalent olfactory-aesthetic connotations that mouth-genital contacts do. It is a technique which can be practised before the intention of the partners is made clear to each other, that is prior to the act of seduction or actual intercourse, and can take place more or less as publicly as mouth kissing. Above all it is familiar to the participants through masturbation. With relation to the last statement it is interesting to see that self-titillation of the vagina is permissible for Roman Catholics. According to the *De rebus venereis ad usum Confessariorium*, 'In the same way it is lawful for the woman to prepare herself by genital stimulation, in order that she may have orgasm more easily. . . . ' (D. Craisson, Paris, 1870, p. 172).

The *Kamasutra* has this to say on the use of the hand on the female sex organs when the woman fails to show enjoyment. ' . . . the signs of the want of enjoyment and of failing to be satisfied are as follows: She shakes her hands, she does not let the man get up, feels dejected, bites the man, kicks him, and continues to go on moving after the man has finished. In such cases the man should rub the yoni (vagina) of the woman with his hand and fingers (as the elephant rubs anything with his trunk) before engaging in congress, until it is softened, and after that is done he should proceed to put his lingam into her. . . . '[62]

There is a whole group of actions in erotic play which come under the heading of painful stimulants. These consist mainly of biting, scratching, gouging, beating, and whipping. There is little doubt that the connection between sexual feeling and pain is well established. Havelock Ellis gives a brilliant exposition of early hypotheses concerning this in Volume III of his *Studies in the Psychology of Sex* (N.Y. 1914). More recent works are C. S. Ford and F. A. Beach, *Patterns of Sexual Behaviour* (London, 1952, 55–65), H. Deutsch, *The Psychology of Women* (London, 1946), and

W. Stekel, *Sadism and Masochism* (London, 1926). Ford and Beach show very clearly that this association of love and pain extends throughout the vertebrate species. One of the most dramatic examples is that of the mole. 'There is perhaps no female who has better reason than the mole for fearing the male. The vulva exteriorly unperforated, is covered by hide as downy as that of the rest of her body; to be fecundated she must undergo a veritable surgical operation. . . . In rutting time, forgetting his hunting, the male starts in quest of a female; as soon as he divines her he starts digging in her direction. . . . Feeling herself hunted the female flees. Hereditary instinct makes her tremble before the tool which shall open her belly, before the redoubtable gimlet-armed penis which has perforated her mother and all her female ancestors. She flees, as the male advances, cross hatching tunnels in which her persecutor may end by losing his way. The male is also educated by heredity; he does not follow the female but circles round her, heads her off, ends by catching her in an impasse, and while she is still running her blind muzzle into the earth, he grips, operates, and fecundates. . . . '(63)

Where pain predominates in sexual stimulation there are necessarily two elements, sadism and masochism. In the case of the former pleasure resides in the infliction of pain, in the case of the latter, in receiving pain. The term sadism is derived from the name of the famous exponent of this type of stimulation, the eighteenth-century Marquis de Sade. Masochism was named after L. Sacher-Masoch, a nineteenth-century Austrian novelist. He wrote a number of novels and stories of which the most famous is *Die Venus in Pelz* (The Venus in the Fur Coat).(64) It is said that it was this book that led R. A. Krafft-Ebing, the famous German sexologist, to use the author's name to describe this form of sexual activity while Masoch was still alive. Krafft-Ebing's definition of masochism in his *Psychopathia Sexualis* (London, 1900, p. 115) is illuminating.

'By masochism I understand a peculiar perversion of the physical *vita sexualis* in which the individual affected, in sexual feeling and thought, is controlled by the idea of being completely and unconditionally subject to the will of a person of the opposite sex, of being treated by this person as by a master, humiliated and abused. This idea is coloured by sexual feeling; the masochist lives in fancies *in* which he creates situations of this kind, and he often attempts to realise them. . . . ' Today we would include 'a person of the same sex' as the masochistic homosexual is a well-known phenomenon. Krafft-Ebing's definition, bearing in mind he is discussing fully developed masochism, which is abnormal, can be contrasted with Helene Deutsch's description of the female personality. ' . . . Woman's entire psychologic preparation for the sexual and reproductive function is connected with masochistic ideas. In these ideas coitus is closely associated with the act of defloration, and defloration with rape and a painful penetration of the body. The sexual readiness, the psychologic pleasure—affirming preparation for the sexual act, draws its masochistic components from two sources—one infantile, regressive, and dispositional, and the other *real*. For defloration is really painful and involves destruction of part of the body. . . . Acceptance of pain associated with pleasure, or of pleasure associated with pain, may result in such a close connection between the two that the sexual pleasure becomes dependent upon pain. Thus feminine sexuality acquires a masochistic character. Actually a certain amount of masochism as psychological preparation for adjustment to the sexual functions is necessary in women. . . . '[65]

The fully developed sadist or masochist is pathological. But, and this is the point made by Dr Deutsch, we all possess these feelings in embryo. Literary or pictorial association or stimulus, through seeing the helplessness of the female and the dominance of the male, may be sufficient to bring them out. The extreme pathological case was vividly shown by Sacher-Masoch in his own life. At one stage in his career he demanded that his wife should be unfaithful to him. For a long time she stood out against his importunities. Eventually he succeeded. The night she was to attend her assignation Sacher-Masoch himself helped to dress her and kept reiterating how he envied her lover-to-be. He obviously enjoyed the humiliation of arranging his own cuckoldom.[66] The masochistic element in women is constantly seen in the acceptances of brutality by prostitutes from their ponces.

Anthropological evidence suggests that sado-masochistic sexual stimulation is of a mutual character. That is both partners experience pleasure from inflicting pain and having pain inflicted. In the case of the Marquesas quoted above where the women force the men to suck their breasts and perform *cunnilingus*, this is followed by biting and scratching on both sides. The same is true of the Trobrianders. ' . . . Gradually the caress becomes more passionate, and the mouth is predominately active; the tongue is sucked, and tongue is rubbed against tongue; they suck each other's lower lips, and the lips will be bitten until the blood comes. . . . '(67) The Trobrianders are also addicted to the infliction of severe scratches on each other while making love. Biting of the eyebrows is also another practice of these people as it is on the island of Ponapé. A somewhat unusual custom is that of the women of the Choroti tribe in Central South America who spit in their partners' faces during intercourse. It is probably true to say that biting, wrestling, and scratching form a part of sexual preliminaries, actually accompany intercourse in a majority of human societies. This is not to suggest that all individuals in such societies use such techniques but that a fair proportion do so.

Biting, the giving of blows, and the use of weapons such as wedges, scissors and so on are dealt with systematically in the *Kamasutra*. The following instructions emphasise the point of mutual enjoyment of pain. 'When a man bites a woman forcibly, she should angrily do the same to him with double force . . . and if she be excessively chafed, she should at once begin a love quarrel with him. At such she should take hold of her lover by the hair, and bend his head down and kiss his lower lip, and then being intoxicated with love, she should shut her eyes and bite him in various places. Even by day and in a place of public resort when her lover shows her any mark that she may have inflicted on his body, she should smile at the sight of it, and turning her face as if she were going to chide him, she should show him with an angry look the marks on her own body that have been made by him. . . . '(68)

The whole section from which that extract is taken is devoted to the kinds and types of bite, the 'hidden bite', the 'swollen bite', and so on. There are other sections dealing with blows to be given, and scratching. But the use of 'pinchers on the breast' and 'scissors on the head' are condemned by the author.

It is quite clear that the infliction of pain as a stimulant was universally recognised in classical India. The situation is not altogether different in the case of our own type of society.

'Towards the peak of sexual arousal there may be considerable slapping and heavier blows, biting and scratching, and other activities which the recipient never remembers and which appear to have a minimum if any effect upon him at the time they occur. Not only does the sense of touch diminish, but the sense of pain is largely lost. If the blows begin mildly and do not become severe until there is definite erotic response, the recipient in flagellation or other types of sado-masochistic behaviour may receive extreme punishment without being aware that he is being subjected to more than mild tactile stimulation. . . .'[69] Kinsey's hypothesis provides an additional (psychological) basis for pain as a sexual stimulant. Both touch and sight are diminished during intense sexual activity with the result that the individual may be unaware of the pain or wounds he is inflicting.[70] Although we have said that pain response in sexual activity is characteristic of mammals in general, the figures adduced by Kinsey show that it is only a minority of people who, at any rate in the U.S.A., respond emphatically in this way. 26 per cent of the women in his sample definitely responded, 29 per cent slightly, and 45 per cent negatively. The comparative figures for males were 26 per cent, 24 per cent and 50 per cent.[71] This would suggest that while sado-masochistic practices are a concomitant of copulation it is only a minority which is strongly affected by them. However manuals of sex instruction give support to such practices. Van de Velde, for example, is enthusiastic about the 'love bite': 'This feeling of the bitten man is complex, interwoven of joy and pain.' He even quotes from Heine's poem *On Hastings Battlefield*:

'And on his shoulder she beheld three scars, and kissed them once again: wounds of no wars, No foeman's hand had smitten— Three little scars, her own white teeth had bitten.'[72]

Unfortunately there are no comparable figures, to those given by Kinsey, for Britain and for European societies. But literary and pictorial sources give a clear indication of the popularity in Europe of flagellation. Havelock Ellis traces the development of flagellation in Europe as an aid to sexual intercourse. He claims that as an erotic stimulant it was hardly known before the sixteenth century.[73] This might be true if we assume that in the extensive religious flagellation which had existed from the earliest days of the Church the erotic element was entirely absent or unconscious. It is debatable.

Flagellation is the one form of sado-masochistic behaviour which can claim to have a large bibliography, by no means entirely scientific in character. This in itself would suggest that it was and is practised on a fairly large scale. The closing down through police action of 'massage' establishments in London, Paris, and New York, from time to time, is some indication of its popularity. There is no

Fig. 10. A seventeenth century Dutch caricature of flagellation

question that violent stimulation of the buttocks through whipping can cause sexual excitement, depending upon the subject. The whole body may in fact be stimulated. Individuals, without becoming pathological, may find a great deal of pleasure in enjoying the mastery over another which whipping connotes. It is noticeable that flagellation is not only a concomitant of heterosexual relationships, but it is even more prominent in homosexual relationships. A factor of some importance which should be considered, not only in connection with flagellation, but in respect of pain and sex generally, is that of conditioning. It is very probable that the individual who is at all suggestible, and at the same time has exhibited no active sado-maschistic desires, will be influenced by a variety of media including the proclivities of his sexual companions, books, and pictures, so that in time he may come to participate fully in painful sexual play.[74]

Most of the sexual techniques we have discussed so far—there are of course some notable exceptions—are found in a great number of widely dispersed societies. One which we have not mentioned so far is massage. This is common in Europe and the Far East. In Europe it became associated in the nineteenth and twentieth centuries with 'perverted' practices. Brothels, as well as so-called clinics, specialised in providing this type of sexual stimulation. Today the association with the perverted is still maintained. There are, however, societies where massage is employed as part of the normal preliminaries to love-making. '. . . The motion begins by passing her open hands gently over the back, rubs a little harder, presses back on the ball of the hand, pushes more and more vigorously and always upward until the chelik nearly falls forward on his face, then rubs down more gently, soothes and quietens the whole body. . . . In some ghotuls there now follows a very intimate form of massage . . . the girl kneels upright or stands behind the boy and bends over him putting her arms around his neck and massages the chest with downward thrusts of the hands, while the boy leans back against her body in great enjoyment. . . .'[75] It is in this way that Murial boys in Central India are prepared for an evening of sexual pleasure.

'The term "petting" is properly confined to physical contacts which involve a deliberate attempt to effect erotic arousal.'[76] If we use that definition it would cover the employment of a great number of the techniques described. A qualification, however, is that the differentiation between petting and normal sexual intercourse is that the latter generally implies full penetration of the vagina by the male organ and subsequent orgasm of the partners. This of course would apply to coitus interruptus and the 'Karezza' method discussed below, whereas petting may produce orgasm without intromission being effected. Petting can therefore be

Fig. 11. An eighteenth century caricature of flagellation

described as the effective use of a variety of techniques, short of actual penetration, in order to produce sexual excitement which may or may not culminate in orgasm. All types of sexual stimulation, however, may be used as the accompaniment of one or the other.

In many societies of widely differing cultures love-making is systematised. That is to say the average boy and girl acquires the knowledge of socially acceptable techniques which are invariably used in conducting a love affair. On the appropriate occasion both will participate in this accepted pattern of love-making. Examples are numerous but there are two societies in which this activity is very fully documented. One is that of the United States, the other the Trobriand Islands. One represents the most advanced type of Western culture, the other is a primitive community.

We have already in Chapter II given some indication of Trobriand behaviour with relation to love-making. In the case of the United States Kinsey and his co-workers resented the criticism which had been made about the petting habits of American adolescents. As they pointed out it is not a specifically American invention, but has existed in all past civilisations, there being literary as well as pictorial evidence of this.[77] This of course is true—there is no society in which some form of pre-coital play has not existed. It is also true that Jewish and Christian codes have condemned activities of this kind which do not lead to sexual fulfilment. In most instances, certainly in the case of the Trobrianders, petting is followed by intercourse. The criticism which is made of American petting is that this is very rarely the result achieved or desired. In the age groups in which petting is a pronounced activity (sixteen to forty), only 35 per cent, or thereabouts, reach orgasm.[78] Although from early adolescence, the percentage of those in the age range of under fifteen to forty having petting experience ranges from 39 per cent in the youngest group to a peak of 88 per cent in the sixteen to twenty-five age group, falling to 70 per cent in the oldest group. This seems to indicate that considerably less than half of those indulging in this form of amatory exploration do in fact achieve orgasm.

The grounds on which both Christian and Jewish injunctions forbid physical contacts of the kind common in petting are very similar. If the assumption is accepted that contact of this kind tends to lead to intercourse, and if such intercourse is only considered lawful to the married, and further, if such contacts increase sexual pleasure, as undoubtedly they do, then they are to be condemned. So runs the argument. The Old Testament specifically condemns nakedness between lovers (Ezekiel, Ch. 16, 36–39). Contemporary Catholic Christian doctrine is quite explicit. ' . . . sexual pleasure, be it complete or incomplete, may be lawfully desired, carried directly or deliberately enjoyed only by those in the state of matrimony. . . . '[79] A seventeenth century view was even stricter. This implied that petting in marriage was permissible if it were for the purpose of showing love, but if for increasing sexual pleasure to be utterly condemned.[80] Many Protestant churches are inclined to a similar view. There is thus considerable pressure against petting in the U.S.A. from the religious bodies, which, in view of the high incidence of petting, does not appear to have had much direct effect. But the consideration cannot altogether be omitted that religious condemnation, although ignored, overtly may have an important effect in promoting conflict in the individual.

For the American youth there is also the law to contend with. A number of states (twenty-seven) possess statutes which make into an offence what they interpret as indecent or improper liberties taken with a minor. While this is an obvious protection for young girls against the depredations of older men, it inevitably includes any males who are guilty of such behaviour in the ordinary course of petting. Some states, such as Michigan and New Jersey, go even further in forbidding any indecent sexual act which takes place in private. Indiana and Wyoming, in their laws against sodomy, include any enticement of a person to commit masturbation. The last would affect a great number of adolescents as apparently 35 per cent of females masturbated after experiencing petting.[81] It is probably true that the majority of young people are unaware of their infringement of the law.

The attitude of the authors of *Sexual Behaviour in the Human Female* is curiously ambivalent with regard to petting. They are amused by the strictures European critics direct against what is almost a national institution in the U.S.A. Legal condemnation is rightly considered absurd in the face of general social acceptance. But they admit that just over a quarter of those females who indulge in petting report having pains in the groin as a result of failing to achieve orgasm after arousal. The masturbation figures we have already quoted on p. 149. Half the sample reported disturbance of one kind or another after petting.[82] The statement then made is that activity of this kind produces sexual tension and there is only one way to relieve this tension, by orgasm.[83] And yet only 35 per cent of females who indulge in petting achieve this. Paradoxically enough, claims are made that the petting experience of orgasm is correlated with a history of successful orgasm experience in marriage. This is somewhat specious as it is based on the facts that only a small minority (13 per cent) of those who reached orgasm as a result of petting failed to do so in marriage, and that 44 per cent of those who had never experienced pre-marital orgasm failed to do so in marriage.[84] This may well be the case but it is quite possible that there are factors affecting orgasm at any time which are not controlled by petting experiences.

Kinsey's conclusions are ' . . . petting provides a great deal more than experience in orgasm. It introduces the female to the physical, psychologic, and social problems that are involved in making emotional adjustments to other individuals. . . . '[85] Presumably the European female, who has not this institutionalised pattern at her disposal for making emotional adjustments, fails by the side of her American sister. However, this would not appear to be the case if emotional adjustment and sexual maturity are to be judged by divorce statistics. The United States has long led the Western world in respect of her divorce rate.

Petting in the U.S.A. has come into being as a result of a combination of factors many of which are unique to that society. For example, the automobile, either owned or borrowed, plays a significant part in both petting and 'dating' and provides opportunity and privacy. The European youngster, in most instances, is not mobile in this sense and thus lacks opportunity. Such factors have not really been assessed in the configuration of petting. The needs and demands for adolescent sexual experience, as we have seen in a previous chapter, are met in a variety of ways according to the cultural context in which they are made. One which is peculiarly American is the 'dating' and petting system. Another is the sexual licence of the Trobriander or the Muria. The clandestine sexual intercourse with a mistress, prostitute, or companion is the European solution.

In this chapter we have dilated on the variety of sexual techniques which man has invented and practised. Some are specifically the result of cultural factors, as the ampallang, others, such as sado-masochistic techniques, have come into being in response to a deep-seated psychological need. All are to be viewed objectively rather than in terms of a subjective good or bad. They are the result of the marriage of the nature of man and his culture.

In the words of the sixth-century Sheik Nefawssi, 'Praise be to God who has placed man's greatest pleasure in the natural parts of woman and has destined the natural parts of man to afford the greatest enjoyment to woman.' That is the principle which is common to all mankind. The principle in action leads to endless variety.

REFERENCES AND NOTES

1. Longus, *Daphnis & Chloe*, translated by George Thornley (1657), London 1933, pp. 118–20.
2. *Daphnis & Chloe*, op. cit., pp. 123–4.
3. *Daphnis & Chloe*, op. cit., p. 125.
4. *Daphnis & Chloe*, op. cit., p. 195.
5. Jules Romains, *The Body's Rapture*, translated by J. Rodker, London 1934, pp. 225–48.
6. A. C. Kinsey and others, *Sexual behaviour in the Human Female*, London 1953, p. 323, and E. Chesser and others, *The Sexual, Marital and Family Relationships of the English Woman*, London 1956, p. 341.
7. L. M. Terman, *Psychological Factors in Marital Happiness*, London 1938, p. 323.
8. The reader will find a useful analysis of the various forms of kiss in E. Crawley's *Studies of Savages and Sex*, London 1929, pp. 113–36.
9. Havelock Ellis, *Studies in the Psychology of Sex*, Philadelphia 1914, Vol. IV, p. 216.
10. J. Jacobs 'Kiss and Kissing', *The Jewish Encyclopedia*, N.Y. and London 1925, Vol. VII, p. 516.
11. Tertullian, *Ad Uxorem*, ii. 4.
12. See Kinsey, *op. cit.*, p. 252.
13. Kinsey, *op. cit.*, p. 252.

14. Act III, Scene XV.
15. Gustave Flaubert, *November*, translated by F. Jellinck, London 1934, pp. 120–21.
16. Kamasutra, Paris N.D., p. 82, English trans.
17. Kamasutra, *op. cit.*, p. 84.
18. R. Lewisohn, *A History of Sexual Customs*, translated by A. Mayce, London 1958, p. 37.
19. Havelock Ellis, *Studies in the Psychology of Sex*, Philadelphia 1913, Vol. VI, p. 510.
20. Kamasutra, *op. cit.*, p. 85.
21. M. Covarrubias, *The Island of Bali*, London 1937, p. 144.
22. Lafcadio Hearn, *Out of the East*, London 1927, p. 80. 1876, 8.22 ff.
23. N. von Miklucho-Maclay, *Verhandl. der Berliner Anthrop. Gesellsch.* 1876, 8, 22, ff.
24. P. Staudinger, 'Reizsteine des Penis auf Sumatra', *Verh. Berliner Ges. f. Anthrop.* 1891, 351.
25. A. B. Meyer, 'Ueber die Perf. des Penis bei der Malayen', *Mitt. Anthrop. Ges. Wein*, 1877, 7, pp. 242–4.
26. R. Lehmann-Nitsche, 'Geskel der Araucaner', *Zeit. f. Ethnologie*, 1900, Bd. 32, pp. 491–2.
27. J. Jacobs, *Eenigen tijd onder de Baliërs . . .* , Batavia 1883.
28. Kamasutra, *op. cit.*, p. 283.
29. Kamasutra, *op. cit.*, p. 284.
30. Kamasutra. *cit.*, pp. 284–5.
31. Kamasutra, *op. cit.*, pp. 285–6.
32. Jules Guyot, *Bréviaire de l'Amour Expérimantal*, Paris N.D., p. 422.
33. Cf. the Venus Kallipygos in the Naples Museum.
34. H. Licht, *Sexual Life in Ancient Greece*, London 1935, p. 311.
35. Athenaei Naucratitae deipnoisophistarum libri', XIII, 590 e.
36. See Licht, *op. cit.*, p. 25.
37. Kinsey, *op. cit.*, p. 253.
38. Kinsey, *op. cit.*, p. 254.
39. See *Their Mothers' Sons*, E. A. Strecker, N.Y. 1946.
40. E. Chesser and others, *The Sexual, Marital, and Family Relationships of the Englishwoman*, London 1956.
41. J. W. M. Whiting, *Becoming a Kwoma*, New Haven, 1941, pp. 125–6.
42. C. du Bois, *The People of Alor*, Minnesota 1944, p. 98.

43. R. Linton, 'Analysis of Marquesan Culture', in *The Individual and his Society*, by A. Kardiner, N.Y. 1939, p. 173.
44. Kinsey, *op. cit.*, p. 258.
45. C. S. Ford and F. A. Beach, *Patterns of Sexual Behaviour*, London 1952, p. 47.
46. Erasmus Darwin, *Zoonomia*, London 1800, Vol. I, p. 174.
47. O. Finsch, 'Über die Bewohner von Ponapé', *Zeitschrift für Ethnologie*, Berlin 1880, XII, 301.
48. F. S. Caprio, *Female Homosexuality*, N.Y. 1954, p. 231.
49. Kamasutra, *op. cit.*, pp. 121–2.
50. See J. J. Meyer, *Sexual Life in Ancient India*, London 1953, pp. 241–2.
51. Kinsey, *op. cit.*, pp. 257–8 and p. 361.
52. See F. May, *Social Control of Sexual Expression*, London 1930.
53. H. Ellis, *op. cit.*, Vol. IV, pp. 21–2.
54. Van de Velde, *Ideal Marriage*, London 1958, p. 148.
55. Van de Velde, *op. cit.*, p. 149.
56. This typifies the whole of Western 'pudeur'.
57. See S. Zuckerman, *Social Life of Monkeys and Apes*, London 1932, and A. C. Kinsey, *Sexual Behaviour in the Human Female*, London 1948, pp. 368–73 and 573–8.
58. Kinsey, 'Female' Volume, London 1953, footnotes, pp. 370–71. Kinsey, 'Male' Volume, London 1948, p. 577.
59. Kinsey, 'Male', Volume, p. 578.
60. See Prince M. zu Wied, *Reise in das Innere N. Amerikas*, Frankfurt 1839, Vol. I, p. 237, Vol. II, p. 107.
   F. de Vaillant, *Voyage dans l'intérieur de l'Afrique*, Paris 1790, Tome II, p. 7.
   J. Adams, *Remarks on the country . . . from Cape Palmas to . . . Congo*, London 1823, pp. 16 and 75.
61. Kinsey, 'Female', *op. cit.*, p. 399.
62. Kamasutra, *op. cit.*, p. 113.
63. Remy de Gourmont, *The Natural Philosophy of Love*, trans. by Ezra Pound, N.Y. 1940, p. 63.
64. L. von Sacher-Masoch, *Le Venue à la Fourrure*, trans. by L. Beaufort, Paris 1902.
65. H. Deutsch, *Psychology of Women*, London 1946, Vol. I, p. 218.
66. See Wanda von Sacher-Masoch, *Meine Lebensbeichte*, Berlin 1906.
67. B. Malinowski, *The Sexual Life of Savages*, London 1932, p. 280.
68. Kamasutra, *op. cit.*, pp. 97–8.

69. Kinsey, 'Human Female', *op. cit.* p. 614–5.

70. *ibid.*, p. 615 for authorities regarding these manifestations.

71. *ibid.*, p. 678.

72. T. Van de Velde, *op. cit.*, p. 140.

73. Ellis, *op. cit.*, Vol. III, p. 130.

74. The reader will find the topic treated at length in Ellis, *op. cit.*, Vol. III, pp. 129–50.

75. V. Elwin, *The Murias and their Ghotul*, Oxford 1947, pp. 377–8.

76. Kinsey, 'Female', *op. cit.*, p. 228.

77. Kinsey, 'Female', *op. cit.*, p. 235.

78. Kinsey, 'Female', *op. cit.*, p. 237.

79. P. O'Brien, *Emotions and Morals*, N.Y. 1950, p. 221.

80. T. Sanchez, *De sancto matrimonio sacramento disputationum*, 1637, Tome I, Bk. IX, p. 302.

81. Kinsey, 'Female,' *op cit.*, p. 263.

82. Kinsey, 'Female', *op. cit.*, p. 263.

83. Kinsey, 'Female', *op. cit.*, p. 264.

84. Kinsey, 'Female', *op. cit.*, p. 265.

85. Kinsey, 'Female', *op. cit.* pp. 265–6.

CHAPTER VI

Courtship

ALTHOUGH man can be differentiated from other animal species in many ways there are some particular aspects in which his social behaviour is in part governed by his biological affinity with other species. One of the outstanding examples of this is seen in courtship.

'These (secondary sexual) characters are very commonly developed among the higher animals, and one may mention as examples the mane of the lion and bison, the ornamental patches of colour and hair in monkeys, the beard in man; the brilliant wattles and plumage in numberless birds, such as the gorgeous feathers of pheasants, peacocks, birds of paradise, and humming birds; the ornamental colours in many fish, butterflies and spiders, the lava-like processes of beetles, the attractive scents of butterflies, the vocal sounds emitted by insects, frogs and mammals, and the beautiful song of birds. Darwin pointed out that these brilliant and striking characters appeal to the senses of the female, and are deliberately displayed to her at the breeding season. Courtship with these animals is often a lengthy and elaborate business, during which the male may perform a regular dance and strike attitudes to display himself to the best advantage. . . . Now it is characteristic of such structures and colours that they develop only in one sex and generally only at maturity; frequently, as in birds, they are periodically renewed at each breeding season. Moreover, they appear only on those parts which are displayed in courtship. . . .'[1]

What is an instrument of nature in other species, man has to create himself by decoration and ornament.

The purpose of the magnificent development of these secondary sexual characters in animals is to ensure that reproduction takes place. The more attractive and healthier male will secure his mate more swiftly. 'Those males will succeed which most effectually stimulate the females. . . . '[2] This then is the biological basis for the often quite fantastic displays during the courtship of animals. There is no doubt that the male sex in most species is granted by nature a general superiority of physique and appearance. The exceptions appear to be mostly confined to the lower animals such as ants, wasps, bees, and the mantis. In man superior strength is granted to the male, but, with regard to decoration and display in courtship, the predominating sex is determined by the particular culture in question. One of the most dramatic comparisons between the sexes in this respect is that of the peacock and the peahen. He dazzles the world with his tremendous magnificence of his tail; she presents a soiled, inferior appearance by his side. There is no equivalent example, among the higher animals, of the female outshining the male. To find a comparison one has to look at the insects and arachnids (spider family). There the gigantic stature of the female mantis dwarfs the tiny insignificant male. Or again, the contrast between the worker-bees and their queen. Man alone, it seems can choose which sex shall predominate, although he too is fulfilling the same biological function once he has made his choice.

The role of the sexes in courtship has been admirably put by Havelock Ellis ' . . . The primary part of the female in courtship is the playful, yet serious, assumption of the role of a hunted animal who lures on the pursuer, not with the object of escaping, but with the object of being finally caught. . . . The primary part of the male in courtship is by the display of his energy and skill to capture the female or to arouse in her an emotional condition which leads her to surrender herself to him, this process itself at the same time heightening his own excitement. . . . '[3]

The role of the sexes in courtship is demonstrated again and again in the behaviour of animal species. The dog chases away his rivals, showing his strength and virility thereby. The bitch retreats coyly; he pursues—the chase continues until copulation. The female role is highlighted by the behaviour of the doe, which retreats from the buck, but does so by running in circles! There may be gentleness and refinement, as in the loveplay of the octopus and of the hermaphroditic slug. There may be extreme cruelty and pain, as is the lot of the female mole, which, as we have seen, after a prolonged erotic chase through innumerable tunnels, has to submit to having her vaginal passage literally torn open by the male. The pleasure-pain principle in relation to sex is present in all animal species. In some it is more prominent than in others. For example, the court-ship of the praying mantis, the scorpion, and the spiders may culminate not only in sexual fulfilment, but in the death of the male through cannibalism.

In all these species the female is bigger, stronger, and more beautiful than the male.

The scorpion's prolonged courtship activities resemble in many ways the habits of adolescents in our own society. The male scorpion sets out on parade to see if he can catch a female's eye. If he succeeds he approaches her and they touch each other. Having proved their mutual liking they set out on a most extraordinary perambulation which may last for hours. The male clasps the female and walks backwards, she following him. They may stop and stare, halt, turn round and go the other way—but always on the male's initiative. Suddenly a rival appears. There is no dis-engagement by the amorous couple. The rival seizes the other side of the lady and a tug-of-war develops. This may continue for some time until one or other gives up. The victor continues on his way. But there are more hazards in store for the lovers. Other females seeing this erotic game may, in an access of jealousy, seize the lady as they walk by. Another struggle develops—somewhat one-sided as the female is bigger than the male. If he survives this new encounter the exhausted lover continues the everlasting parade. He must have strength for he will need it. But there is a pause. 'The foreheads now touch; the two mouths come together with tender effusions. . . . With his forelegs, more delicate, more agile than the others, he pats the horrible mask, which in his eyes is an exquisite little face; voluptuously he nibbles and tickles with his jaws the equally hideous mouth opposite. It is all superb in its tenderness and simplicity. . . . '(4) This might be regarded as the prelude to copulation. It may be: on the other hand, the female may have become bored by the whole process. A hard knock with her terrifying tail and the male disengages himself. All is over for that night. But it can be otherwise and the prolonged embrace dissolves into the accustomed walk. Eventually they may reach an ideal mating place, a stone nicely placed, a broken pot. Now the male pulls with all his remaining strength, and the female with hers, for she exhibits coyness to the end. Breathless they stumble inside the shelter. For hours they remain motionless clasped together. This is the last opportunity the female has to break off the *affaire*. She may leave him there and then. If she stays copulation will, after a long period, take place. When this is over the male must not linger—he must escape. ' . . . By the exercise of nimbleness and decision, he can do so sometimes, not always. He is able to release his hands, for it is his that squeeze; by lifting his thumbs, he unclasps them. But there remains the diabolical mechanism of the combs, an apparatus of sexual pleasure, now a trap. On both sides the long teeth of this interlocking gear, closely fitting and perhaps spasmodically contracted, refuse to come apart as promptly as could be wished. The poor fellow is lost. . . . He allows himself to be pinched by the terrible bride; he perishes without defence. . . . '(5) He is devoured by his consort on the spot. Or the charming bride, having perhaps a full stomach, eats only the head. Or, most frightful of all, she may drag his body about with her all day until she tosses it aside for the ants to gorge themselves.

Perhaps it is more than a coincidence that in the three species quoted the females are bigger and more resplendent than the males, and are cannibalistic. With mankind the occasional larger female may devour her husband or lover in other ways than the physical.

Amongst human beings the sexual urge for courtship is basically the same as in other species. But whereas in the latter case it is entirely an instinctive drive which is concerned, with man the force of instinct is controlled by cultural factors. As we have said, man can choose which sex shall predominate in terms of display, and which shall pursue the other. There are other distinctions.

' . . . Courtship, properly understood, is the process whereby both the male and the female are brought into that state of sexual tumescence which is a more or less necessary condition for sexual intercourse. The play of courtship cannot, therefore, be considered to be definitely brought to an end by the ceremony of marriage; it may properly be regarded as the natural, preliminary to every act of coitus. . . . '[6]

The distinction is an important one. Man can pervert courtship until it becomes, as we shall see, an end in itself; or he may only utilise it as a preparation for marriage and never thereafter. But it is important to appreciate that the content of courtship activities in any society depends upon the values inherent in that society.

It is now generally accepted that the sexual desires of men and women are of the same intensity in the great majority of human, as in animal, societies. Normally the male is the prime mover in human courtship. There are exceptions, but in most societies the woman conceals her eagerness and allows the man to do the wooing.

The Tchambuli of New Guinea represent the complete reversal of the ordinarily accepted male role in society. The Tchambuli women are aggressive, dominant, hardworking creatures. The men graceful, effeminate and interested in acting, dancing, and carving. Sexual initiative is the domain of women. 'Tchambuli young men develop their attitudes towards one another in the highly charged atmosphere of courtship, in which no one knows upon whom a woman's choice will fall: each youth holds his breath and hopes, and no young man is willing to trust another. . . . '[7] That description, reversing the roles, could be taken from an eighteenth-century novel. The woman it is, despite the system of polygyny which prevails amongst these people, who dominates, not only in sexual matters, but in economic affairs as well.

The Tchambuli present a very interesting problem. There are clearly, as Margaret Mead points out, individuals of both sexes who are constitutionally incapable of fulfilling their expected roles. Just as in our own society there are effeminate men who are not necessarily homosexual. But for the majority the pressure of the culture is such that men and women respond in the expected way. The Tchambuli sees that he can rely on the strong character of adult women. The boy in our society models himself on his father, the provider, the protector of women. In other words, it is clear that a particular culture can produce the type of response which is the ideal of the society. If virile males are the ideal, boys will have models to imitate. If effeminate men are the ideal, boys will see the adult manifestation of this before them.

The Tchambuli also illustrate the dangers of loose generalisations about instinctive sexual behaviour of men and women. There are examples of a less extreme nature than the Tchambuli. It has been reported, for example, of other tribes in New Guinea that it is the women who take initiative in sexual matters. An aboriginal tribe of Assam, the Garos, take great exception if a man inadvertently makes advances to a girl. It is regarded as an insult to the kin group of the girl, which can only be removed by a sacrifice. Of the Pueblo Indians of the American South West it was said that '. . . the usual order of courtship is reversed; when a girl is disposed to marry she does not wait for a young man to propose to her, but selects one to her own liking and consults her father, who visits the parents of the youth and acquaints them with his daughter's wishes. . . . '[8] Similarly the Tapieti Indians of South America choose their husbands from a group of dancers. The Brazilian Bororo male is sent a present of magic food by the girl. If he eats it all he is hers, if he eats only a little he wishes time to make up his mind, to leave it untouched indicates outright rejection. North American Indians, such as the Pima, Lillooet, Thompson and Osage, allowed mothers and their daughters the initiative in courtship.

Because of the organisation of Kwoma society, this New Guinea people permits girls to be the instigators in courting and philandering. The boy is scared to make advances as there may be serious consequences. An unwilling girl might scream out she was being raped, and if her male relatives came to her rescue the offender might even be killed.[9]

One of the most extreme forms of sexual invitation made by woman is that of the Kurtatchi of the Solomon Islands. . '. . A woman desiring sexual intercourse with a man who does not make advances to her will, when opportunity arises, lie down in his presence with her legs apart, a position otherwise regarded as indecent. . . . If a woman exposes her genitals, even unwittingly, as in her sleep, the situation is liable to be taken advantage of by any man whose passions may thereby be aroused. . . . The proper behaviour for a woman is to sit or lie with her legs stretched out in front of her, keeping them close together. . . . '[10]

This method of invitation is also used by women of the Lesu tribe in New Ireland, and by the women of the serpent cult in Dahomey. Such exposure is quite uncommon. The majority of societies, even those where female clothing is at a minimum, will only permit such behaviour, if at all, on specifically licensed occasions. The ordinary rule is that women must hide the genital area to avoid sexual provocation of men.

There is a small group of societies where, although convention demands that men should make the first sexual advances, in fact women do so. This is true of the Balinese, the Goajiro Indians of South America, and the Lepchas of Sikkim. The Lepcha boy is initiated into sexual matters by an older woman—the wife of a relative, at the latter's instigation. This is paralleled by the European practice (to which there are frequent references in novels and plays in the heyday of the servant and nursemaid) of the son of the house being initiated by female retainers.

An equal part is played by both sexes in such matters amongst the Trobrianders, the inhabitants of Lesu, and the Kurtatchi in the Solomon Islands.

In general, however, it is evident that in the great majority of humankind it is the male who predominates in courtship. This is understandable when one considers that in most societies the economic and social life of the community revolves round men rather than women. In this extremely important matter, upon which in the long run depends the perpetuation of the group, it is perhaps reasonable to expect that men will exhibit the same apparent control as they do in other spheres. [11] It is possible to establish a correlation between matrilineal societies and female prominence in courtship and sexual matters. That is to say, in those societies where descent is traced through the mother and the husband goes to live with his wife's people (matrilocal residence), feminine initiative tends to be displayed in sexual affairs. Examples of this are found in New Britain and New Ireland in Melanesia, and amongst some Australian Aborigines. A fascinating instance is that of Ancient Egypt, where it appears women supplicated men by letter. These letters ask for rendezvous, and list the writers' charms. Frequently they contain formal proposals of marriage. [12]

In societies where the man woos the girl, a great variety of means are used to impress and win the female. One means, which occurs frequently, is fighting between rivals. This, of course, is common among the mammals and is also found amongst some insects. The advantage of fighting is that it impresses the woman with the strength and virility of the contenders. It pleases her that men should think her worth fighting over. Wrestling between rivals was usual among the Indians of the Canadian North: the winner taking possession of the woman. Such trials of strength could be extended from mere wooing to gaining another man's wife. Amongst the Slave Indians of Canada: ' . . . If a man desire to despoil his neighbour of his wife, a trial of strength of a curious nature ensues; they seize each other by the hair, which is worn long and flowing, and thus strive for the mastery, until one or other cries *peccavi*. Should the victor be the envious man, he has to pay a certain number of skins from the husband-changing woman. . . . '(13) Discovery of your rival in your paramour's tent led, amongst the Siberian Yukaghir, to a duel outside. To the victor went the spoils.

Fighting as a method of wooing is found amongst North American Indians, Siberian tribes, Australian Aborigines, some African peoples, and in Melanesia.

There are other less brutal forms of courtship. The tournament, which did not necessarily lead to death, was popular both in India and Europe, among the nobility, as a means of attaining favour in the beloved's eyes. In classical India this was known as the 'Maiden's Choice'. The victor in the tournament could claim the lady, in whose honour it was held, as his bride. On a more plebeian level there was the Ancient Irish practice. Arthur Young described it in the following way: ' . . . There is a very ancient custom here for a number of country neighbours among the poor people to fix upon some young woman that ought, as they think, to be married; they also agree upon a young fellow as a proper husband for her; this determined, they send to the fair one's cabin to inform her that on the Sunday following "she is to be horsed", that is, carried on men's backs. She must then provide whisky and cider for a treat, as all will pay her a visit after mass for a hurling match. As soon as she is horsed the hurling begins, in which the young fellow appointed for her husband has the eyes of all the company fixed on him: if he comes off conqueror, he is certainly married to the girl, but if another is victorious, he as certainly loses her, for she is the prize of the victor. . . . '(14)

Perhaps the Kirghiz 'love chase' is more romantic than the above. '. . . In this the bride, armed with a formidable whip, mounts a fleet horse, and is pursued by all the young men who make any pretensions to her hand. She will be given as a prize to the one who catches her, but she has the right, besides urging her horse to the utmost, to use her whip, often with no mean force, to keep off those lovers who are unwelcome to her, and she will probably favour the one whom she has already chosen in her heart. . . . '(15)

Unfortunately the romance of the 'love-chase' is only superficial as the winning suitor has invariably already paid his bride-price. He is in fact the bridegroom approved by the families concerned.

The competitive spirit may include tests of endurance. One of the most intriguing is that practised by the Dowgolowi of Kordofan in the Sudan. The woman has two knives attached to each arm so that the blade juts out below the elbow. The rival suitors sit on either side of her on a log with their legs pressed against hers. The girl bends forward, at the same time raises her arms and carefully thrusts the knives into the men's thighs. He who comes out of the trial with the least flinching wins the day.(16)

Another very different form of competition was the public recitation of poetry written by the suitors. This was found not only in the Europe of the troubadours, but amongst the Tuaregs of North Africa.(17)

The idea of competition does not necessarily remain in the sphere of physical strength or intellectual achievement—it can take the form of gifts or presents. The greater or more splendid the gift the more profound the love of the giver. This type of courtship activity is found all over the world. Clearly the kind of gift depends on what the environment has to offer. Thus the chocolates or candy and flowers of Europe and the United States give place to the betel nut of the Far East, and the maize cakes of Central America. The purpose here is somewhat different from that of the ordinary contest. It is not to impress the woman with one's strength and power, but to show how well-off you are, and to give her something which may please her. The resulting pleasure gives you favour in her eyes. As we shall see, marriages in the majority of societies involve not merely the feelings of the couples concerned, but the creating of new relationships between families as well as the exchange of wealth in terms of bride-prices and dowries. This being the case, courtship of all kinds tends to be formalised. For example, the girl will expect presents but they are given her to facilitate what has already been decided. In Europe, when dowries were the rule, this was also true. Today in the West, when marriage is very largely dependent upon the choice of the individual, courtship is much more realistic. The gift can be used as a form of bribery to achieve sexual relations. Dining out in expensive places, visits to the theatre, rides in sports cars, may all be the prelude to the sexual act.

An extremely interesting feature of wedding rites is the so-called marriage by capture, which is discussed in Chapter VIII. In some cases, however, elopement is part of the actual structure of courtship and marriage, for well defined reasons. This is seen in the, at times, necessary elopement which occurs amongst the Tallenisi of W. Africa.[18]

In terms of courtship, however, elopement or abduction has a specific function. It enables the man or the woman to obtain the mate of their choice whatever barriers there may be in the way of marriage. It occurs in societies of all types. The most usual reason for elopement is the inability to obtain the consent of the parents or of the community to the match. Amongst peoples where a bride-price is commonly paid to the woman's family, if the full amount is not forthcoming, then the only way out for the couple is to elope and present the parents with a *fait accompli*. In some societies, such as the Plains Indians of North America, appropriate gifts to the girl's parents made the union legitimate. In others psuedo-elopements, with the connivance of the parents, are arranged. This is to save the expense of an ordinary wedding and occurs in Tibet, Kurdistan, and parts of China. A charming instance of more or less formal elopement is that of some groups of Dyaks in Borneo. If a man fell in love with a girl and for various reasons was *persona non grata* with her parents he would carry her off to his village. The pursuing company would be met with a feast of food and drink at his home. After partaking of this they would go away mollified, leaving the couple together.

In the vast majority of human societies at the simple level elopement is ratified as a marriage when tempers have had time to cool, suitable presents made, and the bride-price adjusted. Elopement demonstrates to the community that whatever other people may say the couple are determined to be married—in time the community gives way, if the regulations can be got round. (See Chapter VII.)

Elopement and abductions have been customary in Europe throughout its history. The reasons are the same as in other societies —the desire of the couple for each other, and opposition to their union from one quarter or another. But there also occurred cases, up to the middle of the nineteenth century, where a man would persuade an heiress of his undying love, elope with her or abduct her, and so gain possession of her fortune. A man who did it more than once in the nineteenth century was Gibbon Wakefield, one of the founding fathers of New Zealand. He was imprisoned for his activities.

In nineteenth century Ireland staged elopements were quite common. The pattern was for the lover and his friends to kidnap the girl at night. She was taken to the house of one of the young man's male relatives. There a party was immediately begun. It appears that the families involved both connived at the elopement. Genuine elopement, as opposed to the latter, was frequently resorted to when a couple ran off together, in defiance of the parental ban, in order to emigrate. But in Ireland, as elsewhere, time produced a softening.[19]

The purpose of courtship, as we have seen, is to effect the sexual union of a couple, either as an end in itself, or as a preliminary to marriage. ' . . . The whole object of courtship, of the mutual approximation and caresses of two persons of the opposite sex, is to create the state of sexual tumescence . . . the most usual method obtaining—a method found among the most various kinds of animals, from insects and birds to man, is some form of the dance. . . . '[20] Rythmic movement of the body to music has been reported from societies all over the world, from the most primitive to the most advanced. Not all societies, however, possess dances which could be described as specifically courtship dances, or indeed dances which express a sexual invitation: a great number do, however. An interesting aspect of such performances is that there is a very common rule that the two sexes do not touch each other during the dance—in fact they tend to dance independently. The sexual symbolism, and thus the invitation, may be demonstrated by either sex. Amongst the Melanesians . . . 'It was during the secular dance, or Kap, that the girls usually lost their hearts to the young men. A young man who was a good dancer would find favour in the sight of the girls. This can be readily understood by anyone who has seen the active, skilful, and fatiguing dances of these people. A young man who could acquit himself well in these dances must be possessed of no mean strength and agility, qualities which everywhere appeal to the opposite sex. Further, he was decorated, according to local custom, with all that would render him more imposing in the eyes of the spectators. As the former chief of Mabuiag put it, "In England if a man has plenty of money, women want to marry him; so here, if man dances well they too want him." In olden days the war dance, which was performed after a successful foray, would be the most powerful excitement to a marriageable girl, especially, if a young man had distinguished himself sufficiently to bring home the head of someone he had killed. . . . '[21] In that extract the author (A. C. Haddon) highlights the connection between blood and sexual pleasure. This relationship is thoroughly discussed by Havelock Ellis.[22] The fascination of blood and things associated with blood appears to be a bye-product of ordinary animal and human courtship.

An unauthenticated description of the part women in the New Hebrides play in such dances is given by an anonymous French army-surgeon (*Untrodden Fields of Anthropology*, Paris 1898, Vol. II, p. 341). The men form a circle around a group of women. The women begin to dance, leaping in the air, exhibiting their genitalia, and imitating the movements of coitus. The men undo their penis girdles, pretend to seize a woman and similarly imitate coital actions. At one stage or another the dancers may masturbate. The New Hebridean dance seems to be at the other extreme to the Melanesians of the Torres Straits. The same pantomime of mock coitus is reported of the Múras and the Pieris of Brazil. The Muras have a danced dialogue: the men sing 'Who will marry me?', the women respond 'All women will marry you'. The Pieris dance completely naked, men and women in two lines. The women rotate their pelvises back and forth while the men thrust forward. But no one touches the other.[23] This type of sexual dance is

typical of a number of widely distributed communities. A somewhat similar pattern is seen amongst some Central Australian
tribes: ' . . . Women are the chief performers; their bodies are
painted with white streaks, and their hair adorned with cockatoo
feathers. They carry large sticks in their hands and place themselves in a row in front, while the men with their spears stand in a
row behind them. Then they all commence their movements, but
without intermingling, the males and females dancing by themselves. The women have occasionally another mode of dancing,
by joining the hands together over the head, closing the feet and
bringing the knees into contact. The legs are then thrown outward
from the knee, while the feet and hands are kept in their original
position, and, being drawn quickly in again, a sharp sound is
produced by the collision. This is also practised by young girls or
by several together for their own amusement. It is adopted also
when a single woman is placed in front of a row of male dancers to
excite their passions. . . . '(24) There is no lack of evidence that
dancing promotes sexual desire.

An exception to the general rule of the sexes dancing separately is
provided by the Alfurs of Ceram in the Molucca Islands:
' . . . The women squat together by the fire, making a deafening
noise with the gongs and the drums, while the young girls, richly
adorned with pearls and fragrant flowers, await the beginning of
the dance. Then appear the men and youths without weapons, but
in full war costume, the girdle freshly marked with the number of
slain enemies. . . . They hold each other's arms and form a circle,
which is not, however, completely closed. A song is started, and
with small, slow steps this ring of bodies, like a winding snake,
moves sideways, backward, closes, opens again, the steps becoming
heavier, the songs and drums louder; the girls enter the circle and
with closed eyes grasp the girdle of their chosen youths, who clasp
them by the hips and necks, the chain becomes longer and longer,
the dance and song more ardent, until the dancers grow tired and
disappear in the gloom of the forest. . . . '(25)

Such contact through touch, as in modern European dancing, is
relatively unknown outside Europe. For example in West Africa
the tribal dances of the Ewe, Fanti, Dagomba, Ga and many other
peoples are characterised by each sex either dancing independently
at different times or, if together, with no contact. This separation of

the sexes in dancing is seen even in the night clubs of contemporary Accra, where, although couples dance together the perennially popular high-life (similar to calypsos), if the tune is played long enough there is a distinct tendency for couples to break away and dance quite independently. Individuals, by themselves, will often invade the dance floor and quietly pirouette around.

In Europe dancing at all social levels has served the identical function it does in tribal society. The dangers were apparent to Richard Burton, who in his *Anatomy of Melancholia* (Part III, Sec. 2) quotes numerous classical and other sources as to the enormities and pleasures which dancing might provoke. He cites Petrarch as saying that it is the spur of lust. 'A circle of which the devil is centre.' Plato, in the *Laws*, advocated dancing schools where the young might meet, and suggested the students should dance naked. On the other hand the Holy Fathers of the Church were very firmly against it. Plato is condemned, as '. . . . the very sight of naked parts causeth enormous exceeding concupiscences, and stirs up both men and women to burning lust. . . .' This condemnation of dancing as an incitement to love was current throughout the Middle Ages. The eleventh century priest might ask his penitent, 'Have you danced and hopped as the Devil taught the pagans to do ?'

But the dancing school and the dance hall, from their inception, have been avenues leading to marriage, and Rousseau, in the *Nouvelle Héloise* (Book IV Letter 10), defended them on this very ground. This has not prevented contemporary churches from condemning dancing and dances. Both the Presbyterian Church of Scotland and the Roman Catholic Church in Ireland pronounce clearly on the matter. With regard to the latter '. . . The clergy, in particular, fulminate constantly, against all-night dances. They object not so much to the jollities as to the opportunities for "walking-out" among the young couples.'[26]

A distinction has to be made between 'polite' or ballroom dancing, and peasant dancing in Europe. The latter has much more in common with similar dances in less advanced societies. Today, however, the significance of many of the movements in dances has been lost. It would, for example, be ridiculous to suggest that Maypole dancers in England today are aware of the sexual symbolism involved in their gyrations round an elongated pole. But in countries with a substantial peasant population, such as those of Central and Eastern Europe, folk-dancing still serves the necessary function of facilitating courtship.

It could be maintained that ballroom dancing in industrial society fufils the same purpose. Rowntree and Lavers quote informants as saying, 'I don't care for the *palais*, I like a dance with a bar. I'm not all that keen on dancing really, but if there's plenty of beer it's all right. It's a good place for picking up a girl.' 'I met my husband at a *palais*. I shouldn't like to be married to a man who wasn't a good dancer. . . . ' 'Oh yes, I'm very keen on dancing. It's good exercise and I meet some nice young women. . . . '(27)

One interesting aspect of the evolution of 'polite' dancing is that in the eighteenth century contact between male and female was minimal in such dance forms as the gavotte and minuet. The advent of the waltz in the early nineteenth century led to greater but restrained contact, as the dance called for fairly violent movement. More modern dances, such as the tango, which is expressive of its name, and foxtrot, drew the partners literally closer together. But the coming of swing, jive, and bebop has restored the individuality of the dancer as a soloist. The more eccentric contemporary forms are akin to the dances we have described among primitive peoples.

Dancing is not only a means of courtship, an incitement to love-making, but a substitute for sexual gratification or pleasure. Booming dance halls and popular television programmes suggest that the 'new' movement in dancing—jive or its equivalent—has an ardent following among teenagers. A writer on the subject (William Sansom) stresses the lack of overt eroticism. '. . . The plain fact is that in the first place jive is in essence the antithesis to romance, and to any traditional idealisation of sex; and otherwise it moves too fast, too acrobatically, too individually to be the vehicle of more direct approach. It is common to see two jivers, who a moment before have been engaged together in the most astounding and intimate-*looking* gyrations, stop when the music stops and return each to their own side of the floor with scarcely a glance at each other, with hardly a "thank you"; the dance, patently, is the attraction, and not the partner. . . . '(28) The meeting of the sexes and the movements of the dance have an erotic basis, but that is all. If, however, it is admitted that continuous rythmic movement in itself is an erotic stimulus, then the 'jive' enthusiast is consciously or unconsciously obtaining some measure of sexual gratification. This is borne out again by the statements of devotees of the cult that their interest is in the dance, not in the people or partners. The girls who partner girls are not necessarily Lesbians. Having a partner is a matter of form—it is a matter of indifference who that partner is so long as he or she can dance. A somewhat extreme example of a twenty-one year old married woman with genital anaesthesia is quoted by Havelock Ellis. She was an enthusiastic dancer: ' "I often felt as though I was giving myself to my partner in dancing . . . and was actually having coitus with him. I have the feeling that with me dancing takes the place of coitus." Normally something of the same feeling is experienced by many young women, who will expend a prodigious amount of energy in dancing, thus procuring, not fatigue, but happiness and relief. . . . '[29]

The evidence seems to suggest that dancing, in all societies, is used as a means to courtship, and as an erotic stimulant leading to mutual or individual sexual satisfaction.

A remarkable group of courtship customs, which can be subsumed under the general heading of 'night courtship' seems to be very largely confined to Europe and Europeans in North America. The basic form of night-courtship is for the young man to visit his beloved and pass the night with her in bed. Sexual intercourse is not supposed to take place. In Norway it is called 'night-running', in Sweden 'frieri' (night courting); in New England 'tarrying' or 'bundling'; in Germany 'probenächte', in Holland 'queesten', in Britain 'sitting-up' and 'running in the night',[30] and 'courting on the bed'. It appears to have been found in most European countries and to have persisted, in some instances, right up to the present day. The background to this very largely peasant custom must be seen in the mediaeval tradition of sexual morality as exhibited in numerous stories and poems such as *Tristan and Isolde*, *Le Chastelain de Couci*, and numerous *chansons de geste*. For example, sexual hospitality, that is providing the guest with one's wife or daughter for the night, was a normal practice.[31] Extremely free speech was also characteristic of the period: 'The conversation and repartee of a mediaeval circle would disgrace a modern tavern. . . . '[32] A fourteenth century book written for the instruction and edification of young girls is full of quite outrageous stories. One in particular, designed to promote decorous behaviour in church, is an account of two young people who copulated on the high altar and were visited with disaster !(33) Looseness in speech and behaviour by our standards was the essential background to mediaeval night-courting customs.

The Norwegian custom of night-running seems to have been so called because of the widely spaced farms in rural areas. The girl would put on a number of skirts and await her lover. He generally made his entry through the window. The couple would spend the night fully clad on the bed chatting and embracing. If things proceeded too far then the young man was under an obligation to marry her.

Night-courting seems to have been found in several Midland counties in England, such as Yorkshire and Cheshire. It was a regular practice in Wales, Ireland and Scotland.(34) In its most developed form it occurs in Germany.

Some variant is found in most German peasant communities. In the Black Forest, as elsewhere in Germany, a distinction is made between 'visiting nights' and 'trial nights', these last being a form of trial marriage which we discuss below. The procedure of a 'visiting night' is as follows: The boy has to make his entry through a window into the girl's bedroom. She receives him fully clothed and they spend time talking together: 'As soon as she has fallen asleep, he must at once go away and only gradually does their intercourse become more lively.'(35) These 'visiting nights' turn into 'trial nights'. 'In due course, the girl gives her lover, amid all sorts of bucolic jesting and teasing, an opportunity to get acquainted with her secret charms; she lets him surprise her lightly clothed, and, at last, grants him everything with which a woman can gratify the sensuality of a man. Yet even then a certain gradation is observed. Very often the girl refuses to grant her lover his final wish until he uses force. This always happens when there are some doubts of his physical strength. . . . '(36) This latter statement seems to indicate that 'visiting nights' are in one way a test of the young man's powers. It appears that these 'nights' are still observed in the Black Forest region. We have had information of this kind from German adolescents from this area.

The Swedish 'frieri' or 'night courting' was very similar to the German practice. It seems, however, to have been more formalised. In the eighteenth and nineteenth centuries Sweden adolescent daughters slept in summer either in huts in the upland pastures, or in barns on the home farm. Young men from the village would go in

organised groups to call on a girl in the special 'girl house'. On arriving
they would begin to have a party. As the evening wore on all would
leave except one who remained all night with the girl. But there
were certain formalities to be observed. Some of the girl's clothing
could be removed, but never her 'skin apron', he must not lie
otherwise than on top of the bedclothes at his first visit, he must
always come in the company of others, and so on. Breaches of these
regulations led to fines and public shaming. For the girl it might
mean she acquired the reputation of having 'slept herself away', and
so would find it difficult to make a suitable marriage. If the visits
progressed presents were exchanged and this was notice that they
were 'courting certain'. It is difficult to assess how frequently night
courting turned into trial marriage, but that it did is certain.[37]

It is said that the New England custom of 'bundling', 'tarrying',
or 'courtship bed' was introduced by Dutch settlers. The custom is
similar to that described in Germany. There are some interesting
variations. The girl might tie her skirts to her ankles to prevent too
much familiarity on the part of the boy. The bed in which she lay
fully clad might have a wooden division running from the top to
the bottom in the manner, and for the same purpose, as the drawn
sword between Tristan and Isolde. Despite such precautions it
inevitably developed into more intimate relations. Pregnancy was
followed by marriage. A nineteenth century American wrote
'. . . the ridiculous and pernicious custom which prevailed among
the young, to a degree which we can scarcely credit, sapped the
foundations of modesty. . . .'[38]

American 'bundling' is discussed at some length by Reg Reynolds in Beds (1952, Ch. 10, pp. 187–210). Various origins are
suggested including a dubious American Indian source. Reynolds's
view is that night-courting customs are not as a whole connected
with trial marriage. This is contrary to the view of Havelock Ellis
whose evidence for this, particularly with regard to Scandinavia,
has been substantiated by Alva Myrdal in recent years.[39] In the
main the evidence seems to suggest that trial marriage is a development out of night courtship, and in some instances, for example in
Germany, the two customs may exist side by side.

The distribution of trial marriage is more extensive than night-
courting. It is found not only in those countries already mentioned
in connection with the latter, but in Jugoslavia and the Philippines,

as well as amongst North American Indians. Historically it appears to have occurred amongst the Egyptians and Greeks. In mediaeval Europe it relates back to the custom of marriage without the benefit of the priest's blessing, which occurred until the time of the Council of Trent. This was in fact marriage by declaration and was legally valid. It should be remembered that it is the couple who marry each other not the priest. He gives spiritual sanction to the union. Thus it is clear that there are strong traditional reasons for the persistence of the custom into modern times. Generally trial marriage consists of a regular sexual association, not necessarily including cohabitation, between an engaged couple. The primary object appears to be to ascertain whether the girl can become pregnant. Thus at the first signs of pregnancy it is incumbent on the man to marry the girl. If he fails to do so a variety of communal sanctions were invoked. If after a specified time she failed to conceive, the relationship could be broken off. This gave freedom to both to seek a fresh arrangement with other individuals. That it was not entered into lightheartedly is seen by the Yorkshire custom in the nineteenth century. 'The solemn words of the fiancé on entering upon such a trial relationship run thus: "If I thee tak I tak thee" (i.e. if thou dost conceive then I will take thee).[40]

In nineteenth century Dalmatia there existed two types of trial marriage. In the first ' . . . The lad cannot or may not, for various reasons, be married at once, before he has taken home the bride. He wants to test her, first of all. He wants to see and be convinced whether she will give birth to children or not. If she brings children into the world, especially if they are boys, then he marries her, if he himself does not die beforehand. If she brings no children into the world, she can and must leave the man's house. . . . '[41] Actually the 'marriage' is a kind of group activity. Two or three boys arrange a rendezvous with a girl in her house. They meet in the kitchen of her house in the late evening. Each of the boys copulates with the girl. The party only breaks up at dawn. If the girl becomes pregnant she chooses one of the boys as the father and he has to marry her. In practice many girls had two or three children before they got married.

The second type is somewhat different. Marriageable daughters are taken to a fair by their mothers. The former wear a special head-dress and a girdle on which hangs a token dowry. A boy will come up and ask the girl to dance. During the dance he will arrange matters. The couple in the late evening go to his parents' home and there spend the night together. If conception does not occur the *affaire* is broken off and the girl will, the following year, embark on a fresh trial. The 'dowry' may very well have been spent during this time which frequently leads to lawsuits for its recovery. Pregnancy assures that marriage will take place.

The incidence of various kinds of trial marriage throughout Germany was remarkably high until well on in this century. No recent study of this has been made, but it would be surprising if there had been a reversal of the widespread approval given to pre-nuptial intercourse in Germany.[42] One feature in the Black Forest type of trial marriage in the eighteenth century was that after a few nights of 'trial' the liaison was quite likely to be broken off and the first boy's place would be taken by another. No stigma attached to this. Community criticism only began to be voiced if the girl had too many lovers in succession. The grounds for this was that such behaviour indicated that the girl must have some frightful, secret defect.[43] This seems an essentially realistic approach to the situation !

Surprisingly enough Britain possessed almost as many variants of trial marriage as Germany. We have already quoted a Yorkshire example. In mediaeval Scotland and Northumbria it was known as handfasting. As in the Dalmatian case trial brides were selected at an annual fair. The relationship lasted for a year. If at the end of the year the girl had conceived marriage was obligatory. If she were not pregnant and the couple wished to part they were free to do so.[44] Trial marriage has also been reported from Wales and Ireland.[45] The most interesting example in England comes from the Isle of Portland in Dorset. This has been excellently treated in Thomas Hardy's novel *The Well-Beloved*, the scene of which is set in the Portland of the 1850's, when the custom was dying out. Apparently the form of trial marriage was similar to those already quoted. It was essentially a test as to whether the woman was fertile or not. The custom was practised by all classes in the 'island'. If conception did not take place the 'marriage' was over. Hardy brings out very strongly the motivation of having heirs for family property which lay behind the practice.

Portland, until comparatively recent times, was virtually isolated from the rest of Dorset. The shingle road connecting it with the mainland was in bad weather, especially in winter, a serious hazard. This may help to explain the persistence of trial marriage in the area until the nineteenth century. Its ultimate decline in that century is attributed to the influx of stone-workers from London— 'foreigners'. These took advantage of the custom but failed to fulfil their obligations, that is refused to marry girls who conceived. The system could only work if everyone was prepared to accept the responsibilities involved. Among these was the insistence on only one lover at a time. So effectively did trial marriage operate that it was claimed that for a considerable period no bastards were born and all proper marriages were fertile.[46]

Both night-courting and trial marriages are typical of closely integrated, well-knit communities. The partners are known to the community and the stranger is not permitted to participate. There may be strong economic motivations for the peasant (a) to postpone his marriage (b) to make sure his future wife will be able to bear children. The latter is not only of importance as regards the survival of the group, but also in relation to the inheritance of property. In Europe the survival of trial marriage almost up to the present day is probably due to its strong traditional background and the relative isolation of many peasant communities.

Courting practices in the contemporary Western world tend to follow a highly idiosyncratic, local pattern, governed by the facilities available (i.e. transport), as well as by traditional thought and feeling. One of the most formalised and intricate of these patterns is that existing in the United States.

'Dating' and its concomitant 'petting' is a peculiarly American institution. It is perhaps too facile to say that the essentially competitive element in dating is a reflection of the highly competitive world that is American society. Nevertheless the accent on competition in American education is no doubt in part responsible for these out-of-school activities which absorb the attention of the vast majority of American youth from the age of twelve until betrothal or marriage. Although garnished with all the trappings of courtship, dating is not strictly speaking courtship proper in the way we have defined it above. (The prelude to sexual fulfilment on a specific occasion or to marriage.) Margaret Mead puts it in this way. ' . . . The clothes, the flowers, the dancing, are all part of the game, but they are to be equated neither with courtship nor behaviour that is primarily sexual, although the pattern of dating does in the end have a profound effect on the later relationships of men and women in America. . . .'(47)

In our opinion it is difficult to dissociate altogether the sexual element from dating. The fact that it is given open encouragement by adults who ignore the sexual implications does not necessarily mean that these are not present. In essence dating consists of a highly competitive system whereby girls are dated by boys, that is the girls go out with the boys to eat, to drink, to dance, publicly —this last is imperative, other people must know how good you are. A girl should have as many dates as possible. A boy must aim to get a heavily dated girl for a date of his—and so on. The boy will present the girl with a corsage, take her in his car, and pay for the evening out. His reward is public acknowledgment of his dating activities and the kiss at parting. There is competition, not only between boys for the popular girls, but between the dated couple themselves. This often takes the form of a verbal competition, in sometimes specialised language, between the boy and the girl, each trying to cap the remarks of the other. Such conversation often has sexual undertones and overtones. Physical intimacy increases as the dates with the same girl progress. Here again is the competitive element. The boy attempts to make each intimacy greater—the girl to combat his advances. Theoretically the result could be stalemate, but clearly this is where technique comes in. Obviously it may end up with a fugitive copulation in the back of a car, but this is not the real purpose of dating. The ultimate objects are the exercise of competitiveness and the approbation of one's fellows. There are other girls who will grant sexual relations but that is something outside the dating system.

The Americans like all other peoples suffer from ethnocentrism. One form it takes is the belief that their dating system is normal courting behaviour. The attempt to put it into practice in Europe, during the war, led to absurd situations. On the one hand English girls were outraged at what they regarded as premature attempts at seduction; on the other hand the young G.I. who found his girl-friend ready for intercourse on the first date was disgusted.

The long-term effect of sexual mimicry in an unreal situation, and the perversion of continuous petting with no proper sexual outlet, inevitably results in frustrating marital situations. One effect is the apparent inability of American women to participate fully in sexual activity after marriage. Divorce statistics and the popularity of psychiatry may very well be an indication of the sexual maladjustment consequent upon dating. The land of 'bundling' and the 'Blue' laws of Massachusetts can claim the honour of developing a system of pseudo-courtship which places great strain on the individual, and which has as its only merit the fact that it is time-consuming.

Trial or temporary marriage in a more sophisticated form than that already discussed has been popular in Scandinavian Europe since the nineteenth century. In part this started as a revolt against the imposition of the marriage tie by church and state. A book which did a great deal to advance the cause of sexual freedom in this respect, in both Scandinavia and Germany, was *Love and Marriage* (Berlin 1894, N.Y. and London 1911), by the Swedish writer Ellen Key. At one time individuals in Scandinavia would announce their 'free marriage', that is their intention of living together, by an advertisement in the newspapers. Such activity has been attributed to the effect of *Love and Marriage*. In England Carpenter was one of the pioneers in the advocacy of sexual relations without ties. Since the 1914 war the effect of Freud's writings in this respect has been incalculable. In the U.S.A., in the twenties, B. B. Lindsay, judge of the juvenile court in Denver, advocated a form of companionate marriage.[48] Bertrand Russell in England has suggested a similar type of marriage. [49]

Quite apart from intellectually motivated movements of this kind it is probably true that the industrial working class in Europe and America, from the nineteenth century onwards, has practised this type of trial union, partly from economic reasons.[50] There is little doubt from the evidence of the Kinsey Reports and other evidence that pre-nuptial sexual intercourse is now practised by large sections of the population in Europe and America. What in fact originated in a rural-peasant background has now established itself on both an intellectual and non-intellectual basis in industrial society.[51]

The desire of men to have some experience or knowledge of a physical kind concerning their future brides before marriage is illustrated by the following examples from entirely different cultures.

Sir Thomas More wrote in his *Utopia* (New York, N.D., p. 200) '. . . Before marriage some grave matron presents the bride naked, whether she is a virgin or a widow, to the bridegroom, and after that some grave man presents the bridegroom naked to the bride. We indeed both laughed at this, and condemned it as very indecent. But they, on the other hand, wondered at the folly of the men of all other nations, who, if they are but to buy a house of small value, are cautious that they will see every part of him . . . and that yet in the choice of a wife, on which depends the happiness or unhappiness of the rest of his life, a man should venture upon trust, and only see about a hand's breadth of the face, all the rest of the body being covered, under which may be hid what may be contagious, as well as loathsome. . . .'

According to John Aubrey's *Brief Lives* (London 1939, p. 316) More put his theories into practice. '. . . Sir (William) Roger, of Eltham in Kent, came one morning, pretty early, to my lord, with a proposall, to marry one of his daughters. My lord's daughters were then both together in a truckle-bed in their father's chamber asleep. He carries Sir (William) into the chamber and takes the sheet by the corner and suddenly whippes it off. 'They lay on their Backs, and their smocks as high as their armpitts. This awakened them, and immediately they turned on their Bellies. Quoth Roper, "I have seen both sides" and so gave a patt on her Buttock he made choice of, sayeing, "Thou art mine." Here was all the trouble of the wooing. . . .'

The other example is to be found in Sebastian Munster's *Cosmography* (1548): 'One finds also certain Indians who have such a custom. If a poor man cannot give his daughter a dowry and she has yet reached marriageable age, he takes drum and pipe and repairs with his daughters to the market just as if he were going to war, and, when everybody runs up as to a public show or play, the daughter raises her dress at the back up to her shoulders and lets herself be seen from behind, then she raises it to her breast in front and lets the front of her body be seen also, and then the one whome she pleases takes her for his own and does not buy her blindly. . . .'

Contemporary British courting customs have not, so far as we are aware, been subjected to the extensive analysis that American petting has undergone at the hands of sociologists. Such information as is available is meagre. There is, however, little doubt that such customs have not been elaborated into a highly formalised pattern as in the American case. The pattern is divided according to the class of the individuals participating. Thus the traditional working-class 'parlour' as a place where courting may take place does not figure in upper-class courtship.

The picture given by one study of working-class marital habits is that courtship is largely a matter of the haphazard.[52] Chance encounters in the street, dance-halls, cafés, public houses, and so on, may lead to an attachment. The relationship develops against this public background rather than in the home. The authors state that, '. . . sex did not play an important part in courtship, and an important reason for refraining from sex relations was a lack of any urgent desire.'[53] This may very well be true, but another factor to be taken into consideration is the lack of facilities for such intercourse, except in the streets or parks. Sexual desire has to be fairly strong to attain gratification in such a public manner.

It appears as if there has been a definite shift, at this level of the society, from the home as a place of courtship, as compared with the nineteenth century. This is probably due to the greater attractions offered by public places of entertainment today.

Another striking element in the British pattern of working-class courtship is the absence of passionate feelings. Individuals appear to start a relationship for no better reason than it is the expected thing to do. Intense feeling for each other does not figure prominently. The romanticism engendered by the film or books does not appear to take on reality in human relationships. Presumably if the romantic element is absent in courtship it would hardly figure in the later marriage.

Elsewhere we have shown that in one section of the English working class (miners) there is conflict between the group of 'mates' and the courting couple. This we would suggest is characteristic of any industrial community which is male-dominated: 'But the strongest competitor for the attentions and time of the group's members is, of course, sex interest. Between the ages of fifteen and eighteen the youths will have only casual girl-friends. "I don't bother with girls. Sometimes I'll pick one up at the dance on a Saturday, perhaps take her out on a Sunday, and never see her again," was a typical comment. At this stage youths will be anxious for any sexual experience, and occasionally this will be accom-

plished, but they are not yet skilled in the approaches to girls; they
are awkward and embarrassed in the presence of girls—a state of
mind which shows itself in a blustering and jokingly aggressive
attitude. . . . Nearer the age of twenty, of course, when the young
men are beginning to develop serious sexual affairs, and their
stories of success are more likely to be believed, the attraction of the
opposite sex becomes a real danger to the solidarity of the group.
. . . After the first few months of intensive wooing the love affair
either breaks off or becomes more pedestrian, with prospects of
permanence. Eventually the young man begins to insist on one or
two nights "with the lads" and it is at this stage, *not necessarily after
the marriage*, that the struggle for the interest and attention of the
husband begins. . . . One young man of twenty-three, even
though his holidays coincided with those of his fiancée, booked
her accommodation at Blackpool and paid for the whole of her
holiday. "I'm not having her hanging around all week through my
holidays ! . . . "(54)

The impression which emerges from a consideration, at least of
adolescent miners, is that not only is there conflict between the
male 'group' and the couple, but courtship itself is a half-hearted
affair which very quickly loses whatever little attraction it had
initially. If the romantic element is at a discount in the early stages
of courtship, it has completely disappeared after the first months of
marriage when the man re-appears in his 'group' and functions as
before.

Courtship practices at this level in the society do not reflect
directly the romanticism of films and magazines. What has
developed, against a given environmental background, is, on the
part of the woman, a twofold attitude. One in which she finds
recompense for the lack of romance in her fiancé or husband in
these same sources of synthetic love, the other an approximation
of the male attitude that sex is something "in itself". Most people
are familiar with sexual life as it is portrayed in the cinema, but only
those who are assiduous readers of women's magazines and
novelettes can claim to know the romanticism which they purvey.
In such literature detailed pictures of ordinary life, which give the
reader a sense of security, are opposed to stories of sin and shame in
which good always triumphs. As Hoggart has pointed out the
working class in Britain operates from a solid ethical basis.(55)

Escapism in literature is produced in just this matter—identification, 'they're people just like us', and the portrayal of the exotic or remote, 'that's what I'd be if I could'.

A rather different aspect of the influence of literature on the female reader is the enquiry column of the popular press. The advice given enquirers is never to permit sexual intercourse before marriage. E. S. Turner in his *History of Courting* gives some amusing, but at the same time revealing, examples of questions and answers on this theme.[56] An interesting comparison can be made between this type of sought advice and the figures for pre-marital pregnancies given by Alex Comfort in his *Sexual Behaviour in Society*.[57] It would appear that many readers are seeking advice after the event—are in search of justification for their behaviour. This is connected with what was said above. Women's attitude is changing, in respect of sex relations, from romantic notions to seeing sex 'in itself', rather than romance, as the aim, not only of courtship, but of marriage.

The attitudes and behaviour revealed by such research as has been made into this sector of working-class life exhibit a number of contradictions. The resolution of such contradictions, which would indicate a clearly defined series of patterns, waits upon more detailed investigation and analysis.

So far as we are aware no serious study has been made of middle and upper-class courting habits in Britain. Some obvious inferences, however, can be drawn from the existence of associations at these levels of society which do not appear amongst the working-class. For example, it is fairly clear that the tennis club, or its equivalent, plays an extremely important part as a background for courtship in the middle-class. Again the social gatherings of different kinds which are normal in these classes have no place in the lower class. The sexual opportunities presented by 'parties' in Bayswater or Belgravia have not an equivalent in the predominantly working-class towns of the Midlands and North.

Information of a more detailed kind is forthcoming in the form of fiction and the drama. How the presentation of courtship in these forms tallies with reality it is difficult to ascertain. Can Kingsley Amis's *Lucky Jim* and John Braine's *Room at the Top* be taken as a truthful representation, or even an approximation, of life in this particular respect? Is John Osborne's *Look Back in Anger* a reflection of typical sex relations in certain sections of the society? The answer to such questions lies in the fact that such novels and plays are being written. To that extent they reflect a climate of opinion which has its origin in actual behaviour.

To achieve the object of one's passion is the aim of courtship. As we have seen the means adopted for this end are infinitely varied. But beneath all the extravagance of variety lies the fundamental instinctive drive to gain possession of the desired person which is common to all mankind. The variation is due to the accident of culture.

The Australian Aborigine, whirling his bullroarer around his head in the hope of charming a woman to his side, is motivated by the same feelings as the German peasant creeping up a ladder to a tryst with his girl in her bedroom.

REFERENCES AND NOTES

1. E. S. Goodrich, *Living Organisms*, Oxford 1924, pp. 133–4.
2. *ibid.*, p. 134.
3. Havelock Ellis, *Studies in the Psychology of Sex*, Philadelphia 1913, Vol. III, pp. 68–9.
4. J. H. Fabre, *The Life of the Scorpion*, translated by A. T. de Mattos and B. Mill, London 1923, pp. 130–31.
5. *ibid.*, pp. 150–51.
6. Havelock Ellis, *op. cit.*, p. 237.
7. M. Mead, *Sex and Temperament*, London 1935, p. 258.
8. H. H. Bancroft, *Native Races of the Pacific States*, N.Y. 1875–6, Vol. I, p. 547.
9. J. A. Whiting, *Becoming a Kwoma*, O.U.P. 1941, pp. 74–5.
10. B. Blackwood, *Both Sides of Buka Passage*, Oxford 1935, p. 125.
11. For a discussion of the historical inferiority of women to men see Simone de Beauvour's *The Second Sex*, London 1953.
12. W. Max Muller, *Der Liebespoesie der alten Aegypter*, Leipzig 1899, pp. 8 and 40.
13. W. H. Hooper, *Ten Months among the Tents of the Tuski*, London 1853, p. 303.
14. Arthur Young, *Tour in Ireland* in Pinkerton's *Collection of Voyages and Travels*, London, 1808–14, Vol. III, p. 860.
15. E. Schuyler, *Turkistan*, London 1876, Vol. I, pp. 42 *et seq.*

16. C. T. Wilson and R. W. Felkin, *Uganda and the Egyptian Sudan*, London 1882, Vol. II, p. 310.

17. H. M. and N. K. Chadwick, *The Growth of Literature*, Cambridge 1940, Vol. III, p. 659.

18. M. Fortes, *The Web of Kinship*, Oxford 1949, pp. 91–2.

19. C. Arensberg and S. T. Kimball, *Family and Community in Ireland*, Cambridge, Massachusetts, Harvard University Press 1940, p. 212.

20. Havelock Ellis, *op. cit.*, p. 53.

21 A. C. Haddon, *Reports of the Cambridge Anthropological Expedition to Torres Straits*, Cambridge 1904, Vol. V, p. 222.

22. Havelock Ellis, *op. cit.*, pp. 121–8.

23. J. B. von Spix and C. M. Martius, *Reise in Brasilien*, Munich 1823–31, Vol. III, p. 117 and Vol. I, pp. 373–5.

24. E. J. Eyre, *Journals of Expeditions into Central Australia*, London 1845, Vol. II, p. 235.

25. W. Joest, *Welt-Fahrten*, Berlin 1895, Bk. II, p. 159.

26. Arensberg and Kimball, *op. cit.*, p. 214.

27. B. S. Rowntree and G. R. Lavers, *English Life and Leisure*, London 1951, pp. 282–3.

28. W. Sansom, 'A Public for Jive' in *The Public's Progress*, London 1947, p. 60.

29. Havelock Ellis, *op. cit.*, p. 57.

30. Eric Linklater gives an account of 'running in the night' in *White Maa's Saga*, London 1930.

31. *Le Chevalier à l'épée*, edited by E. C. Armstrong, Baltimore 1900, pp. 18 *et seq.*

32. C. H. Pearson, *The Early and Middle Ages of England*, London 1861.

33. *Le livre du chevalier de la Tour Landry pour l'enseignment de les filles*, translated by Thomas Wright, London 1868, pp. 71–2 and 51–2.

34. F. C. J. Fischer, *Über die Probenächte der teutschen Bauermädchen*, Berlin 1780.

35. *ibid.*

36. *ibid.*

37. Alva Myrdal, *Nation and Family*, London 1945, pp. 42–3.

38. H. R. Stiles, *Bundling*, Albany N.Y. 1869, p. 6. See also M. C. Crawford, *Social Life in Old New England*, Boston 1914, p. 199; W. Irving, *A Humorous History of New York*, London 1821, p. 175; C. W. Janson, *The Stranger in America*, London 1807.

39. Havelock Ellis, *Studies in the Psychology of Sex*, Philadelphia 1913, Vol. VI, pp. 380–3.

Alva Myrdal *op. cit.*, pp. 42–3.

For the reader who wishes to pursue the topic of American Bundling further there is an excellent bibliography in *Beds*, R. Reynolds, London 1952. See also footnote in A. C. Kinsey, *Sexual Behaviour in the Human Female*, London 1953, p. 232.

40. G. von Bunsen, *Das Zusammenleben der Brautleute auf Probe in Yorkshire*, Verh. d. Berlin Gesellschaft f. Anthrop., Ethnol. u. Urges., 1887, p. 376.

41. A. Mitrovič, 'Zeitehen in Norddalmatien', *Anthropophyteia*, Berlin 1907, Bd. IV, pp. 37–45.

42. See M. Michels, *Sittlichkeit in Ziffern*, Munich 1928, and M. Marcuse, *Uneheliche Mütter*, Berlin 1907.

43. F. C. J. Fischer, *op. cit.*

44. Neil McCullum, *It's an Old Scottish Custom*, London 1951, pp. 173–4. *Brand's Antiquities*, London 1900, pp. 87–8.

Walter Scott's *The Monastery*.

C. Rogers, *Scotland, Social and Domestic*, London 1869, p. 109.

45. Oswaldus de Barri, *The Itinerary of Bishop Baldwin thro' Wales*, London 1806, p. 346.

G. L. Gomme, 'Exogamy and Polyandry', *Archaeological Review*, London 188, Vol. I, p. 391.

46. E. Hutchins, *History and Antiquities of Dorset*, London 1868, Vol. II, p. 820.

47. M. Mead, *Male and Female*, London 1950, p. 285.

48. B. B. Lindsey, *The Companionate Marriage*, London 1928.

49. Bertrand Russell, *Marriage and Morals*, London 1929.

50. See Charles Booth, *Life and Labour*, London 1912, Vol. VI, p. 41.

C. E. Collett, *Educated Working Women*, London 1902.

F. Henriques, 'Sub-cultures in English Society', in *Researches and Studies*, Leeds 1953.

51. For a review of companionate and trial marriage see E. E. Westermarck, *The Future of Marriage in Western Civilisation*, London 1936, Chs. VI and VII, pp. 104–50.

Ivan Bloch, *The Sexual Life of our Time*, London 1909, Ch. XI, pp. 236–78.

Havelock Ellis, *op. cit.*, pp. 381–419.

52. E. Slater and M. Woodside, *Patterns of Marriage*, London 1951, p. 102.

53. *ibid. op. cit.*, p. 272.

54. N. Dennis, F. Henriques and C. Slaughter, *Coal is our Life*, London 1956, pp. 221–3.

55. R. Hoggart, *The Uses of Literacy*, London 1957, p. 107.

56. E. S. Turner, *History of Courting*, London 1954, p. 271.

57. A. Comfort, *Sexual Behaviour in Society*, London 1950, p. 90.

CHAPTER VII

Regulation of Sexual Life

UNRESTRICTED sexual licence cannot be tolerated in society. Its existence would lead to perpetual dissension. On this ground alone it is necessary for sexual relations to be ordered. An equally strong reason for order of this kind is the necessity to assure inheritance of property, and the perpetuation of the society. All these are grounds which apply wherever society occurs. Thus no society exists—or has existed—where general promiscuity is the norm. Occasions of ritual sexual licence undoubtedly take place in different societies, but these in fact serve to emphasise the rules governing behaviour at other times. To achieve order and regulation in sexual behaviour some form of marriage is necessary. Marriage assures the sexual rights of the partners in each other, and ensures the creation and care of a family to inherit property and to help perpetuate the society.

A nineteenth century view, which has stultified much of the thinking about marriage and the family, was that which we can call the evolutionary hypothesis. The theories advanced by Huxley and Darwin in the nineteenth century concerning the evolution of species greatly influenced anthropologists who were only, at that time, beginning to establish their discipline. Almost as a reflection from the biological thought of the period they too began to be interested in origins. Their concern was to discover the origins of the human institutions, such as marriage, the family, and property. These early anthropologists, such as Lewis Morgan in the United States, Bachofen in Germany, and J. G. McLennan in Britain, all postulated that marriage and the family had evolved from a primal state of general promiscuity. In time it was believed, this had given way to various forms of marriage of which the most advanced was that of monogamy. It all fitted a little too neatly into the Victorian scheme of things—into theories of the perfectibility of man. This view was later taken up by Frederick Engels in his book *The Origin of the Family, Private Property and the State*, first published in 1884. Unfortunately this has led to much loose thinking, with regard to marriage and the family, on the part of Marxists. B. Briffault was probably the last serious student to accept the hypothesis of an original state of promiscuity. In *The Mothers* (London 1927) he assembled a vast compendium of facts concerning marital and other customs. If Briffault's theories are left on one side *The Mothers* is a most valuable compilation of ethnological facts.

Why should there been have so violent a reaction from what was once so popular a hypothesis? Let us see what evidence there was for it. Lewis Morgan, in his researches amongst North American Indians, had found that individuals, who were obviously not biologically related, called each brother or sister, mother and son, and so on. This led him to assume that such nomenclature was the contemporary relic of what had once been a real state of affairs. In other words, savage peoples in the nineteenth century called each brother and sister because at one time general promiscuity had existed, so that no man knew who was his brother—in fact everyone was your brother, literally. Morgan, in fact, provided the means to destroy his own hypothesis. Anthropologists subsequently showed, in other societies they studied, that Morgan's contribution to what is called the classificatory system of relationship was of paramount importance. This system is one which is found all over the world and is based precisely on the forms of address upon which Morgan formulated his hypothesis of promiscuity. Briefly, a majority of human societies divides all people into categories using the names of blood relatives. Thus all the children of several sisters may call each other sister; or all the sons of brothers may call each other brother, and all the individuals of the biological father's generation may be termed father, and so on. This was a discovery of fundamental importance to anthropology and the original credit must go to Lewis Morgan. Yet, as we said, this discovery of classificatory kinship destroyed the theories of primal promiscuity; for it is quite clear that, in those societies where it exists, it has the precise and definite social function of ordering relationships; this function has no apparent connection with its hypothetical origin. The importance of kinship can be seen if it is remembered that the great majority of modern field studies made by British anthropologists are concerned with some aspect of kinship.

In the absence of any historical records whatsoever, any theory about the sexual arrangements of early man must of necessity be based upon conjecture. Science can predict the future, but you cannot recover the past unless it is there to be recovered. In the lack of any kind of record anyone's guess is as good as anyone else's. Observation from nature, that is, for example, from the behaviour of anthropoid apes, suggests that they live in pairs and are not promiscuous. In their case, as well as in that of human beings, the infant's long period of maternal dependence clearly affects the type of family unit. It must be of a permanent or semi-permanent nature.

It is safe to say that we will never discover how Cro-Magnon man and all the other predecessors of contemporary man conducted themselves in matters of marriage and the family. Historical conjecture of the kind which concerns itself with Atlantis or sexual communism is a pleasant pastime, but it has absolutely no scientific validity. The Victorians thought their society perfectible, and that they could discover the answer to all things *in time*. The nineteenth century climate of opinion helps to explain the boldness of anthropologists in claiming to discover such things as the origin of the family. Anthropologists have now swung entirely the other way: instead of grandiose theories explaining the origins of society, they now offer painstaking monographs devoted to the minute, detailed description and analysis of an individual society, which may number less than an hundred people. The result is that sometimes the reader feels that only the writer can understand what he has written. It was said of Bronislaw Malinowski, one of the greatest of modern anthropologists, that he had done so much work on the Trobriand Islanders he thought of man as a Trobriander. Change the island or society and the same might be said of many living anthropologists. In our view there is need today for students of society to collate the vast amount of material produced by anthropologists in the last forty years, and on that basis propound hypotheses concerning human society as a whole.

The reader, we hope, is now prepared to accept the view that, however attractive the idea may be, there never was in fact a stage of primal promiscuity. What we possess, with regard to all social institutions, is evidence from existing societies, and accounts of past ones. From these we can build up a picture of social life and thus of marital arrangements in societies of widely divergent types.

Irrespective of the form or forms of marriage which exist in a particular society, there are certain elements which appear to be fairly evenly distributed. Marriage itself can be defined as 'a socially recognised union between persons of opposite sex'. [1] The majority of societies regard marriage as a form of contract not only between the individuals involved but between the families. The contract is concerned with both the mutual rights and duties of all those implicated, and with property. Property in this context means status, position, title, as well as land and goods. In other words much more is at stake in marriage than the mere happiness of the partners. This may be contrary to the current ideas of marriage in Europe and America. Such ideas, however, are a comparatively recent phenomenon, fostered in part by the mass media of communication. For the vast majority of mankind marriage remains essentially on a contractual basis. If mutual love and property can be combined so much the better; if they cannot the situation must be accepted.

The contract may vary in detail and type, but it is found in all societies of all kinds, from the most primitive to the most advanced. The largest group of such societies is that in which it appears superficially that the wife is purchased. That it so say a payment is made by the bridegroom's people to the bride's people. A much smaller group consists of societies where payment, that is a dowry, is made to the husband. It is to this group our own society belongs.

Wife purchase must not be interpreted literally. The man does not buy the woman in the sense that he would a slave or an article. He cannot, for example, dispose of her as a commodity. What in fact he is purchasing is her child-bearing capacity. This is why some communities permit divorce if the wife is barren. In any case the payment made is often offset in part by a gift made by the family of the bride. The former is generally known as the bride-price. Bride-price is really a more sophisticated form of daughter-exchange and marriage by service.

Daughter-exchange is literally what it says. Families will arrange to exchange their marriageable daughters. In many such cases no bride-price is paid. For example, in some Australian tribal groups this is the normal method for obtaining a wife. [2] It is found also amongst the Kiwai Papuans, and is fairly general in New Guinea. In all these instances no payment is made, thus there is a definite economic saving. In the Australian case, however, because of the extremely strict and complicated rules concerning prohibited degrees of marriage, it may be the only method by which a wife can be obtained. Other societies such as those of ancient Arabia, and the Senufo and Mossi of the French Sudan, use daughter-exchange as an alternative to paying the bride-price.

The classical case of marriage by service is that of Jacob serving his uncle Laban for fourteen years in order to obtain his daughters Leah and Rachel as his wives. It is in fact an extremely widespread custom, being found in North and South America, Polynesia, South and West Africa, Afghanistan, Siberia, and amongst the aboriginal inhabitants of China, India, and Japan. In many of these societies the period of service may be the only method by which you can obtain a wife (Ainu of Japan, and Siberian tribes). In others it is an alternative to payment (Indian aboriginal tribes). The period of service required may vary from a few months to several years, as in Jacob's case. What the potential husband is doing is assisting the girl's family unit, and in a sense proving his worth. For example, some communities (in Brazil and India) will permit the aspirant to sleep, but not copulate, with his future bride. There are instances where the period of servitude is prolonged after the actual marriage until a child is born. This occurs amongst the Gonds of Central India and some North American Indians. Where polygyny is practised the period of servitude may apply only to the first or principal wife as it does amongst some Brazilian and Siberian peoples.

This type of servitude can also be regarded as an alternative for payment of a bride-price. Its usage is similar to that of daughter-exchange in that it may be the only way of obtaining a wife, or it may be an alternative method. There may in fact be a combination of the two as occurs amongst the Yukaghir of Siberia, where not only service but a payment of reindeer is demanded. [3] Another Siberian people, the Kamchadal, emphasise a different aspect. The period of service is regarded as one of probation in which the young man has to prove himself. Parental approval will mean he wins his bride. Disapproval results in a small payment to him, and he is asked to leave. It is probably true that wherever a period of service is demanded the element of testing is present.

Of the different methods of obtaining a wife discussed so far payment of some kind is the most widespread. The variation in the amount paid or value of the presents made is considerable. The Vedda of Ceylon, some tribes of Malaya and the Philippines, as well as some Australian aboriginal groups, merely demand a token payment of food, a present, or a weapon. On the other hand many North American Indian tribes place the transaction on a much more commercial basis. The gifts made must be of real value—blankets, horses, and so on. In the case of the Apache and the Hupa Indians of California, the value of the gifts made on behalf of a wife was supposed to reflect the actual worth of the woman, so that it was important to pay as much as possible in order to obtain a prestige-bearing wife.

Wife-purchase is common throughout Africa. The payment made in cattle raising areas is almost inevitably livestock. According to the society there will be an accepted tariff. Nadel cites the following for one group of Nuba of the Sudan: 'A certain Albina . . . who married in 1938, paid forty goats, two cows, one gun, thirty spears, and twenty cakes of tobacco, or, in money, £27. He paid the whole bride-price in the course of a year. This is the highest bride-price I recorded; but a bride-price amounting to £24 to £25 is quite common, and a bride-price of about £18 was positively, or, rather apologetically, declared to be exceptionally low.' [4] Similar instances could be cited for tribal groups in

Uganda, South-West Africa, Kenya, as well as of West African peoples such as the Ewe and Ibo.

The principle seems to be that whatever the society regards as of value, either intrinsic or apparent, will be used in the bride-price transactions. Thus amongst Siberian peoples furs and rein-deer are prominent gifts. In Melanesia and Polynesia the emphasis is upon the special shell money which is much used for ceremonial exchange.

When the bride-price is handed over to the father of the girl it does not necessarily mean that he has the exclusive right to it. In many instances he has to share it with other relatives, or has to give them presents. This is the case amongst the Aleutians, the Osage Indians of North America, the Baganda of Uganda, many Siberian tribes, and in Melanesia. The mother has a special claim in other primitive groups. For example the East African Masai and Akamba, the West African Ibo, and some tribes of Madagascar, allow the mother of the bride a large part of the bride-price. This element of sharing is reflected in the extension of the responsibility for the bride-price from the groom's father to other relatives. In some cases this may involve the whole clan to which the groom belongs, as occurs in the Central Celebes, Ceram, and Buru in Indonesia. According to Seligman the Mekeo tribes of New Guinea made up the bride-price by donations from both the paternal and maternal relatives of the groom. [5] The stress need not necessarily, however, be placed upon relatives, real or fictitious. The Altai of Siberia have the practice of organising a subscription among the friends of the groom. This, of course, removes the responsibility from the latter's father. [6]

Payment of the bride-price by instalments figures in some societies. Thus the Tungus, Yakut, and Ostyak of Siberia permit the groom to sleep with his future wife when he has made certain payments. The Akamba of East Africa and the Batta of Sumatra will allow the marriage to take place while payments are still being made. But such practices may lead to the situation whereby the debt is never paid off and permanently affects the economic position of the family. This obtains in some of the aboriginal tribes of Burma. In other cases the husband, if there are instalments outstanding, does not have full rights over his wife and the children she may produce.

9a. Love and wine.

9b. The Cocotte; after Doré.

10a. The kiss. From a
nineteenth century
drawing.

10b. The kiss of love. From an
eighteenth century
engraving.

11a. Nineteenth century German romanticism.

11b. Passion. Early twentieth century lithograph.

12a. Eighteenth century French romanticism; after Fragonard.

12b. Blessing the nuptial bed. Eighteenth century engraving.

13. From the erotic "Posizioni" series. Attributed to Guilio Romano.

14. *In Flagrante Delicto*. Nineteenth century engraving.

15. Conceptions of the bust in the nineteenth century.

16a. The ideal can be built up.

16b. Nature and art;
Nineteenth century
French painting.

As we have suggested the payment of bride-price cannot be regarded cynically as merely a commercial transaction. The giving of material objects, animals, or money for a woman demonstrates that she is of value. Everything else in life is valued according to its use, and so is the woman. The element of purchase is concerned with the child-bearing capacity of the woman rather than the woman herself. Another consideration of some importance is that the bride-price, to some degree, acts as a safeguard for the woman, for in many societies it is returnable if the wife runs away or is divorced. To appreciate the values inherent in this custom of making a payment for a wife the opposite situation should be considered, where the bride-price is obligatory but the man is unable to pay it, yet marries. In such a situation the girl is counted worthless, in every sense of the word, and the children as father-less. [7] This is actually the case among the Hupa Indians of California. The woman has her value and this must be paid for.

Payment of bride-price seldom exists on its own. In the majority of cases there is some reciprocal payment. This may be only at the token level or, on the other hand, it may function as a fully developed dowry system. Throughout North America, wherever the bride-price is demanded, some return is made to the groom or his family. This is also true of the Siberian tribal peoples, and of Polynesia and Melanesia. Some Indians of British Columbia have an arrangement whereby the gifts exchanged are of more or less equal value. Amongst the Siberian Yukaghir, on the occasion of the first visits of a newly married couple to the wife's relatives, the latter return the reindeer which have come into the family as a bride-price. But it is in New Guinea and Melanesia that this type of gift-exchange really flourishes. According to Malinowski the return made is of such a nature that there is always a small balance in favour of the bride's family. [8] In some few cases the return exceeds the bride-price paid (tribes of the Nilgiri Hills in South India, and some Canadian Indians). The return may not necessarily be made in terms of gifts. For example, the father of the bride may have to provide such a splendid marriage feast that the bride-price he has received hardly covers expenses. This is said to happen in the Herero tribe in South Africa.

At the stage when the contribution made by the family of the girl begins to exceed the payment made by the boy's family the concept of the dowry is beginning to emerge. But in fact there does not appear to be any society at the simple level, whichever type of wife purchase may obtain, in which the woman is sent forth dowerless. What she brings with her may not be susbtantial but it is her property.

The pagan tribes of Europe exhibited the same pattern as that of other simple societies—wife-purchase in conjunction with a limited form of dowry. This was the case in Wales, Ireland, Gaul, and Germany. The Welsh tribes' dowry system was more fully developed: it was, for example, the duty of a father to provide a marriage settlement (Gwaddol).

The classical societies of India, Greece, Rome (though here it is debatable), Arabia, China, and Israel, all possessed a form of wife-purchase in addition to a dowry. The type of development which took place within such societies can be illustrated by the case of the Greeks. Aristotle claimed (*Politica*, ii. 8) that in early times wife-purchase was the rule. But in his own day, and certainly later, it became the custom for a father to endow his daughter with at least a tenth of his goods. [9]

But it is in Rome that the dowry system, which is really husband-purchase, reached its most developed form. Some scholars (Rossbach, Sohm, Leist, Schrader) have maintained that the very earliest form of Roman marriage involved a real or symbolic bride-price. Others (Marquardt, Karlowa) have denied its existence altogether. With regard to dowries there is a great deal of legislation which shows clearly how the system operated.

In the Europe which existed after the fall of Rome, wife-purchase was a normal practice. It was termed *Weotuma* by the Anglo-Saxons. The laws of the Anglo-Saxons, both pagan and Christian, give precise instructions as to the amount to be paid for a woman according to her rank and as to whether she was a virgin or a widow. The latter was always available at a lower price. The legislation of Ethelbert of Kent came very near the practice of contemporary simple societies in permitting the use of cattle for wife-purchase. A very ordinary contingency which frequently arises was guarded against by King Alfred. 'If any one deceive an unbetrothed woman, and sleep with her, let him pay for her, and have her afterwards to wife . . .' More exceptionally perhaps Ethelred provided that 'If a freeman have been familiar with a freeman's wife, let him pay for it with his wer-gild (compensation paid for a homicide), and provide another wife with his own money, and bring her home to the other . . .' [10]

In Germany the practice was of a similar nature almost until the end of the mediaeval period. Norway enacted legislation of this type as late as the end of the sixteenth century. Amongst the Slav peoples wife-purchase was the ordinary preamble to marriage. Both in Albania and Yugoslavia it lingered on until the beginning of the nineteenth century. Thus the original post-Roman European scene, as regards payment for a wife, was very similar to the one we find in contemporary simple societies, where a simple payment is made to the relatives of the bride. But from the sixth century A.D. there was a gradual change. The next stage was the bulk of the money or goods being settled on the wife by the husband, her people taking only a token. An important element here is the creation of provision for the wife in case of divorce or death of her spouse. The rediscovery, at a later period, of Roman Law and its emphasis on the dowry implemented the process, so that in time, with few exceptions, Europe evolved a fully developed dowry system. The shift from wife-purchase to husband-purchase is complete when the responsibility for the dowry is no longer that of the husband, as in the intermediate stage, but has become the duty of the wife's parents. [11]

In most European countries the influence of the Catholic Church was behind the application of the dowry. The interest of the church was primarily in the widow. As Sir Henry Maine puts it: '. . . The provision for the widow was attributable to the exertions of the Church, which never relaxed its solicitude for the interest of wives surviving their husbands—winning, perhaps, one of the most arduous of its triumphs when, after exacting for two or three centuries an express promise from the husband at marriage to endow his wife, it at length succeeded in engrafting the principle of Dower on the Customary Law of all Western Europe . . .' [12]

Today it is mainly in Latin countries that the possession of a dowry remains a prerequisite of the young marriageable girl of all classes. It is, of course, precisely in such countries that the Roman Catholic Church is extremely influential. In Britain and America, with the increasing fluidity of marriage and the decline of class hostility, the dowry is no longer prominent. When it does occur it is in cases where considerable amounts of property are involved.

It should be remembered that where the dowry is in force it is not always an easy burden to bear. For peasant families in bad economic conditions it may mean years of saving and scraping. In such societies to offer a dowerless girl in marriage would bring shame on all concerned. Obviously in these circumstances a variety of expedients and devices are adopted to scrape together a reasonable sum. A somewhat unusual method, which at any rate removes the burden from the girl's parents, is the practice of earning one's dowry by prostitution. Herodotus cites the instance of young women in Lydia obtaining their marriage portion in this manner. The Lydian case is apparently connected with forms of temple or religious prostitution found in various parts of the world. Other examples come from the Kabyle and Ouled Nail tribes of North Africa. [13] Amongst these peoples it is the custom for unmarried girls to travel to the cities and act as prostitutes for a definite period. Then they return with their rewards and, one hopes, become contented brides with sizeable marriage portions. This practice shows an essentially realistic and logical approach to the problem of obtaining a dowry. But for successful operation obviously the would-be husband's complaisance must be assured.

It is of some interest to note that marriage by purchase in Britain persisted with varying frequency from Saxon times until late in the nineteenth century. The popular magazine with which Dickens was associated, *All the Year Round*, on December 20th 1884, reported twenty cases in which the price given for women varied from twenty-five guineas to a penny. In the eighteenth century such sales of women, for they were little else, were cited in the market intelligence of *The Times*. For example the issue of July 22nd 1797, contains this announcement: 'By an oversight in the report on Smithfield Market we are not in a position to quote this week the price of women. The increasing value of the fairer sex is considered by various celebrated writers to be a sure sign of increasing civilisation. On these grounds Smithfield may raise a claim to rank as a place of special advance in refinement, for at its Market the price of women has lately risen from half a guinea to three guineas and a half...' What had been an essential part of the traditional marriage system of the Saxons became by the eighteenth century a degraded device by which husbands got rid of unwanted wives. The legality of such sales and subsequent unions is obscure. They appear however to have had as much validity as the notorious 'Fleet Prison' and Gretna Green marriages, and can be regarded as part of the general chaos of the English marriage laws which persisted until the reforms of the late nineteenth century. Although the money involved in such transactions might be as little as a penny, custom, or the law demanded that certain formalities should be complied with. The sale had to be conducted publicly before witnesses. It generally took place in the market place the woman being led round for everyone to see with a rope or halter round her neck, bids were taken, and she was knocked down to the highest bidder. The attitude of the mass of the people towards such sales was curiously ambivalent. On the one hand magistrates who attempted to frustrate such auctions were sent about their business. On the other the husband-vendors were frequently assaulted by the market crowds. An early nineteenth century observer, de Jouy, in his *L'Hermite de Londres* gives a most interesting account of wife purchase in a chapter entitled 'Vente de Femmes à Londres'.

One of the most striking contrasts between so-called savages and ourselves is in the field of kinship. It is not too much of an exaggeration to say that for the vast majority of human societies kinship is the pivot. In Europe and America kinship relationships undoubtedly exist, but they are at a minimum and are generally concerned with immediate, close relatives. Our relationships with other individuals are determined by a great number of factors— work, money, interests, and so on—which have nothing to do with kinship. To a very great extent, in simple societies kinship, that is a real or fictitious relationship to other individuals, is the major determinant of social relationships. Radcliffe-Brown expresses it in this way: ' . . . At every moment of the life of a member of an Australian tribe his dealings with other individuals are regulated by the relationship in which he stands to them. His relations, near and distant, are classified into certain large groups, and this classification is carried out by means of the terminology, and could not apparently be achieved in any other way. Thus in any part of the continent when a stranger comes to a camp the first thing to be done, before he can be admitted within the camp, is to determine his relationship to every man and woman in it, i.e., to determine what is the proper term of relationship for him to apply to each of them. As soon as he knows his relation to a given individual he knows how to behave towards him, what his duties are, and what his rights . . .'[14]

In other words the knowledge of kinship enables you to behave as a person should in society. In many instances the range of relationships is so wide that it must be a phenomenal task to memorise them all. The Chagga of East Africa have this problem and solve it in the following way: 'From birth the child is taught the proper terms for addressing his relatives. He is told about paternal and maternal grandparents, uncles and aunts, before he understands one word of his language. It is the mother and nurse who teach the child to use the terms in appropriate situations . . . Father, mother, elder siblings (brothers and sisters) and nurse admonish the impolite child and advise it . . . It is not to be wondered at that children are masters of kinship etiquette when they are six years old and that at fourteen they know most of the terminological subtleties.'[15]

Perhaps it is a misnomer to speak of these societies as simple!

To understand how kinship operates it is necessary to see how primitive society is organised. If we take the largest single unit of the tribe, we find that it is composed of a number of clans. In many cases the clan is totemistic, that is has a special relationship with a representative of an animal or vegetable species. The tribe itself is made up of individuals all claiming descent from a common ancestor. Membership of the clan is determined in the same way. Each clan has a founding ancestor or ancestors. As every individual has two parents he has membership of a maternal and a paternal clan. In many societies either the paternal or the maternal clan is emphasised. In others, such as the Akan peoples of Ghana, both are emphasised. The mother's clan creates your social position, family, and what you inherit; but your father's clan has possession of your soul which governs your conduct: this is the explanation the Akan give.

The clan is further divided into lineages and sub-lineages on the same principle of tracing descent through a common ancestor. A minor lineage or sub-lineage is made up of extended family groups which in turn are composed of individual households.

Inside this framework of tribe, clan, and lineage, there is the system of classificatory relationships. All people, according to their generation and blood relationship, either real or imagined, are grouped in different categories. Thus, as we stated earlier, all female relatives of your mother's generation will be addressed as mother. Or all male relatives of your own generation will be brothers. According to your place in the system there are duties owed to you and duties to be carried out; there are rights which are yours and rights which are others. The system, in fact, represents a perfect pattern of how one ought to, and in fact must behave. It may sound confusing and complicated, but as we have seen children master it at a very early age and never err thereafter.

We have, of course, only outlined the system in an elementary way. But while it would not apply to all societies which are organised on a basis of kinship—for there are countless variations —it gives a general indication of such organisation.

Whom you marry is to a great extent determined by clan membership. A society may practise exogamy, that is the individual has to marry someone from outside the group. The Baganda of Uganda are a good example. They are divided into thirty-six clans, amongst whom inter-marriage takes place. On the other hand the rule may be one of endogamy, which compels marriage within the group or clan. Amongst the Riffs of North Africa the clan groups are isolated from each other and we find that they are in fact endogamous through necessity. Other instances of endogamous societies have this characteristic of relative isolation. Exogamy, which is far more common, tends to be associated with larger social units having more varied contacts. Endogamy serves to keep property and power within the clan, a useful social function. But the primary reason for its existence may be the pressure of the environment leading to isolation. This is certainly true in the case of the Riffs of Morocco and the Yukaghir of Siberia. For clans at the simple level nations, racial groups, castes and classes may be substituted at the more advanced level of society. These operate in the same way in promoting exogamy or endogamy. One of the earliest injunctions against the inter-marriage of nations is contained in the Old Testament. *The Book of Deuteronomy* (Ch VII), in forbidding inter-marriage with the Canaanites, states the practical reason that such marriage may turn men from God. Other prohibitions are contained in the *Books of Ezra* (Ch. IX, Verse 1 *et seq.*) and *Nehemiah* (Chs X, V 30, and XIII, V 23). This biblical abhorrence of marriage with Gentiles has persisted to the present day amongst Jewish people.

Racial endogamy, as opposed to group endogamy, appears to have occurred with as much frequency as its opposite. Where legal marriage has been forbidden, however, as in the south of the U.S.A. between whites and Negroes, it has not prevented the occurrence of extra-legal relationships. In fact it is true to say that wherever the European has been in contact with non-European peoples both marriage and concubinage have ensued. The same pattern is observed in the case of another nation which travelled great distances from its homeland, the Arabs. The problem, if it is a problem, did not disturb most simple societies as they existed in relative isolation.

The Hindu caste system has endogamy as one of its chief characteristics. It operates in such a way that you may not marry outside the sub-caste to which you belong. There may be, however, what is called hypergamy. This is the rule that when a caste is divided into a hierarchy of sections a girl may marry a man from a superior section. Caste may be defined as a rigid religious and social division of society into groups. The Hindu system has religious validation stemming from the most ancient period of India's history. In contemporary India, however, with enormous social and economic changes taking place, the system is being greatly modified.

In the primitive world the existence of endogamy or exogamy is governed by kinship relations and the total environment of the particular society. In the Western world class, status, and economic values operate to the same end.

The operation of endogamy or exogamy is further complicated by the existence of incest prohibitions. These vary from simple injunctions preventing marriage between close blood relatives, as in our own society, to involved rules concerning blood and social kin which sometimes narrows the field of possible choice to an impossible extent, as amongst some Australian tribes. The extent and variety of these prohibitions is enormous. There have been several hypotheses which have attempted to explain the almost obsessional preoccupation with incest regulations which is characteristic of many societies. None has been really adequate in accounting for the variety of forms exhibited. Old theories, such as the natural sexual aversion of blood relatives to each other and the instinctive aversion based on unconscious fears of inbreeding, are valueless. [16] One dramatic theory, unfortunately not in accordance with ethnological facts, is that given by Freud in *Totem and Tabu*.

Restriction on the choice of a mate is again apparent in the customs of the *levirate* and the *sororate*. The levirate is the custom whereby a man inherits, that is to say must marry, his brother's widow. This is an extremely widespread practice found in a variety of peoples all over the world, ranging from the aboriginal tribes of India to the Bedouin Arabs. The sororate is the custom whereby if a man's wife dies he marries her sister. This is less extensive both in its incidence and distribution. It occurs mainly among North American Indians though it is found in Melanesia and Africa. In many societies either the levirate or sororate may be compulsory as amongst the Maori, the Ewe of West Africa, and the Tlingit of North America; in others, such as the Navaho, there is only social resentment if a widower fails to take a second wife from amongst his wife's kinsfolk. A variation on this theme is provided by some African societies and the Caribs of Central America. In these groups a man sometimes inherits his father's wives, with the exception of his mother.

The explanation of the levirate and sororate lies in what may appear to be a necessity, that is the perpetuation of the original marriage bonds. They help to maintain the relationships created by the original marriage, and strengthen property ties already created.

For the majority of peoples, as we have seen, marriage is not at all a simple matter. Financial transactions apart, it may be obligatory to select your bride from a certain group of females, or you may have to tread so warily to avoid the stringent incest prohibitions which hedge your choice, that to speak of free choice is ridiculous. From our point of view it appears that the individual in primitive society is bowed down beneath the complexity of his marital and incest regulations. Whether this is so or not is a debatable matter; but that the individual is not always prepared to accept the situation is well illustrated by the systematic evasions of the incest tabus practised by various societies, such as the Trobrianders. [17]

In contrast Western society, with its paucity of incest prohibitions and low incidence of arranged marriages, appears to give the individual absolutely free choice in selecting his or her partner. At the same time it as is well to note that marriages in our kind of society tend to follow class and status lines, if not with the rigidity of the simple society, at least with great frequency.

The young man in a tribal society having theoretically selected his bride from amongst those available, or having merely decided to embark upon matrimony, may be faced by a further problem. Negotiations cannot be opened direct with the parents of the bride to be. If one remembers that marriage for a great number of peoples exists not merely to satisfy the needs of two individuals but to create new and important relationships, involving not only the partners but also property, the desirability of a go-between or agent to help arrange the marriage appears to be reasonable. A further very important reason for the existence of the go-between is that negotiations may break down. If this happens neither family loses face as they have not been directly involved. The latter reason may help to explain the widespread incidence of the marriage agent in Chinese society. But the activities of the go-between are by no means confined to China. He exists throughout the world in many different types of society. African, Indian, Polynesian, Siberian and Arab peoples, as well as many North and South American Indians, all employ this most useful member of society. In Europe the peasant societies of Finland, Germany, Poland, Russia and Yugoslavia were prominent in their use of the go-between. His activities in Europe still persist in a somewhat attenuated form. The matchmaker in more sophisticated European circles performed more or less the same role as the go-between. The difference being that the matchmaker did not wait to be approached by an interested party but tried to provoke interest.

Today in our world of free choice the matrimonial agency has taken the place of the go-between and matchmaker. The sanction extended to it by the society is by no means wholehearted, and it has certainly not attained the important status of the go-between in classical China.

In simple society the go-between or agent may deal with his opposite number rather than with the family direct. Gorer describes his activities in this way. '. . . A marriage is never arranged by the parents of the child concerned; were the parents to do so, either the parties would die young or the marriage would break up. In Lingthem (a village in Sikkim) the marriages are usually proposed by the "Mandal" (headman) and negotiated through the intermediary of the child's uncles and grandparents on both sides, and especially the father's elder brother or, if such a man does not exist, anyone who stands in a similar relationship . . . All the real marriage negotiations are carried on between two "bek-bu" (between-men) representing each side. Any experienced and tactful man, with the exception of the spouse's father, who knows the correct things to say and the correct way to say them and has sufficient vocabulary of "tong-bor" (elegant circumlocutions) may take this role . . . The first preliminary to arranging a marriage is a visit of the bek-bu by himself to the girl's village; on this visit he will take him with a load of "chi" (a drink fermented from millet). He will go to some neighbouring house—never the house where the girl lives—and will discover what man of the village is acting as the girl's bek-bu; To this man he will give the load of chi and start negotiations for the marriage. The girl's bek-bu will discuss the proposition with the girl's family—particularly her uncles—but the father and mother are also unofficially consulted. As a matter of form the girl's family will belittle the match on the first conversation, saying they do not yet wish to get rid of their daughter, that the proposed match is not good enough, and so on. If they do not know the boy proposed, they will send to make enquiries about his character, as to whether he is a good and industrious worker, peaceable and generous. The girl's father will always refuse at the first discussion and usually at the second; if they have not agreed when the subject is broached for the third time the negotiations are called off. If they do agree the bek-bu will present them with a ceremonial scarf and a rupee and a date will be set for the formal "asek" (betrothal), dependent on the lama's horoscope not being completely unfavourable. This preliminary is called "kachyoung" . . .' [18]

This description of the Lepcha go-between is a good example of the function the latter performs in society. Clearly the world-wide incidence of marriage agents in greatly different societies makes it difficult to give a typical example of their activities, but nevertheless the procedure of the Lepcha bek-bu, in its essentials, can be regarded as typical. The equivalent practice in our own type of society can still be observed in rural Ireland where a neighbour acts as the go-between or matchmaker. [19] If all the hazards—incest barriers, go-betweens, and so on—are overcome the individual, according to his society, may have the choice of one or more particular forms of marriage. These are monogamy, which is the union of one man and one woman; polygyny, the union of one man and X number of women; polyandry, the union of one woman and X number of men; and 'group marriage', where X number of men are united with X number of women. Polygamy, which is a term somewhat loosely used, merely means plurality of spouses so can apply to both polygyny and polyandry. In the popular mind polygamy has come to be synonymous with polygyny, possibly because there has been a traditional aversion to it in the West.

In Malinowski's view marriage is essentially the union of two people for the purposes of sexual satisfaction, procreation, co-operation, and other aims. He writes: 'Monogamy is, has been, and will remain the only true type of marriage. To place polygyny and polyandry as "forms of marriage" co-ordinate with monogamy is erroneous. To speak about "group marriage" as another variety shows a complete lack of understanding as to the nature of marriage . . . As a rule a polygynous co-habitation is a successive monogamy and not joint domesticity; children and property are divided, and in every other respect the contracts are entered into individually between two partners at a time . . . Both polyandry and polygyny are compound marriages, consisting of several unions combined into a larger system, but each of them constituted the pattern of a monogamous marriage . . .' [20] Malinowski also denies the existence of true 'group marriage'. The view that marriage is essentially the union of two people of different sex, and that polygyny and polyandry are really a series of successive monogamous unions may be substantially correct, but it is confusing. A somewhat different approach to marriage is that of R. Linton, the American anthropologist. He distinguishes four 'ways' of marriage, much as we have done above. [21]

It seems obvious that there must be a nomenclature by which we distinguish one kind, type or way of marriage from another.

With regard to 'group marriage', although its proper manifestation no longer takes place in any living society, there is considerable evidence as to its former existence in the Marquesas Islands in the Pacific. [22]

Because of Western tradition, with its emphasis on Christian marriage, there has been a tendency for writers on the subject to regard other forms of marriage as inferior. This was given a quasi-scientific boost in the nineteenth century when a stage of primal promiscuity was postulated from which man evolved through group marriage, polyandry and polygyny to the blessed state of monogamy. Such theorising, as we have tried to show, is highly fallacious. To speak of evolution in forms of marriage is nonsense. Each type must be seen as part of a particular social structure, fulfilling its necessary and proper function in the society in which it exists. One form does not *develop* into another. Nor is one form inferior to another. All are fulfilling the same purpose—satisfying the sexual, procreative and familial needs of men. Critics of polygyny, who suggest that it lowers the status of women, should look more closely at life as it is lived in a polygynous household, where the unfortunate husband may be browbeaten by an alliance of his wives. The truth of the matter is that in all types of marriage there are cases of happiness and cases of acute misery.

Monogamy and polygyny are the two outstanding types of marriage and are to be found all over the world. In some societies, such as our own, the acceptance of monogamy prohibits the existence of polygyny, which is punishable at law. In contrast to this, in all polygynous societies, such as those of the Arab peoples, monogamy is an acceptable alternative. This is through necessity.

It would be superfluous to elaborate the functioning of a monogamous household: polygyny, on the other hand, does not seem to be understood by the ordinary person in our society. Polygyny is practised in a great number of human societies of widely divergent types. At one pole are the Islamic peoples; at the other the Australian aborigines. Lloyd Warner has suggested that amongst the Murngin tribes of Northern Australia constant blood feuding reduces the number of men and so makes polygyny open to all. [23] The Murngin attitude towards polygyny is given by Warner as

'. . . A man wants as many wives as he can get and still keep his peace with the other males of his clan. The average is about three and a half for middle-aged men; but there is a recorded case of one native with seventeen wives, the majority having been obtained by stealing them or killing their husbands . . . There is a close correlation of having many wives with fighting strength . . .' And '. . . Murngin polygyny implies that a man will acquire wives throughout his lifetime. Through the operation of tribal laws a very old man frequently gets young girls for wives. All these women are "arndi" (within a forbidden relationship) to his sons, but often young men cohabit clandestinely with their father's younger wives. These must be only tribal relatives of the sons' actual mothers. Even so, the practice is considered wrong, but the feeling is not strong enough to prevent a sexually active son from cohabiting with a father's wife. Should the old man discover it, he would be very angry and reprove his son by calling him a dog, etc., but it is generally agreed that an old man beyond the age where sexual life interests him would not "growl very hard" . . .' [24]

There is no doubt that where polygyny is the socially desired ideal the husband's prestige increases with the number of wives he has.

Evidence from another society, that of Alor in the East Indies, shows a different but equally important aspect of polygyny: '. . . Jealousy on the part of women has direct cultural outlets and aggressive expression. When a man takes a second wife, for example, it is considered good form for the first one to quarrel about it. As might be expected, these quarrels are often phrased in terms of property. The first wife will ask how a man can afford to pay a bride-price on another woman when he has paid so little for her. Or she will claim that the pigs he has given for a second wife were in large part raised by herself . . . After a few reproaches of this sort the first wife seeks out the second. They exchange insults for a time and then begin pulling, tugging and beating each other. Immediately all the women of the village become involved. Each wife has a certain number of belligerent allies, and in addition there is always a large group of women who try to separate the combatants but who manage, in their role of peacemakers, to land some very effective blows. A whole village may be in a turmoil of struggling women waging a shifting warfare in the mud or dust of the dance place for as long as from two to four hours. Men at such times are inclined to stand out of range and watch the tide of battle with mixed amusement and contempt . . . Naturally some battles may be much less violent than others, depending on how much real jealousy motivates a woman utilising this formal cultural outlet. More than once a senior wife who is in earnest makes life so uncomfortable that the junior wife finally insists on a divorce, but even a wife who has urged her husband to buy another woman will go through the forms of a quarrel . . . The effect of this cultural pattern is to afford women a very direct and relatively harmless emotional outlet.' [25]

In almost all polygynous societies the first woman a man marries ranks as the senior wife. Deference is due to her from the other wives, and she has certain rights and privileges denied to them. In many instances it is only with her consent that another wife can be taken. In Alor '. . . In the case of plural wives, separate households are established, and a man is supposed to divide his attention labour and gifts equally among them. Any slight on his part may result in reproaches directed toward him and quarrels among the wives. A duty of the senior wife is to cook for the husband's guests and to take the initiative in contributing food to his feasts. The feasts are supposed to be held at the house of the senior wife. These duties may at times be considered in the light of privilege and any infringement may make the second wife feel that she is imposed upon . . .' [26]

The husband in a polygynous marriage has to arrange things well if he wishes to have a peaceable life. There is always the possibility that the wives will, if driven to it by his behaviour, cooperate to make his life quite unbearable. A good example of well planned polygynous households comes from the Kipsigis of Kenya. They are a cattle rearing people. All the agricultural work is done by women, so that it is advantageous for a man to have several wives. As his herds grow so will the number of his wives. The cattle are distributed over a considerable area for fear of disease and raiding parties. Individual homesteads are set up in different areas, complete with wives and children. The husband then spends his time on tour, as it were, visiting his different establishments. The friction exhibited amongst the Alorese is thus carefully avoided by the Kipsigis. [27]

Choice of the preferred form of marriage amongst less advanced peoples is to some extent determined by economic causes. Thus in the first instance a man must be able to afford the necessary bride-price before he can embark on a second marriage. In societies where women are an asset from the point of view of work (as in a large number of African agricultural communities) it is clearly advantageous to have more than one wife. Similarly amongst the food gathering and hunting aborigines of Australia women play an equal part with men in these activities and polygyny is the norm. But in some societies which depend almost entirely on hunting in difficult conditions, such as the Veddas of Ceylon and a number of South American Indian tribes, polygyny would create serious difficulties for the husband, thus such peoples tend to be monogamous. But there are many anomalous examples of peoples living in conditions which theoretically should promote polgyny but who are in fact monogamous. The monogamous Pygmies of the Congo are surrounded by polygynous tribes. The opposite also occurs—polygynous tribes existing in economic conditions where monogamy would be advantageous. The Greenland Eskimo are an example.

The economic factor does influence the incidence of polygyny in simple societies, but it does not *create* it. The main factor affecting the incidence in any society is the number of marriageable women. Unless there is a surplus some men are bound to be monogamous.

From the studies that have been made, it appears that in societies which are polgynous it is always a minority of men who have more than one wife. One writer has estimated that among the Eskimo the ratio is one polygynous household to twenty monogamous ones, and that this is approximately the same for India, China, and Islam. [28] This is undoubtedly due to economic conditions. But there will always be cases where an individual is monogamous through choice.

Western man practises monogamy. He can understand, and may even desire, polygyny, but he is baffled by polyandry. The idea of sharing his sexual rights in a woman, outside of a brothel, is anathema. Nevertheless there have been, and are, societies in which polyandry has been the preferred form of marital union. The classical example is that of the Todas of the Nilgiri Hills in South India.

'. . . The Todas have a completely organised and definite system of polyandry. When a woman marries a man, it is understood that she becomes the wife of his brothers at the same time. When a boy is married to a girl not only are his brothers usually regarded as the husbands of the girl, but any brother later born will similarly be regarded as sharing his older brother's rights. In the vast majority of polyandrous marriages at the present time, the husbands are own brothers . . . In a few cases in which the husbands are not own brothers, they are clan-brothers, i.e., they belong to the same clan and are of the same generation . . .

'The arrangement of family life in the case of a polyandrous marriage differs according as the husbands are, or are not, own brothers.

'In the former case it seemed there is never any difficulty, and that disputes never arise. The brothers live together, and my informants seemed to regard it as a ridiculous idea that there should even be disputes or jealousies of the kind that might be expected in such a household. When the wife becomes pregnant, the eldest brother (of the co-husband) performs the ceremony of giving the bow and arrow (by which the paternity of the child is established) but the brothers are all equally regarded as the father of the child . . .

'. . . When the husbands are not own brothers, the arrangements become more complicated. When the husbands live together as if they were own brothers there is rarely any difficulty. If, on the other hand, the husbands live at different villages, the usual rule is that the wife shall live with each husband in turn, usually for a month at a time, but there is very considerable elasticity in the arrangement . . .' [29]

The custom of giving the bow and arrow mentioned above establishes paternity for the purposes of tracing genealogical descent.

If, as we said earlier, the existence of polygyny is dependent upon a surplus of women, in the same way polyandry is dependent upon a scarcity of women. In most societies the balance between the sexes does not vary a great deal. Artificial means have to be reverted to to produce a scarcity, i.e., resort to female infanticide. There seems to be little doubt that the Todas practised this in the past and, at the time the above account was written (the early twentieth century), were being forced to give it up by the authorities. The resultant increase in the number of women in our own day has destroyed the classical picture of polyandry as described by W. H. R. Rivers in *The Todas*.

On the north-eastern borders of India the Lepcha also practise polyandry in a limited way. Gorer describes it thus: '. . . It is permissible for a man who feels himself unable to cope with his field-work, either on account of physical weakness or because he has other work which takes him a great deal from the neighbourhood, to invite an unmarried younger brother to live with him to share his fields and wife. The co-husband is co-opted without any sort of ceremony, but thereafter he is no longer free in the choice of a wife of his own, if he desires one . . . The co-husbands sleep with their common wife on alternate nights, but all the children are presumed to be gotten by the first husband, and he alone has to observe the pre-natal precautions; an exception is only made to this rule if the first husband's prolonged absence makes his paternity a physiological impossibility . . . There are some obvious advantages for a first husband in co-opting a second husband: it is an easy way to get rid of a wife of whom you are tired; it gives an extra adult worker and a caretaker for your property and wife when you have to be absent. The position of second co-husband on the other hand seems to offer few attractions except to the poor, and unambitious, undersexed man, and it is understandable that there are few examples of such polyandry . . .' [30]

It must be remembered that the Lepcha attitude towards polyandry is to some extent affected by their admission of both polygyny and monogamy in their scheme of marital relations. In this they follow the pattern of Tibetan marriage, which also allows the other two forms of union. According to some authorities the economic factor is of considerable importance in establishing the forms of marriage. [31] The majority of land in Tibet is in the form of family holdings. Division and sub-division of these has been so great that no further splitting up into viable units can take place. One son tends to become a priest. The others marry one woman and the ensuing family lives on the holding. In time the sons as a whole inherit the farm. To provide for this situation there is the usual female infanticide. But women apparently do not resent the situation by any means. An Indian writer in the nineteenth century reports a Tibetan wife as saying 'In Tibet the house-wife is the real lady of all the joint earnings, and inheritance of all the brothers sprung from the same mother, who are all of the same flesh and blood. The brothers are but one, though their souls are several. In India a man marries several women who are strangers to each other.' [32] Certainly a very reasonable point of view.

Tibet presents a picture of a society which has adjusted its type of marriage to the economic condition of the individuals participating in the pattern. In other words the majority of the lowest economic group tend to be polyandrous, the middle section favour monogamy, and the rich nobility indulge in polygyny.

In Europe there appear to have formerly existed limited forms of quasi-polyandry. For example, according to Plutarch the Spartan law allowed an impotent husband to engage a substitute to produce an heir. In addition a Spartan man who wished to have children but had no desire to marry could, with the consent of a husband, use the latter's wife for the purpose of producing children. [33] *The Laws of Manu* (IX, 59) also gave permission for a substitute to be employed in the same circumstances. Both Xenophon and Polybius state that fraternal polyandry existed in Sparta. [34] The employment of a substitute when the husband is impotent occurs in old German custom. [35] It has probably existed all over Europe but has never been given open recognition. Artificial insemination by donor would seem to be the latest variation on supplying a very old need.

What has been called cicisbeism could be regarded as a variant of polyandry. This was the custom which gave public sanction to a wife's lover. Eli Reclus, in his *Primitive Folk* (pp. 66–67), published in the late nineteenth century, states that upper class Florentine women could have the right to claim a lover written into their marriage contract. But it was at the Viennese court in the early eighteenth century that the cicisbeo or acknowledged lover was really given his due '. . . . The established custom is for every lady to have two husbands, one that bears the name, and another that performs the duties. And these engagements are so well known, that it would be a downright affront, and publicly resented, if you invited a woman of quality to dinner, without at the same time inviting her two attendants of lover and husband, between whom she always sits in state with great gravity. These sub-marriages generally last twenty years together, and the lady often commands

the poor lover's estate even to the utter ruin of his family . . .'
Husbands 'look upon their wives' gallants as favourably as men do
upon their deputies, that take the troublesome part of their business off their hands; though they have not the less to do; for they
are generally deputies in another place themselves . . .' [36]

The attitude seems remarkably sophisticated. It is possible to
lament that the custom has not persisted into our own day in which,
of course, exactly the same events take place, but the parties have
to resort to subterfuge to preserve the proprieties.

Another interesting variant of polyandry comes from the Nairs
in South India. The Nairs were of Dravidian stock but have become intermixed with other Indian peoples such as the Tamils.
Originally they were a warrior caste, but in the last century came
to include a variety of menial occupations. Their claim to fame in
anthropological literature rests on the virtual exclusion of marriage as it is ordinarily understood. The young Nair girl, before
puberty, is married to a nominal husband—a stranger. This marriage remains entirely formal and in three days is terminated by a
divorce. The girl is now ready to embark upon her career of love
—for this is what it amounts to. She can take as many lovers
simultaneously as she wishes. The lovers contribute to their
mistress's support by presents and money. But this establishes no
hold over the woman. At any time she may dismiss a particular
lover by returning his last gift. Cohabitation is met by arrangement among the lovers, or by order of precedence in time.
'. . . They cohabit with her in their turns, according to their
priority of marriage (sic), ten days, more or less, according as they
can fix a term amongst themselves, and he that cohabits with her,
maintains her in all things, necessary, for his time, so that she is
plentifully provided for by a constant circulation . . . And all the
time of cohabitation she serves her husband as purveyor and cook,
and keeps his clothes and arms clean . . .' [37]

As regards the children of such unions, authorities from the
sixteenth century onwards have disputed as to whether they were
recognised by individual lovers or not. In any event they were not
fatherless in a social sense, for the mother's brother acted towards
them very much in the way a normal father would.

The apparent virtue of the Nair system is that it provides the
maximum amount of freedom for both men and women; for the

lovers were as free as the woman to enter a number of liaisons simultaneously. The arrangement could be broken by either party at any time. Provided sexual jealousy is kept at a minimum, and the children are adequately cared for it is difficult to think of a more satisfying arrangement for both sexes. As it is the Nair system remains unique. So far as is known it has no counterpart in the world. [38]

Polyandry has not the world-wide distribution of monogamy or polygyny. It appears in fact, in its institutionalised form, to be largely confined to the Indian sub-continent—where it is found in both the south and north—Tibet. There are a few isolated examples in the Pacific area (Marshall Islands).

'Group marriage', the last of our four main categories of marriage, is even rarer in its incidence. The only well authenticated example is that of the people of the Marquesas Islands in the Pacific. Linton describes the Marquesan household '. . . The household consisted of the main husband, the wife or wives, and a series of subsidiary husbands . . . The second husband outranked the other subsidiary husbands and took charge of the household in the absence of the head. He also exercised preferential sexual rights with the wife, either with the first husband's permission or during his absence. In the chief's establishment all the husbands would have certain sexual rights with the chief's wife, but when there were a good many husbands they lived in another house and were called over at the will of either the chief or the wife, and rewarded for good service by a night's pleasures. In theory all members of the household had sexual rights, even servants had access to the head wife if they so wished; actually, the first husband ran things and distributed favours, although it was to his advantage to see that his underlings were sexually satisfied, so that they would work for his house and not wander off with other women . . . The household also included the children of the women, either real or adopted, and old people . . . [39]

Although the Marquesans denied that they practised female infanticide, for such a system to function it was necessary to have a preponderance of males. So that in all probability it was secretly practised. Another feature of some interest is the more extensive rights of the main and second husbands over the wife or wives.

It was formerly suggested that some Australian peoples possessed

the institution of group marriage, notably the Dieri and Urabunna. As recently as 1952 Professor E. O. James in his *Marriage
and Society* (pp 32–34) maintains this view. But from the evidence
it would seem that, while a particular group may have exclusive
sexual rights, within itself, the group is by no means a permanent
union. Amongst the Dieri, while he is in camp, the main husband
has exclusive rights, except at periods of general sexual licence.
But in his absence all those men who stand in 'Noa', that is in a
relationship of spouseship to the woman, can have intercourse
with her. She is a 'Pirrauru' or group-wife to these men, but they
do not form a permanent household as in the Marquesan instance.
A similar pattern is observed amongst the Urabunna.

For the Dieri ordinary marriage is between one man and a
woman, but in addition sexual rights may be extended to those
who have the relationship of Noa to each other. In practice a man
may have several Pirrauru wives, and a woman several Pirrauru
husbands. But the woman can only be the chief wife of one man
at a time. On the other hand the man can have more than one
main wife at a time. A woman, before she can embark on Noa
sexual relationships, must have been married in the ordinary way.

For the Urabunna the rights of access of the men to a particular
woman can only be freely exercised in the absence of her main
husband. When the husband is in camp his permission must be
obtained.

This Australian pattern allows the main household, polygynous
or monogamous, to perform its familial functions, but at the same
time permits extra-marital activity to take place in a socially
approved manner. [40]

The fact that a number of societies, such as the Chuckchee and
Tungu, extend sanction to temporary sexual unions within a
specified group does not indicate the existence of 'group marriage'.
Such extensions are generally found in most polyandrous groups.
But true group-marriage on the Marquesan model remains an
exceedingly rare phenomenon.

Two somewhat exceptional types of marriage deserve to be
considered here. The first concerns the Nuer of the Southern
Sudan. The Nuer are a cattle rearing people who are patrilineal,
that is they trace their descent through the male line. They have a
peculiar institution which Evans-Pritchard has termed 'ghost-

marriage': 'If a man dies before he has married a wife, or if, having married a wife, she does not bear male children (even after his death), one of his kinsmen must marry a wife to his name. Daughters are not regarded as heirs, because à daughter becomes one of her husband's people and her children belong to her husband's lineage . . . The obligation to marry a wife to the name of a dead kinsman is invariably carried out when the dead man has any close kinsmen to interest themselves in saving his name from oblivion. No initiated male (wut) should be allowed to lie in his grave unremembered by his children and Nuer say that if an uninitiated boy dies " after his testicles have fallen", that is after he has reached puberty (juil), he must be married to a wife . . . When asked why they marry wives to dead men the Nuer say that until a man marries and begets children he has not reached full manhood, and that a man desires children who keep his memory green and to whom he can make his wants known in dreams. A ghost likes to think of people asking "Whose son is that?" and being told in reply that it is the son of so-and-so. Thus his name continues on the lips of men. They also say that if the kin of a dead man neglect to provide him with a wife he will haunt them. In discussions with the Nuer on this they almost invariably stressed anger of the ghosts as the sanction for their obligations to dead kinsmen. "The ghosts are bad and if you do not marry them to a wife they will not spare you." A ghost will bring evil upon (cein) the family of a man who fails to do his duty.

'This is a vicarious marriage. The vicarious husband acts as though he were the true husband in the ritual that precedes and brings about marriage, and in domestic duties when he and his "wife" begin to share a house. In his physiological and domestic roles he is husband in all but the strict legal sense . . .' [41] Apparently the Nuer refer to a woman married in this way as the wife of a ghost and the children as children of a ghost. This 'ghost family' consists of a trinity composed of the ghost, his wife, and the man who acts for the ghost, together with the children. [42] There are many families of this kind as many youths die before marriage (owing to constant feuding) and many do not have male children.

The reasons for this somewhat strange marital arrangement are very well defined by the Nuer themselves in the statement quoted above 'that a ghost likes his name to be invoked as a father', etc.

Nuer 'ghost marriages' are one solution to the problem of ensuring the perpetuation of a man's name if circumstances has denied him male children of his seed.

A somewhat different conception of marriage from that of the Nuer 'ghost marriage' is found amongst certain Siberian tribes, notably the Buryat, Yakut, Chuckchee, Koryak, and Kamchadal. The religion of these peoples is Shamanism. A 'shaman' is an individual who acts as an intermediary between a man and the spirit world. A characteristic of the shaman is the ability to have epileptic fits, either genuine or simulated, during which he communes with the spirit world. There is an extensive spirit world, part good, part evil. Spirits which combine both good and evil are called Kelets, and it is they who compel a man to become a shaman. One of the most extraordinary features of Shamanism is its ritual homosexuality. The Kelets are homosexual.

A Kelet will adopt the role of husband to a homosexual shaman and more rarely that of a wife to one who has retained his normal sex. This activity is not confined to spirits, for both men and women shamans enter into homosexual relationships with humans. But in all cases this is in obedience to the commands of the spirits. It appears that this is a fundamental of Shamanism as it appears in those tribes whose culture has least been corrupted by foreign influence.

Amongst the Chuckchee the change of sex is called 'soft-man being': transformation entails changes of clothing and occupation. In rare cases the 'soft-man' begins to feel himself a woman, seeks for a lover, and sometimes marries. Such unions appear to be as durable as others. 'The 'man' goes hunting and fishing, and the 'woman' does domestic work. Opinion differs as to actual sex activity. Some writers maintain they practise sodomy, others that they have mistresses in secret and produce children by them.

Each 'soft-man' has a special protector among the spirits who plays the part of a supernatural husband, the Kelet husband of the transformed one. Sometimes the untransformed shaman has a Kelet wife in addition to his own. The spirit is held to be of a physical nature as traditions exist of Yakut men shamans bearing children or animals.

Not every shaman, however, is a homosexual, but there is a real tendency for them to become so. Other perversions, if homosexuality be a perversion, occurs amongst these people, but homo-sexuality is the only one which has been an object of magical worship.

But curiously enough ordinary or non-shamanic homosexuality is severely disapproved in these societies; it is only tolerated as part of the shamanistic character. In fact public opinion is really against these shamans, but as they are very dangerous they are not opposed and so outward objections are not made.

Exception has to be made of one people, the Kamchadal, amongst whom homosexual men, not necessarily shamans, enjoy an even higher degree of consideration than homosexual shamans in the other societies mentioned. This appears to be a blending of worship of the pathological and of the supernatural.

These societies are unique in their elevation of the epileptic and homosexual to the position of intermediary with the spirit world. [43]

Marriage in one of its varying forms having been achieved the individual is faced with the ultimate problem: where shall he live? In most societies there is no choice. If the society is matrilineal, that is, traces descent through the female line, he will reside in or near the household of his wife's people. This is known as matrilocality. There are a few exceptions to this rule. For example the Yukaghir of Siberia are patrilineal but practise matrilocality. Matrilocal residence inhibits polygyny, except where the man marries sisters. If, on the other hand, the society is patrilineal, in the majority of instances patrilocal residence will be the rule. The distribution of both matrilocal and patrilocal residence is world-wide.

Marriage is necessary for the regulation of sexual life and stability in society. What form it takes and what regulations govern the aspirant to matrimony are dependent upon the culture of the particular society. There is no scale of values against which to measure the merits and demerits of different forms of marital union. They must be viewed solely in the context in which they occur.

REFERENCES AND NOTES

1. R. Linton, *The Study of Man*, New York 1937, p. 173.
2. A. Radcliffe-Brown, *Three Tribes of W. Australia*, J.R.A.I., Vol. XLII, London 1913, p. 156.
   B. Malinowski, *The Family amongst the Australian Aborigines*, London 1913, pp. 36 *et seq.*
3. W. Jochelson, *The Yukaghir and the Yukaghirized Tungus*, publication of the Jesup North Pacific Expedition, New York 1908, Vol. IX, Part I, p. 93.
4. S. F. Nadel, *The Nuer*, Oxford 1947, p. 219.
5. C. G. Seligman, *The Melanesians of British Guinea*, Cambridge 1910, p. 363.
6. M. A. Czaplicka, *Aboriginal Siberia*, Oxford 1914, p. 117.
7. P. E. Goddard, *Life and Culture of the Hupa*, University of California Publication in American Archaeology and Ethnology, Berkeley 1903, Vol. I, No. 1, p. 56.
8. B. Malinowski, *The Natives of Mailu*, Trans. Royal Society, South Australia, Vol. XXXIX, Adelaide, 1915.
9. Isaeus, *Oratio de Pyrrhi Levititate*, para. 51.
10. 'Laws of King Aethelbert' in *Ancient Laws and Institutes of England*, London 1840, Ch. 77, and R. Wright, *A History of Domestic Manners and Sentiments in England during the Middle Ages*, London 1862, pp. 55–6
11. For discussion of particular aspects of this topic in Europe see F. Pollock and F. W. Maitland, *The History of the English Law before the time of Edward I*, Cambridge 1898.
    R. Sohn, *Das Recht*, Weimar 1875.
    H. Maine, *Ancient Law*, London 1905.
    J. Grimm, *Deutsche Rechtsallerthümer*, Leipzig 1899.
12. Sir Henry Maine, *op. cit.*, p. 186.
13. E. Doutté, *Magie et Religion dans l'Afrique du Nord*, Algiers 1909, p. 560.
14. A. R. Radcliffe-Brown, *The Social Organisation of Australian Tribes*, Oceania Monographs, No. 1, Australia 1931, p. 95.
15. O. Raum, *Chagga Childhood*, London 1940, pp. 167–75.
16. For a review of hypotheses concerning incest prohibitions see 'The Definition and Prohibition of Incest', by L. A. White, *American Anthropologist*, Vol. 50, 1948, pp. 416–35.

17. B. Malinowski, *Crime and Custom in Savage Society*, London 1932, pp. 77–84.
18. G. Gorer, *Himalayan Village*, London 1938, pp. 317–8.
19. C. Arensberg and S. T. Kimball, *Family and Community in Ireland*, Cambridge, Mass. 1940, pp. 107–14.
20. B. Malinowski, *Article on Marriage*, 14th ed. Ency. Brit., Vol. 14.
21. R. Linton, *The Study of Man*, New York 1937, p. 181.
22. E. S. C. Handy, *The Native Culture of the Marquesans*, B. P. Bishop Museum Bulletin No. 9, 1923.
    R. Linton, 'Analysis of Marquesan Culture' in *The Individual and His Society* by A. Kardiner and R. Linton, New York 1939.
23. Lloyd Warner, *A Black Civilisation*, New York 1958, p. 5.
24. Lloyd Warner, *op. cit.*, 2nd ed., New York 1958, pp. 72 and 77.
25. C. Du Bois, *The People of Alor*, Minneapolis 1944, pp. 110–11.
26. C. Du Bois, *op. cit.*, pp. 111–2.
27. R. Peristiany, *The Social Institutions of the Kipsigis*, London 1937, pp. 73–5.
28. R. Linton, *The Study of Man*, New York 1934, p. 183.
29. W. H. R. Rivers, *The Todas*, London 1906, pp. 515–7.
30. G. Gorer, *Himalayan Village*, London 1938, p. 171.
31. R. Linton, *The Study of Man*, New York 1934, p. 183.
    C. H. Desgodins, *Le Thibet d'aprés la correspondance des missionaires*, Paris 1885, p. 244.
    F. Kingdon Ward, *The Land of the Blue Poppy*, Cambridge 1913, p. 57.
32. Sarat Chandra Das, 'The Marriage Customs of Tibet', *Journal of the Asiatic Society of Bengal*, Calcutta 1893, Vol. LXII, Part III, p. 161.
33. Plutarch, *Vita Lycurgi*, XV, 9 and 10.
34. Polybius, *Historia*, XII, 6 to 8.
34. Xenophon, *Lacedaemoniorum respublica*, 1, 9.
35. Otto von Gierke, *Der Humor im deutschen Recht*, Berlin 1876, p. 56.
36. Lady Mary Wortley Montagu, *Letters and Works*, London 1861, Vol. I, p. 244 *et seq.*
37. A. Hamilton, *New Account of the East Indies*, in Pinkerton's *Collection of Voyages and Travels*, London 1811, Vol. VIII, p. 375.
38. There are numerous writers on the Nair, among them A. Hamilton (see 37 above).
    D. Barbosa, *Description of the Coasts of E. Africa and Malabar in the*

beginning of the 16th century. Translated by H. E. J. Stanley, London 1866.

James Forbes, *Oriental Memoirs,* London 1813.

J. N. Bhattacharya, *Hindu Castes and Sects,* Calcutta 1896.

39. R. Linton in *The Individual and his Society* by Linton and A. Kardiner, New York 1939, p. 155.

40. B. Spencer and F. J. Gillen, *Native Tribes of Central Australia,* London 1899.

41. E. E. Evans-Pritchard, *Some Aspects of Marriage and the Family among the Nuer* in Rhodes-Livingstone Papers No. 11, pp. 5–6. Northern Rhodesia 1945.

42. *ibid. op. cit.,* p. 7.

43. M. A. Czaplicka, *Aboriginal Siberia,* Oxford 1914.

CHAPTER VIII

Marriage Rites and Ceremonies

ONE of the distinctions between marriage and illicit sexual unions is the publicity which is given to the one but not the other. Publicity might be said to be one of the main objectives of marriage ceremonies. By observation, knowledge and participation, the community is given notice that a wedding has taken place. The ceremonies, as well as fulfilling this primary purpose, are concerned with a great variety of particular aims, ranging from the avoidance of spiritual dangers to ensuring the fruitfulness of the union. Clearly what occurs is that the values attached to the institution of marriage in a particular society are brought out and emphasised by the rituals associated with the wedding.

In all societies, but particularly in those at the pre-literate level, marriage is a time of crisis. Such a crisis is not only concerned with the marital pair but with their families and the community in general. As we saw in the last chapter, marriage is not only the affair of the two people directly involved but may be concerned with complicated financial transactions, between the two families. The aspect of crisis is reflected again in the fears attached to the formation of a new family unit. The couple at marriage change their former status. Just as at initiation they cease to be children, so at marriage they enter into a new life with new responsibilities. In the wider sphere of the community a marriage is a matter of concern to all. In essence it is the method through which the community itself is perpetuated. Marital relationships therefore tend to be controlled and regulated by the community. The seal of approval is given on the one hand by the marriage contract which establishes the legal aspects of the union; and on the other by the spiritual ratification of the union.

Malinowski sums it up in this way: 'In reality marriage is the most important legal contract in every human society, the one which refers to the continuity of the race; it implies a most delicate and difficult adjustment of a passionate and emotional relationship with domestic and economic co-operation; it involves the co-habitation of male and female, personally attracted and yet in many ways for ever incompatible; it focuses in a difficult personal relationship of two people the interests of wider groups: of the progeny, of their parents, of their kindred, and in fact of the whole community . . .' [1]

It is against this background of crisis, readjustment, change and responsibility that we have to consider the, at times, amazing variety of marriage rituals and ceremonies throughout human society.

The factors like crisis, which we have mentioned above, find their expression in ritual. In a small minority of human societies, however, such expressions are at a minimum. This is the case in some groups which exist at the subsistence level such as the Australian Aborigines, the Bushmen of South-west Africa, and the Eskimo.

The Australians with their complicated system of social relationships do not have a wedding ceremony in the ordinary sense of the term. It could be said that the rite of female circumcision takes its place. After this has been performed, the woman has sexual connection with the group of men who have sexual rights over her. This concluded, she joins the man designated as her husband and they set up a joint household. It is possible to suggest that as the individual in the Australian system has a limited choice of possible brides this, together with daughter-exchange and infant betrothal, renders elaborate notifications in the form of ceremonies unnecessary.

The attitude of many groups of Eskimo towards marriage is essentially realistic. Divorce is easy and frequent, but despite this children are well cared for. The ease with which the marriage bond can be broken, in many instances the man has merely to tell his wife to go home to her own people, is reflected by the simple way in which the joint home is created by the mere fact of its establishment.

Similarly the Bushman bridegroom merely goes off with his bride-to-be. When they return to the village they live together as man and wife.

Such people as these, however, are exceptional in their apparent indifference to the ceremonial of marriage. To the vast majority of human communities marriage is an event which demands appropriate celebrations.

It is convenient to make certain divisions in the extraordinarily variegated pattern of marriage rites. One very large group consists of those rituals of a magico-religious nature which fulfil a protective or propitiatory function. Possibly rites which are specifically religious, such as those which bestow blessings on the couple, and those which symbolise the sacramental bonds of marriage, should be included in this category. Another group is made up of ceremonies which symbolise the union of the couple by various means: eating, drinking, the exchange of rings, and so on. A third section covers the achievement of material objectives, such as fertility in the woman, economic prosperity, and the consummation of the marriage. Lastly there are those rites which symbolise change of status, such as mock abductions and sham fights. No doubt many other categories could be cited, but those quoted cover the major types of ceremonies.

As we have said such divisions are largely a matter of convenience. The danger in creating too precise an array of categories is that the meaning of particular rites may have changed in the course of time. In addition, many rituals are in fact the result of emotion and feeling rather than logical thinking. People very often perform actions for which they cannot give a satisfactory reason. Our understanding is not helped by inventing logical reasons where none originally existed. It is also as well to bear in mind that rites such as those we are discussing are often capable of more than one meaning or interpretation.

Two elements, symbolic reluctance of the bride and her family to the change of status involved in marriage, and sexual modesty are involved in the staging of sham fights and abductions. It was mistakenly thought in the past that these wedding episodes represented survivals of ancient 'marriage by capture'. The latter has been practised in a number of societies, not as a normal method of obtaining wives—it is too strenuous for that—but as a by-product of warfare. Some examples will make clear how change of status and modesty are symbolised.

Amongst the Banyankole of East Africa the bridgeroom is accompanied to the hut where his bride awaits him '. . . He takes her right hand and leads her from the house and out of the kraal to the assembled guests. A strong rope is produced by one of her relatives and tied to one of the bride's legs. Sides are then chosen by members of the bride and bridegroom's clans and a tug-of-war takes place. The bride's clan struggle to retain their sister, and the bridegroom's clan strive to carry her off. During this contest the bride stands weeping because she is being taken from her old home and relatives; it is the correct thing to do. The bridegroom stands by her, still holding her hand, and when the final pull is given in his favour he slips the rope from her ankle and hurries her away a few yards to a group waiting near with a cow-hide spread on the ground. The bride sits upon this and the young men raise her up and rush off with her in triumph to the bridegroom's parents' house, chased by friends and relatives . . .'[2] This tug-of-war indicates very effectively the apparent reluctance of the woman's family to lose her to another group. Her maidenly modesty is demonstrated by her tears which are as obligatory on this occasion as they are in funeral rites.

The pattern exhibited by the Roro of New Guinea is somewhat different, and in some ways more dramatic. In his absence, the partisans of the groom approach the bride's parents' house with great clamour: '. . . The bride rushes out and runs away as fast as she can, and although she is soon overtaken and caught, she defends herself to the best of her ability, with hands, feet and teeth. Meanwhile a sham fight rages between the adherents of the bride and bridegroom. In the midst of the commotion is the bride's mother armed with a wooden club or digging stick, striking at every inanimate object within reach and shouting curses on the ravishers of her daughter. Finding this useless, she collapses weeping for the loss of her child. The other women of the village join in the weeping. The girl's mother should keep up the appearance of extravagant grief for three days, and she alone of the girl's relations does not accompany the bride to her father-in-law's house . . .' [3]

Genuine regret obviously may enter the picture—the tears may be real—but it is mainly a ritual occasion. This is clearly brought out in the following account of an African people, the Nuba: '. . . In Heiban the last step of courtship—or first step of the marriage ceremonial—takes the form of a (conventionalised) capture of the bride . . . the bride in Heiban continues to sleep in the girls' hut till the day of the "capture". Warned by her mother the girl knows what to expect, though neither mother nor daughter know previously when to expect it. One morning, when the girl is as usual working in the field, the bridegroom collects four or five friends, all young men and mostly unmarried, to go out and kidnap the bride. All is done most realistically: there is a genuine struggle, the bride, aided by her girl friends, will fight tooth and nail and resist as best she can. Eventually the men will chase away the other girls, haul the kicking bride up in the air, and carry her off to the house of her future mother-in-law. There the girl spends the day, ostensibly reconciled to her fate. But the same evening she will be taken back to her own mother's house, from where she will be finally married. This last turn proves convincingly the conventional nature of this marriage by capture . . .' [4]

In some societies this particular aspect of wedding ritual is not so heavily emphasised. This type of struggle may, however, involve disadvantages for the groom. For example amongst the aboriginal Gonds of Orissa in India, the bridegroom carries his bride on his back from her village to his own. His male friends act as a body-guard which is very definitely needed. The entourage is subject to a running attack by the girl friends of the bride who use sticks and stones to bombard them throughout the journey. On reaching the groom's village the hostile female host is driven off, and all is well. [5]

It is not always the case that the bride's modesty is greater than the groom's: the Andamanese bridegroom is generally very shy at his wedding and his friends are always ready to stop him in case he runs away. At one point in the ceremony he is conducted to his bride and made to sit on her lap—the formal method of greeting in the Andamans—and it is at this juncture that he may run off. [6] There is no mimic battle as part of the wedding celebrations amongst these people. On the other hand the real or apparent reluctance demonstrated may symbolise the importance with which the Andamanese regard the entry into the married state.

Sham fights and abductions are by no means confined to the pre-literate peoples. There are numerous European examples (in Russia, Yugoslavia, Finland, Greece). A direct parallel of the Malay custom of barring the path of the bridal procession by means of a rope or cloth is found in many European societies. In Italy this is known as *fare la barricata* and in Holland as *keeren*. Before the barrier is withdrawn the bridegroom has to pay a ransom. This practice appears to be a substitute for actually fighting for the bride. Similar instances are reported from Gloucestershire in England, and from Wales. In Scotland, Ireland, and Wales of the eighteenth century, sham fights and pursuits were common at peasant weddings. In Wales, the bridegroom on his wedding morning formed a posse of his friends; they asked for the bride to be delivered up to them but the request was treated with scorn. A mock battle between the partisans of the couple then followed. Then the bride mounted behind a near relative and galloped off. The groom and his friends pursued them until exhaustion set in and he was allowed to 'capture' his bride.

Crying, as a symbol of modesty and of the fear of exchanging virginity for the married state, is a fairly common phenomenon in our own society. Tears are not, of course, obligatory as in those instances already cited, but many people feel that they are most appropriate on such occasions. Both the mothers (especially the bride's mother) of the couple are also approved of if they weep. This becomes ironical if the match is the result of protracted scheming on their parts. Female tears are expected at many European weddings. Peasant belief in Germany carries this a stage further: the weeping of the bride is regarded as essential to her future happiness. 'She who cries not before, must cry afterwards.' In parts of Russia and Yugoslavia there was a similar belief.

One other type of custom seems to belong to this category of wedding rites. This is the substitution of a false bride for the real one. The pattern is for the groom's party to be given a disguised girl in place of his betrothed. After the bridal procession has gone some way the girl throws off her disguise and runs away; the procedure may be repeated several times. It is a custom found amongst the Beni-Amer of North Africa. In Europe some type of substitution was practised amongst many peasant groups. For example the Transylvanian bride hid behind a curtain with two married women and the groom had to guess which was his bride. Breton custom dictated that there should be a succession of substitutes beginning with a little girl and finishing with the grandmother. Amongst the Estonians the somewhat strange practice obtained of the bride's brother, suitably dressed, impersonating the bride.

A possible explanation of such practices of simulated abductions and crying is that they demonstrate the internal solidarity of the opposing groups, and the antagonism inherent in any social situation which is one of crisis and change.

In a very different category are those rites the purpose of which is to achieve some positive objective, such as the breaking of the hymen.

A number of customs observed at weddings appear to have as their object to facilitate consummation of the marriage: 'Among the Aith Yúsi, a Berber tribe south of Fez, after the bride has been painted with henna, an egg enveloped in a kerchief is tied round her forehead; it is then broken by the women who painted her, and is left there till she is washed. This is done in order that her hymen shall be broken by her husband as easily as was the egg. Next morning she is washed with water containing some henna, while seated on a weaving-stool and a pack saddle—on the former because when she was a little girl she was, in accordance with the customs of her tribe, taken three times underneath the two upper cross-bars of a weaving-stool after the web was ready, in order that no man should be able to destroy her virginity, and the magical effect of this procedure must naturally be cancelled before her wedding . . .' [7]

Egg-breaking is commonly used to symbolise the breaking of the hymen. It is found in Persia, Java and Bali. In Europe, in seventeenth century France and contemporary Sicily, eggs were trodden on by the bridal couple before they entered their new

home. As a symbol at weddings eggs possibly have several signi-
ficances, but when they are broken immediately prior to the act
of consummation there is little doubt as to the meaning.

The breaking of fragile objects in general seems to serve much
the same purpose. Pottery and glass articles are favourites. These
may be broken by the guests as in some parts of Morocco, or by
the bridegroom as in America. Amongst the Zulu the bride breaks
a spear. The Matabele bride crushes a calabash. European practice
in peasant communities is very similar, glasses and pots being
broken in Scotland, Yorkshire, Germany, Czechoslovakia and
Yugoslavia. The Jews have traditionally had the breaking of a
glass at the wedding ceremony. This is performed either by the
officiating rabbi or by the groom. It is in the Serbian practice,
however, that the meaning of the symbolism is most openly
expressed. The bridegroom's father late at night at the end of the
wedding feast leads the bridal pair to their room. The door is
closed. He then toasts the couple with a glass of wine and throws
it at the door. When this is done the guests with tremendous noise
attempt to break an egg which has been placed in a sack. This
symbolises the consummation of the marriage. [8]

The cutting of cords and the untying of knots are tokens of the
same type as the breaking of objects. In parts of Morocco the
bridegroom before he copulates has to undo seven knots in his
bride's knickers. [9] This is paralleled by the Roman custom of the
bridegroom having to undo the 'Herculean knot' in the bride's
girdle before he achieved his desire. [10]

One of the commonest of symbolic ways of inducing fertility is
the throwing of some kind of seed over the bridal couple. In our
own society we are familiar with confetti—clearly a substitute for
corn—and with rice which are thrown at the couple. It is doubtful
however, whether the well-wishers know the real purpose of their
actions! Grain throwing is found all over Europe, in India, Siberia
and the Far East. In some instances the meaning is made explicit.
For example, in pre-revolutionary Russia the clerk at the wedding
after sprinkling hops on the head of the bride said he hoped she
would be as fruitful as they were. In Sicily peasants say that if
barley is thrown this indicates the birth of boys, and wheat the
birth of girls. The classical Chinese practice of placing nuts and
fruits at the four corners of the marriage bed was said to indicate

the coming of fruitfulness of the bride. Similarly the Christian Maronite custom of the bride being pelted with corn and raisins is indicative of the hoped for fruitfulness of her womb. In the Shetland Isles it was formerly the practice for the mother of the bride and other female relatives to go to meet the bride, taking with them a broken cake of seeds and sugar. This was scattered over the girl's head. [11]

The symbolism of fertility in the use of seeds can be extended from the womb to material prosperity in general. This seems to be the case in many societies. It is a very good example of the duality of this type of symbol. The connection between the seed germinating in the earth and the sperm germinating, as it were, in the womb is obvious. In the same way the idea of the seed growing in the earth symbolises the growth of prosperity, For in peasant societies prosperity is equated with good crops. To produce healthy children is to ensure prosperity by means of their work, and so on—there are a great number of analogies.

Promotion of the woman's fertility and the achievement of material prosperity may depend upon the aversion of evil. The symbolic offerings of grain, rice, fruit and nuts have also a propitiatory purpose. Thus seed throwing or its equivalent may have a trifold function. All or any can be present according to the particular social context. Long ago the danger was pointed out of assuming that similar rites in different societies had an identical function. Nevertheless there is a great deal of evidence to suggest that in a great number of societies seed throwing has the functions we have attributed to it.

A custom which has a far less wide incidence, and seems to be quite specific, is the handling of a little boy by the bride, or his actual presence in the bridal bed, in order to induce fertility. In classical India, amongst the Masai, and the Suk of East Africa, a child, prior to the couple retiring on the wedding night, is placed on the lap of the bride. Amongst some Muslim communities of Eastern Europe a boy is rolled to and fro on the bed before the couple appear. In Sweden the bride should spend the night before her wedding with a boy in her bed. The symbolism is quite clear. The presence of the boy will induce others to be born.

Eggs and fish are other articles which are used in a variety of ceremonies in many different societies for securing the fruitfulness of the bride's womb, and the future prosperity of the family.

The object of this type of ceremony is undoubtedly to produce material benefits. This is shown in the rites to promote mutual good behaviour in the couple. For example in Eastern Europe, Rumania, Bulgaria, Rhodes and Sparta, honey is smeared on either the bride or groom's face or lips that they may become as sweet as it is. In Sparta the doorway is also covered with honey so that the couple will not quarrel. [12] The relationship desired for the couple is seen in those rites which demonstrate the authority of the husband. In Morocco the husband may tap the wife several times on the head with his sword, or smack, or kick her gently. In Slav countries it was the custom for the bridegroom to give his bride a symbolic beating; later she would pull off his boots for the first time. The antithesis of this is seen in those customs in which the wife asserts her authority over her husband. This is typified by the struggle of the bride at German peasant weddings to have her hand uppermost when the priest joins the hands of the couple. Similarly in Sweden and Finland the bride attempts to place her foot in front of the groom's during the ceremony. These and similar rites to achieve mastery in the home, and to promote happiness within it, have definitely material and desirable objectives.

One of the most important categories of wedding ceremonies is that concerned with emphasising the union, the new bond which has been created between the couple. The most obvious is that of the use of rings to symbolise the union. The incidence of the ring for this purpose is very widespread. It is found in India, East and Central Africa, as well as in Europe. The exchange of rings, common in Southern Europe, replaced the ancient Teutonic custom of breaking a coin—each half being kept by the bride and groom. There is no need to expatiate on the symbolism of the ring as representing unity.

Unity can be demonstrated in other ways. The joining of the hands is almost as common as the use of rings in a number of societies. It is prevalent in Ethiopia, New Guinea, India and Burma, as it was in classical Rome and, of course in Christian Europe. What is not so common is when the symbolic unity of clasping hands is carried a stage further. In Portugal and in parts of Eastern

Europe the priest ties the hands of the couple together with his stole. The practice also occurs in South India, while the Parsees use a frail twine for this purpose. In Ceylon a chain is used. Amongst an aboriginal tribe in that country, the Veddas, a piece of string is tied by the bride round the groom's waist. The string is regarded as an important symbol of the union and the husband keeps it all his life. [13] Heads may be symbolically knocked together, as occurs amongst some of the Negrito tribes of the Philippines, to achieve the same purpose. Perhaps the most curious 'joining' rite is that of some Chinese communities where the couple's hair is tied together, thus demonstrating their future inseparableness. [14]

The unity of the couple can be shown in more subtle ways: the practice of lovers exchanging tokens, presents, or articles of clothing is extremely common; the more extreme custom of complete exchange of clothes at weddings is fairly rare. Transvestism, that is the adoption of the clothing of the opposite sex, is an extremely complex subject. Various explanations have been given in the past as to its meaning in different contexts and it covers a far wider field than marriage rites. There are, for example, associations with magic—the idea that to produce a change in nature, man must change his own nature. Ritual homosexuality and changes of status are also concerned with transvestism. But our concern is with its apparent purpose in connection with wedding ceremonial.

Amongst the East African Masai the bridegroom has to wear the clothes of his wife for a month after the wedding. According to Mary Kingsley, a similar custom prevailed amongst some West African peoples. There is no indication, however, that the bride dressed up as a man. [15] On the other hand, the bride in ancient Sparta lay on her couch, dressed in the cloak and shoes of a man, awaiting her husband. [16] Similar instances can be quoted from eighteenth century Wales, and from European countries, where the bride is dressed as a man. [17] It is possible that the symbolism in such cases is not only concerned with the sacramental union of the couple but has supernatural connotations. It is difficult to be dogmatic with this type of custom which has so many possible interpretations.

The use of blood in marriage rites is similar to its function in creating blood brotherhood—people who are not related are brought into a special relationship either by the mingling of their

blood or by drinking each other's blood. The marriage rite may
be quite dramatic. In parts of Brittany the bride, after the church
ceremony, cuts herself beneath her left breast. Her husband then
sucks some of the blood. [18] Some tribes of Bihar in India have the
custom of mingling the couples' blood in food which is then eaten
by them. The couple may, however, merely be smeared with
blood, as occurs in Bengal. The importance of such ritual is that it
emphasises the union in an unmistakable manner.

Eating and drinking at the wedding feast again expresses the
unity of the couple. Commensal rites, as they are called, have a
wide field of application in demonstrating the union of those
concerned.

The eating together by the bride and groom in some instances is
the only rite performed at a marriage. This was so for the Navaho
and Pawnee Indians of North America. The bride prepared some
food with her own hands; she and the groom ate this together, and
they were then regarded as man and wife, with no further ceremony.

A simple meal is prepared for the couple amongst the Berbers of
Southern Morocco. The groom tries three times to push some of
the food into the bride's mouth. She in bashful play tries to stop
him. Then in turn she does the same thing to him. [19] This type of
ritual eating is found in a considerable number of societies in New
Guinea, Malaya, Fiji, India, and South-east Asia, as well as in
European communities (Italy, France, Switzerland, Germany,
Sweden, Russia). In the same way the ritual of drinking together
is equally widely distributed, being found in Brazil, Polynesia,
India, and Indo-China. The couple either exchange drinking cups
or use the same vessel. This last is the form which is popular in
many European countries.

The meaning of the ritual becomes plain in both the classical
Chinese custom, and that which obtained in Russia prior to the
Revolution. In classical China the couple ate a part of the animal
sacrificed at the wedding. They then drank out of cups made
of halves of the same melon, drinking from each other's half.
'They now formed one body, were of equal rank, and pledged to
mutual affection.' [20] The ritual of the Russian Orthodox Church
contains directions for the priest to mix wine and water in a silver
ladle. This is held to the mouths of the bridal couple who take

turns in sipping it three times, 'That the husband and wife must share everything in joy and grief.' [21]

If marriage is a matter of concern to the whole community it is necessary that the wedding should be given proper publicity. At its simplest, it may be the mere announcement by one or other of the couple that they are to take a spouse. This was formerly done by the bride amongst the Maoris. Similarly a simple declaration was the only requisite for marriage among the Kubus of Sumatra. In many societies a more elaborate form requiring witnesses is obligatory. The Sunni Muslims require a minimum of two witnesses, the Parsees five, and for Patrician marriage in classical Rome ten witnesses as well as the officiating priests were necessary. For a civil marriage in contemporary Europe and America only two witnesses are required. Sometimes the required publicity is obtained by the presence of an official such as the chief or headman or, in our case, a registrar. But there are examples where public proof of the sexual consummation of the marriage is necessary. This may entail the performance of the initial sex act in front of the wedding guests, as occurs amongst the Bantu Kavirondo. A little more privacy is assured by the Koita of New Guinea: the Koita bridegroom informs the bride's mother that he is prepared to marry and 'That night the bride prepares a sleeping mat for the bridegroom, who now comes to her publicly, before the house is quiet for the night . . .' [22] In Europe this type of publicity given to the union is not unknown. Up to the eighteenth century in Germany, in many communities, a marriage was only held to be legally valid when proof was forthcoming from witnesses that the couple had been in bed under a blanket. The Slav peoples tend to insist on the newly married going to bed in front of witnesses. This also obtained in Southern Sweden where, in addition, up to the end of the eighteenth century, the couple were undressed before the invited guests. [23]

Probably the most general form of publicity is the wedding feast, which is found in all types of societies all over the world, from the most simple to the most advanced. This has the advantage of not only celebrating the union of the couple, but of creating new bonds, and reinforcing old ones which existed between the two families and the representatives of the community in which they live.

As we have said, marriage is a time of crisis and danger for the couple: they are to enter a new state of happiness, but there are forces which will try to prevent this. Thus we find that a large category of rites of a magico-religious character is concerned with the protection from and the propitiation of evil forces or spirits. Evil may be outside or external. Again, it may reside within the bride and be a danger not only to herself but to others. This danger must be destroyed by purification, symbolic purging, or assault.

The most obvious symbolism employed is that of firing guns over the heads of the bridal pair to ward off or destroy evil spirits. This is the case in West Africa, Siberia, Morocco and was formerly so in Sweden, Germany and England. Elsewhere, arrows are a substitute for guns, as in classical India and China.

A far more important aspect of such ceremonies is that which is specifically religious. The classical civilisations of India, Greece and Israel all demanded the presence of a priest or priests: the function of the priest was to make a sacrifice and implore a blessing on the couple from the gods. This created a sacramental bond between them and, at the same time, warded off evil influences. In ancestor worshipping societies, like many in Africa, offerings or sacrifices are made to the ancestral spirits who are implored to accept the newcomer to their ranks. These sacrifices establish the bond of the bride with the groom's clan and, at the same time, the union is blessed. Elsewhere, amongst the Parsees and in Tahiti, God is invoked for his protection and blessings. In all such societies the priest is clearly acting as an intermediary between the couple and the spiritual world. If the marriage is to be successful he must sanction and approve it.

Christian Europe up to the Reformation tolerated the existence of non-sacramental marriage *without* the blessing of the priest. There is no reference in the Gospels to the forms of marriage. According to Tertullian the Church did not actually forbid unblessed marriages, but disapproved of them. [24] The dogma of the sacramental nature of marriage based on St Paul's views developed slowly over the centuries and was only fully recognised by the twelfth century. However, it is not until the Council of Trent in 1545–63 that the Church laid down that a valid marriage had to be celebrated by a priest in front of witnesses. It is as well to remember that current Roman Catholic doctrine still maintains the view that it is not the priest who marries the couple, although he administers the sacrament—it is the couple who actually marry each other. Thus if a Catholic couple were deprived through circumstances of the ministrations of a priest it would be perfectly proper for them to live as man and wife providing their intention were genuine, and they sought out a priest to bless the union as soon as it was possible to do so. [25]

The Reformers such as Luther, Calvin and Melanchthon had

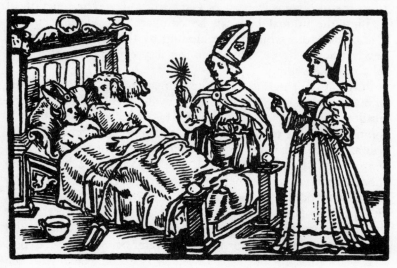

Fig. 12. The blessing of the nuptial bed

clear-cut views about the non-sacramental nature of marriage. Due to their activities, helped by such political events as the French Revolution, marriage in the Protestant countries began to lose its religious connotation, so that in the contemporary Protestant Western World civil and ecclesiastical marriages have equal validity at law. In this, Europe follows Muslim and Jewish tradition. In neither does the absence of a rabbi or mullah invalidate the marriage. Religious blessing is left to the discretion of the partners. [26]

The nuptial mass and the blessing constitute the core of Roman Catholic ceremony today. But prior to the Reformation in England the priest had other functions: 'On the evening of the wedding day when the married couple sat in state in the bridal-bed, before the exclusion of the guests who assembled to commend them yet again to Heaven's keeping, one or more priests, attended by acolytes swinging to and fro lighted censers, appeared in the crowded chamber to bless the couch, its occupants, and the truckle bed, and fumigate the room with hallowing incense . . .' [27] This practice apparently obtained all over Roman Catholic Europe and even lingered on in Protestant Norway until the seventeenth century; it still obtains in parts of Germany today. The function of blessing the nuptial bed can be compared to another current Catholic custom which is the blessing by the priest of a new or newly bought house. This exorcizes any evil spirit which may inhabit the dwelling.

Purification, particularly of the woman, forms a necessary part of many marriage ceremonies. Thus bathing, as symbolic of purification before the actual wedding, becomes an important preliminary. This is true in Morocco and amongst some Bedouin tribes. Hindu India also recommended a bath for the bride. The Parsees insist that both the bride and groom take a bath in the morning and afternoon before the marriage. The custom of the bridal bath occurs in classical and modern Greece and in Slav Europe. The Rumanian peasant bride had to bathe in running water in the summer, but in the winter she was excused what would have been an exercise in fortitude, the water being brought to her.

A somewhat curious type of rite is that connected with the disguising of the couple. The object here appears to be to distract the attention of the evil spirits and, possibly, in some cases, to neutralise the danger of initial sexual intercourse.

A good example of the latter type occurs amongst the Tamil Brahmans of South India. On the fourth day of the wedding ceremonies the bride dresses up as a boy and, in company with another girl dressed as the bride, they process through the streets. On their return the false bridegroom insults the real bridegroom, the latter being addressed as a servant. He may be treated as a thief—the false bridegroom passing judgment on him. [28] Presumably the evil spirits are deceived by these manoeuvres and the marriage can then proceed in the normal way. There is another explanation—that transvestism of this kind decreases the sexual dangers which are associated with marriage—to change your sex symbolically destroys the power of the opposite sex because you become identified with it. Similar practices in Morocco, Israel and Denmark to the one quoted bear this out.

Individuals other than the couple may impersonate them and thus draw the evil (which to them is harmless) on themselves. This occurs amongst the Somali of East Africa, in Northern India, and in some European countries.

The Somali custom follows this pattern: the couple are confined in the nuptial chamber; in the house seven unmarried young men and seven young women are married in pairs in mock fashion; the pseudo-wives have now to obey their pseudo-husbands; the couples may exchange clothes: 'The girls dress up their partners, using padding to make the disguise as complete as possible; and then, assuming all the airs of husbands, they flog their partners with horsewhips and order them about in the same manner as they themselves had been treated by the young men . . .' These proceedings go on for a week. At the end of the week payment is made to the impersonators by the bridegroom. [29]

The European pattern is somewhat different. Usually in the Slav and Teutonic countries when the bridegroom or his friends call for the bride a false bride is given to them. This 'bride' may be an old woman, a little girl or even a man suitably disguised. The idea of the pseudo-bride in Europe is admirably discussed by G. M. Godden in 'The False Bride', *Folklore*, Vol. IV, (1893). The idea is exactly the same as in the Somali case—to distract attention from the bridal couple. The reasoning is that evil spirits will always attack those about to enter great happiness—they must be diverted. There are, as we have said, other customs where transvestism takes place, such as those concerned with priestly function. The purpose of exchanging clothes in that context is quite different.

Substitution of this kind is sometimes carried a stage further to include the inanimate or animal.

Tree-marriage occurs in classical Greece. At the festival of Daedala an oak, selected by divination, was cut down and dressed up as a bride; the tree bride was then taken in procession. This ceremony was apparently traced back to the mock marriage of Zeus to an oak. [30] The counterpart of this ceremony is found in Hindu India. In some parts of India if the bridegroom's 'stars' form a stronger constellation than the bride's it is thought advisable that she should first marry a peepul tree (*ficus religiosa*). In the North West Provinces amongst the Gadariyas if a girl's hair resembles a snake (is curly) she has to be married to a thorn bush before she can marry a man. The snake evil which she is thought to possess will be vented on the bush rather than her proper husband. These are instances of ordinary substitution. But there are other circumstances in which tree-marriage may be necessary. For example in the Punjab a Hindu cannot be legally married a third time but may marry a fourth time. The law is got over by making him marry a Babul tree (*acacia Arabica*) as his third wife. He is then free to marry for the fourth time. In the same area if a man keeps losing his wives through 'accident' or illness he must marry a bird before he embarks on ordinary matrimony again. Tree-marriage is also practised in Madras for similar reasons. The custom there forbids a younger brother to marry before an elder. If the elder is no great catch through physical or other defects, the younger may have to wait a long time. To avoid this situation the elder brother marries a plantain tree with due ceremony. The priest then cuts down the tree which is mourned by the family in the appropriate manner. As the elder brother is now widowed the younger can get married.

Other instances occur in North-west India amongst aboriginal tribes, where the bridal couple have to clasp a tree or are tied to it. This brings in the concept of transferring the fertility of the tree to them. This is paralleled in the Yugoslav customs of the bride dancing three times round an apple tree to which her veil has been tied. A pitcher of water is placed under the tree into which money is at first thrown. Then the girl kicks over the pitcher.

Among certain groups of people other objects may be used as substitutes for a bridegroom. Thus dancing girls in Goa are married to daggers before they take up their activities. In the same way Indian courtesans who are daughters of courtesans marry flowering house plants. They look after their vegetable husbands and when they die mourn them appropriately. Amongst the Gonds of Bastar if a woman's husband has been killed by a tiger and she wishes to remarry she must first be formally married to a dog or a weapon. The Gond belief is that the former husband's spirit has entered the tiger and will try to kill the new husband. Now he will either carry off the dog or be killed by the weapon.

It is of some interest to note that tree-marriage occurs amongst

Hindus whose religion is firmly based on metempsychosis, or the transmigration of souls through the animal and vegetable world. [31]

Another protective custom which is common in Europe and America as well as in China, Israel, and Egypt, is that of veiling the bride, or covering the bridal couple. In classical China an old woman who had borne many children held an umbrella over the bride. The canopy under which the couple are married is used in synagogues and Orthodox Christian churches. A deviation from the canopy, a piece of cloth, used to be held over the bridal couple at the benediction in both Catholic and Protestant Europe. European veiling of the bride is clearly connected with this. The contemporary use of swords or rifles to form an arch under which the bride and groom pass after the ceremony serves the same protective purpose—to guard against danger from the heavens. A similar custom was that of the miners of Fifeshire in Scotland; formerly an arch of green boughs was held over the bridal couple as they made their way to the kirk. [32]

Evil may come from the earth as well as from the heavens. This accounts for the very widespread practice of the bride, and less frequently the groom, being conveyed to the wedding ceremony so that she or he does not touch the ground. This occurs in Morocco, Germany and Finland. Groom and bride may be carried, as happens amongst the Indian tribes of San Salvador and Guatemala, and aboriginal tribes of Bengal. In Cyprus the groom arrives either on horseback or is carried on the crossed arms of his friends. Covering the floor may serve the same purpose: a number of different peoples cover the approach to the groom's home, as do the Yugoslavs or the Greeks of Epirus. In Britain the red carpeted steps of the church are a familiar sight. A charming old Kentish custom at Cranbrook was to strew the path of the couple when they left the church with symbols of the groom's profession. For a carpenter there were wood shavings, for a butcher sheep skins, for a shoemaker bits of leather, and so on. [33]

Allied with the practice of covering the ground is that of carrying the bride over the threshold. This has a much wider incidence, however, being found in classical Rome, China, Egypt, Greece, France, Germany and Britain. There is no doubt that the threshold itself is associated with spirits and thus is dangerous. The carrying of the bride over it may be a simple prophylactic against its inherent dangers. In some cases, for example, in Wales and Scotland, this becomes explicit. It is possible there are other and more recondite explanations: 'Why do they not permit the new-married woman herself to step over the threshold of the house, but the bridegroom lift her over? What if the reason be that they, taking their first wives by force, brought them thus into their houses, when they went not in of their own accord? Or is it that they will have them seen to enter into that place as by force, not willingly, where they are about to lose their virginity? (Plutarch, *Questiones Romanae*, 29). As we saw, marriage by capture was a dubious method of obtaining wives, so that perhaps more emphasis should be placed on Plutarch's second suggestion. [34]

To canopies and veils may be added the practice of throwing shoes. The provenance of this appears to be mainly European—though in the past in Turkey the bridegroom had to battle his way through a positive storm of shoes to reach the nuptial quarters. It is a custom which is found in Britain, Denmark, Germany and classical Greece. It can be equated with the former practice in the same countries of throwing a shoe or slipper after a person who goes on a journey. In connection with weddings it is probably an additional form of protection from evil influences. Various suggestions have been put forward as to the origin and exact meaning of shoe throwing but none of them is very satisfactory. [35]

There are positive advantages to be gained for those who participate in weddings. There can be benefits which are quite unconnected with the event being celebrated. In Morocco the bride when offered a bowl of milk dips a finger in it to taste a few drops, then blows on the rest so as to impart a magical quality to it. It can now be used mixed with other milk as a charm against witchcraft or to make butter plentiful. The bread or dried fruit used to throw over the couple is collected by people to put under their corn on the threshing floor as this will benefit them. The Moroccans also insist on viewing the blood-stained sheet after the marriage has been consummated. When this occurs individuals wipe their eyes on the dried stains, as this is believed to be most beneficial to the eyes. [36]

The principal advantage, however, to be gained from eating or wearing something of the bride's is in promoting your own wedding; this is fairly common throughout Europe. The Breton bride

gives away the bread and butter given to her; the recipients eat it
in the hope that they will be married within the year. There was
the Northumbrian custom of the wedding ring dropped into a
posset. The unmarried girls rushed to see who should discover it
—the winner being the first to get married. There were many
other similar practices which utilised stockings, pieces of veil, and
clothing. Perhaps the most widely spread is that of sleeping with
a piece of wedding cake under the pillow so that you dream of
your future husband.

The dispensing of the bride's token may not always be unorganised. Swedish girls are married in a crown or coronet: at one
stage in the proceedings the bride is blindfolded; the unmarried
girls dance round her; the bride now takes off her coronet and puts
it on the head of a girl. This is the one who will be first married.
The latter places it on the head of another girl and so on until in
turn everyone has been crowned. Then the bride is chaired and
drinks a toast to maidens that they may soon become
brides. [37]

Another fairly common practice in Europe is for the bride to
kiss or be kissed by all the men present. [38] But any contact with
the lucky one is regarded as being auspicious. Such customs show
that although the couple must be protected from evil they can
bring good fortune to others.

A fairly general belief is that there are times when evil spirits are
less active than others. Thus we find in a number of societies,
almost all Europe, India, China, Burma, Ceylon, Japan and Indo-
China, certain days and months are to be avoided. For example,
in Italy, Greece, France, Scotland and Germany, to marry in May
was regarded as singularly unlucky. This is summed up by the
Scottish saying 'O marriages in May Bairns in decay.' [39] The
antithesis is also found in that some months are considered lucky.
The waxing of the moon is a time to be chosen amongst the Swedes,
in Germany and in Burma. This leads to fruitfulness. Days of the
week are the subject of local superstitions—every day being regarded as unlucky somewhere. For example in seventeenth century France the belief was that a Wednesday marriage ensured the
groom becoming a cuckold; Italians avoided Fridays and Tuesdays
as days when evil was about; whereas for the Germans Tuesday
was a favourite day. The Sabbath, whether Christian or Muslim,

was above suspicion. The choice of day seems to be largely a matter of local caprice and fashion.

If it be granted that bride and bridegroom are about to enter a new, special, and holy state it seems reasonable to expect some form of abstinence to be exercised before the consummation of the marriage. This agrees with the fairly widespread idea that for any major change or event man should prepare himself mentally and physically in order to combat evil influences. Thus in many societies certain restrictions are placed on the couple prior to, during, and after the ceremony.

The keeping of silence is one typical form of abstinence. For example silence is imposed on the bride at the wedding ceremony in Morocco. Sometimes partial silence is obligatory until the birth of the first child, the wife being forbidden to speak to anyone with the exception of her husband. This is the practice in Armenia and among some Caucasian tribes such as the Ossetes. Albanian custom forbids the wife to converse with the husband in front of other people until a child is born. Similar customs have been reported from parts of East Africa and Yugoslavia. Various explanations of the ban on speech for women at this time do not appear to be satisfactory. Sir John Frazer discusses these at length, but ends his exposition with the statement that we do not yet understand the motivations behind this practice. [40]

Continence for a long or short period after the wedding is of frequent occurrence in a number of societies. This may take the form of abstaining from coitus on the first night or two subsequent nights, as amongst the Baganda and Bayankole of East Africa. North American Indians extended the period of continence to a considerable length of time. The Thompson Indians of British Columbia abstained for four nights after the marriage, the Nootka for ten nights, and the Tlingit for as much as a month. Some cases were even reported of continence for as long as a year. [41] Similar periods of continence occur in Melanesia, Australia, Indonesia, Burma and India. The orthodox Hindu was enjoined, 'For three nights they shall eat nothing pungent or seasoned with salt; they shall sleep upon the ground and preserve chastity ... On the fourth night a food offering is to be made and the marriage consummated . . .' [42] Apparently, according to Hindu tradition, the longer the time of abstinence the more favoured the child that was eventually born. A year's continence practically guaranteed the birth of a god. The obverse of this is seen in the disregard of a similar prohibition in the Ragnar-Lodbrok Saga where King Ragnar refuses to postpone his pleasure. The child born, 'was loveless and as though there was gristle where the bones should be . . .' [43]

Mediaeval Christianity also ordained abstinence for three nights after the wedding—the so-called Tobias nights. The Fourth Council of Carthage in A.D. 398 enacted that consummation was to be postponed until the night after the marriage. [44] Later enactments extended the period to three nights. The basis for this appears to be the story of Tobias as it is given in the Vulgate, the Roman Catholic version of the Bible. The three nights were set aside for the devil, Asmodeus, who if given these would not further troub the bridegroom as he does in the story.

'. . . Now it happened on the same day that Sara, daughter of Raguel, in Rages a city of the Medes, received a reproach from one of her father's servant maids, because she had been given to seven husbands, and a devil named Asmodeus had killed them, at their first going in unto her . . .' Later on in the story Tobias asks for the hand of Sara: '. . . Now when Raguel heard this he was afraid, knowing what had happened to those seven husbands, that went in unto her: and he began to fear lest it should happen to him also in like manner: and as he was in suspense, and gave no answer to his petition, the angel said unto him: Be not afraid to give her to this man, for to him who feareth God is thy daughter due to his wife: therefore another could not have her . . .' Tobias then burns some liver on the fire which the angel orders him to do . . .' Then the angel Raphael took the devil, and bound him in the desert of upper Egypt, Then Tobias exhorted the virgin (*sic*) and said to her: Sara, arise, and let us pray to God today, and tomorrow, and the next day: because *for these three nights* we are joined to God: and when the *third night is over*, we will be in our own wedlock . . .' The story goes on to tell how Sara's father does not really believe that Tobias will survive the ordeal of being married to Sara, so he prepared a pit for his body which he fills in with great rejoicing when he finds his new son-in-law alive. [45]

The traditional period of abstinence persisted in European peasant populations up to the eighteenth and nineteenth centuries. It has been reported from Alsace-Lorraine, Brittany, Italy, Germany, Estonia, Scotland and Switzerland. It has been suggested that the church was merely grafting her injunctions on to a very old pagan belief. This is a view advanced by Sir James Frazer in his *Folklore in the Old Testament* (London, 1919, Vol. 1). Looking at the variety of cultures which have rules of nuptial continence, Westermarck argues for a differentiated origin in individual cases. [46] He maintains that there is a common Muslim belief that evil spirits may slip into a woman while she is copulating—the result may be a child who is a villain. [47] This is in line with the adventures of the unfortunate Sara with the demon Asmodeus. The Muslim belief is paralleled in Indian tradition that devils were apt to behave in this unseemly fashion.

But whatever reasons may be developed for nuptial continence, and there are many, as we have seen, looking at it today it seems to have quite a sound psychological basis. The experienced man who marries a virgin would be well advised to indulge in continence for a period. The result of such restraint is beautifully described by Jules Romains in his novel *The Body's Rapture* [48] which is the story of a couple who develop an overwhelming physical relationship.

We have not attempted to describe all the infinite multiplicity of marriage rites—clearly impossible in a single chapter—but rather to indicate some of the more significant trends in the pattern. The following accounts of weddings seem appropriate at this juncture.

The Kwoma, a New Guinea tribe, have the minimum of ceremony attaching to their weddings: 'A Kwoma weds soon after he becomes adult. Adolescent courtship, culminating in the trial marriage in which the girl comes to live with the boy's parents, is finally terminated, if all goes well, by a special ceremony which makes the couple man and wife. The boy's mother determines when this ceremony shall take place. If she is satisfied with the girl and knows that her son is also, she tells her to cook the food for the afternoon meal. Hitherto the betrothed has cooked food only for herself, and the boy's food has been prepared by his mother or sisters. The mother chooses an occasion when the boy is away from the house, so that, when he returns, he begins eating his soup unsuspectingly. When he has nearly finished his first bowl, his mother informs him that it was his betrothed who cooked the meal and that he is now married. At this announcement, it is expected that the boy will rush from the house and exclaim as he spits out the soup: "Faugh! It tastes bad! It is cooked terribly." ' (49) Thus the Kwoma are married; simple but effective.

Arrangements are very different amongst the Nuer, a tribe of the Nilotic Sudan: '. . . Marriage amongst the Nuer is brought about by payment of bridewealth and by the performance of certain ceremonial rites . . . The chief ceremonies are the *larcieng*, the *ngut*, and the *mut*: the betrothal, the wedding, and the consummation . . .' After the betrothal ceremony which consists of part payment of the bride price of cattle, made in ritual fashion, and which is an occasion of general feasting and dancing, the wedding takes place some weeks later: 'Both sides want to complete the marriage without undue delay. The bridegroom's people want their wife and the bride's people want their cattle so that they themselves can marry . . .' Thus preparations are made. 'The main features of a wedding are discussions about cattle in the morning and the invocation over the cattle of the bridewealth (*twoc ghok*), and the wedding dance, and the wedding sacrifice, in the afternoon and evening: '. . . While the discussions are going on in the cattle byre, the youth of the bridegroom's village charge into the homestead, chanting and skirmishing as they come. They rush the kraal and the bridegroom hurls his spear at his mother-in-law's *buor*, (a mud windscreen) while the girls of the bride's village attack the visiting youths in mock combat and try to catch the bridegroom and seize his wedding stick. If they succeed he will have to pay them a calf . . . The bridegroom may also throw a spear into the threshold of the byre. This goes to his father-in-law . . .' People begin to arrive and wish the dance to begin and it will go on the whole of the afternoon, half the night, and begin again the next morning.

When the dance begins, or a little before, the ritual of receiving the bride-wealth is performed. The bride's ancestors are called to bear witness that she is married openly with such and such number of cattle, and that she will bear her husband a male child. Offerings of tobacco are made to God (*Gwandong*).

'Towards sunset or on the following morning, the wedding ox provided by the bride's father, is sacrificed by the master of ceremonies or a senior kinsman. He rubs ashes on its back and speaks to it, saying: "We do not kill you for an evil thing, we kill you about a good thing," . . .' The greater part of the meat is divided and distributed by the bridegroom between the relatives on the father's side and mother's side.

'. . . A large part of the night is spent in dancing and flirting and love-making, The bride and the girls of her homestead are cooking while the bridegroom, who is fasting, is seeing that his companions are being properly looked after. On the following morning beer is served, pots being distributed to the bridegroom's kin . . . who share the beer with members of their age-sets. After a meal the youths resume dancing and their elders, fortified with beer, probably start once more on the seemingly endless cattle talks . . .'

The third public ceremony, the *mut* (consummation) is the one which generally makes the union legally binding. The day has to be prepared for, since beer has to be brewed. At dawn on this day the bridegroom and his male friends, chanting, go to fetch the bride. They may find that the bride's mother has prepared beer for them. It is necessary for them to ask her permission to take her daughter, and she asks for presents such as a spear or tobacco. These are given her and the bridal procession of youths and girl companions of the bride suitably bedecked sets out. They chant poems on the way, which are frequently in praise of the groom. There is a great deal of horse play among them. Near the village the boys go on ahead. Young men now come out of the bridegroom's village and lead them to the kraal where they serenade the groom's mother: '. . . After a while a kinsman of the bridegroom places a tethering-cord across the inner threshold of one of the huts and the bridegroom crawls over it, followed by the bride, the best man, and a special girl friend of the bride. This action is said to make the marriage fruitful. Then, towards evening, takes place the rite of consummation. '. . . The bride retires to a hut wearing a special goatskin cap and here the bridegroom joins her. His age-mates seek him out and say to him: "Come now, let the people go to bed, come and loosen the bride's girdle." He is bashful and gets the business over as quickly and inconspicuously as he can. He enters the hut and gives his bride a cut with a switch and seizes her thigh, she refusing his advances and crouching by the wall of the hut. He strikes her with a tethering-cord, snatches the cap off her head, breaks her girdle, and consummates the marriage. Reluctance is imposed on her by custom and she pretends to resist even when she has known her husband before in the gardens. It is not expected that a bride will be a virgin . . . His duty done, the bridegroom leaves the hut, sometimes the bride's girl friends rushing at him and beating him with their fists as he emerges. The rest of the evening is given to the favourite pastimes of Nuer youth *muong* and *lum* visiting with the girls and making love to them . . .'

The next morning certain obligatory rites have to take place; the sacrifice of the ox, if this has not already occurred, the lustration and shaving of the bride's head. The 'cow of the consummation' may be an ox, a goat, or merely beer depending on the financial state of the groom's father—the wedding at this stage has already cost him a great deal. The ancestors of the groom are invoked by his master of ceremonies, ' "Now you see your ox; you are this maid; let her be a good wife; let her bear many children, many sons, let her work well in her husband's home, milk the cows, dry the cattle dung, let her be a faithful wife and not a profligate." . . .' The ox is then speared and cut up by the bride's people and divided in the customary fashion. After this the bride may be anointed with butter by the master of ceremonies.

This is followed by the lustration. The bride's girl friends sit in a hut with a pot of warm water. A girl washes her hands in the water and then drops a bracelet she is wearing into the pot and she then passes the pot to one of the husband's relatives outside. He washes his hands and retrieves the bracelet. The whole process is repeated by all the maidens with all the close kinsfolk of the husband. 'Any person who can claim kinship with the husband can demand a bracelet. If a man's dip into the pot reveals a poor bracelet he does not hesitate to upbraid the girl who put it there and he may select a better one from those on her arm . . .'

The last ceremony is the shaving of the girl's head by a member of the husband's family. This may be done privately, as it is essentially a family matter. The rite denotes a change in her status. It is spoken of as 'the removal of the hairs of maidenhood'. The wife now takes off all her ornaments which are distributed amongst her husband's kinsfolk, and she is dressed anew in finery given by her husband: 'She belongs to his, and not her father's people now and it is for them to adorn her . . .'

Although this is the end of the wedding ceremonies the marriage is not regarded as a proper one until a child is born. The couple continue to lead their separate lives as before, the husband visiting his wife in pretended stealth at night. They do not set up house together. This does not happen until a child has been born and weaned. After this the husband builds a hut for his wife in his father's homestead facing the family kraal. Now they are a fully fledged married couple: 'She comes to her husband's home not as a wife but as a mother whose breasts have suckled a child of their lineage . . .' [(50)]

A Japanese village wedding is a very different sort of affair: 'Marriage is primarily a social and economic arrangement between two families. A friend of the family, frequently a woman, is asked to act as a *naishōkiki* (secret finder out) when the family feels a boy is of the right age to marry. The job of the *naishōkiki* is to find a suitable girl, that is suitable from the point of view of 'family', etc. Elaborately casual arrangements are made for the couple to meet by chance. If they dislike each other, no more is done. If they are mutually attracted matters proceed. The next step is to select a *nakaudo*, a go-between. It is he who takes over from the *naishōkiki*; arranges the wedding, and performs the marriage ceremony.

The nakaudo is generally a prominent member of the community. Preparations have to be made well in advance of the wedding—a kitchen may have to be done up for the bride to work in, and the wedding clothes and trousseau must be ready. The day has to be chosen carefully so that it is a lucky one. There is great excitement on the day before the ceremony, and on the following morning. The feast has to be got ready, and all the womenfolk have to have their hair elaborately dressed. In the morning relatives start arriving, the women first, to help in the house—they do not participate in the banquet, only greet the guests. Male relatives arrive later on and behave as guests—not helping. Everyone brings their formal clothes to change into at a later stage. Gifts, specially wrapped, are bought, of clothes, fish and kaés (rice wine). The latter is brought in red lacquer buckets. The fishman prepares the banquet food. He arrives early with elaborately decorated gift boxes, and a great deal of fish.

'Her hair done up and decorated with a special set of pins, the bride has her bath and is finally dressed in her very formal kimono, her elaborate coiffure covered with a white piece of silk (*tsunka-kushi*, the "horn concealer"), a traditional purse containing a mirror, pin, and crystal ball, and a fan tucked in her very wide and very tight belt . . .'[51]

The groom's party consisting of the groom, his parents, the go-between, and his wife who takes charge of the bride, now arrive. They have with them presents of saké, tea, and rice cakes for the bride. They first drink a cup of tea, then the gifts are accepted by the bride's mother who places them in the corner where the other gifts and the trousseau are set out.

The banquet begins when the bride's male relatives come to the house. The banquet is an extraordinary meal as all the various fish soups and other foods are only tasted. So much so that after this and the banquet which follows at the groom's house, an ordinary meal has to be served to the guests. Saké is drunk, however. Now the whole party complete with gifts is loaded into a hired bus which proceeds to the groom's house. Before the same ritual (complete with banquet) which took place at the bride's is gone through the marriage ceremony, the *san-san-ku-do*, is performed.

The couple are taken into a separate room and the go-between directs the proceedings. This is the marriage ceremony of the 'three-three-nine times drink': '. . . Two children pour out the saké in three small pours from a special container into a tier of three cups, one on top of the other. First the groom has a drink out of the smallest cup, then the bride, then the same is done with the second and the third cup. Drinks are also exchanged between the bride and the groom's father; and there are also exchanges with the nakaudo and his wife. A small serving girl brings in some dried seaweed and cuttlefish of which a small amount is handed to each to be wrapped up in a tiny piece of paper and put away . . .'

Now follows a ceremony the significance of which has apparently been forgotten: a small strip of dried fish in a red and white paper folded in a special way is given to the groom's father; it is called *Noshi*. The nakaudo declares 'the noshi has been received'.

At the banquet which follows, the bride is present but the groom stays in a back room until near its end. Formality is the rule, all

sitting on their heels, until he comes in. The end of the banquet is
indicated by a serving girl taking round fish (presented by the
bride) together with a special cup of saké. The bridegroom's father
then declares that the ceremony is over. Now everyone can relax.
People move about, the bride changes into a kimono from her
trousseau, and the women guests change into gayer informal
clothes. Singing and dancing begins, drinks are exchanged, and so
on. At this juncture some young men with their faces covered by
towels bring in a stone (god) Jizō which has some obscene verses
pasted on it. They demand shōchū (pickle and rice). They then put
down the Jizō and go into the kitchen where they are given some.
This is said to keep the bride from running away. Some days later
on the Jizō is back in his proper place beside a path, and decorated
with a new bib by the bride.

A great deal is drunk and broad jokes made about the couple;
men and women dance in an abandoned way; games are played
and there is great merriment. Extreme formality marks the open-
ing stages of a wedding—it ends with complete informality. The
party lasts until eleven or midnight. After the guests have been
served with supper and rice, they are ready to go home. Now the
bride, as hostess, will serve tea made of the two measures brought
to her by the groom and with the groom's family will come to the
gate to see off her parents. Thus she assumes her role of daughter
in the new household . . .' (52)

It is noticeable that in the case of the Nuer who see life in terms
of cattle, the wedding ceremonies accentuate, in terms of the ox
sacrifices and the bridewealth of cattle, the social significance of
these animals. In contrast the Japanese villager whose life depends
on fish and rice emphasises these (saké is rice spirit) in his wedding
ceremonials. The point we wish to emphasise is that marriage ceremonies embody the cultural values inherent in a particular society.

The formality of the Japanese can be contrasted with the orgiastic element in Bánaro weddings.

The Bánaro live on the banks of the Ceram river in New Guinea.
On reaching puberty, Bánaro girls have to get married: they do
this in sets of four according to clan relationships in association
with a system of daughter exchange. For about nine months prior
to this the girls are imprisoned in a cell in their family house and
fed on sago soup; on the day of their marriage they are released,

and as they come out they are pelted with coconuts by the women and pushed into the river. When they emerge they dress and are decorated with various bits of finery. This is the signal for a dance of the women to begin. But it is in the evening that the wedding 'ceremonies' really get under way. The men collect together in the village and decide how to distribute the girls amongst them. It is done in this way: the groom's father should really deflower the bride but he feels 'ashamed' to do this so he requests his clan friend, his '*mundu*', to act for him. This being agreed upon, the girl's mother hands her to the groom's father saying that he will conduct her to the goblins. The goblins of the Bánaro are a kind of tutelary deities. The girl is taken to the goblin hall and told to go in. The mundu is already there waiting for her. He takes on the role of the goblin and he leads her to the place where the big bamboo pipes are hidden. These pipes are of great significance in the ritual life of the Bánaro. Women are absolutely forbidden to look at them—to do so is to die. In front of the pipes the mundu deflowers the girl. The mundu then leads the girl outside to where the groom's father is waiting to take her to her mother's home. He slinks off by himself as he is said to be 'ashamed' to meet anyone. The bridegroom's father returns to the goblin hall, for now it is his turn to deflower a girl, the girl being his mundu's son's bride. So the process continues with the other two girls.

While all this is going on the bridegrooms are being kept in a special house and watched by their mothers' brothers. This sexual ritual in fact concludes the marriage. For the groom is not allowed to copulate with his bride until a child is born. When this happens the mother says, 'Where is thy father? Who had to do with me?' The groom answers, 'I am not his father, he is a goblin-child'. Her reply, which seems appropriate, is: 'I did not see that I had intercourse with a goblin'.

By the time the child is born the groom should have finished building a house. The couple move into this without further ado and are accepted as a proper married couple by the community. The sexual rights of the fathers over the brides does not cease after marriage but are exercised on special, solemn occasions in the goblin hall. (53)

The unfortunate Bánaro bridegroom does not appear to figure in the wedding ceremonies at all. But we should remember that for these people to get married in any other way would be unthinkable.

Each culture in the world has developed its own unique way of achieving the enduring union between the sexes which we call marriage. The function, as we have tried to point out, is everywhere the same. The means adopted are infinitely various.

REFERENCES AND NOTES

1. B. Malinowski, Article on 'Marriage', *Encyclopedia Britannica*, 14th ed., Vol. 14, p. 945.

2. J. Roscoe, *The Northern Bantu*, Cambridge 1915, p. 120.

3. C. G. Seligman, *Melanesians of British New Guinea*, Cambridge 1910, p. 268.

4. S. F. Nadel, *The Nuba*, Oxford 1947, pp. 111–12.

5. S. C. Macpherson, *An Account of the Religion of the Khonds in Orissa*, London 1852, p. 55.

6. A. R. Radcliffe-Brown, *The Andaman Islanders*, 2nd Ed., Cambridge 1933, p. 74.

7. E. Westermarck, *Marriage Ceremonies in Morocco*, London 1914, p. 232.

8. L. Rejacsich, *Das Leben, die Sitten und Gelräuche, der in Kaiserthume Osterreich lebenden Sudslaven*, Vienna 1873, p. 161.

9. E. Westermarck, *op. cit.*, p. 232.

10. S. Festus, *De verborum significatione quae supersunt*, ed. C. O. Müller, Leipzig 1837, p. 63.

11. G. F. Black, *Country Folklore, Orkney and Shetland Islands*, London 1903, Vol. III, pp. 209 *et seq.*

12. J. Piprek, *Slawische Brautwerbungs—und Hochzeitsgebräuche, (Ergänzungsheft. X [zu Band XX] der Zeitschrift für oesterreichische Volkskunde)* Stuttgart 1914, p. 144.

13. C. G. and B. Seligman, *The Veddas*, Cambridge 1911, p. 97.

14. Y. K. Leng and L. K. Tao, *Village and Town Life in China*, London 1915, p. 107.

15. Mary Kingsley, *West African Studies*, London 1901, p. 131.

16. *Lycurgus*, XV, 48.

17. T. Moore, *Marriage Customs*, London 1814, p. 37.

18. F. C. Conybeare, 'A Brittany Marriage Custom', *Folklore*, London 1907, Vol. XVIII, p. 448.

19. E. Westermarck, *op. cit.*, p. 258.

20. *The Li Ki*, translated by James Legge, Oxford 1885, ix 3; xli, 2, p. 258.

21. H. C. Romanoff, *Sketches of the Rites and Customs of the Greco-Russian Church*, London 1869, p. 204.

22. C. G. Seligman, *The Melanesians of British New Guinea*, Cambridge 1910, p. 77.

23. N. L. Nicolovius, *Folklifvet i Skytts Härad in Skane, vid början af detta arhundrade*, Lund 1868, p. 144.

24. Tertullian, *Ad uxorem*, ii, 9 in J. P. Migne, *Patrologiae Cursus*, 1.1415 *et seq.*, Paris 1844–64.

25. For a discussion of the development of Christian marriage see *Christian Marriage*, G. H. Joyce, S.J., London 1933, Ch. III, pp. 103–45.

26. The views of the Anglican Church on marriage are well expanded in H. Hensley Henson's *Christian Marriage*, London 1927.

27. J. C. Jeaffreson, *Brides and Bridals*, London 1872, Vol. I, p. 98.

28. E. Thurston, *Ethnographic Notes on Southern India*, Madras 1906, pp. 2 *et seq.*

29. J. S. King, 'Notes on the Folklore and some Social Customs of the Western Somali tribes', *Folklore Journal* (1888) Vol. VI, pp. 121 *et seq.*

30. Pausanias, ix, 3.

31. For a survey of tree-marriage in India see W. Crooke, *The Popular Religion and Folklore of Northern India*, London 1896, 2 vols.

32. J. E. Simpkins, *Country Folklore*, London 1914, Vol. VII, p. 392.

33. W. Crooke, 'Lifting the Bride', *Folklore*, London 1902, Vol. XIII, p. 245.

34. The significance of the threshold in folklore is dealt with by H. C. Trumbull in his *The Threshold Covenant*, N.Y. 1896.

35. See J. Brand, *Observations on Popular Antiquities*, London 1888.

36. E. Westermarck, *Marriage Ceremonies in Morocco*, London 1914, pp. 360, 185 and 159.

37. L. L. Lloyd, *Peasant Life in Sweden*, London 1870, p. 27.

38. C. Rogers, *Scotland, Social and Domestic*, London 1869, p. 112.

39. J. E. Simpkins, *Country Folklore*, London 1914, Vol. VII Fife, p. 182.

40. J. G. Frazer, *Totemism and Exogamy*, London 1910, Vol. IV, pp. 233–7.

41. *Jesuit Relations and Allied Documents*, translated by R. G. Thwaites, Cleveland 1896–1901, Vol. XIX, pp. 68 *et seq*, and Vol. XXXVII, pp. 154, *et seq*.

42. Grihya-Sutras, ii, 67, translated by H. Oldenberg, *The Sacred Books of the East*, Oxford 1886–92, vols. XXIX–XXX.

43. A. Edzardi, *Volsunga and Ragnars-Saga, nebst der Geschichte von Nornagest*, Stuttgart 1880.

44. Concilium Carthaginense quartum, 13 in J. P. Migne, Partologiae cursus, Series Graeca, LXXXIV, 201, Paris 1857–66.

45. *The Holy Bible*, translated from the Latin Vulgate, first published at Douai, 1609; *The Book of Tobias*, London 1899, pp. 513–24.

46. E. Westermarck, *History of Human Marriage*, London 1921, Vol. II, pp. 560–1.

47. El-Bukhārī, *Sahih*, LXVII, 66, translated by T. Houdas and L. Marçais, Paris 1880, Vol. III, p. 578.

48. Translation by John Rodker, London 1934, pp. 230–45.

49. John A. Whiting, *Becoming a Kwoma*, Oxford 1941, p. 125.

50. This account is based on that given by E. E. Evans-Pritchard in *Kinship and Marriage among the Nuer*, Oxford 1951, pp. 60–74.

51. Woman, being evil, is supposed to have horns, these are concealed in the bride by the tsunkakushi.

52. John F. Embree, *A Japanese Village, Suye Mura*, London 1946, pp. 151–6.

53. R. Thurnwald, *Bánaro Society, Memoirs of the American Anthropological Association*, Vol. 3, No. 4, 1916. The description of the Bánaro wedding ceremonies is based on the above.

CHAPTER IX

Divorce

MARRIAGE is a necessary means for the regulation of sexual life in society. But if marriage becomes, or is thought to become, intolerable for a variety of reasons, society offers a solution. This solution is either in terms of separation or divorce. Separation in one sense is only a partial solution; it does not leave the partners free to undertake other marital relationships, and thus fulfil their proper roles in the society. Divorce on the other hand is literally the termination of the marriage and thus bestows freedom of action on the two people involved.

The intolerableness of a marriage is not something which can necessarily be left to the discretion of the couple. It may, for example, be considered both in personal and public interest that a marriage be dissolved on the grounds of childlessness. But, as we shall try to show, grounds for divorce vary enormously, from the whims of a spouse to matters which are the concern of the society at large.

Despite the almost world-wide incidence of divorce it should be remembered that in most human societies marriage is regarded as permanent. It is only when what has been described by Linton as

255

the breaking point has been reached that divorce is liable to occur. [1] When that stage comes depends upon the values and beliefs of the particular society. As Linton says the breaking point may be very high as in Britain today; or very low as in some parts of the United States. [2]

There are exceptions to the concept of permanence in marriage. Trial marriages, however, come into rather a different category. They are entered into for a specific purpose—to ascertain the suitability or otherwise of the (generally) female partner, as we have shown in Chapter VI. But a marital union can be based on a temporary contract for very different reasons. The Muslims of the *Shī'a* sect who are found mainly in Persia and Arabia possess a temporary form of legal marriage. This may be contracted for a definite period of time—a day, a week, a month, a year, or a number of years. This is called Mu'tah. No rights of inheritance are created in either party, but children are legitimate and inherit in the normal way. Mu'tah is distinguished from ordinary Muslim marriage in other ways: the husband need not maintain his wife unless this is stipulated in the contract; he may refuse to have children, which right does not exist in ordinary marriage; nor has he the usual Muslim power to divorce his wife at will. On the other hand before the stipulated period has run its course the union may be dissolved by mutual consent of the partners.

This type of marriage possibly arose in order to supply the need of pilgrims going to Mecca. [3] Such pilgrims, many travelling without their womenfolk, are supposed to remain continent throughout their journey. A temporary marriage in Mecca may well have served a useful purpose. At the least it prevented recourse to prostitutes. The *Sunnî*, the other great Muslim sect, do not recognise the legality of Mu'tah in any way.

The utilitarian approach of the Shî'a Muslims to the problem of sexual relations appears to be almost unique. It has been reported in the past that the Eskimo of Ungava in the Hudson Bay region of Canada took wives for a limited period. [4] But the Eskimo practice does not seem to have been institutionalised as it is amongst the Shî'a Muslims. Other cases quoted from the North American tribes may have been confused with the ease of divorce existing amongst such peoples as the Iroquois. Other reputed instances from Indonesia and West Africa appear to be examples of trial marriages.

Societies in which divorce does not exist are comparatively rare. At the pre-literate level the Veddas, an aboriginal tribe of Ceylon, are an outstanding example. They have this proverb , 'Death alone separates husband and wife'. According to the Seligmans, '. . . Anything like a formal divorce is unknown . . .' [5] In the same way the Bahuana of the Congo do not tolerate divorce. Some Indians of the Matto Grosso in Brazil, the people of Chatham Island in the Pacific, the Lisu tribes of Indo-China all maintain the indissolubility of marriage. But when all the instances amongst simple societies are considered the number still remains small.

Roman Catholic societies, that is societies in which Roman Catholicism is the dominant legal and religious force, form the largest group of communities which reject divorce in the ordinary sense. The early Church had debated the possibilities of allowing divorce. The evidence from the Gospels is contradictory. (Compare Matthew V. 32 and XIX. 3). The early Fathers condemned divorce, but it certainly existed for a considerable period on grounds of adultery or fornication. However, by the twelfth century the doctrine was beginning to emerge that a Christian marriage was indissoluble if it had been consummated. This was a view very strongly advocated by St Augustine some centuries before. It eventually prevailed, being asserted as dogma at the Council of Trent, the first post-Reformation Council, in 1545–63. Its dogmatic validity was reasserted by Popes IX and Leo XIII in the nineteenth century. The doctrine here is that marriage, when consummated, becomes a sacrament symbolic of the union between Christ and the Church, and as such is indissoluble. The phrase 'when consummated' is of great importance for it allowed, and allows, a Pope to annul a marriage if unconsummated. Annulment is also permissible when some canonical impediment to the marriage, which may vary from duress to relationship within the prohibited degrees, exists. A notorious case in the recent past was that of the Marchese Marconi, the inventor of wireless. It was held in that instance that the wife had been forced into the marriage against her will. But as Lord Bryce put it—throughout European history the rules concerning impediments to marriage were so complicated and diffuse that almost any marriage could be declared invalid. [6]

Contemporary Roman Catholic societies can be divided into two kinds: the first are those communities where although the Church is predominant in religious affairs the state is secular and opposed to it at many points.

The conflict is not only one between the Church and the State but also between individuals and the Church. In Portugal divorce has been permitted since 1910 but infrequent recourse is had to the law for the reasons we have suggested. In Central America, Guatemala, Salvador, and Costa Rica introduced divorce legislation in the 1890s and Mexico at the beginning of the twentieth century. In all these cases, as well as in the Catholic parts of Germany, it is possible for the practising Catholic to obtain a divorce on grounds established by law but in defiance of the church. In fact few do so with the result that divorce statistics for these societies are amongst the lowest in the world. (See Table II) at the end of the chapter.

The second kind of society is composed of those where there is almost complete identity of interest between Church and State. Examples are Eire, Spain and Malta. In these countries, through the influence of the Roman Catholic Church, divorce does not exist. It is difficult to assess the degree of identity of interest between lay and ecclesiastical authorities. However, it is of interest to note that Brazil, Chile and Columbia also exclude divorce.

As we have stated divorce appears to have been tolerated, if not openly approved, by the very early Church. This developed in time into almost entire disapproval. In contrast to Western Christianity the Eastern or Orthodox Church took a somewhat different view. Most of the Slav countries (Poland is an exception), including Russia, as well as Greece, had as their official religion a form of Orthodox Christianity. The latter appears to have had a much greater identity of interest with the secular authorities. One of the fruits of this union is that divorce has always from the early times had the complete sanction of church and state. Thus divorce laws have existed in the Slav countries of Europe for a long period.

In the West the early Protestant reformers such as Luther and Melanchthon disputed the doctrine that marriage was a sacrament which could be dissolved only by death. Their legacy in this respect is that all the countries where the Reformation was successful today admit divorce as a legal, and sometimes religious, solution to the problem of an unsatisfactory marriage. Though, as we shall see, the grounds for divorce vary a great deal.

England in contrast to Scotland was somewhat out of step with continental Europe in this matter. She has never been sure whether to admit this solvent of marital disunity. The case of Lord Northampton in 1548 (his second marriage after a legal separation was upheld by Parliament) appeared to show that divorce after all was possible. But in 1602 in the Foljambe case the courts ruled that remarriage to another person after legal separation was not permissible. This looked as if England although having a reformed church was destined to follow the strict letter of Roman Canon Law. However, by the end of the seventeenth century the law changed its mind and divorce could be obtained by Special Act of Parliament. (Cases of the Earl of Macclesfield, 1697 and Duke of Norfolk, 1700). This remained the only means by which a divorce could be effected until 1857. [7]

For the spouse who wished to set aside the bonds of matrimony matters were not all simple. First of all, before he could get someone to initiate his Bill in Parliament, he had to satisfy the authorities that he was of irreproachable character, and that he had already obtained a legal separation in the ecclesiastical court. Moreover, his sole ground for petitioning was adultery. For a wife divorce was practically impossible: she had to prove incestuous as well as adulterous intercourse on the part of her husband if her plea was to succeed. The whole procedure was so long and complicated, besides running into thousands of pounds in costs, that it is not surprising that from the seventeenth century until 1857 only three hundred and seventeen divorce bills were passed. The first case of a woman obtaining a divorce by Act of Parliament occurred in 1801.

In 1857 a Court for Divorce and Matrimonial Causes was set up. To it was transferred all the authority of the ecclesiastical courts in matters of marriage and divorce. The dissolution of marriage now came within the scope of the ordinary citizen. But the grounds for a plea were still severely limited. A husband could only obtain a divorce for adultery. A wife's position was even more difficult. If she wished to put forward the adultery of her husband its aggravated character was insisted upon; that is its combination with desertion, rape, incest, sodomy, or bestiality.

Extension to the permissible grounds for divorce had to wait until 1923. In that year Lord Buckmaster's Matrimonial Causes Act was passed. This put the wife on the same level as the husband in that she could now obtain a divorce on the ground of simple adultery. Further reform came in 1937 when Sir Alan Herbert's Act established what is the basis of the present law. From that time a divorce has been obtainable by either spouse for adultery, desertion for at least three years, cruelty, and insanity for at least five years preceding the petition. In addition, the wife alone can proffer charges of rape, bestiality or sodomy against her husband. He cannot retaliate in kind unless he can demonstrate that such practices by injuring his health amount to cruelty. No petition whatsoever may be presented, unless the circumstances are quite exceptional, until the marriage has lasted three years.

The course of events was quite different in Scotland: the Reformation there had been far more radical, and the Church was greatly influenced by the continental Reformers. Thus we find that the courts were granting divorces in the sixteenth century. Far in advance of England by 1573 divorce was allowed for desertion by either partner. The basic ground, again in contrast, was simple adultery by either partner. It is not always appreciated that the legal system of Scotland differs in many respects from that of England: divorce legislation is only one example.

Curiously enough the Matrimonial Causes Act of 1857 did not extend to Ireland. That country continued with the necessity of a Special Act of Parliament to create a divorce, on the same grounds as in England, until the creation of an independent Eire. Today divorce is not permitted at all.

For the average citizen in Britain divorce is now within his economic means. The grounds are, by American standards, still severely limited. But the possibility remains and the statistics grow. Throughout the nineteenth century, and indeed until comparatively recently, an extremely severe social stigma attached to the parties in a divorce suit, particularly the woman, whether innocent or guilty. One's friends were inclined to avoid one, your business might suffer, as might your prospects of employment or promotion. For the woman it might mean, at any rate before 1914, complete ostracism. After two major wars there have been tremendous changes in this respect. In fact there are now only two major disabilities attaching to the ordinary divorced person apart from the barring of the way to ecclesiastical preferment. One is perhaps more important than the other: you cannot apparently obtain a ticket for the Royal Enclosure at Ascot, nor can you apparently be considered as a suitable candidate for the hand of a member of the Royal Family.

Although the law in Britain now gives full recognition to divorce the Church of England continues to exhibit the same vacillation which characterised it in its early centuries. It appears incapable of making a final pronouncement to be enshrined in a canon. Bishops express individual views for and against. The layman is bewildered by the controversy amongst clerics as to whether the guilty party should be allowed to remarry in a church or not: to most people such disputes are essentially academic. The range of opinion in the Anglican Church is so great that there is bound to be some clergyman somewhere who will grant you the sanction of his church.

The United States inherited British canonical reforms. With the emphasis in the American Constitution on freedom it is not surprising to find that all the States of the Union have divorce laws. South Carolina is a paradoxical case: it probably has the smallest Roman Catholic population of any State yet it did not permit divorce until 1948; there must obviously be special reasons for this anomaly. In some States the grounds for divorce are as strict as they are in Britain. For example in New York State it is obtainable only on grounds of adultery. In others it appears as if the merest suggestion of incompatibility will produce the desired result. When the vastness of the country, the number of nationalities which make it up, the great recent period of expansion, and the changing quality and texture of life are all taken into consideration it is not unreasonable to find that the divorce rate in the United States is amongst the highest in the world. All these factors as well as others dependent on premarital sexual habits may affect the durability of a marriage, and in weak marriages the result may be divorce.

The ambivalence towards divorce existing in nominally Christian communities can be compared with attitudes and conditions in pre-Christian Europe. In Homeric Greece divorce appears to figure very little. Some authorities have suggested that it was virtually unknown. [8] But in later periods it became normal practice. Procedure was essentially simple. All that was required was repudiation of the wife by the husband either with or without witnesses. The wife was then sent back to her father's house with her dowry. However guilty she might be her dowry was inviolate. According to Demosthenes an adulterous wife had to be divorced, otherwise the husband was guilty of atimia or infamy. [9] Similarly the repudiation of a barren wife was regarded as a social duty. Clearly this existed for the same reasons as obtain in simple societies —the necessity of ensuring the perpetuation of the community.

From the wife's point of view procedure was more difficult. She had to make a declaration before a magistrate, giving the grounds for her plea. What was more onerous was the fact that no matter how guilty the husband might be the children always remained with him.

The situation with regard to the Romans was much more involved. To begin with they had at least three different types of marriage. The most sacred was known as *confarreatio*: this was a most solemn and binding contract confined to the patrician class. Divorce was possible by means of *diffarreatio*, an equally solemn rite. It is probable that so dreadful were the implications of the dissolution of this type of marriage that it was seldom invoked. A marriage, which gave the wife into the power or 'manus' of her husband could be dissolved at any time at the behest of the husband. The wife appears to have had no rights whatsoever in the matter. However, the Censors (magistrates) and public opinion could, and did, control this authority of the husband if it was flagrantly abused.

The third, and most common, type of marriage was that in which the wife did not pass into the power of her husband. It could be terminated either by mutual consent or by the initiative of either partner. An official statement, a *repudium*, had to be made before witnesses by the partner who was bringing the proceedings. But, and this is of some importance, both husband and wife had absolutely equal rights.

If a marriage took place but the wife remained in the power (potestas) of her father the latter could at any time demand the return of his daughter, and thus dissolve the union. The wishes of the spouses were entirely irrelevant. Legislation at a later stage limited the power of the father by prohibiting his breaking up a happy marriage.

Unlike the Greeks, the Romans were most liberal in their attitude towards children. Their early laws gave discretion to the magistrate to dispose of the children to either parent. Justinian's reforms produced a result very similar to the arrangements under modern British law.

In the early periods of Roman history divorce was not popular. As Rome grew and expanded divorce became more and more fashionable until it reached its peak under the later Empire. Of historical figures we know that Ovid and Pliny the Younger were each married three times; Caesar and Antony had four wives in succession, and Pompey five. This propensity of the Romans for divorce has been attributed to the general decay of morals in the society. This may have been a contributory factor. There are, however, other factors to be considered, such as the general unbalanced state of the society in its latter days. [10] But whatever the incidence of Roman divorce at any given time it is true that for most people living under their dispensation the divorce laws were just and humane.

The classical Hindu attitude towards divorce is similar to that of Roman Catholicism in its later stages. Marriage, strictly speaking, was, and is, regarded as a sacrament which cannot be dissolved. The adulterous wife could be set aside by what amounted to a judicial separation as she could not remarry. The law was, however, considerably modified in practice. It was admitted on certain specified grounds that either party could remarry. For example the husband could divorce a wife who wasted his entire property, procured an abortion, or attempted to kill him. A wife had the same remedy if her husband entered the religious life, became impotent, or was expelled from his caste. But the guidance of the law was contradictory: the Laws of Manu state that a wife given to drink, or who is rebellious, diseased, mischievous, or wasteful may be superseded by another. And in another place they say, '. . . Neither by sale nor repudiation is a wife released from her husband . . .' [11] A potential wife also had to be a virgin. Such anomalies gave all the advantages to the husband.

It was only the Brahmins, the highest caste in Hinduism, who consistently adhered to the letter of the law. Obviously enough, in the vast area of India with its differing local customs considerable variety with relation to divorce is much in evidence. The Abbé Dubois wrote, '. . . A Hindu can only put away his legitimate wife for one cause, and that is adultery . . .' [12] Whereas in South India all castes admit divorce for reasons other than adultery, in some cases by mutual consent. The contemporary Hindu situation can be compared with that of the nominal adherents of the Anglican Church who have the law on their side in this matter, but may run into trouble with their local church.

In direct contrast to Hinduism, Burmese Buddhism does not emphasise the sacramental aspect of marriage at all: it is essentially a civil contract. [13] Such being the case dissolution is comparatively easy: adultery and desertion are common grounds; the disposal of children is in line with contemporary British practice. Altogether the Burmese attitude towards divorce appears extremely enlightened. For whereas divorce itself is easy, the rights of all parties concerned are safeguarded. In this connection a profitable comparison could be made between the relationship of Buddhism and Hinduism, and that between the Reformed Churches and Roman Catholicism in regard to divorce. In both cases the reformed religion (Buddhism can be seen as a reformed Hinduism) has a considerably more permissive attitude towards the dissolution of marriage.

A further point is that although the grounds for divorce in Burma are as wide as in the United States, the incidence is a great deal lower. A possible explanation might be that Burmese society, despite apparent contradictions, is of a much more stable character than that of the United States.

The ancient Semitic peoples all permitted divorce, with a bias very heavily in favour of the husband. The Babylonians according to the Laws of Hammurabi allowed the husband to get rid of his wife at will. If caught in adultery the wife and lover were drowned. A woman who had borne children fared better at the dissolution of the marriage. Her marriage portion was returned to her, and her husband made her an allowance to bring up the children. A barren, divorced woman had both her dowry and marriage portion given back. But the foolish wife '. . . Who has set her face to

go out and has acted the fool, has wasted her house, has belittled
her husband . . .' got nothing at all, and could be turned into a
servant. [14] A blameless woman could petition for divorce or
separation before the magistrates. If her case were found to be
true, that her husband had belittled her, '. . . She shall take her
marriage portion and go off to her father's house . . .' [15] If the
plea turned out to be untrue the wife was more or less thrown out
of the house penniless.

Babylonian divorce was obviously not to be trifled with from
the wife's point of view. Men had no such qualms so that such
records as there are show the incidence of divorce was quite high.

Another Semitic people, the Jews, formerly emphasised the
right of a man to divorce his wife at any time. Exceptions to this
were: if he wrongly accused her of promiscuity before marriage,
or if he had fornicated with her before her marriage. Clearly these
were limitations on the husband rather then advantages for the
wife.

From early times right up to the eleventh century Hebrew jurists
and rabbis disputed in factions over whether divorce could be
granted to a husband on grounds other than the adultery of his
wife. The two main factions took the passage in Deuteronomy
(xxiv. 1), which says 'When a man hath taken a wife, and married
her, and it come to pass that she find no favour in his eyes, because
he hath found some uncleanness in her: then let him write her a
bill of divorcement, and give it in her hand, and send her out of
the house, she may go and be another's man's wife.' The difficulty
was in the interpretation of uncleanness, one faction maintaining
that this could only mean sexual immorality, that is adultery. The
other's reasoning was more 'liberal' for they suggested it meant
anything which the husband disliked. It was this view which
prevailed in the end. [16]

After the eleventh century there is a marked change. A truly
liberalising influence seems to have been at work: for although a
woman could be divorced not only for adultery, but for a number
of reasons varying from disregard of ritual to insulting her father-
in-law in her husband's presence, it was laid down that she could
not be put away for trivial reasons unless she consented. Again,
contrary to the Old Testament which gives no rights of this kind
to the wife, the Mishnah permitted the wife to initiate proceed-

ings. [17] If the court was convinced the husband was compelled to agree to a divorce. Once this right was admitted it led to a gradual extension of the grounds on which a wife could sue. In addition a guilty husband had to return the dowry. But a guilty wife was cast adrift without it. With regard to children, at one time they remained with the mother whether she was guilty or not, but a male child over six reverted to the father. Later, custody was left to the discretion of the court.

Like the Jew of the Old Testament the pre-Muslim Arab could put away his wife at pleasure. This custom is known as *Talaq* and, although ratified by Mohammed, was also condemned by him as a cruel and horrible thing. For Talaq to be effective the husband must be in his right mind! Some Muslim sects also insist that he must have a positive intention; others, that even accidental or drunken pronouncements are sufficient. The same differences of opinion are expressed over the procedures to be followed in divorce. Some opinion maintained that any form of words used by the husband would do; other views were that there must be a precise statement. Again, there was dispute over the validity of the verbal form against the written form, over the necessity for witnesses, and so on. [18] At the present time as the type of Mohammedanism professed in different parts of the world varies, so does the Islamic law and practice of divorce.

For a wife it is impossible to divorce her husband. But she can ask her husband to divorce her by offering to give up her dowry and thus break the marriage contract, a practice known as *Hula*. If conditions are really intolerable the wife can plead to this effect before the court. The judge has power to grant a divorce. This, however, cannot be regarded as a right of the wife since the most stringent examination of the case is made and all accusations have to be thoroughly substantiated.

Thus it is possible to say that in contemporary Islam, divorce is really a male institution with the wife cutting a very poor figure. What statistics exist indicate that the incidence of divorce in Muslim countries is high: Egypt with a population of nearly 23 million had 70,000 divorces in 1952; the Muslim population of Algeria, approximately 9 millions, had over 14,000 in 1953. These high figures may be a result of the essentially simple and cheap way divorce can be achieved in those countries.

The pagan tribes of Europe all appear to have admitted divorce as a solvent of marriage. In pre-Christian Ireland, either spouse could sue on a variety of grounds. There was also divorce by mutual consent. The Brehon Law Tracts are quite explicit in connection with the rights of women to a divorce: '... There are with the Feine seven women (that is seven grounds on which women could bring proceedings) who, though bound by son and security, are competent to separate from cohabitation, whatever day they like; and whatever has been given them as their dowry, is theirs by right: a woman of whom her husband circulates a false story; a woman upon whom her husband gives circulation to satire until she is laughed at; a woman upon whom a check blemish is inflicted; a woman who is sent back and repudiated for another; a woman who is cheated of bed rites, so that her husband prefers to lie with servant boys when it is not necessary for him; a woman to whom her mate has administered a philtre when entreating her (that is when courting her), so that he brings her to fornication; a woman who is not able to receive her desire in the community of marriage, for every woman among the Feine on whom there is this bond (marriage), and who gives her proper co-operation for it, is entitled to her desire ...' [19]

If the Brehon Tracts are taken as typical it seems very clear that pagan Ireland in this matter was not only superior to her Christian successors but well ahead of society existing today. The categorical statement concerning the woman's rights 'to receive her desire in the community of marriage' is quite unique. It has only recently been recognised, in a negative sense, in the United States under the heading of incompatibility: it has yet to be recognised in Britain. Surely this right is fundamental to the achievement of a happy marriage? Failure to achieve it would appear to be one of the most reasonable grounds for divorce in any society.

The pagan Irish certainly reached a peak of enlightenment in a most remote period of European history. The same type of liberality is exhibited by pagan Wales. Separation could take place at any time after the marriage, at the instigation of either partner or both. In cases where the wife committed adultery, or behaved improperly with another man the husband could divorce her, and her property remained with him. On the other hand her property remained with her if she divorced him for having leprosy, being impotent, or having fetid breath. [20] It looks as if these tribal societies were extraordinarily aware of the minutiae which go to make up the daily round of married life.

Amongst the contemporary primitive peoples who permit divorce, two divisions can be made. The first kind would consist of those where divorce is infrequent or rare; the second of those where it is common.

Among the first kind, the Lepchas of Sikkim are prominent. As Gorer says, '. . . Most consummated marriages are stable and divorce or separation is very rare . . .' [21] The fact that at a divorce all the movable property in the household, as well as animals and children, has to be divided may serve as a very real deterrent. But the general context of Lepcha society with its somewhat unusual marriage system must also be considered. In addition there is the rare fact that 'Adultery, without really marked preference, is not a reason for divorce; and no anxiety is felt or expressed about the paternity of a man's children . . .' [22] Such factors help to explain the low incidence of divorce.

The reluctance to resort to divorce is to be found amongst societies all over the world. It is found, for example, in Siberian tribes such as the Yakut and Koryak who lead a semi-nomadic existence. It is not possible to establish a correlation between nomadism and stability in marriage, for with other nomadic peoples in Siberia, such as the Chuckchee, divorce is easy and popular. This raises a very interesting problem, since the way of life and religion of most of these Arctic peoples is essentially similar.

Many of the hill tribes of Assam, such as the Nagas and Kukis, have an extremely low incidence of divorce. This was also true of the Maoris, and of the tribes in some parts of New Guinea, besides some North American Indian tribes such as the Natchez. An African example of this reluctance to resort to divorce is that of the Masai. Malinowski in describing the group of Australian Aborigines he studied was never quite sure on this point. He stated that he was unable to decide whether a wife was repudiated after she had outlived her useful life, or whether unions tended to be life-long. [23]

But although communities of this kind are not excessively numerous they are distributed throughout the world. So far as we are aware, the social and psychological factors underlying enduring marital unions have not been studied.

Of the second kind, where divorce machinery exists and is commonly and frequently used, the number of societies is much greater. The distribution is as wide as in the first group.

Possibly the most extreme instance of the popularity of divorce comes from the Maldive Islands in the Indian Ocean. There, apparently, divorce was formerly a popular pastime. Men were in the habit of divorcing and remarrying the same woman three or four times in their lives.

The Sea Dyaks of North-west Borneo exhibit a similar attitude towards the dissolution of marriage: the majority of men of middle years appear to have had several wives in succession. Seligman states in connection with the Southern Massim (Dyaks) of New Guinea '. . . there is no doubt that formerly many perfectly valid marriages lasted only a short time . . .'[24] The propensity for divorce is found in such diverse peoples as the Kiwai Papuans, the inhabitants of the Marshall Islands in the Pacific, some Indian tribes of Bolivia, and the Chuckchee of Siberia.

On the islands of Buka and Bougainville in the Solomons group in the Pacific, the inhabitants typify this free and easy attitude towards divorce. 'Divorce is easy and frequent. The woman has as much right to demand it as the man, and neither party can deny it to the other . . .'[25]

Procedure is essentially simple: a wife may be sent back to her people by her husband; if this occurs he can demand the return of the ceremonial currency he gave to the former at the wedding. If the wife leaves the husband, which is just as common, this currency is not returnable. However, in many cases it is returned as 'a matter of family pride'.[26] The mother in every instance takes the children with her. As they are a matrilineal people, and thus trace descent through the maternal line and emphasise maternal relatives, this is to be expected. On the woman's remarriage, which is usual, the new husband undertakes full responsibility for the children. In some instances they may be cared for by the wife's sister.

These Melanesian people can change partners easily. There is no stigma attached to the divorced. The freedom of the wife not to return the ceremonial currency if she leaves her husband may be a powerful factor in promoting action. Again, the children are adequately cared for if the union is dissolved. In other words the woman can act with impunity.

The situation is somewhat different amongst the Nuba of the Southern Sudan. In the great majority of African societies divorce is of common occurrence, This is so for the Nuba: '. . . But, whatever the reasons, the husband will decide to divorce his wife only if he can be sure either that her father or brothers are able to refund the bride-price or that she will find another husband from whom the bride-price could then be recovered. If neither is very likely, the husband would argue that he might just as well keep his wife . . .' [27]

The Nuba practice of thinking out the economic implications of dissolving a marriage is in complete contrast with the almost feckless attitude of the people of Buka .This regard for the bride-price, which is the money or its equivalent paid by the prospective bridegroom to the bride's family, and which may be considerable, appears to be present in the majority of simple societies. The amount may vary considerably, but the fact remains that at the stage when divorce is liable to occur it may very well have been disposed of or spent. To return it, or its equivalent, may be an onerous or impossible task. For example, one of the commonest forms the bride-price takes in Africa is cattle. To return the original cattle or others may mean disturbing and reducing your herd. This is a serious matter—affecting among other things your social prestige. Of course you may restore your fortunes by another marriage: it is rather like gambling on the Stock Exchange; divorce may deplete your fortune, but remarriage may increase your profits.

Another factor which should be considered is the passion for litigation which seems to be inherent in many African societies. Where there are fully developed traditional courts of law, as in West Africa, a divorce suit may provide opportunity for demonstrating wit, cleverness, as well as social prestige. This factor may very well influence the incidence of divorce amongst such peoples.

It is possible that a correlation could be established between polygyny and the frequency of the dissolution of marriages. It is true to say that in those societies, as in Islamic communities and in Melanesia, where divorce is easy and frequent, polygyny also exists. The practice of having more than one wife at a time certainly increases the possibility of adultery by a wife, which is the commonest ground for divorce. The husband may inadvertently or deliberately neglect a wife. She in revenge or idleness will take a lover. Discovery of the *affaire* may end the marriage. There is also the attitude on the part of the husband that the possession of several wives diminishes the importance of the marital tie with any one of them. In other words divorce might be said to have less significance in such societies than amongst monogamous peoples such as ourselves.

So far we have discussed the existence of the means for dissolving marriages. We have mentioned various grounds for divorce but these require elaboration.

While the greater part of mankind admits the necessity of a solvent for the disastrous marriage, the definition of disaster, as it were, varies tremendously. There are, of course, many grounds of divorce which are peculiar to a particular people. The breaking of a tabu is an example. But other grounds, more general, have a wide distribution.

Under the heading of disease we find leprosy is frequently cited: this disease is endemic in India, Asia and Africa. It is of course one which prevents cohabitation. Other skin infections, including venereal disease, may be cited as is the case in some Melanesian societies, and the states of Illinois and Kentucky in the United States. Britain, in 1937, admitted new grounds for a decree of nullity in marriage: these included venereal disease (which must be given to the other partner), insanity and epilepsy if they existed at the time of the marriage.

In Europe Norway includes insanity as a plea in a divorce suit, and allows annulment in cases of leprosy and epilepsy. Denmark lists insanity and venereal disease if it has been communicated to the other spouse. Finland does not define specifically, only in terms of incurable contagious disease. Portugal has wider terms. Any incurable contagious disease, or any disease which creates sexual aberration is included, in addition to insanity. On the other hand Germany and Switzerland admit only insanity. The recognition of insanity, either at the time of the marriage or after a term of years, as a plea, appears to be confined to the Western world, and to India and Pakistan.

Throughout the less advanced societies barrenness is almost universal in its occurrence as a ground for dissolving marriage. The motives behind this are fairly obvious: all communities depend upon effective replacement if they are to survive as entities; in primitive conditions replacement is heavily emphasised. Barrenness in a woman is a serious matter. The barren wife must give way to the potentially fruitful wife. In addition to effective survival there may be important religious or ritual demands which can only be met by bearing children.

In contrast, the legal codes of Europe and America are without this particular provision. Clearly, advanced societies have less reason to emphasise this aspect of marriage, since the material conditions of life are far less hazardous amongst them. Individuals in European countries have succeeded in the past in obtaining annulments on the grounds of barrenness; titles and property were the background to such cases. But it has never been admitted as an ordinary plea for divorce. The European is more concerned to combat artificial barrenness, that is the refusal to have children, by prohibiting the sale of contraceptives. This is certainly the case in France, Belgium and Holland; and in America in the states of Connecticut, Massachusetts, Minnesota, Mississipi, Nebraska, New Jersey and Ohio.

Inability to copulate with one's spouse is a lawful ground for divorce in several primitive societies. The Bushongo of the Lower Congo allow the wife to rid herself of an impotent husband. The Bakongo in the same area permit an impotent husband to try and find a substitute; if he can do so the marriage may continue, if not the wife may divorce him. Similar reasons are at work here as in the case of the spouse's infertility. One point in this context is that rarely, if ever, at the less advanced level is the failure to have children attributed to the husband. This, of course, is due to lack of physiological knowledge.

In Western societies there is a reluctance to recognise this plea. Parts of Canada, Nova Scotia and New Brunswick; Australia, under the heading of physical incapacity; and the majority of jurisdictions in the United States, are amongst those which permit impotence as a ground for divorce. On the other hand, Britain and some other countries will declare a marriage null and void, which is not the same as a divorce, if it has not been consummated by virtue of the impotence or wilful refusal of the spouse. If a plea of nullity is admitted this a tantamount to declaring that no marriage took place. The point here is that initial capacity may give way to later impotence.

From a commonsense point of view, failure to perform the sexual act would seem a most reasonable ground for dissolving a marriage. Speculation as to feelings and attitudes behind this refusal to accept the sexual aspect of marriage is not very reward-ing. The British attitude might be said to be due in part to the traditional repugnance against discussing sexual behaviour. The difficulty of producing reliable evidence that the individual, al-though at one time potent is now incapacitated, undoubtedly has some bearing on the matter.

Desertion by either party is another very widespread reason for divorce in simple societies. The effect of desertion is to deprive the wife and children of support without giving the freedom to re-marry. Economic security may only be restored by remarriage, so legal dissolution is necessary. Here the advanced society is at one with the savage. For desertion is also recognised by a large number of Western nations as reasonable ground on which to dissolve a marriage, although in many instances a definite period is set before the law can be invoked. For example, Britain and New Zealand require a three year period, and Denmark a two year period.

The incidence of cruelty as the basis of divorce is fairly wide-spread in savage society. It is found amongst the Basuto of South Africa, the Kavirondo of East Africa, the Ewe and Yoruba of West Africa, the Sakai of Malaya, and in many groups in Melan-esia. Of course it is nearly always the cruelty of the husband to the wife which is meant. In fact there does not appear to be an instance where simple cruelty by the wife can be cited. Perhaps an indict-ment of a woman on these grounds is too much for the 'face' or pride of primitive man. The same male squeamishness is not noticeable in the case of Western communities. In most European countries where divorce is permissible cruelty, that is ill-treatment, is a normal plea. The laws do not seem to distinguish between husband and wife in this respect. This also applies in the United States where cruelty is defined in different ways, from homicidal assault to displays of violent temper. For example in Florida a divorce may be granted for violent and ungovernable temper exhibited by either partner. In Britain, where it is admitted as a plea, it constitutes an extremely difficult ground to establish. It may even be associated with social class. For instance wife beating and foul language may be a norm in one section of the society, but may be held to amount to cruelty at another level. Happily or unhappily the savage does not indulge in these refinements of distinction.

Adultery by the wife is by far the commonest cause for divorce throughout the world. It is found in all types of society irrespective of the simplicity or complexity of their culture. In advanced societies adultery by a husband can also be put forward by a wife. It is usually simple adultery but in some instances as the Australian State of Victoria, in the case of either spouse, it must be aggravated. That is it must be accompanied by incest, cruelty, bigamy, desertion, rape, sodomy or bestiality.

Primitive societies as a rule do not give a wife equality with her husband in respect of adultery. Apparent exceptions are the Southern Massim of New Guinea, and the inhabitants of Ceram in the Moluccas.

Reasons for the emphasis on female adultery are not far to seek: the act is regarded by most peoples as a betrayal of the sexual trust placed in the wife; associated with this is the destruction of the individual male's sole rights in the woman. Such a betrayal may result in pregnancy and the production of illegitimate offspring. Such children are not only a permanent reminder of a spouse's infidelity, but may disrupt the line of inheritance, as well as being an insult to the husband's honour. Inheritance is possibly the most important factor. Property, in the widest sense, is sacred and the legitimate family ensures its appropriate method of transmission. Female infidelity casts doubts on the efficacy of inheritance. Such reasoning, both conscious and unconscious, helps to explain the prevalence of female adultery as a grounds for divorce.

On the other hand acceptance of male adultery as a proper plea by a wife would be to admit women to equality in marriage. Such equality would entirely upset the conception of marriage held by many of the less advanced peoples.

The views of a Lord Chancellor (Lord Cranworth) in the mid-nineteenth century aptly express the feeling of many peoples in relation to this, as it were, double standard with regard to adultery. 'A wife might, without any loss of caste, and possibly with reference to the interests of her children, or even of her husband, condone an act of adultery on the part of the husband; but a husband could not condone a similar act on the part of a wife. No one would venture to suggest that a husband could possibly do so, and for this, among other reasons . . . that the adultery of the wife might be the means of palming spurious offspring upon the husband, while the adultery of the husband could have no such effect with regard to the wife'. (*Hansard*, 1857, Vol. 145, col. 813.)

Despite the general anxiety about orthodox inheritance there are some exceptions to this widespread attitude regarding female adultery. The Todas, a small Southern Indian aboriginal tribe, are a somewhat strange people. They practise fraternal polyandry, that is a group of brothers may marry one woman. A man will divorce a woman if she is foolish, or if she will not work. Intercourse with men other than her husbands is not regarded by them as a serious matter. They will not divorce a woman for this reason. It may well be that their rather exceptional social structure promotes this indulgence of female adultery amongst the Todas. After all when your sexual and other rights in a woman are shared by others, to increase the number is hardly reason for concern. [28]

The Lepchas of Sikkim also have this tolerance of female adultery. Again polyandry is in evidence but it is practised on a more limited scale than amongst the Todas. A Lepcha may invite an unmarried younger brother to live with him and share his fields and wife. [29] The brother may either be a real one or one socially regarded as such. As the co-husband is inferior to the chief husband in many ways such marriages are not popular. The situation is further complicated as the Lepcha also practise polygyny, again in a limited way. But whatever type of union the Lepcha individual favours, he is, as we said above, indifferent to his wife's adultery.

More moderate examples of the toleration of female adultery exist: amongst the Dinka, an African polygnous society, the law will not permit a husband to divorce an unfaithful wife, provided she stays in his compound; the Morans, an aboriginal people of Assam, will allow the plea of the wife's adultery to be made by the husband only if her lover is of a lower caste than her own.

All these instances, however, can be regarded as exceptions to what is tantamount to the general rule of female infidelity being accepted as a cause for the dissolution of marriage.

If one leaves the field of what might be termed universal grounds of divorce, the variety of pleas which exist are quite bewildering. The impression is that practically every item of human behaviour has been somewhere at some time allowed as just cause for divorce.

Miss Blackwood collected the following list from the people of Buka. [30] Grounds for the husband: persistent refusal on the part of the wife to cook his food, or continued slowness in doing so; refusal of sexual intercourse; bad skin disease; adultery. Grounds for the wife: husband's failure to take his share in the work of providing food for the household; persistent cruelty and severe beating; inability to perform the sexual act. These are all down-to-earth and practical reasons which are typical of those existing in widely separated societies of this kind. A point of some importance is that the failure of the husband to act out his proper economic role may cause the ruin of the family, so that divorce in such a situation would be a real remedy.

Similar lists to that for Buka could be made out for many other societies. The Tanala of Madagascar, according to Linton, permit a man to divorce his wife for not cooking rice well. In the ordinary course of marriage she may be beaten, but if he pulls out her hair or teeth she may leave him and the marriage is at an end. [31]

In European or American societies mere failure to support a wife does not lead to the remedy of a divorce. There are other more or less adequate legal means of compelling maintenance. Thus there is not the same urgency as at the simple level of society for dissolving the marriage. Divorce may be necessary at that level so that the wife may have her status clarified, and possibly seek another man to support her.

Although not as basic, the same type of particularisation quoted for the Melanesians of Buka exists in the West. The legal codes of pre-1914 Serbia, and contemporary Kentucky provide examples. In Serbia, if a wife visited beer gardens or similar places or spent the night in a strange place, she could be divorced. This conjures up the alarming activities which must have taken place in these Serbian drinking dens. In Kentucky today, mere lewd or lascivious behaviour is sufficient reason to grant a divorce to a husband. One wonders what criteria are used to define the lascivious or lewd. A group of South and Central American countries have a provision which superficially appears somewhat strange. Chile, Venezuela, Mexico, Costa |Rica and Panama all allow a wife to divorce her spouse if he attempts to prostitute her. Costa Rica and Panama go further and extend it to attempts to prostitute the children of the union. The provision suggests the likelihood of the occurrence which seems remote.

Consumption of alcohol on the part of the wife is regarded in parts of India as just ground for divorce. In Sweden, in cases of habitual drunkenness of either spouse, the court may dissolve the marriage. The people of the Shan States in Burma permit a wife not only to cast aside a husband for the same reason but she may retain all the household goods and property. Thirty-eight out of forty-nine states in the United States permit either partner to obtain a decree for habitual drunkenness. Australia and New Zealand have similar legislation. Britain does not specifically allow this, but no doubt a case could be made out under the heading of cruelty.

Britain is also amongst those Western countries which refuse divorce to spouses whose partners have been, or are, in prison. In other European societies, such as Portugal, the plea of imprisonment is admissible but it must be for a major crime such as homicide or immoral conduct. France demands that the crime must be of a most grave nature, such as treason, which deprives the person of civil rights. Whereas in the United States in most jurisdictions conviction for felony is sufficient, Norway, Holland, Sweden and Denmark do not specify offences but prescribe lengths of time.

The equivalent to the above grounds in simple societies would be a permissible dissolution of the union if either spouse broke an important tabu. Such cases do occur but not with great frequency. The discovery after marriage of an inadvertent violation of an incest tabu would be a typical example.

Divorce by mutual consent, that is the expressed desire of the partners to end the marriage, is permissible as we have seen in many societies both simple and classical. Amongst contemporary advanced societies Belgium permits this if certain conditions are fulfilled. For example, the wife must not be over 45, and the unconditional consent of the parents or other senior relatives of the couple has to be obtained. A curious example is that of Austria which formerly permitted this type of divorce to Jews alone.

Norwegian law stipulates that a union may be dissolved if a joint application is made after a year's separation. Sweden, Greece, New Zealand and Panama also have legislation with reservations which grants divorces by consent.

The theoretical objection to mutual consent in divorce in our kind of society is that it would lower the value of the institution of marriage in the eyes of most people. Further, that it would interfere with the economic arrangements made at marriage; and that it would increase the divorce rate. None of these results would be desirable.

The argument that the ease of divorce by consent cheapens marriage is not borne out by the facts. Norway can be taken as a reasonable example of a country which permits marriages to be dissolved in this way. In 1954 there were 2,103 divorces; this in a population of 3,392,000. In contrast, Denmark, with a population of 4,406,000 does not permit this type of divorce, yet in the same year there were 6,686 divorces. In both countries the evidence suggests that the institution of marriage is respected in the same way.

Another aspect should be considered. There are in Europe few restrictions on entering marriage: mere compliance with the age of consent is sufficient. If it is necessary to stabilise marriages it would be more logical to make entry into matrimony much more difficult, but at the same time make its dissolution easier by such means as divorce by consent.

Interference with contractual economic arrangements made at marriage is not a valid objection to permitting divorce by consent. Today few marriages in Western society are of this kind. Property is now much more fluid and unconnected with land than it was in the nineteenth century. Marriages are nowadays more a matter of individual choice rather than property transfers.

It is the possibility of increasing the divorce rate which is the most powerful argument against divorce by consent. Let us see if in those countries that permit this type of divorce the rate is greater than in those which do not.

TABLE I

(Figures relating to 1954)

Countries which permit divorce by consent	Divorce rate per 1,000 of popn.	Countries which do not	Divorce rate per 1,000 of popn.
Belgium ..	.. 0·45	England & Wales ..	0·62
Norway ..	.. 0·62	Denmark ..	1·52
Sweden ..	.. 1·20	Dominican Rep. ..	0·45
Panama ..	.. 0·46	W. Germany ..	0·90
Holland ..	.. 0·52		

In view of these figures that argument has as much weight as that in favour of capital punishment on the grounds that its abolition increases the homicide rate.

The admission of sodomy and of bestiality as grounds for the dissolution of marriage does not figure prominently in the legal codes of the West. There are some anomalies in respect of this: in Australia (that is in the area of jurisdiction of the Commonwealth of Australia) a husband may divorce his wife for sodomy or bestiality only in South Australia, Western Australia, Papua and New Guinea. For a wife to divorce her husband for the same offence it must be accompanied by adultery. Although this applies in all the Australian States it seems highly unfair to the wife. Canadian legislation on this topic gives the wife the right to sue on the grounds of attempted sodomy, but not the husband. This applies in all the Canadian provinces except Saskatchewan, Nova Scotia, Quebec, New Brunswick, Prince Edward Island and, of course, Newfoundland where there is no divorce at all.

The Parsee Marriage and Divorce Act of 1936 which applies only to the Parsee community in India states that 'rape or an unnatural offence' is an admissible plea in the courts. This is in distinction to ordinary Indian legislation which makes no mention of the matter. In the United States there is no specific mention of sodomy in any of the States' divorce laws, although it figures prominently as a sexual offence in almost all State codes of law. But North Carolina and Alabama cite a crime against nature. It appears to be forgotten that, generally speaking, sodomy is widespread throughout the animal world. Missouri and Arkansas list intolerable indignities. No doubt sodomy could well come under these headings. The British anomaly we have already discussed.

None of the countries quoted above make any reference in their laws to consent to sodomitical act. This is probably because sodomy is held to be an offence in itself, therefore one cannot consent to participation in it. This is certainly true in Britain where sodomy is in the same legal category as grievous bodily harm to which you cannot consent. On the other hand if married couples wish to indulge in such practices it seems unreasonable that the law should have the power to interfere. It is even more unreasonable that sodomy consented to by a wife at the time can later be used as a plea in divorce proceedings against her husband. Norway alone, so far as we are aware, makes a provision of this kind in her divorce laws. 'Unnatural offences' if consented to at the time render a later plea invalid. In our view this is most enlightened legislation.

A somewhat minor ground which is admissible in a few societies is when a spouse is converted to a religion different from his or her partner. In Europe this was the case under old Serbian law and was probably due to the presence of Muslim communities in Serbia side by side with Christians. It is embodied in the laws of both the Hindu and Parsee communities in India. In them conversion, for example to Christianity, would give the right to the non-Christian spouse to institute proceedings. With the latter-day religious tolerance or indifference of the West, it is not surprising that religious conversion does not figure as a ground for divorce. An apparent exception to this is is the legislation in Kentucky and New Hampshire in the United States. This specifies that a spouse may sue for divorce if the other partner joins a religious sect which does not believe in cohabitation.

Although incompatability is popularly believed to be a sound plea for divorce in many parts of the United States it is not stated as such in any of the jurisdictions there, except that of New Mexico. What in fact occurs is that pleas of incompatability are made under the heading of cruelty or gross indignities. New Mexico has a European counterpart in Yugoslavia which has also enshrined incompatibility in her divorce laws.

Perhaps the oddest plea which is found in the law books is that of keeping a concubine at home. Many societies cover this type of activity under a general concept of adultery, or the keeping of concubines in general, as is the case of Panama. Belgium is apparently the only country which regards the installation of one's mistress in the matrimonial home as sufficiently heinous to be particularised in her divorce laws. It is a provision which opens up all sorts of unlikely speculations. Was it at one time, or indeed is it still, fashionable in Belgium for respectable bourgeois to keep their mistresses at home?

The most sensible approach, in our opinion, to the problems of grounds for divorce, is contained in the Pakistani laws affecting Muslim women. A Muslim wife may claim to have her marriage dissolved if it was so provided for in the marriage contract. This is a provision, or some modification of it, which might well be adopted by Western states. If introduced it might even deter the over-enthusiastic from rushing into matrimony.

The aftermath of divorce is the position of the wife and children. This is far less of a problem in simple societies than in those of our own type. In some primitive groups, for example the Lengua Indians of Paraguay and the Karens of Burma, divorce is not permitted at all if children have been born of the marriage. But this is an extreme position not frequently found. In the great majority of such societies the family structure is such that divorce does not necessarily entail great hardship for the woman and children. The large extended family group to which the woman may return offers support and consolation. If the man has moved into the woman's family group, divorce merely means that he moves out, and there is the minimum of disturbance to the family. What it amounts to is that kinship relations are so extensive in life at the simple level that divorce does not create great difficulties of maintenance and welfare for the ex-wife and children. Even in the cases where the children remain with the husband there are other women connected to his household who can act as mother-substitutes. We would suggest that the family structures of primitive groups create a cushioning effect on the dissolution of a marriage.

It is far otherwise in Western society. The family structure in our midst is extremely atomistic, each unit is on its own, and usually comprises only father, mother and children. The result is that divorce creates a problem of some magnitude both in economic and emotional terms. With regard to the former, divorce legislation tends to include the provision of maintenance of the innocent spouse by the guilty, that is alimony. France provides that the guilty spouse must give the equivalent of one-third of his or her income to the innocent. In Britain the matter is left within the discretion of the court. Germany specifies that the latter must be maintained in his or her accustomed way. In the case of a guilty husband it applies only if he cannot maintain himself. Few innocent husbands in Germany, we would suggest, have the temerity to apply for alimony. Not because they may not need the money, but rather because of the social reluctance of the male animal to demean himself by accepting the support of a woman.

Alimony does ensure that children are adequately taken care of in the material sense. What legislation does not do is to ensure joint parental care; in the circumstances this is impossible. This is where the so-called savage scores very strongly over Western man. The price we pay for the individualistic, free, family unit is only appreciated when such a unit is dissolved. The strongest argument against divorce in the West is that the children almost inevitably suffer.

Many people are disturbed by the real increase of divorce in the West. It is regarded as an indication of a sick society. But there is another way of looking at this increase: Alva Myrdal, the Swedish sociologist, has suggested that 'with life expectancy increased and age at marriage remaining approximately the same, the prospective duration of marriage itself has increased, thus making the demand on lifelong, faithful marriage quantitatively more exacting for the modern couple.' [32] This could be interpreted as meaning that the longer a marriage lasts the more exacting it is. However Mrs Myrdal is careful to point out that this should not be over-emphasised, but considered. She goes on to say that a little over one-half (approximately 1,280) of all divorces in Sweden during 1931–35 were of couples who had been married ten years or more. And that one in five of all divorces took place after twenty years.

This is one aspect of the increase in divorce incidence. There is another which is perhaps more important. The changing economic structure of the Western nations has destroyed in the last two hundred years the connection of the mass of the people with the land. Industrialisation disrupted the ancient ties of the family to the land through inheritance and marriage. Part of these changes has been the growing economic independence of women. Their participation in many fields of activity which were until recently closed to them is a modern phenomenon. With that economic freedom has come an increasing social freedom. The result is that the contemporary Western woman is now demanding not only equal pay with men, but equality in marriage. If she fails to attain it there is a tendency to resort to divorce; for this she cannot be entirely blamed, for it is logical.

If all who were concerned in the dissolution of a marriage were merely the spouses, the matter would rest there. Unfortunately in many cases children are involved and they are liable to suffer. Not in any material sense, for generally adequate provision is made for that, but emotionally. This is a problem which appears insoluble. A partial solution might be to restrict the liberty of spouses to resort to divorce in cases where it meant the more or less permanent deprivation, for the children, of one parent. That is to say that in those instances where the partners to a marriage had children and were contemplating remarriage after divorce, possibly a majority of cases, pleas on the usual grounds would be permissible. But where remarriage was not a probability and there were children of the union, a plea could not be made.

The Czechoslovak law of 1950 on divorce sums it up: 'Divorce is based on a deep and permanent dissension between a man and a women on important grounds. It may not be granted, however, if this is contrary to the interests of minor children.' (33)

We have by no means attempted to cover the whole enormous field of divorce. But it is hoped that sufficient evidence has been presented to show the variegation of the world pattern of types of divorce, and the pleas that may be entered. Also, to show that the Western contribution to the pattern is only one among many. That there are anomalies cannot be denied; that there could be improvements and extensions is bound to cause debate according to the reader's social and ethical views. But it should be remembered that the accident of birth and upbringing alone accounts for this view or that.

TABLE II

(Figures for 1954 unless otherwise stated).

Country	Estimated Population in 1000's	Number of Divorces	Divorce rate per 1000
Aden	150	1,156	7·71
Egypt	21,473	69,538	3·24
			(Figures for 1952)
Ceylon	8,520	1,908	0·22
Iran	21,181	25,404	1·20
Israel (Jews only) ..	1,499	2,142	1·43
Turkey	23,441	10,155	0·43
Japan	88,000	76,759	0·87
Austria	6,969	9,227	1·32
Belgium	8,819	3,999	0·45
Bulgaria	7,467	4,475	0·60
Czechoslovakia ..	12,952	11,280	0·87
Denmark	4,406	6,686	1·52
Finland	4,191	3,492	0·83
France	42,951	28,664	0·67
W. Germany ..	49,689	44,750	0·90
Hungary	9,690	12,144	1·25
Norway	3,392	2,103	0·62
Poland	26,761	12,409	0·46
Portugal	8,693	1,068	0·12
Sweden	7,213	8,588	1·20
Switzerland ..	4,927	4,437	0·90
England & Wales	44,274	27,471	0·62
Scotland	5,123	2,200	0·42
Holland	10,615	5,525	0·52
Yugoslavia	17,267	16,053	0·93
Australia	8,987	6,457	0·72
Hawaii	522	1,256	2·41
New Zealand ..	2,093	1,536	0·73

Country	Estimated Population in 1000's	Number of Divorces	Divorce rate per 1000
U.S.A.	162,417	379,000	2·35
Virgin Islands, (U.S.A.	24	123	5·12
Puerto Rico (U.S.A.	2,229	4,686	2·10
Dutch West Indies	181	150	0·85
Jamaica	1,518	325	0·21
Venezuela	5,608	924	0·16
Alaska	208	537	2·58
Zanzibar and Pemba	277	1,755	6·33
S. Rhodesia (Europeans)	159	318	2·00
S. Africa (Europeans)	2,803	4,011	1·43

NOTE: The following quotation is relevant to the above Table. It is from the *United Nations Demographic Yearbook for* 1957, page 40: '... Crude divorce rates are a measure of the frequency of marriage dissolution by divorce, or conversely of additions to the marriageable population by this means. But because of basic differences in the marital status and age composition of populations, crude rates do not measure the risk of divorce among married persons or couples. They give only a general idea of the trends over time and the gross differences between countries in levels of divorce in the total population. They are limited always by the international variations in the meaning of the term "divorce".'

REFERENCES AND NOTES

1. R. Linton, *Study of Man*, New York 1937, p. 176.
2. *ibid. op. cit.*, p. 176.
3. C. S. Hurgronje, *Mekka*, The Hague 1888–9, Vol. II, pp. 5 and 109 *et seq.*
4. *Annual Reports of Bureau of American Ethnology*, Vol. XI, p. 189.
5. C. G. and B. Seligman, *The Veddas*, Cambridge 1911, p. 100.
6. Lord Bryce, *Studies in History and Jurisprudence*, Oxford 1901, Vol. II, p. 434.
7. O. R. McGregor, *Divorce in England*, London 1957, pp. 10–11.

8. L. Beauchet, *Histoire du droit privé de la République Athénienne*, Paris 1897, Vol. I, p. 376.

9. Demosthenes, *Opera, Oratio contra Neaeram*, para. 87, ed. J. T. Vremel, Paris 1843.

10. O. Kiefer, *Sexual Life in Ancient Rome*, London 1938, pp. 33–4.

11. *Laws of Manu*, translated by G. Buhler, *The Sacred Books of the East*, Oxford 1886, Vol. XXV, p. 46.

12. Abbé Dubois, *Hindu Manners, Customs and Ceremonies*, Oxford 1906, p. 211.

13. J. D. Mayne, *A Treatise on Hindu Law and Usage*, Madras 1914.

14. *Laws of Hammurabi*, translated by C. H. W. Johns, Edinburgh 1903, p. 27.

15. *ibid. op. cit.*, p. 27.

16. D. W. Amram, *Jewish Law of Divorce*, London 1897, pp. 24, 52, and 46.

17. D. W. Amram, *op. cit.*, p. 118.

18. Ameer Ali, *Mohammedan Law*, Calcutta 1908, Vol. II, pp. 511 and 516.

19. *Ancient Laws and Institutes of Ireland*, London 1865–79, Vol. V, p. 293.

20. 'Vendotian Code', ii, 18, 31, *Ancient Laws and Institutions of Wales*, London 1841, p. 39.

21. G. Gorer, *Himalayan Village*, London 1938, p. 157.

22. *ibid. op. cit.*, p. 157.

23. B. Malinowski, *The Family among the Australian Aborigines*, London 1913, p. 65.

24. C. G. Seligman, *Melanesians of British New Guinea*, Cambridge 1910, p. 510.

25. B. Blackwood, *Both Sides of Buka Passage*, Oxford 1935, p. 109.

26. *ibid. op. cit.*, p. 110.

27. S. F. Nadel, *The Nuba*, Oxford 1947, pp. 125–6.

28. W. H. R. Rivers, *The Todas*, London 1906, pp. 525 and 529.

29. G. Gorer, *Himalayan Village*, London 1938, p. 171.

30. B. Blackwood, *op. cit.*, p. 110.

31. Linton, *op. cit.*, p. 176

32. Alva Myrdal, *Nation and Family*, London 1945, p. 38.

33. 'Act relating to the Rights of the Family' quoted in United Nations *Survey of Legislation on Marriage, Divorce and Related Topics Relevant to Population*, New York 1956, p. 89.

34. Based on tables contained in the United Nations *Demographic Yearbook*, New York 1957.

NOTE: The greater part of the information in this chapter regarding contemporary divorce rates and legislation is based on the United Nations reports cited under 33 and 34 above. A comprehensive survey of divorce regulations in Western Europe is to be found in the *Minutes of Evidence of the Royal Commission on Marriage and Divorce*, 1911. For a liberal view of divorce see the *Minority Report of Lord Walker to the Royal Commission on Marriage and Divorce*. A fairly comprehensive survey of divorce amongst the less advanced peoples is given in Ch. XXXIII of E. Westermarck's *The History of Human Marriage*, London 1921.

CHAPTER X

Coitus and Tabu

FOR THE American or European the place and time for coitus are governed by what might be termed rational or practical considerations. He has to be careful that he does not offend against the laws concerning indecency; he cannot copulate in a public place, or indeed in a private place such as a garden if it is overlooked. The sexual act in an automobile would come under the same stricture. The attitude current in our type of society is that behaviour of this kind not only offends against public decency, but, and this is perhaps equally important, in England at any rate, would give rise to behaviour likely to lead to a breach of the peace on the part of the onlooker.

Restrictions relating to public decency prevent the majority of people from indulging themselves in public. Nevertheless a great number, possibly of the younger age groups, are known to copulate at all times and in all places. Evidence for this is to be seen in the discarded condoms or sheaths which litter the streets, alleyways, and parks of the cities of Britain after weekends in the summer months. Such public copulation does not seem to occur so much from choice as from lack of suitable private premises. Individuals are driven to take the risk of discovery by lack of means to be private. For with the exception of the eccentric or perverted it is possibly true to say that the average European male and female when performing the sexual act wishes to be alone. This is an attitude which is prevalent in most, but not all, human societies.

In general it can be said that for the majority of Europeans or Americans most sexual activity takes place indoors in a bedroom in private. Two factors, climate, which acts as a deterrent for a large part of the year, and regard for public decency, are operative. This last is obviously a product of sexual moral conceptions as to what is proper or improper behaviour. Such conceptions are themselves rooted in the whole complexus of Judeo-Christian thought which has come down to us.

The time when coitus takes place on the other hand is governed by much more mundane considerations.

Night, when the children are safely in bed and there is no other duty or obligation to fulfil, appears to be the time of choice. Exception must be made here of the large number of men who in provincial towns in Britain go home for their mid-day meal. This gives them the opportunity of satisfying their sexual appetites during the day. There is a tendency here for class differentiation to enter the picture. It appears that it is mainly working-class and lower middle-class people who have their mid-day meal at home. Whereas upper-class business men and executives do not have this opportunity, as lunch becomes part of their business day. In Jamaica, a colonial society, the mid-day break and lunch at home is taken by the majority of people irrespective of class. There is accordingly daytime opportunity for sexual gratification.

Sunday afternoon is another time when class-differentiation seems to operate: many working class people in England will say jokingly that they were conceived between mid-day dinner and tea on a Sunday afternoon. There is this much truth in the assertion that Sunday afternoon after the meal of the week is a time for relaxation and somnolence. The children are about their own occasions, and, as at nights during the week, there are no other calls upon the individual's time.

All such considerations as we have discussed are determined by essentially rational or practical issues, fear of the law and the existence of opportunity. Quite other factors in addition to these are operative in non-European and so-called savage societies.

The influence of the rational and irrational on the time and place of coitus is admirably illustrated by classical Indian injunctions: 'At the time of the ritu do thou, O Lord of the earth, approach thy wife happy under a constellation bearing a masculine name, at a propitious time, during the best even-numbered nights. But go not to the unbathed woman, to the sick one, to the menstruating one, nor to her without desire, nor to the angry one, not to one in ill-repute, not to one with child, not to one uncomplaisant, not to her that longs for another man or is without love (or that is unwilling) not to another's man's wife, not to one that is faint with hunger, not to one that has over eaten. Nor do thou thyself be weighed with such qualities as these. Bathed, wearing a wreath and scented, bursting with strength (*sphîta*), not wearied or hungry, filled with love and tender inclination, let the man go to sexual union. The fourteenth and the eighth day of the half-month, the day of the new moon, as also the day of the full moon and also the day when the sun comes into a new house of the zodiac—these are the Parvan days, O ruler of princes. The man who on these Parvan days partakes of oil, flesh, and woman goes after death to hell, where dung and urine must be his food . . . Neither outside the vulva, nor in the vulva of another (not human) being, nor using medicines (exciting or strengthening the manly powers), nor in the house of a Brahman, a god, or a Guru, let a man give himself up to love's pleasures, nor near holy trees . . . Nor by cross roads, nor in places where many roads meet, nor in graveyards, nor in groves, nor in water, O lord of the earth. Neither on the Parvan days named, nor in either twilight, nor troubled by urine or stool, must the wise man go to the joyful union. Copulation on the Parvan brings misfortune on men, that by day brings evil (or: sin) that done on the ground has sickness after it, and calamitous is that done in the water . . .' (Vishnu-purana, iii, II 110 ff.)[1]

That is an admirable catalogue of do's and don'ts for the would-be lover. Suitably prepared and dressed the lover should only approach his beloved on certain nights. To do otherwise is to invite calamity. There is a further prohibition which forbids sexual intercourse in a vehicle. (Laws of Manu, XI, 175). Petting couples in the United States and elsewhere who indulge in this type of activity in automobiles obviously are not aware of the spiritual dangers which beset them. The moving vehicle, the train, coach, car, or boat, seems to have exercised an extraordinary fascination for the European as a setting for copulation. It figures prominently in contemporary fiction. Two classical examples are to be found in Flaubert's *Madame Bovary*, and Maupassant's *Bel Ami*. Emma Bovary and Léon attain fulfilment for the first time in a coach with drawn blinds driven all over Rouen throughout an afternoon.

It is possible that this fascination for copulation in a moving vehicle has a physiological basis. Informants, both men and women, have stated that a long railway or bus journey tends to excite them sexually. The rhythmical movement of the seat against the buttocks would undoubtedly tend to act as an erotic stimulus.

The Hindu injunctions we quoted above are representative of what may be considered as a very widespread attitude towards sexual intercourse.

In the total range of human societies there are an infinite number of tabus connected with sex. For the primitive, sexual connection is often thought to be dangerous as well as unclean. The danger lies in the extraordinarily widespread belief that intercourse is weakening for the man. For example the Creek Indians of North America believed that it exercised an enervating effect and thus made them less fit to be warriors. This weakening effect, which of course is part of the nominal physiological process after copulation, is often associated with uncleanliness. Thus amongst some peoples copulation must be followed by a ritual cleansing as in some South American Indian tribes. This fear of sex on the part of the male becomes prominent as when continence is enforced at times of crisis such as childbirth. It can be extended far beyond a particular time, in fact for considerable periods. Many societies regard a woman as unclean after childbirth for a period which may last until the child is weaned, or even longer, as amongst the Cheyenne Indians. This attitude is reflected in the practice of Muslims all over the world of remaining continent while making the pilgrimage to Mecca. Other examples of the 'unmanning' belief concerning intercourse are found amongst many American Indian societies, and in the case of Europe there was the Greek belief, in classical times, that intercourse with a woman before battle made a man cowardly, but intercourse with a boy was encouraged as this did not impair one's martial qualities!

Considerations of this kind—fear, uncleanliness—determine in part the time and place that savage man chooses for sexual intercourse.

Although the great majority of peoples, except at times of ritual licence, tend to copulate in private there are some examples to the contrary. Captain Cook reported that copulation was publicly performed in Tahiti. The French explorer La Pérouse makes a similar statement concerning Samoa. It was reported of ancient Thessaly that women had no objection to any kind of sexual act being performed publicly. Xenophon and Diodorus both tell of the Mosnhi, a people of Pontus in the Black Sea, that 'the men have intercourse with the women in front of everybody . . .'

In contemporary societies, those of Formosa and the island of Yap near the Philippines are the only ones where similar practices exist. The indigenous Formosans appear to have no inhibitions against copulating in public in the daytime. They do, however, dislike the presence of children. On the other hand the Yapese will copulate almost anywhere at any time, and do not object to the presence of other people. If we disregard these instances it seems clear that the great majority of peoples demand some degree of privacy. Since the belief is current that coitus is possibly both dangerous and fearful for the participants, privacy becomes a reasonable requirement.

Granted the savage demands privacy does he in fact succeed in finding it?

Housing in most primitive societies generally consists of an isolated hut for each family, or communal dwelling houses for several families. In neither can the privacy which is characteristic of European housing be easily obtained. Some societies overcome this difficulty by the institution of open-air intercourse. For example, many Pacific peoples such as the Buru Islanders will copulate by day in a secluded part of the forest. An additional reason in their case may be the one they themselves offer, that they are too tired at night after the day's labour.

Privacy in one's hut is, of course, obtainable in the sense that no other adults may be present, but there are inevitably children.

This consideration does not appear to loom very large in the parents' minds. We should bear in mind that this indifference to the presence of children in the face of sexual appetite is not common to savage society alone—the same indifference is reproduced in over-crowded working-class housing conditions in Europe and America. The hut may be said to provide relative privacy, that is freedom from the presence of other adults who would witness the dangerous act and possibly be able to work magic against one as a result. It is thus preferable to the open air which may render the act visible to others, and, unless you are an indigenous Formosan or Yap Islander, this is undesirable.

But privacy is by no means always assured within the hut. The following account by A. R. Holmberg of the Siriono, a polygynous Indian tribe of Eastern Bolivia, shows the extreme form that lack of privacy can take: 'Much more intercourse takes place in the bush than in the house. The principal reason for this is that privacy is almost impossible to obtain within the hut where as many as fifty hammocks may be hung in the confined space of five hundred square feet. Moreover, the hammock of a man and his wife hangs not three feet from that of the former's mother-in-law. Furthermore, young children commonly sleep with the father and mother, so there may be as many as four or five people crowded together in a single hammock. In addition to these frustrating circumstances, people are up and down most of the night, quieting children, cooking, eating, urinating, and defecating. All in all, therefore, the conditions of sexual behaviour in the house are most unfavourable. Consequently intercourse is indulged in more often in some secluded nook in the forest.

'. . . Unmarried couples and potential spouses, of course, must take advantage of whatever opportunities arise. A favourite spot for sexual indulgence between potential spouses, when there is one near the camp, is a patch of ripening maize, which is generally both near at hand and secluded . . .' [2]

The unfortunate Siriono are undoubtedly driven to seek the forest as their living conditions are so appalling.

On the other hand where the house or hut provides reasonable accommodation as is the case with the Hopi, the rationalisation offered is that legitimate copulation must take place in the house—anywhere else would be unthinkable. The Hopi are Pueblo

Indians of the American south-west and have rock and cave
dwellings as well as substantial structures of dried mud (adobe)
divided into rooms. It is easy to see that they are arguing from
what in our society would be a comfortable middle-class background. Other people such as the Lango of Uganda have a similar
point of view, but again their housing, while not of Pueblo
standards, is immeasurably superior to that of the Siriono. Thus
we can say that in many instances preference for either outdoors or
the hut as a place for copulation is determined by essentially
utilitarian reasons. One people, the Kiwai, near the southern
coast of New Guinea formerly inhabited communal 'long houses',
which are a characteristic pattern in New Guinea. In recent years
due to a number of external factors families have begun to live in
individual houses. Whereas formerly copulation took place out of
doors the tendency today is for the house to become the setting
for sexual intercourse.

The utilitarian attitude is, however, by no means universal. The
Gonds, an aboriginal tribe of the Central Provinces of India, refuse
to copulate in their houses on the grounds that to do so will cause
them to lose their possessions. This clearly has to do with the
danger associated with the act—its debilitating effects on the man.
The Gond rationalisation is that the goddess of wealth lives in the
house and she is liable to be outraged if forced to witness copulation. Similar reasoning is apparent in the case of the Yurok, a
Californian Indian tribe, who believe that sexual activity in the
house will prevent their making a material success of life. Such
ideas, while not utilitarian in the ordinary sense, are examples of
the belief in the possible disgust of the supernatural beings for
human sexual activity. There are other societies where an aesthetic
attitude determines the place of coitus.

In Polynesia there is a tendency in some communities, such as
the inhabitants of the island of Pukapuka, to choose a quiet part of
the forest for their love-play and its consummation. The people
of Wogeo off the northern coast of New Guinea almost invariably
copulate for preference in the forest or on the beach. But such
regard for the surroundings is not typical amongst married couples
in most societies. The aesthetic element only becomes prominent
when lovers as opposed to the married are considered.

Lovers in most savage societies have to seize the opportunity whenever it occurs. This applies equally well to the conduct of an adulterous *affaire* or of liaisons between the unmarried. Obviously in the case of adultery the house or hut of either party is hardly likely to be safe from detection. Thus some secluded spot in the jungle or elsewhere is invariably chosen. The 'bush' offers the opportunity of clandestine assignations which are impossible in living quarters. Adultery in any society is never openly tolerated unless it is for ritual purposes or is part of the institution of sexual hospitality. This being the case the 'place' for adultery is nearly always outside the house.

With liaisons between the unmarried the picture is much more variegated. There is a rough division between those societies which encourage pre-marital sexual intercourse, such as the Muria of Central India, and have special institutions for this purpose; and those in which such activity takes place, but is not actively encouraged, yet nevertheless tolerated, as amongst certain of the Pueblo Indians of the American south-west. A third group would consist of societies where any sexual contact between the sexes before marriage is stringently avoided and breaches of the tabu are severely punished. Some peoples of Madagascar, the Iroquois Indians of North America, and the society of Lifu in the Loyalty Islands in the Pacific would belong to this third category.

Love affairs appear to occur amongst all peoples, and in some savage groups the conduct of an affair is characterised by great refinement of taste. The setting chosen is frequently one of beauty as the following quotation shows: '. . . The *Kwakwadu* has a wide meaning. It signifies a collective excursion, or party of several couples setting out on a love picnic; the being together of two people who are in love with each other—a sort of erotic *tête à tête*; the caresses and approaches before the final union . . . We shall attempt to reconstruct the behaviour of a pair who have left such a party. The scrub surrounding the village, which is periodically cut for gardens, grows in a dense underbush and does not everywhere offer a desirable resting place. Here and there, however, a large tree, such as the butia, is left behind for the sake of its perfumed flowers, or there may be a group of pandanus trees. Pleasant shady places, too, can be found under an old tree in one of the groves which often mark the site of a deserted village whose fruit trees, coco-nut-palm, and big banyans make an oasis within the stunted tropical undergrowth of recent cultivation. On the coral ridge (*raybwag*) many spots invite a picnic party. Cavities and hollows in the coral, rocks of queer or attractive shape, giant trees, thickets or fern, flowering hibiscus make the raybwag a mysterious and attractive region ... The roar of the breakers on the fringing reef, the dazzling sand and foam from the blue sea provide the favourite surroundings for native love-making ... In such places the lovers enjoy the scent and colour of the flowers, they watch the birds and insects, and go down to the beach to bathe ... All such pleasures—the enjoyment of landscape, or colour and scent in the open air, of wide views and of intimate caress of Nature—are essential features in their love-making ...' [3]

The Trobriand youths described by Malinowski in that passage belong to that group of societies which actively encourage pre-marital sexual activity. The daytime and afternoons are the times for a kwakwadu, but at night the young lovers are catered for in the bukumatula or village dormitory, where they can make love as much as they like. In other words, as sexual liaisons amongst the unmarried are encouraged by the society, the choice of the place of assignation is governed by the aesthetic pleasure of erotic play—on a coral reef by day, and the half secrecy of the dormitory by night.

In those societies which condone but do not openly encourage young lovers there are frequently customs such as that possessed by the Hopi Indians. This is known by the Hopi as *Dumaiya*. The young man, suitably disguised, is able to pay visits at night to homes of the girls he loves. If the girl sleeps alone, and this is probable in Pueblo society, he can spend the whole night with her and have intercourse with her. The parents generally know of such visits. Nevertheless the boy will leave before dawn so that he will not make the affair known to everyone. If, in fact, they are caught together no serious punishment results. The parental attitude is apt to be governed by whether the boy is a suitable prospective bridegroom or not. Both boys and girls may have several lovers, and courtship is conducted in this semi-clandestine way in the girl's home. If in time she becomes pregnant she will choose her favourite lover, and in most cases a match is arranged between the respective families. Apart from the Dumaiya the Hopi unmarried lovers rely on chance encounters away from the public.

The Lepchas in that part of Sikkim which borders on Tibet have a somewhat down to earth attitude with regard to the management of sexual affairs: '. . . Lepcha sexual experience can be divided into four categories: legitimate copulation with one's spouse, which almost always takes place in the house; semi-legitimate copulation with potential . . . spouses, which usually takes place either in the house during the husband's temporary absence, or in casual encounters in the forest or field-house, since it is considered tactless to allow the husband to witness such copulations; thirdly, intrigues with unmarried girls which entail clandestine visits by the young man at night; and lastly, sudden and clandestine encounters which may or may not be adulterous, in the fields or forests or at big feasts. The last named are always excessively hurried and rather romantic; hurried because there is the fear of being surprised and romantic because they are unforeseen and unprepared . . . If unmarried and unrelated men and women wish to sleep together, the man will find out from the girl her exact sleeping position in her house; then at his own home he will wait till he can hear everybody sleeping, creep out on hands and knees, run to her house, which may be a couple of villages away, and creep in beside her. He must return to his own home before cockcrow. Normally if a man is surprised he will run away and not come back again; but it occasionally happens that these originally clandestine intrigues become socially recognised and the lover goes to live, either temporarily or permanently, with his mistress, particularly if she is past the age of child bearing . . . If the woman is of child bearing age she will more often go to live with her lover, especially if he is an householder in his own right . . .' [4]

The Lepcha appear to have thought the problem out very efficiently. As we have seen in a former chapter their marriage system is somewhat exceptional.

From the evidence it does appear that the place of coitus is dependent upon a number of factors such as housing, the attitude of the society in question towards pre-marital sexual intercourse, and who are the parties concerned. Clearly these same factors govern the time at which intercourse will take place. If the place is outdoors the day is generally chosen, night is excluded as there is the fear of the dark and its association with the supernatural which is very widespread amongst all societies. In addition the chance encounter which leads to copulation invariably takes place in the daytime as people do not venture forth at night.

If the place is indoors then coitus is really only possible at night when other residents in the house or hut are presumed to be asleep. This applies equally to the village dormitories which are only inhabited at night. In other words, when it is permitted, or semi-clandestine intercourse, the time is generally the night. Exceptions to this like the Siriono, Formosans, and Yapese have been noted. When the intercourse is illicit or not sanctioned, the casual encounter is by day.

Frequency of intercourse is not a topic which easily finds explicit expression amongst pre-literate peoples. There is, in fact, little philosophy of sexual practice as occurs in the case of advanced societies. Frequency at this level of society is governed, apart from the capacity of individuals, by extra-sexual factors. We have enumerated some of these which are based on tabus connected with fear of the sex act on the part of men. Women may become tabued and unclean during menstruation, pregnancy, and after childbirth. Such tabus concerning continence are fairly widespread. But there are others which appear to have only a local incidence.

A Melanesian practice found in several island communities is for men to abstain from intercourse before going fishing or engaging in new agricultural work. This last is true of the Trobrianders and the Koita tribe of Papua. Continence before fishing expeditions is observed by the people of the Manus Islands, and Caroline Islands. There is, however, an isolated case from North America. Nootka men of the north-west coast had to abstain from their wives for a period of *months* before embarking on whale fishing. [5]

The principle at work seems to be that almost any action the outcome of which is important but uncertain is liable to be assisted by sexual continence. The psychological complications of this can best be understood by comparing a European couple in which the male partner has serious business worries. It is unlikely that he will make a satisfactory lover, and in the interests of the couple's relationship it is best that he should refrain. The importance of continence and other creative acts is vividly portrayed by certain Australian aborigines. One of the central beliefs of these people is that all animal and vegetable species must be renewed by man in the appropriate ways. If this fails the species will die, with consequent disaster for the people who depend upon them for their livelihood. The individual who is generally responsible for such rites is called the *Alatunja* or headman. His role is a decisive one. In one tribe, the Kaitish, it is incumbent upon him to remain continent throughout the period of the rites. [6] In the same tribe this restriction is extended to all the initiated men who partake in the rain-making ceremonies.

One, somewhat strange, custom obtains in the island of Wogeo off Northern New Guinea. Here, as in classical India, individuals should not engage in intercourse unless both are in a fit and proper state. Among the Wogeo, menstruation acts as a means of cleansing—after a woman has menstruated she is clean. For a man 'cleanliness' or protection from disease, is not so easily obtained. Logically enough he undergoes a process of 'male menstruation': for this the individual periodically makes a cut in his penis and the blood is allowed to flow; intercourse is forbidden to him until the wound is healed which may take as long as two months after the operation. 'Male menstruation' is brought about prior to any serious undertaking, such as burial of a corpse, building a house, and so on. [7] This type of purificatory rite is also found amongst the Arapesh tribe in New Guinea. [8]

The range of activities, preparation for which may involve continence, is very large. It includes seed-planting (the Bakongo of Central Africa), the preparation of poison (the Masai of East Africa) ironworking (Fanti of West Africa), the making of pots (Naga of North-west India), and gathering peyotl (Huichol Indians of Mexico).

Apart from the almost universal tabus on intercourse during menstruation and after childbirth, there is another period of continence which appears to occur in widely separated groups. This is the time before battle. It has been reported of a great number of African societies such as the Zulu, the Konde of Nyasaland, the Ba-Ila of Rhodesia. Such abstinence occurs in the Caroline Islands, New Britain, the Manus Islands, and in Papua. [9]

A further group of prohibitions relating to sexual intercourse is concerned with death. For a bereaved spouse in many societies, coitus is forbidden for varying periods. There may be a difference of extent in the obligatory period for the widower and the widow. Among the Kongo of Central Africa, for example, the latter has to wait up to two years before re-marriage. The man, however, can re-marry as soon as he has buried his wife. The ban on coitus may extend to immediate relatives of the dead person. This occurs amongst the Jivaro Indians of South America. In extreme cases the whole community has to remain continent until the funeral is over, as is demanded by custom in Lesu in the Pacific. [10]

A somewhat rare injunction with relation to coitus occurs amongst the Kwakuitl Indians of British Columbia. After the individual has eaten human flesh as part of a special ritual he is subject to a number of restrictions. For example for sixteen days he may not eat hot food, for four months he may not blow on hot food to cool it, for a year he cannot gamble or work. Sexual relations with his wife are forbidden for the same period. [11]

From the examples we have quoted it seems clear that frequency of intercourse is, as we have suggested, governed by factors other than the strictly sexual. The picture which some people may have of the 'savage' indulging his unbridled passion on every possible occasion has to be revised. A comparison could very well be made between the effect of 'Saints' Days' in Catholic countries on the working year, and the innumerable days on which you are compelled to abstain from your wife in the simple societies. In both cases the effect on activity in considerable. In this connection it appears that the celebration of feast days in Russia with their concomitant drunkenness and absence from work on the following days is causing severe disquiet to the Soviet authorities (1958).

The Zuni Indian (American south-west) regulations regarding abstinence give some indication of the limitations which may occur in a society at the simple level. Coitus is forbidden for ten days during the winter solstice and for four days subsequent to the planting of prayer sticks. In addition it is forbidden during the performance of religious dances and ceremonies. It should be added that these people are famous for the complexity of their religious ceremonies and the frequency with which they are held. If to these restrictive occasions are added those which we have mentioned such as menstruation and childbirth it becomes apparent that days on which sexual intercourse is permissible are somewhat limited.

Apart from tabus imposed by man, the environment in which a people lives and the occupation pursued may be a determinant in such matters. Hunting societies demand that males shall be absent for considerable periods in search of game. Cattle rearing may demand absence while the herdsman are away at pastures some distance from the village. There are many other instances.

In general we can say that frequency of intercourse for the simple peoples is determined, apart from individual capacity, by man-made tabus, and by environmental factors. (12)

When the advanced societies are considered it is seen that frequency of coitus has from early times been a subject of debate, legislation, and tabu. This is a somewhat paradoxical situation as amongst 'primitive' peoples the influence of superstition and magic has clearly a great deal to do with sexual tabus; but in the civilisations where man has developed speculative thought, it is strange that a matter which logically should be left to the individual's capacity and initiative has been argued about and legislated about by both lay and ecclesiastical authorities.

Amongst the earliest regulations dealing with the frequency of intercourse are those contained in the Laws of Manu. There it is laid down for Hindus that only two weeks in each month were to be permitted as days of sexual pleasure. We have already mentioned the Parvan or forbidden days. Another ancient lawyer, Zoroaster, prescribed intercourse once in nine days. Solon was equally parsimonious in allowing three times a month. At a considerably later period, the Koran enjoins once a week. The Jewish Talmud goes into details according to the occupation of the individuals concerned. There is a decreasing frequency from the virile but not hardworking youth who was permitted intercourse once a day to the scholar with a quota of once a week. The labourer occupied an intermediate position with an allotment of twice a week.

Havelock Ellis quotes the above restrictions to maintain a thesis that the frequency allowed can be correlated with the amount of sexual stimulation which exists. (13) That is to say as stimulation increases so does the permitted frequency. This is not really tenable in the face of evidence as to extent and degree of erotic stimulation in early civilisations. Evidence from Hindu and Greek sources only would seem to indicate that sexual stimulation was as great if not greater than in the Middle Ages, or in contemporary Europe. The erotic poetry, love-magic, and orgiastic festivals of the Greeks, are sufficient indications that these people did not suffer from a lack of sexual incentives.

A point, however, which Ellis makes a little later, is of much greater validity. He suggests that the classical regulations on this topic were entirely inspired by men, and if women had had any influence the permitted times would have been subject to much greater variation, since the variations of the sexual impulse are greater in women. [14] He cites the two extremes of Queen Zenobia who allowed her husband intercourse once a month if she were not pregnant, and a Queen of Aragon who solemnly declared that six times a day was proper in marriage! There is considerable clinical evidence to support the view that coitus does not leave a woman physically weakened as it does a man, and that there is extensive variation in the capacity of different women for sexual intercourse.

To understand the sexual regulations of the Middle Ages it is necessary to appreciate that the Early Church was, from one point of view, obsessed with the sinfulness of carnal desire. There are innumerable references in the works of the Holy Fathers which inveigh against concupiscence and adulate chastity. Marriage was apparently no more than tolerated. Tertullian puts the case nicely: marriage 'consists of that which is the essence of fornication'; on the other hand chastity 'is a means whereby a man will traffic in a mighty substance of sanctity.' [15] Again the fact that the Council of Gangra in the fourth century A.D. had to condemn anyone who supported the view that a married Christian could not go to heaven is indicative of the strong feeling in favour of chastity. [16] To restore the balance a later Council, that of Mediola (A.D.390), excommunicated a monk for his denial of the doctrine that virginity was more worthy than marriage. [17] As St Justin says, marriage is only permitted to man as necessary for the perpetuation of the human race, and as an imperfect curb on his licentiousness. [18] In the twelfth century Peter Lombard is maintaining tha to love one's wife is a sin worse than adultery. [19] Thomas Aquina is not so extreme; he merely says that although marriage is no contrary to the love of God it is nevertheless an obstacle to it. [20

It is against this background of belief and doctrine that some of the most curious documents in European history have to be examined. These are the series of Penitential Books which appeared throughout the Middle Ages. The earliest books of this kind date from the Celtic Church of Ireland. They were primarily intended as guides for confessors. Every transgression is given its appropriate penance. It appears, however, that a disproportionate amount of space is given up to sins of a sexual nature—fornication, sodomy and bestiality. For example, in the Anglo-Saxon Penitential of Theodore (A.D. 668–690) the two longest sections are devoted to fornication and marital questions. [21] No aspect of sexual misbehaviour is left to the imagination. The confessor was thus in a strong position to deal with his penitents. There is little doubt that these books are unique in more than one way: they do represent one of the few examples of an attempt to control the sexual life of human beings by legislation, and the ultimate sanction of eternal damnation. The saintly authors, among them Bede and Dunstan, were no doubt following in the steps of the Holy Fathers—but the Penitentials remain a monument to the mediaeval sense of sin. [22]

Curiously enough the Penitential Books were not officially sanctioned by the Popes. [23] The clergy's attitudes towards them were ambivalent: in A.D. 813, the Council of Chalons decreed that priests should give penances for sins according to the official canons, 'paying no attention to the books called Penitentials, whose errors are as certain as their authorship is uncertain. [24] Another Council at Paris in A.D. 829 ordered bishops to make enquiries into the Penitentials used in their dioceses; those that conflicted with the official canons should be burnt. [25] On the other hand, the Council of Aix in A.D. 802 stated that a necessary qualification for the priesthood was a thorough knowledge of the Penitentials; this was an opinion endorsed by Hatto of Basel (A.D. 806–836). What emerges is that confessors really needed an exact tariff of sins and penances to expedite their work. So although the Penitentials were reformed in later years to comply with canon law, the older unreformed books continued to be in popular use among the clergy. [26]

'To have intercourse except for procreation is to do injury to nature' (Clement of Alexander, *Paedagogus*, Bk. II. Ch. X), is not an attitude which is peculiar to Christianity. Many peoples believe that sexual intercourse is polluting, and this belief demands abstinence before undertaking a critical activity or participation in a religious ceremony. So far as the Church was concerned the result was a whole series of prohibitions affecting the frequency of marital coitus.

In the first place intercourse was forbidden on Sundays, feast days, and fast days—this would involve Fridays and possibly Wednesday. Failure to abstain meant a variety of penances and, for the persistent offender, a special version of hell-fire. According to the *visio* of Alberic, a twelfth century work, a molten lake of lead, pitch, and resin was reserved for such sinners. [27] A strict interpretation of Lent as a period of fasting would naturally prohibit sexual union for the period prior to Easter; the same would apply to Advent before Christmas. If to these usual days be added the obligatory abstinence before taking communion, and various other special times, the period of continence demanded of the medieval couple extended to nearly half the year. For example the Penitential of Theodore states that a couple must abstain for three nights before taking communion, for forty days before Easter, and for forty days after the birth of a child of either sex. [28] Whether in fact these prohibitions were observed in practice it is impossible to ascertain. The Church had no means beyond the confessional of knowing if the injunction had been kept. Obviously a religious couple would feel impelled to abstain on the required days, and if they offended would confess. But there must have been a great number who, in defiance of spiritual dangers, transgressed the regulations. For the bold, to flirt with hell-fire must have added a piquancy to marital relations.

The mediaeval obsession with control of sex reaches its logical conclusion in the heretical sect of Cathari which flourished in South-eastern France in the twelfth century. One of their principal doctrines was the denial of sexual intercourse to the initiated. For them carnality hampered spiritual development—the next step was obvious. [29]

Although the profound effect of the Early Church in such matters could never be entirely destroyed the Renaissance undoubtedly did much to render attitudes more permissive. One of the results of the Reformation in the sixteenth century is the beginning of the process whereby sexual offences cease to be the concern of the ecclesiastical courts and become a matter for the civil authorities. The change in attitude is exemplified by Luther's pronouncement that intercourse twice a week was the mean at which married couples should aim. He is not concerned with feast days and fast days; for him it is a question more of hygiene than of spirituality. Luther's advice has been endorsed by numerous authorities since his day.

In Britain from the Reformation to the present day sexual attitudes have undergone great changes and modifications. Puritanism is replaced by the licentiousness of the Restoration. The freedom of the eighteenth century is followed by the restraints of the

Fig. 13. A mediaeval woodcut depicting sexual intercourse

Victorian age. But throughout all these changes there is no attempt to impose regulations regarding legitimate sexual intercourse—fornication and adultery is properly a matter for the courts, but how frequently a man indulged himself with his wife is left to him to decide.

There is one factor which affects frequency of intercourse, and which is part physiological and part social: this is menstruation. The menstruating woman in primitive society is commonly regarded as unclean and tabu. Intercourse is strictly forbidden to her. The menstrual tabu is compounded of different elements: there is the idea amongst some peoples that the flow of blood at this time is connected with hymenal blood; from this it is inferred that the menses are caused through intercourse with an evil spirit or spirit animal, or through such a being biting the woman. This is a belief found in Australia, New Guinea, and elsewhere. It is a belief which is not entirely confined to such peoples. Havelock Ellis quotes a Portuguese custom that women wear special drawers at this time to prevent their being bitten by lizards.

What is far more general is the acceptance of the idea that women are essentially unclean during menstruation, and moreover capable of causing great evil to men who are contaminated by them. As Frazer puts it: 'Thus the object of secluding women at menstruation is to neutralise the dangerous influences which are supposed to emanate from them at such times.' [30] In practically all societies at this level there is complete segregation at the first menses; there may later be a slight relaxation of the tabu on subsequent occasions.

The French sociologist Durkheim in the course of an essay on the origins of incest suggests that the awe in which menstruous blood is held is part of the extremely widespread conception in all types of societies that all blood is of a sacred and divine character, and thus tabu. Of the menstruous woman he wrote: 'A more or less conscious anxiety, a certain religious fear, cannot fail to enter into all the relations of her companions with her, and that is why all such relations are reduced to a minimum. Relations of a sexual character are specifically excluded. In the first place, such relations are so intimate that they are incompatible with the sort of repulsion which the sexes must experience for each other; the barrier between them does not permit of such a union. In the second place the organs of the body here specially concerned are precisely the source of the dreaded manifestation. Thus it is natural that the feelings of aversion inspired by women attain their greatest intensity at this point. Thus it is that of all parts of the feminine organisation it is this region which is most severely shut out from commerce . . .' [31]

Another authority W. Robertson-Smith, indicates the widespread incidence of this tabu: 'The impurity of menstruation was recognised by all the Semites, as in fact it is by all primitive and ancient peoples. Now among savages this impurity is distinctly connected with the idea that the blood of the menses is dangerous to man, . . . Similar superstitions are current with the Arabs, a great variety of supernatural powers attaching themselves to a woman in this condition. Obviously, therefore, in this case the Semitic taboo is exactly like the savage one; it has nothing to do with respect for the gods but springs from mere terror of the supernatural influences associated with the woman's physical condition . . . ('32)

Some examples of the awe in which menstruous woman is held will make clear its world-wide incidence.

In Central Australia the Luritcha tribe believe that to cohabit with a menstruating woman produces a bodily degeneration. (33) The people of Mangareva in the Pacific assume that any contact with a woman at this time produces blindness. (34) Suk warriors of the Nilotic Sudan cannot eat anything touched by a menstruating woman or their virility will be lost. (35) ' "When a woman has her menstruation the evil spirits are angry with her".' This is the firm belief of the Bolivian Toba Indians. (36)

Some peoples believe that the menses cannot take place unless sexual intercourse has occurred. This has been reported of the Déné Indians of Canada and of some tribes in Madagascar. (37) There are very few instances in which a society allows or enjoins sexual intercourse at the time of the monthly period. This is reported of the Maori, the people of Truk in the Carolines, the Walapai Indians of Arizona and the A-Kamba of East Africa. Of these last it is said: '. . . When a married woman menstruates, the husband cohabits with her that night, the idea being that she will probably conceive. (38)

As we have seen coitus at menstruation was tabu for the Semitic peoples. The Jews had very strong prohibitions to this effect. There is, for example, the injunction in Levitcus, XV, 24: 'If a man copulateth with her in the time of her flowers, he shall be unclean seven days: and every bed on which he shall sleep shall be defiled.' The Hebrew attitude can be said to be in part responsible for the European-Christian attitude towards intercourse with a woman during her period: this is very largely one of revulsion. Against this is the opinion of Catholic theologians such as Sanchez and St Alphonse Liguori which permitted it. (39) In most people's minds it is associated with uncleanliness. This in part may be based on the idea, which was still current until recently, that to have a bath or to wash the affected area was dangerous. On the other hand the actual smell of a menstruating woman may act as a powerful sexual stimulus in the case of some men. [40] Again, there are women who experience great sexual desire at the onset of the menses and as it is ending. It would be extremely difficult to assess exactly how far menstruation affects the frequency of intercourse in societies such as our own. An inspired guess might be that in a majority of instances it acts as a deterrent to coitus.

In this connection Schapera's account of the menstrual tabu amongst the Kgatla tribe in South Africa is pertinent. The Kgatla have a belief in what they describe as 'hotness'. 'Hotness' is a condition of the blood which may be brought about by various actions, including coitus, and events such as being widowed or, if you are a doctor, having a patient die. For a man to copulate when he is hot may lead to impotence or becoming crippled. [41] 'The main prohibition for all married people, however, is during the wife's menstrual periods. In addition to fearing the consequences to which I have already referred, women say that they themselves feel no sexual desire at all during this time, and therefore strongly object to having intercourse with their husbands.' [42]

This, if we bear in mind the supposition that some women are likely to feel in a state of sexual excitement during their period, could be regarded as an example of cultural conditioning. In the same way, European women, having the tradition that intercourse is distasteful to men at this time, would repress their desires.

There are other limitations on frequency imposed by custom: the sexual tabu on the pregnant woman is almost as wide in its incidence as that on the menstruous woman; it exists in societies in all parts of Africa, (e.g. Bakongo, Nandi, Masai), is a common practice in Melanesia, and is found in North and South America. [43] The rationalisations given are similar to those regarding menstruation: that the woman is impure at this time, the child would be born deformed, the mother's milk would be soured, ill luck would dog the father in his occupation, and so on. Of course the tabu on intercourse is only part of a wider complex of tabu which imposes restrictions on both husband and wife at this time. [44]

Although the pregnant woman in most societies is regarded in a special way there are some tribal groups which allow, and even require, that the husband should copulate with her while she is in this condition. For example the South African Kgatla, recommend intercourse at this time on the grounds that it promotes the growth of the foetus. [45] The Arapesh of New Guinea require continual cohabitation for the first two months of pregnancy. After this period the child is regarded as being firmly placed in the womb. [46] The most extreme instance is where pregnancy actually increases the frequency of coitus. This is found among the Ekoi and other tribes of Southern Nigeria. (Intercourse is, in fact, more frequent during these months than at any other time). It continues until the actual birth. [47]

The same pattern of tabu is repeated in connection with the period after the birth of a child. The mother is dangerous and unclean and no intercourse can take place until she has been purified. Apart from ritual cleansing, the passage of time in itself will restore the mother to her original, uncontaminated position. The estimate of the requisite time before this can happen varies a great deal. A general rule is that the tabu on copulation lasts until the child is weaned. This may be for only a year as it is among the Masai, and Bambala of East Africa. Or it may extend for two or three years as occurred in the Buganda of Central Africa, the Huron Indians of North America, and the Fijians. There are instances where the time of tabu may be as long as five or six years. This has been reported of the Pawnee Indians of North America and some Indian tribes in Paraguay. [48] The logic of tabu in this respect is the same as in the case of menstruation and pregnancy— the woman is unclean. This is exemplified in cases where the actual birth must take place away from the community. The Arunta of Australia, the Arapesh of New Guinea, the people of Wogeo in Melanesia, the Tlingit Indians of Alaska, all have this requirement. [49]

Superficially it appears that the tabu on copulation after a childbirth is extremely onerous. In practice, the effects are almost entirely mitigated by the existence of polygyny in almost all the societies where such tabus exist. If a man does not possess another wife recourse can always be had to the illicit affair. It should be noted that the tabus concerning menstruation, pregnancy and childbirth affect intercourse only with the woman in question— the husband is thus free to copulate with another wife or any other woman.

In mediaeval Europe abstinence was demanded, as we have said, for forty days after a birth, but for the contemporary European there are few tabus in the primitive sense which control intercourse during pregnancy or after childbirth. The factors involved for abstinence and against it are essentially medical and psychological. Van de Velde in his *Ideal Marriage* (pp. 260–8) sums these up most effectively. He points out that very few physicians give advice to patients as to whether they should refrain from intercourse during pregnancy, or when sexual relations should be resumed after the birth of a child. It is probably true that in a majority of instances among the lower classes neither period acts as an effective deterrent. The feelings of the woman may be entirely ignored.

This is not altogether borne out by the study made of American wives by K. B. Davis.[50] He found that twenty-six and two-fifths per cent experienced intercourse throughout the whole period of pregnancy; sixty-two per cent for part of the period; eleven and six-tenths per cent had no coital experience at all during the pregnancy.

As we have said the advice given by Luther has not been improved upon. Most writers on the subject since his day have endorsed his opinion. But the implication behind their suggestions as to frequency of intercourse is that it is basically a matter of desire and capacity. Of course husband and wife may not by any means be complementary in this respect. The opinions of one early twentieth century sexologist are worth quoting if only on the grounds of their complete opposition to contemporary thought on the subject. Dr. E. H. Kisch has the following to say: '... When affected with intense sexual excitement, a woman is much more unfavourably situated than a man, since man claims the right to indulge in sexual intercourse whenever he feels disposed, and has, moreover, ample opportunity for sexual gratification. A woman, however, properly endowed with self-respect, will understand how to bridle her senses. Bodily exercise, moderate, stimulating diet, intellectual occupation with serious matters, the avoidance of equivocal literature and of sensual dramatic representations, cold bathing and the use of a hard mattress and light bed-clothing— these means will co-operate powerfully toward the prevention of excessive sensual desire ...'[51] Comment is superfluous.

It is interesting to note that the two authorities who have probably had, in Britain at any rate, more influence on sexual practice than any others, are in disagreement over this question of frequency. The late Marie Stopes was a firm believer in a female cycle or rhythm of desire. That it to say that women experience a period of sexual indifference followed, after an interval, by a period of intense desire. This led her to say, 'the mutually best regulation of intercourse in marriage is to have three or four days of repeated unions, followed by about ten days without any unions at all, unless some strong external stimulus has stirred a mutual desire . . .' (52) Van de Velde denies the existence of such a period in ordinary women. He suggests it may occur in some women, but it is unsafe to generalise from this. (53) In his view frequency should be dictated by mutual desire.

Certain eccentric religious groups as late as the nineteenth century had emulated the example of the mediaeval Cathars in excluding coitus from their scheme of things. Examples are the Russian Skoptzi, notorious for their mutilation of the female breast, and castration; and the millenary American New Harmony colony. But such extremism is rare in recent times. What is perhaps more relevant is the advice given to Roman Catholics: for either spouse to make immoderate demands is regarded as unlawful. 'Moderate' is defined in Luther's terms but, and this is an extremely sensible admission, if it does not endanger health, almost every night can also be considered 'moderate'. In other words demands should be adjusted to capacity. (54)

The law in the United States takes notice of unreasonable demands for coitus in connection with suits for divorce and other matters. The presumption of proof, in the case of divorce, appears to be with the spouse who is suing. Opposing decisions have been given so that it is difficult to see what in fact would constitute excessive demands in a legal sense. In one case a wife pleaded that for twenty years her husband '. . . abused me with sexual intercourse at all times . . . If I refused he would bribe me with money . . .' (55)

There is another and negative aspect of coitus which is recognised in both moral and legal codes in the contemporary western world. Jewish and Christian codes lay down the principle that there is an obligation for both spouses to engage in coitus. Persistent denial by either spouse is considered a mortal sin according to Roman Catholic doctrine. [56] The Jewish code states that there must be mutual consent—the husband must not force his wife. [57] These moral injunctions are borne out in the law both in Britain and the United States. The legal doctrine is that failure to grant coitus can lead to an action for the restitution of conjugal rights. If the spouse still refuses after such action then there may be grounds for divorce. The law thus operates at the two extremes: it lays down that intercourse must take place in a marriage, but it does not say how frequently this should occur. At the other extreme it is concerned with excessive demands.

We have attempted to show how the frequency of sexual intercourse is determined by tabu, religion, convention, and moral and legal codes as extra-sexual factors. In the last analysis these are governed by the innate capacities of particular individuals. The law and tabu can order you when not to copulate; they cannot force you beyond your capacities in the other direction.

If all these determinants are taken into consideration we have still to assess the *actual* frequency of coitus. With regard to simple societies such information as exists is mainly unreliable, with one or two notable exceptions. There are sound reasons for this. 'Primitive' informants are no way exceptional in that they demonstrate an ordinary human failing: of a tendency to boast in matters of sexual prowess. We, ourselves, have had this type of experience during fieldwork in the West Indies. One informant refused to retract his statement that as a commercial traveller in Jamaica he had copulated every night with a different woman. There is a simple alternative: either the man was a liar or a sexual athlete. The unreliability of informants can be associated with the fact that in most field reports no mention is made of the age-groups which are being considered. Thus the evidence as a whole tends to be suspect. The table on page 313 has been based on reports quoted by Ford and Beach: [58]

The reader will know how to diminish the record as it appears at the bottom of the table.

Against this must be set the accounts of anthropologists such as Geoffrey Gorer who give precise statements as to the effect of age on frequency of intercourse: 'In their youth and young manhood (the period Lepchas call *Fleng*) Lepcha men would appear to be

TABLE I

People	Locality	Frequency of Coitus
Keraki	New Guinea	Once a week
Lesu	New Ireland	Once or twice a week
Hopi	America (south-west)	Three or four times a week
Crow	Plains Indians of North America	Every night but find it weakening (sic)
Siriono	Eastern Bolivia	Once a day
Aranda	Australia	3–5 times a night
Ifugao	Philippines	Several times a night
Thonga	East Africa	With three or four wives in one night
Chagga	East Africa	Ten times a night

remarkably potent; trustworthy people said that when they were first married they would copulate with their wives five or six, or even eight or nine times in the course of the night, though they would then be tired next day. I have got no comparable information from women, but such statements were often made in mixed company without the women present making any comment or in any way expressing incredulity. This potency diminishes around the age of thirty, but copulation once nightly is still the general rule for married couples . . .' [59]

Until there are studies made which will try to overcome the problems of authenticity and age-grouping, the assessment of coital frequency in such societies will remain difficult. One way of overcoming the former problem would be to check the information obtained from men by a male anthropologist with similar material elicited from women by a woman anthropologist.

These problems are not altogether absent from studies made of and by contemporary Americans. In one such research project, that made by Dickinson and Beam in the Twenties, no ages were given for the 526 couples investigated. Results varied from daily, or oftener, in the case of approximately sixteen per cent of couples to less than once a year in the case of twelve per cent, with a frequency of once or twice a week accounting for nearly forty-one per cent. [60]

The factor of age was found to have considerable effect on frequency in the researches made by Kinsey and his colleagues. For women: '. . . The average (active median) frequencies of marital coitus in the sample had begun at nearly three (2·8) per week for the females who were married in their late teens . . . They had dropped to 2·2 per week by thirty years of age, to 1·5 per week by forty years of age, to 1·0 per week by fifty years of age, and to once in about twelve days (0·6 per week) by age of sixty . . .' [61] For males the figures are closely comparable.

Another American study, dating from 1938, is that of Terman. He found a median frequency of 7·2 a month under the age of twenty-five. This dropped to 4·1 a month between thirty-five and forty-four. Over fifty-five the frequency was 1·2 a month. [62]

Two British studies with different sized samples gave somewhat different results. The study made by P. A. McCance and his colleagues published in 1937 gave a frequency of 1·2 a week in a sample of fifty-six wives, aged twenty to forty-seven. [63] Slater and Woodside's report on working-class marital patterns (1951) gives a frequency of twice a week for 200 couples. [64]

To build up a picture of the incidence of coitus amongst married couples in the Western world it would be necessary for a great many more studies to be undertaken in different societies. For example, so far as we are aware, there are no reports on this topic concerning Latin countries. It is possible that such research might reveal significant differences between predominantly Anglo-Saxon communities and Latin groups.

The adoption of a particular position for coitus may, as we have shown, be dependent upon circumstance. It is even more evident that the use of any position is the result of cultural factors rather than any 'natural' disposition on the part of man. In the case of Oriental peoples there is a considerable literature which conveys information relating to coital postures. [65] If such literature is any indication the Arabs, Persians, Indians and Japanese must display a surprisingly varied sexual technique. Many of these positions remain in the realm of fantasy or the gymnasium, but others can be regarded as reasonable variants.

There is considerable evidence in the form of drawings, paintings, sculpture and pottery from the early periods of man's history which indicates the type of coital posture which has existed in a particular age. Unfortunately we have no means of knowing

whether in fact they represent normal practice, or the unconscious
desire of the artist. Clearly where there is literary corroboration,
as in the case of certain Pompeian wall paintings, we can accept
that such postures were normal.

One of the earliest representations of coital activity is an engraving on the walls of the Grotte des Combarelles in the Dordogne in
France. This shows a man with an erect penis approaching a woman

Fig. 14. Drawing in the Grotte des Combarelles in the Dordogne

from behind—the woman is bending forward with a penis pro-
truding from the cleft of her buttocks. The drawing dates from the
Aurignacian period of the late Old Stone Age, 40,000 years ago.
It demonstrates that this method of intercourse was known to
Aurignacian man but in the absence of other evidence nothing
more can be deduced.

This engraving may be compared with another in the Laussel
Shelter in France dating from the Solutrean period which ante-
dates the Aurignacian. The Laussel engraving is somewhat difficult
to decipher. For some time it was believed to represent the birth of

a child: a more modern interpretation is that it depicts a fairly difficult coital position which is in use amongst some Australian aborigines. [66] The woman is on her back, the man squatting between her legs. The woman is drawn forward until there is genital contact. A variant of this is for the man to bring up the upper part of the woman's body into contact with his breast. It appears to be similar to the Indian Yab-Yum position which is frequently depicted in erotic cave paintings, and obviously requires considerable skill if it is to be successful. The brothel paintings of Pompeii also depict a variant of this.

Another prehistoric rock drawing, that from Bohuslan in Sweden, shows two couples standing up and copulating. [67] This position is also found in Greek and Roman erotic pictures.

Nearer to our own time (approximately 3000 B.C.), seals from Ur of the Chaldees show a copulating pair with the woman on top of the man. [68] This is a position which is frequently depicted in the classical art of a number of civilisations, such as those of the Aztecs and the Peruvians, and in India, China, and Japan. At an early period it is found in Pompeii as well as in Greek vase paintings. The conclusions to be drawn are that this position was probably the most widespread alternative to the face-to-face postures, which is the norm in relatively large sections of our society.

The wall paintings of Pompeii illustrate a number of different positions. We have already mentioned some: the man effecting entry from the rear of the woman, the method which is in use amongst Australian Aborigines, and the face-to-face posture. Others include the man kneeling and the woman placing her legs on his shoulders, and the woman sitting on the man with her back to him, besides several variants of male entry from the rear, e.g., the woman standing, kneeling and lying down. Literary evidence that these coital positions were in use in Greece and Rome comes from a variety of sources. Aristophanes, Ovid, Martial, Lucian, Horace, and Apuleius, are among the most well known. [69] For example, Ovid in his *Art of Love* has this to say: 'Let each woman know herself; from your own bodies fix your methods; one fashion does not suit all alike. Let her who is fair of face recline upon her back; let those whose backs please them be seen from behind. Milanion bore Atlanta's legs upon his shoulders; if they are comely let them be taken thus. A small woman should ride astride . . . A woman whose long flanks deserve to be seen should press the coverlets with the knees, her neck bent backward somewhat. If her thighs be youthful and her breasts without blemish, her lover should stand, and she herself be slant-wise on the couch . . . There are a thousand modes of love; a simple one, and least fatiguing, is when the woman lies upon her right side, half reclined . . .' [70]

It is interesting to see that Ovid relates his suggestions to the appearance of the woman, and is concerned about fatigue. The position which was most recommended by another Latin author, Lucretius, was that the woman should bend forward and the man approach from the rear—the so-called quadrupedal variation. [71]

According to Havelock Ellis the earliest known work on coital positions is an Egyptian papyrus of 1300 B.C. in the State Library at Turin. Apparently it lists fourteen different postures. [72] In contrast the Indian erotic work *Ananga-Ranga*, dating from the twelfth century A.D., gives thirty-two, and the Islamic *Perfumed Garden*, forty. These last two works in common with the *Kamasutra* cannot be described as pornographic in any sense. In fact they are infused with a genuine poetic feeling. The same cannot be said of the work of the sixteenth century Italian, Pietro Aretino. By his industry in pornography he made Venice into a centre for this type of literature. He is most famous for his *Sonetti Lussuriosi* illustrated by Giulio Romano. Romano produced sixteen drawings depicting different sexual positions and Aretino supplied a poetical text to accompany each picture. These are notorious for their grossness and essentially vulgar choice of language. It says a great deal for his depravity that even a Renaissance Pope could not tolerate them. The work was banned and has remained so up to the present time. [73]

We have already discussed the Church's attitude towards sexual intercourse. It is not surprising in the light of that attitude to find that experimentation outside of what was regarded as normal intercourse (i.e., the position where the woman is supine and the man on top of her) was condemned. For example the Penitential of Angers gave forty days' penance, that of Egbert three years, others gave penances of seven years for adopting the 'quadrupedal' posture. [74] Medieval medical opinion was that it tended to induce abortion. [75] Two aspects of sexual intercourse seem to have agitated the minds of theologians from the earliest times. One is

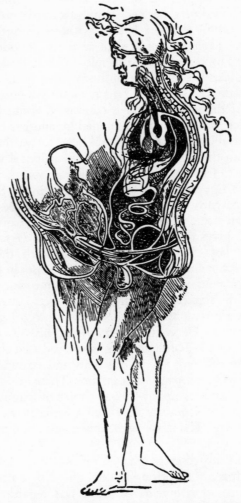

Fig. 15. Leonardo da Vinci's famous *Venus Obversa*

that the employment of variants might lead to enhancement of the pleasure. This would be sufficient to condemn them, as the purpose of coitus is not so much for pleasure as for the perpetuation of the human race. The other develops out of this—variations might hamper conception. How such views were interpreted depended upon particular theologians. Thomas Aquinas severely condemns any variation as mortal sins; whereas Sanchez at a later date is content to classify them as venial. [76] The most usual variant in Western Europe has been that in which the positions of the couple are reversed. This was, by theologians, probably the most condemned. It contained all sorts of evil: the seed would run back from the womb so preventing conception. Equally important it allowed the woman a position of superiority over the man which was quite unthinkable.

The strength and persistence of these Christian strictures can be seen at work today. Kinsey states that a considerable number of people, particularly from the lower educational groups, consider the reversal, as it were, of sexual roles a definite perversion. He says further that there may be unconscious homosexual fears which this usual variant implies. [77]

Modern Catholic theologians have adopted somewhat more lenient views than their predecessors. Arregui states than an unnatural position (that is one different from the woman lying on her back) is only a venial sin. If there is a good cause (e.g. medical reasons) it is not a sin at all. [78] Davis implies that the woman lying on her back is the most proper posture; but other positions are permitted if conception is not endangered. [79] Such opinions are certainly more enlightened than the utter condemnation by mediaeval theologians. But it should be remembered that such condemnation took place against the background of the horror of sexuality which characterised the Church for centuries.

In contrast to Christianity the Koran gave Muslims much greater freedom of choice in this matter: 'Your wives are your tillage: go into your tillage in what manner so ever you will.' But this precept is contradicted by a Muslim saying: 'Cursed be he who maketh woman heaven and man earth.' In fact Muslim theologians appear to have been as much opposed to this elevation of the woman as Christian ones. [80] They have stronger reasons as the whole Muslim philosophy insists on the natural superiority of man.

Modern Jewish thought on the subject of coital positions is similar to Christian views. A man '... should have intercourse in a most modest possible manner ...' [81] For the woman to be above the man is considered immodest and so forbidden.

A nineteenth century sexologist, F. K. Forberg, claimed in his *De figuris Veneris* that there were no less than ninety positions for sexual intercourse. [82] This appears to be one of the highest estimates ever made. Contemporary authorities are much more modest in their assessments.

Fig. 16. Erotic scene on base of a Greek vase

Van de Velde in his *Ideal Marriage* lists ten 'possible' positions. [83] These vary from the normal or habitual posture where the woman is supine to the 'equitation' method of Martial where the woman sits astride the man facing him. Each position is commented on in detail with the stimulation afforded in each case to the man and woman described. This is probably the most adequate treatment of postures in coitus which is available to the ordinary person. They all appear to be not only possible, but essentially practical.

17. Flagellation: from a nineteenth century engraving.

18a. An English eighteenth century brothel.

18b. A nineteenth century
Parisian brothel.

19a. The private room. A nineteenth century lithograph.

19b. "The Rape." After an engraving by Fragonard.

20a. An orgy. From a caricature by Thomas Rowlandson.

20b. English erotic engraving by Newton.

21a. French caricature of
Priapic worship.

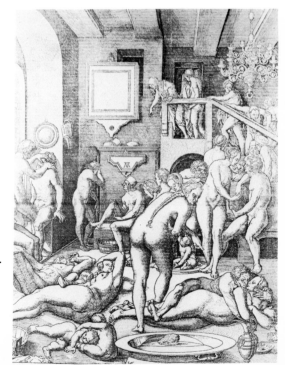

21b. The Bagnio.

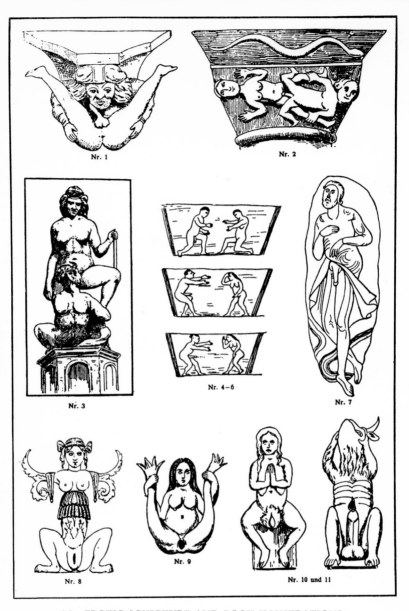

22. EROTIC SCULPTURE AND BOOK ILLUSTRATIONS:

1. Sculpture in the cathedral at Tregnier (France). 2. Bas-Relief on a church in Pairon (France). Disobedience of Adam and Eve. 3. Sculpture in the porch of the L'Isle Adam Church. 4-6. Scenes from a tapestry in Bayeux Cathedral (France). 7. Fresco in the church of St. Savin (France). The Drunken Noah. 8. Ornament in the Raphael room in the Vatican. 9. Sculpture in the north door of the Schotten Church in Regensburg. 10-11. Fountains at the Bishop's Palace in Sens (France).

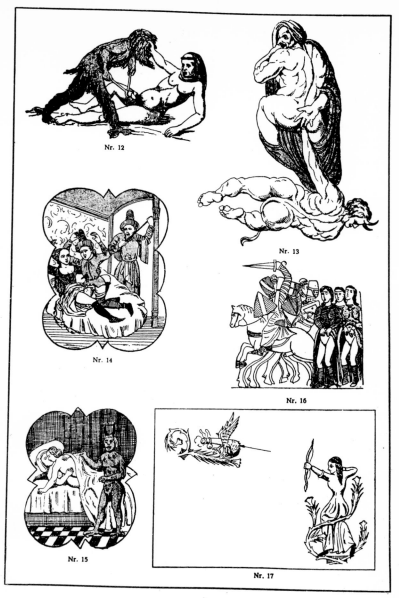

Nr. 12

Nr. 13

Nr. 14

Nr. 16

Nr. 15

Nr. 17

23. EROTIC SCULPTURE AND BOOK ILLUSTRATIONS:

12. Punishment of a monk's fornication from a painting in the church of the Madonna del Arena (Padua). 13. Punishment of Sodomy, after Michel Angelo. 14-15. Miniatures from a Bible of Charles V. 16. Miniature from a French manuscript of the twelfth century. 17. Letterheads from a book on Canonical Law of the year 1400.

24. TWO DRAWINGS BY PICASSO.

What is the contemporary practice as opposed to the theory? There do not seem to be any studies of this regarding Britain. In the case of the United States, Kinsey's researches showed the following results.

TABLE II [84]

Positions Frequently used	IN PRE-MARITAL COITUS Total sample	IN MARITAL COITUS Total sample	Decade of birth Bf. 1900	1900– 1909	1910– 1919	1920– 1929
	%	%	Per cent. of females			
Male above ..	Usual	100	100	100	100	100
Male above: only position used	21	9	16	10	7	6
Female above ..	35	40	35	38	48	52
Side	19	31	37	31	34	29
Sitting	8	9	6	9	9	10
Rear entry ..	6	15	10	12	18	16
Standing	4	4	4	4	5	4
No. of cases ..	478	2451	345	603	894	607

These researches seem to indicate that the preferred method in both groups, pre-marital and marital, is the female being supine. It is interesting to see that the percentage of those using the 'reversed' position rises by ten per cent from the pre-marital group to the marital group. There is, in fact, an increase in the use of all the variants, with a corresponding decrease in the 'normal' position, by the married group. Reasons for this are varied, but obviously the security and opportunity of marriage must increase the desire for experimentation. In the same way familiarity in marriage may produce both boredom and experimentation.

It is significant that the highest percentage of females (fifty-two per cent) who used the 'female above' position comes from the youngest age group. In fact this age group represents a much more active interest in positions outside the 'normal' than any other.

This, of course, is in a sense to be expected as it is the group which is least affected by tradition and the conventions of the past. Research in other Western societies would no doubt reveal a comparable trend. We can thus assume that in the future the dead hand of the theologians in these matters will be entirely eliminated and man will be free to experiment as he will.

Another aspect was brought out by Kinsey in his previous research concerning the human male.[85] There appears to be a correlation between the educational standard of the male and the employment of *certain* coital techniques. For example there was a definite increase in the percentages, using the position of the female above, from the lowest educational grade to the highest—from 17·1 per cent to 34·6 per cent. But with regard to the standing position there was a decrease from the lowest grade to the highest from 7·5 per cent to 3·6 per cent. The same type of decrease from the lowest educational grade to the highest is noticeable as regards the sitting position from 7·7 per cent to 6·1 per cent. Unfortunately there are no tables in the later volume to which the original findings could be related. But it seems as if education is a factor which affects choice of coital position.

Although, as we have tried to show from the evidence of advanced societies, a great number of coital positions are theoretically possible, the vast majority of mankind seems to prefer to employ a few established postures he has faith in. To do anything else requires the skill and technique of a gymnast which few possess. Other factors from the female point of view may influence choice.

If the mechanics of coitus are examined, the reasons for this conservatism, as it were, become apparent. From the male point of view it is necessary for the penis to be inserted in the vagina and while there to be moved in such a manner as to produce friction against the vaginal walls. This movement in time gives rise to ejaculation and thus orgasm. In the case of the male all this is obvious in that the glans of the penis is its most sensitive area and friction against it acts as a stimulant. On the other hand, as regards women, the situation is much more complex. Authorities differ as to whether the stimulation of the clitoris is necessary for the female to achieve orgasm. Again there is debate about the actual sensitivity of the vaginal walls. What does emerge is the fact that probably in a majority of women clitoral stimulation forms a vital part in the mechanics of sexual stimulation.

This being the case it would be reasonable to assume that those positions will be favoured which on the one hand are easy to embark upon, and on the other exert the maximum amount of pressure on the clitoris. If this is accepted it helps to explain the worldwide incidence of what is called the 'normal' or usual position of the woman supine and the man on top. It is depicted in the sources we have already mentioned. A particularly notable example is found in Twelfth Dynasty graves in Egypt. The other most widely distributed technique is where the positions of the couple are reversed. Its popularity is equally well attested. In the case of the 'normal' position, moderate stimulation for both parties is provoked, and it is easy to perform. The 'reverse' position provides maximum stimulation for the couple, but requires an uninhibited attitude for proper performance.

Anthropological data from simple societies suggests that there are two positions upon which variations are embroidered—face-to-face, and male entry from the rear. Entry by the man from the rear does not normally exert clitoral pressure as the clitoris lies above the vagina; however, it can be achieved when the man lies on his back and the woman sits on him facing his feet. By leaning forward and moving backwards and forwards the clitoris will rub against the underneath of the penis.

The basic positions which appear to be dominant are those composed of types of the face-to-face posture. This is the case for many societies in Polynesia, Indonesia, East and Central Africa, and the aboriginal peoples of North America. The preferred variant amongst several of these communities is for coitus to start with the woman lying down and the man kneeling between her legs. He draws her towards him so that her legs are across his thighs. The next stage is for the man to pull the woman into an upright posture with the result that they embrace in a half kneeling position. Apparently this is a posture in which the clitoris is subjected to a great deal of pressure and therefore stimulation. This method is universally used throughout the whole of the Pacific Islands area.

The Goajiro, a South American Tribe in Colombia, the Masai of East Africa, and the Kwakuitl tribe of the North-west Coast of America appear to prefer lying on their sides facing each other.

The advantage of this position is that it allows equal freedom of movement to both the man and the woman, and this encourages mutual stimulation. Two peoples, in the Western part of the Caroline Islands in the Pacific, the Palanese and the Yapese, have as their dominant form of intercourse the method whereby the woman squats over the supine man. In Pukapuka in Eastern Polynesia the most favoured method is for the man to kneel with his legs under him. The woman faces him placing her legs on his thighs. This does not allow the same freedom of movement as for example the Masai method.

The general pattern in all societies as regards methods of coitus is fourfold: there is first of all the predominant method regarding which in most cases it is impossible to trace the origin; secondly, there is a series of limited alternatives which provide variety, particularly in marriage; thirdly, methods are adopted on a basis of idiosyncratic or individual preference. This last category is often determined by pre-adolescent sexual play. For example, individual male choice of methods entailing entry from the rear are often determined by experience of this form of pseudo-intercourse among children. Fourthly, methods governed by factors external to the act itself such as the need for discretion or pregnancy.

With regard to the methods alternative to the preferred one, one of the most common is for the woman to sit or squat on the supine man. The Hopi favour this type of intercourse, as do the Trobrianders, and the Wogeo people off the coast of New Guinea. It is in fact a common and widespread alternative.

Malinowski describes the Trobriand methods in this way: 'The woman lies on her back, the legs spread out and raised, and the knees flexed. The man kneels against her buttocks, her legs resting on his hips. The more usual position, however, is for the man to squat in front of the woman, and, with his hands resting on the ground, to move towards her or, taking hold of her legs, to pull her towards him. When the sexual organs are close to each other the insertion takes place. Again the woman may stretch her legs and place them directly on the man's hips, with his arms outside them, but the far more usual position is with her legs embracing the man's arms and resting on the elbows . . .' [86]

The third category of individual choice is very difficult to assess as the practices involved are so numerous, and in many instances

are of incredible ingenuity. Here indeed the *Kamasutra* and
Aretino come into their own. For while pictorial examples from
wall paintings in the brothels of Pompeii and the caves of Ellora in
India seem to involve anatomical difficulties, adaptations of these
are perfectly possible given time and practice. For example, the
writer has witnessed an unbelievable performance, there is no
other word, in Jamaica, where the participants adopted a variety
of postures which would have risked dislocation in the case of
ordinary individuals. It is safe to assume that this type of intercourse is aberrant. Where intercourse is governed by external
factors, various considerations are involved. If discretion is the
paramount need, for fear of observation by children or adults, the
side by side position tends to be adopted. The incidence of this is
again very widespread. It is found in many African societies, such
as the Azande of the Southern Sudan, and amongst the Lepchas
and the Trobrianders. It is a position which does not permit of
excessive stimulation, but one where movement is essentially
quiet. In pregnancy, or when there is some physical disability in
either of the partners, male entry from the rear is a preferable form.
This is the case in the number of European societies as well as
amongst the people of Alor in Timor in the East Indies, some
Australian Aborigines, and the Crow Indians of North America.
In the sexual act performed in this manner the man may stimulate
the clitoris manually both before and after he has achieved entry.

For the quick, casual, sexual encounter, the primary regard is
for a coital position which allows for swift disengagement. This
resolves itself into standing postures. The most common is for the
man to enter the woman from behind while she bends forward as
in a game of leap-frog. Alternatively the woman can support
herself on her hands and knees. In Dobu, which is an island in the
Trobriand group; in the Marshall Islands in the Pacific, and in
Tibet this is considered the ideal arrangement for a fugitive copulation. Obviously the couple can spring apart very quickly and
thus disguise their behaviour. One method practised in the central
group of the Caroline Islands calls for comment: the couple stand
facing each other and the woman places one leg on the man's
shoulder, entry by the man is then effected. This appears to call for
some gymnastic training on the part of the woman. We may add
that its occurrence has not been reported from elsewhere. Simple

consideration will show that to achieve entry in a standing position with the couple face to face is extremely difficult. It is possible if the woman places her knees apart and the man stands in a semi-bending position between her legs. Movement is extremely restricted and difficult. It appears to belong more to the category of the idiosyncratic than to that of everyday usage. A variant of this is depicted in an obscene drawing by the early nineteenth century artist Fuseli which is in the British Museum.

The actual description of a copulation which follows applies to unmarried lovers, but would probably equally apply to behaviour in the early stages of marriage. The individuals concerned are of the Kgatla tribe in Bechuanaland. The informant was a young teacher.

'The boy and girl sit together outside her hut talking, until her parents go to bed. Then he pleads with her to sleep with him, and because she is shy she will at first refuse, but when he says she refuses it because she does not love him, she will consent. She goes into the hut to spread her blankets on the floor, and then calls the boy to come in. He sits on a chair, and she sits beside her blankets, and they talk. Then he puts out the light in the hut, takes off his clothes, and gets into the blankets; he calls to the girl to come to him, and she also gets into the blankets, and then takes off her clothes.

'As they lie together like this, the girl turns her back on the boy, while he faces towards her. Then he begins to trouble her by feeling her body, he fondles her buttocks and breasts, and all over stroking her. She keeps stirring her body uneasily, and she will keep on saying: "What are you doing? Leave me alone, why do you feel me all over?" The boy will keep reassuring her, saying, "What are you afraid of? I am just admiring your body." Sometimes he kisses her, but many girls will not allow him to do so, for they regard the kiss as an awful thing, then he tries to touch her vulva, and she will jump, because she does not like him to do that, and she will tell him not to insult her, because she does not want her private parts to be seen. But the boy will say to her, "I am not insulting you, I am just caressing your body to make you feel well"; but she will refuse to let him do so at first, but when she gets hot, then perhaps she will not mind so much.

'Sometimes it happens that the girl takes the initiative. She begins to feel the boy's body in the same manner; she is hot, but afraid to ask him to start doing it now, so she tries to arouse him, and may catch at his penis to make it stand, and may even put it at the mouth of the vulva. But some girls have much shame, so that even though they are hot they simply lie still and pretend not to be troubled, so that the boy must be the one to begin.

'When they are both hot, the boy gets on top of the girl. She lies on her back and opens her legs, and he will begin to feel for the vagina with his hand and put his penis in. If he does not find the vagina he will ask the girl to show him; and sometimes she catches the penis and puts it in, but sometimes she refuses and says, "You can find it for yourself," and this is due to shame. Then they begin to copulate. The boy presses hard on her, he breathes deeply and perspires freely. And while the boy is working, the girl sometimes folds her legs over his back and clasps him firmly, but sometimes she is nervous and simply lies still. If she is still young, she feels sore, and she will begin to cry softly, "You are hurting me, be gentle, be slow, it is enough"; but the boy will just continue, and then she keeps quiet, she is feeling the sweetness of it. Some girls, if already much used to this thing, keep quiet altogether, and say nothing, but others, because they like it very much, keep saying, "Push harder, man". The boy, as he keeps pushing, talks softly of the pleasure he is getting: "Oh, you are treating me well tonight, my wife, my love; when I used to say you must love me, I meant that you must treat me like this; oh, how nice it is! One can die of it." And just when he ejaculates, he says, "Man it is so nice that I could cut off my neck; oh, what a wonderful sweetness, it is coming out of my ears!" He gives a deep breath and becomes weak and loose all over. Sometimes he ejaculates into the girl, sometimes outside. And sometimes the girl, after he has ejaculated, will hold firmly with her hands and not allow him to get off, telling him to continue, because she feels the sweetness, but he will refuse, and tell her he cannot do so because his semen is all out. And when she is absolutely convinced that he will not continue, she will let him get off.

'Now they will lie down again next to each other. If she is a good-mannered girl, she will always have a towel near her pillow, and as soon as they lie down she quickly takes it and cleans his genitals and her own, and wipes the sweat from their bodies, so that the blanket should not be stained. They keep quiet for a while, then the girl embraces the boy: "You boys have it hard, you keep on breathing hard and working at this." But the boy will say, "Yes, it is hard work, but it is also very nice, so much so that one could cut off one's neck." And the girl says, "Oh, is that so? But you boys are naughty, and you have terrible wishes, you can't even lie quietly for a short time before you must be at it. You boys are thieves, why can't you just stay without it?" And the boy will reply, "We cannot stay without it, we are not doing it blindly, we have it hard unless we can do so."

'Sometimes he copulates with her three or four times that night, and then he leaves early in the morning so that he may not be seen by the people. And once they have slept together like this, they begin to love each other very much almost as if they were man and wife . . .' [87]

That description although essentially practical in its details is also extremely poetic, and shows that the Kgatla feel the significance of sexual passion in a very similar way to the European.

An important aspect of intercourse is the expected role of the sexes. Again there appears to be a fairly definite division amongst societies as to the role to be played by either sex. If we assume, which is undoubtedly true, that the sexual appetites of men and women are equal, it would appear that where for example, the woman is supposed to be passive during coitus this is due to the demands of the particular culture rather than to any natural deficiency on her part. This is certainly the case with Lepcha women. While copulating these women lie completely motionless and relaxed. The Lepcha claim that the woman participates in this way and has an orgasm, though in fact she gives no overt sign that this is so. This sexual role of passivity for woman has its origin in the extremely matter of fact attitude that Lepchas have towards sex. They appear to equate sex activity with eating, and to assume that both are necessary for survival, and that both are of the same emotional significance. Their culture does not have room for strong, passionate attachments between individuals. This in Lepcha eyes would interfere in the ordinary business of living. One does not become too excited about food providing it is there, so why make a fuss about sex? The male attitude is essentially objective and helps to assign a passive role to women. For the men sex forms just as much a topic of conversation and jokes as it does amongst European men. But it is man who is dominant and active. The Lepcha man in fact reminds one of a Victorian middle class paterfamilias. [88]

Other societies such as the Apache Indians of North America, and the Colorado Indians of Ecuador have similar ideas regarding the ideal role of woman in copulation. In the case of the Apache who were essentially a male directed society organised for pillage and warfare, it is reasonable to assume that the culture enforced this passive sexual characteristic on the woman as a means of gratifying the excessive male attributes of the men. They went so far as to demand that no emotion at all be displayed by the women while coitus was taking place. In none of the societies mentioned in this connection does the male tolerate the woman taking the initiative in any way. This would be to reduce the male status and equate him with the female.

In complete contrast with such peoples are the Tchambuli, a lake dwelling tribe in New Guinea. Amongst them, apparently, the sexual roles are very largely reversed: that is to say, it is the women who decide who shall be their lovers and husbands, and who in fact take charge of sexual proceedings.

'Tchambuli young men develop their attitudes towards one another in the highly charged atmosphere of courtship, in which no one knows upon whom a woman's choice will fall; each youth holds his breath and hopes, and no young man is willing to trust another . . .' [89]

Despite the fact that in Tchambuli society property descends in the male line, and a man pays a bride-price for his wife, as Margaret Mead says, '. . . It is the women in Tchambuli who have the real position of power in the society . . .' [90] Both fishing and trading as well as manufacturing (mosquito bags for trading purposes) are carried out and controlled by women. Such factors would clearly help to determine the sexual role of the women. Much as the Apache men completely dominated their women so the contemporary Tchambuli female almost entirely dominates her man.

Another category of society is that which demands equal participation of the man and woman in sexual activity. A notable example is the Trobrianders. The women are expected to make as vigorous a contribution to copulation as the men. Malinowski gives an account by a male Trobriander: '... When I sleep with Dabugera I hug her with my whole body. We suck each other's lower lip, so that we are stirred to passion. We suck each other's tongues, we bite each other's chin, we bite cheeks and caress the armpit and the groin. Then she will say: "my lover, it itches very much ... push on again, my whole body melts with pleasure ... do it vigorously, be quick so that the fluids may discharge ... tread on again, my body feels so pleasant ..." ' [91]

That passage expresses the mutual role of the sexes in intercourse amongst these peoples. If we were to attempt to assign our own society to any of the categories above, there is considerable evidence to suggest that it would fall within the group which demands passivity from the woman. Our society is very largely male-directed and the cultural values we hold demand that woman should fulfil a somewhat receptive sexual role. Most men are indeed frightened by any overt sexual move on the part of the female, and not far from their minds is the thought that they are dealing with a nymphomaniac. To allow dominance, initiative, or even equality in the sexual act is to destroy our male superiority, or so our reasoning goes. But it seems clear on the other hand that in those societies where there is mutual responsibility for sexual activity, the act of coitus yields the greatest pleasureable results. It is possible that as woman's status both socially and economically becomes equal with that of man in the Western world this last bastion of male aggressiveness will fall.

The achievement of sexual satisfaction by both partners follows and can be correlated with the type of roles adopted in intercourse. That is to say in societies where passivity is expected of the woman (Lepcha), she is supposed to have an orgasm simultaneously with the man. Whether in fact this is so seems doubtful. In the Trobriands and in the Kgatla account quoted it is obvious that failure by the man to produce an orgasm in the woman would be regarded as lamentable. Their sexual technique is such that failure would not seem to be much in evidence. Other peoples such as those of the Caroline Islands and the Crow Indians of North America have a similar attitude, with its ensuing pattern of satisfaction for both sexual partners.

In the case of our own type of society the pattern fulfils that of

the expected passivity in woman. Dickinson and Beam in their
A Thousand Marriages have the following table:

TABLE III [92]
Wife's Experience with Orgasm as Reported in 442 Cases

Orgasm during coitus 'Yes' (frequency not stated)	40%
Usually	2%
Sometimes	15%
Rarely	10%
Formerly, not now	4%
Following coitus by masturbation involving clitoral stimulation	3%
Not experienced with husband	26%

These figures are somewhat alarming, but are borne out by
Kinsey and others. [93] They are certainly indicative of the general
attitude towards woman's sexual role in Britain and America.
Unfortunately there is no corresponding statistical evidence from
savage societies but arguing on the lines suggested, that there is a
correlation between the sexual role which woman adopts and the
amount of sexual satisfaction achieved by her, it is reasonable to
assume that investigation into frequency of female orgasm in
such societies would show similar correlation.

The ideal is perhaps for the woman to exhibit a becoming reti-
cence and at the same time to gain and administer full pleasure. The
people who come nearest to this are the Baiga, an aboriginal tribe
in Central India: '. . . "We sleep," says Dhan Singh, "on separate
beds . . . If I go to sleep without doing it my girl wakes me up."
"What are you sleeping for?" she asks. "Whom have you been
with today?" But if I am awake we wait till all is quiet. Then a
ripple passes between us. She coughs to show she is ready. Then
we go on the floor together. She doesn't remove all her clothes.
She lies on her back with her legs in the air. I kneel against her. It
knows its place; it makes no mistake. Like an arrow it goes straight
to its home. If it misses, the man is impotent. She puts her legs
round my waist. She makes no response. She wants it, but she
mustn't show it. So long as her breast is round like a fig, you hold
it, and press it; when it is loose as a sack, you let it go. Once you
are there, pressed to her, for ever . . .' [94]

It is a coital method which is mentioned in the Hindu erotic books, and has obviously been practised by individuals in a number of societies. But it is only in the United States that a whole community acted upon it as a matter of principle.

Man has always tried to achieve some way of prolonging the sexual act in order to allow his partner to reach orgasm and to prolong his own pleasure. Simple ways consist of doing some other act while copulating, such as smoking or eating or reading. The Hindus recommended concentration on some subject totally unrelated to sex, such as eternity. The most difficult method, involving tremendous self-control, is that of *Karezza*. Marie Stopes describes it in her book *Married Love*: 'The idea being, that after mutual passion has been aroused and union effected, instead of encouraging the excitement by movement and so on, an attempt to reach complete calm, both mental and physical should be made. This is achieved by the cessation of physical movement, and the centering of thought on the spiritual aspect of the beloved . . . Extremists in the practice of this idea would go so far as to prevent ejaculation on all occasions, but others use it only to increase the length of time between the occasions when ejaculation takes place . . .'[95]

The Oneida community of New England founded in 1846 were certainly extremists. They believed in 'free love', but every man was not allowed to make every woman pregnant. With this purpose in view a man would, while making love, insert his penis in his partner's vagina. There it would remain for an hour or more while the woman experienced orgasm. At the end of this time he withdrew without having experienced orgasm and all was over. The founder of the community, J. H. Noyes, in his pamphlet *Male Continence* (New York, 1872) explains that procreation must never be haphazard, and the only way to ensure that is to adopt this method of intercourse. Of course it has the advantage of allowing the weaker vessel, the woman, to indulge her pleasure without conception, the man remaining literally continent. It is a sobering thought to reflect, as Noyes pointed out, that the community was organised from the most respectable families in Vermont. The founder also claimed that the community suffered no nervous troubles as a result of this practice!

A similar practice is that of the man so controlling his desire for orgasm that the woman would experience several orgasms over an extended period. This was debated as to whether it were permissible by Christian theologians in the seventeenth century. [96] Whereas the Karezza technique as practised by the Oneida community is open to severe criticism on medical grounds the former method is, if possible to maintain, extremely beneficial to the woman.

This chapter has attempted to analyse some of the factors affecting coital activity in human society. The point to be emphasised is that whatever sexual customs are involved they can only become meaningful when viewed within their context. Each society, on the basis nature has provided, determines for itself the times, methods, and frequencies of sexual intercourse, as well as the roles demanded of the sexes. The act of coitus itself is culturally conditioned.

'. . . Panting with desire, she said: "Prove yourself, old Zacharias, prove yourself, sinewy father!"

'At this explicit appeal, Beauty-Spot seized the girl by the thighs and aimed a great stick of conserve in the direction of the gates of triumphs; then riding towards the crystal corridor, he halted at the gate of victories. After that he left the main road and spurred vigorously by a short cut to the mounter's door; but, as the nerve failed a little before the narrowness of this wicket, he turned then and, staving in the lid, found himself as much at home as if the architect had built on the actual measures of both. He continued his pleasant expedition, slowly visiting Monday market, the shops about Tuesday, Wednesday bazaar, and the stall of Thursday; then, when he had loosened all there was to loosen, he halted, like a good Mussulman, at the beginning of Friday. Such was the voyage of discovery which Beauty-Spot and his little boy made in the garden of girlhood . . .' [97]

REFERENCES AND NOTES

1. J. J. Meyer, *Sexual Life in Ancient India*, London 1953, pp. 244–5.
2. A. R. Holmberg, *The Siriono*, an unpublished PH.D. thesis in the library of Yale University, quoted by C. S. Ford and F. A. Beach in *Patterns of Sexual Behaviour*, London 1952.

3. B. Malinowski's *Sexual Life of Savages*, London 1932, pp. 274–5.

4. G. Gorer, *Himalayan Village*, London 1938, pp. 327–8.

5. G. M. Sproat, *Scenes and Studies of Savage Life*, London 1868, p. 227.

6. B. Spencer and A. J. Gillen, *The Northern Tribes of Central Australia*, London 1904, pp. 293, 295.

7. H. I. Hogbin, *Oceania*, V, 1934–5, 330 f.

8. M. Mead, *Anthropological Papers of the American Museum of Natural History*, XXVII, 346 f.

9. For a review of conditions demanding continence in pre-literate societies see H. Webster, *Taboo*, Oxford 1942, pp. 132–9.

10. C. S. Ford and F. A. Beach, *Patterns of Sexual Behaviour*, London 1952, pp. 75–6.

11. F. Boas, 'Social Organisation of the Kwakuitl Indians', *Annual Report of the Smithsonian Institution* 1895, Washington 1897, p. 537.

12. The point that almost any ceremonial occasion demands sexual abstinence is emphasised by L. Hubert and M. Mauss in 'Essai sur le sacrifice', *L'Année Sociologique* 1899, pp. 50–51.

13. Havelock Ellis, *Studies in the Psychology of Sex*, Philadelphia 1913, Vol. VI, p. 532.

14. Ellis, *op. cit.*, p. 533.

15. Tertullian, *De Exhortatione Castitatis*, 9 & 10, J. P. Migne, *Patrologiae Cursus*, Paris 1844–64, Vol. II, p. 689, *et seq.*

16. *Concilium Gangrense*, Canon I in P. Labbe, *Sacrorum Concilium collectio*, ed. J. D. Mansi, Venice 1759–98, Vol. II, p. 1106.

17. *Concilium Mediolanense*, Labbe-Mansi, *op. cit.*, Vol. III, p. 689 *et seq.*

18. St Justin, *Apologia* I. J. P. Migne, *op. cit. Series Gracea*, Paris 1859–66, Vol. VI, p. 373.

19. Quoted by G. R. Taylor in *Sex in History*, London 1953, p. 52.

20. Thomas Aquinas, *Summa Theologia II*.

21. 'Penitential of Theodore' in A. W. Haddon and W. Stubbs, *Councils and Ecclesiastical Documents*, Oxford 1871, Vol. III, pp. 175–204.

22. An extremely useful analysis of the sexual aspect of the Penitentials is given in G. May, *Social Control of Sexual Expression*, London 1930.

23. G. H. Joyce, S. J., *Christian Marriage*, London and N.Y., 1933 p. 339.

24. *Conc. Chalons*, II, c. 32, Labbe-Mansi, *op. cit.*, Ch. XIV, p. 101.

25. *Conc. Parisien*, VI, c. 32, Labbe-Mansi, *op. cit.*, Ch. XIV, p. 559.

26. G. H. Pertz, *Monumenta Germaniae historica*, Leges, Hanover 1837–75, Vol. I, p. 107.

27. Albericus, *Visio*, ed. C. de Vivo, Ariano 1899.

28. 'Penitential of Theodore', *op. cit.*, 1, 2, 3, p. 199.

29. S. Runciman, *The Mediaeval Manichee*, Cambridge 1947.

30. J. G. Frazer, *The Golden Bough*, abridged edition, London 1923, p. 106.

31. E. Durkheim, 'La Prohibition de l'inceste et ses origines', *L'Année Sociologique*, 1898, pp. 50–56.

32. W. Robertson-Smith, *Religion of the Semites*, London 1894.

33. G. Roheim, 'Women and their Life in Central Australia', J.R.A.I. LIII, 1933, p. 212.

34. H. Laval, *Mangareva*, Paris 1938, p. 225.

35. M. W. H. Beech, *The Suk*, Oxford 1911, p. 11.

36. R. Karsten, 'The Toba Indians of the Bolivian Gran Chaco', *Acta Academiae Aboensis Humaniora*, Åbo 1923, p. 28.

37. J. Gette, 'On the Superstitions of the Déné Indians', *Anthropos*, Vienna 1911, VI, p. 700.
    A. and G. Grandidier, *Histoire . . . de Madagascar*, Paris 1875, Vol. IV, Pt. II, p. 133.

38. C. W. Hobley, *Ethnology of Akamba and other East African Tribes*, Cambridge 1910, p. 65.

39. Quoted by Havelock Ellis, *op. cit.*, p. 533.

40. H. Van de Velde, *Ideal Marriage*, London 1958, pp. 256–7.

41. I. Schapera, *Married Life in an African Tribe*, London 1940, pp. 194–5.

42. *ibid. op. cit.*, p. 200.

43. J. H. Weeks, *Among the Primitive Bakongo*, London 1914, p. 148.
    A. B. Ellis, *Ewe-speaking Peoples*, London 1890, p. 206.
    M. Merker, *Die Masai*, Berlin 1904, p. 50.
    A. C. Hollis, *The Nandi*, Oxford 1909, p. 66.
    C. G. Seligman, *Melanesians of British New Guinea*, Cambridge, p. 582.
    P. F. X. de Charlevoix, *Voyage to North America*, Dublin 1766, Vol. II, p. 41.
    H. M. Bancroft, *Native Races of the Pacific States of North America*, N.Y. 1875–6, Vol. II, p. 267.

44. See M. Fortes, *The Web of Kinship*, Oxford 1949, especially pp. 162–6.

45. I. Schapera, *A Handbook of Tswana Law and Custom*, London 1938, p. 154.

Married Life in an African Tribe, London 1940, pp. 198–9.

46. M. Mead, *Sex and Temperament*, London 1935, p. 31.

47. P. A. Talbot, *The Peoples of Southern Nigeria*, Oxford 1926, Vol. II, p. 354.

48. E. Torday and T. A. Joyce, 'Notes on the Ethnography of the Ba-Mbala, J.R.A.I., XXXV, 1905, p. 410.

Merker, *op. cit.*, p. 50.

R. W. Felkin, *Proceedings Royal Society of Edinburgh*, 1886, XIII, p. 745.

P. Le Jeune, in *The Jesuit Relations and Allied Documents*, Cleveland 1897, Vol. VIII, p. 127.

B. H. Thomson, *Fijians*, London 1908, p. 175 *et seq.*

W. B. Grubb, *Among the Indians of the Paraguayan Chaco*, London 1904, p. 63.

49. F. J. Gillen, *Report on the Work of the Horn Scientific Expedition to Central Australia*, London and Melbourne 1896, Part IV, p. 166.

M. Mead, *Anthropological Papers of the American Museum of Natural History*, XXXVII, p. 414.

H. I. Hogbin, *Oceania*, V, 1934–5, p. 331.

H. J Holmberg, *Acta Societatis Scientiarum Fennicae*, Helsinki 1856 IV, p. 317 *et seq.*

50. K. B. Davis, *Factors in the Sex Life of Twenty-two Hundred Women*, N.Y. 1929.

51. E. H. Kisch, *The Sexual Life of Woman*, translated by M. E. Paul, N.Y. 1931, p. 174.

52. M. Stopes, *Married Love*, London 1931, p. 73.

53. T. Van de Velde, *Ideal Marriage*, London 1958, pp. 253–4.

54. H. Davis, *Moral and Pastoral Theology*, N.Y. 1946, Vol. 4, pp. 258–9.

55. Quoted by Kinsey, *op. cit.*, footnote 17, pp. 369–70.

56. Davis, *op. cit.*, pp. 78–9.

57. S. Ganzfried, *Code of Jewish Law*, London 1938, pp. 329–30.

58. Ford and Beach, *op. cit.*, pp. 78–9.

59. G. Gorer, *Himalayan Village*, London 1938, pp. 329–30.

60. Ford and Beach, *op. cit.*, p. 77.

61. Kinsey, *op. cit.*, pp. 348–9.

62. M. L. Terman, *Psychological Factors in Marital Happiness*, London 1938, pp. 270–1.

63. R. A. McCance *et alia*, 'Physical and Emotional Periodicity in Women', *Journal of Hygiene*, 1937, pp. 571–611.

64. E. Slater and M. Woodside, *Patterns of Marriage*, London 1951, p. 165.

65. Vatsyayana, *Kamasutra*, Paris, N.D. (Sanskrit)
Sheik Nefawzi, *The Perfumed Garden*, Paris, N.D. (Persian)
Anon., *Love and Women Amongst the Arabs*, London 1896.
'Hikatsu-sho', *The Japanese Book of Secrets*, circa 1845.

66. H. Ploss and M. & P. Bartels, *Woman*, London 1935, Vol. 2, pp. 61–62.

67. C. G. Brunius, *Försök till Förklaringar ofver Hällristningar*, Lund 1868 Taf. V.

68. L. Legrain, 'Ur Excavations', *Archaic Seal Impressions*, British Museum publication, London 1936, Vol. III.

69. There are numerous references in Aristophanes *Lysistrata*.
Ovid, *Art of Love*, 771–808, Horace *Satires*, aa 7, 49–50, Martial XI, 104, Lucian, *Lucius or the Ass*, 8–10, Apuleius, *The Golden Ass*, II, 16–17.

70. Ovid, *Art of Love*, translated by J. H. Mozley, London 1929, p. 173.

71. Lucretius, *De rerum natura*, Book IV, 1258.

72. Havelock Ellis, *op. cit.*, Vol. VI, p. 557.

73. The story of Aretino and his works is given in R. Lewinsohn's *History of Sexual Customs*, London 1958, pp. 155–8.

74. Ellis, *op. cit.*, p. 556.

75. *ibid. op. cit.*, Vol. V, p. 148.

76. *ibid. op. cit.*, Vol. VI, p. 555.

77. A. C. Kinsey *et alia*, *Sexual Behaviour in the Human Male*, London 1948, p. 374.

78. A. M. Arregui, *Summarium theologie moralis ad recentem codicem iuris canonici accommodatum*, Bilbao 1927, p. 531.

79. H. Davis, *Moral and Pastoral Theology*, N.Y., 5th edition, 1946, Vol. 4, p. 254.

80. Ellis, *op. cit.*, Vol. VI, p. 556.

81. S. Ganzfried, *Code of Jewish Law*, translated by H. E. Goldin, N.Y. 1927, Vol. 4, p. 14.

82. F. K. Forberg, 'De Figuris Veneris', *Manual of Classical Erotology*, Brussels 1884.

83. T. Van de Velde, *op. cit.*, pp. 186–215.

84. Based on Table 101 in Kinsey, *op. cit.*, *Female*, p. 400.

85. Kinsey, *op. cit.*, *Male*, p. 372.

86. Malinowski, *The Sexual Life of Savages*, London 1932, p. 283.

87. I. Schapera, *Married Life in an African Tribe*, London 1940.

88. A. Gorer, *Himalayan Village*, London 1938, p. 332.

89. M. Mead, *Sex and Temperament*, London 1935.

90. *ibid. op. cit.*, p. 253.

91. B. Malinowski, *The Sexual Life of Savages*, Kegan Paul, London 1932, p. 287.

92. R. L. Dickinson and Beam, *A Thousand Marriages*, Baltimore 1931.

93. Kinsey, *op. cit*, *Female*, pp. 379–91.

Although we have used the term *orgasm* with reference to women in a general sense to mean the climax of sensation it should be appreciated that authorities are by no means united in their views as to how it can be precisely defined. Generally a distinction is made between vaginal and clitoric orgasm. *True* orgasm can only be of a vaginal nature. E. Bergler and W. S. Kroger in their *Kinsey's Myth of Female Sexuality*, New York 1954, maintain that Kinsey added a further, false category of 'pubic area' orgasm (pp. 74–5). The authors attack the whole basis of Kinsey's theories.

94. V. Elwin, *The Baiga*, London 1939, p. 265.

95. Marie Stopes, *Married Love*, London 1930, pp. 191–2.

96. Zacchia, *Quaestiones medico-legales*, *Avenione*, 1655, Bk. VII, Tit. III, Quaest. VI.

97. *The Book of a Thousand Nights and One Night*, J. C. Mardus and E. Powys Mathers, London 1923, Vol. II, pp. 180–81.

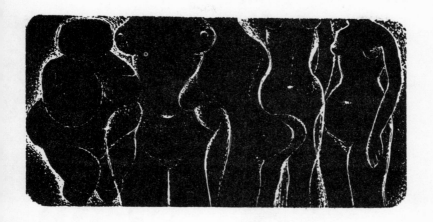

CHAPTER XI

Beauty

THE Venus of Brassempouy, the Venus of Willendorf, and the Venus of Laussel are all over-blown, blowsy, sexually exaggerated representations of the human female forms. They are among the earliest depictions of humanity. That they represent prehistoric man's ideal of beauty is debatable but possible. As we shall see the ideal of beauty is governed by a series of social factors so that however exaggerated the lady of Willendorf appears her very exaggerations may have been that which was desired.

Still within this same remote time of pre-history the Cycladic dolls from the Mediterranean typify a beauty with which we are much more familiar. Here in terms of the European aesthetic are grace and appeal of line.

The breasts are small and compact. There is no distortion of belly and thighs as in the Venuses. In fact these figures from the Cyclades Islands are the complete antithesis of the Willendorf Venus. As we hope to show, both are representative of the variations in the concept of beauty, not only in Europe, but throughout the world.

'She was a slight Egyptian admirably waisted, straight as the letter Alif and with Babylonian eyes, her hair was darkness, but her white was the white of silver in the mine or of a peeled almond. She shone so in her sombre robe that you would have taken her for a Summer moon on a Winter night. How then would she not have breasts of white ivory, a harmonious belly, a glory of thighs, and buttocks like cushion? Would there not be a thing rose-balmed in front of them, like a small scent-bag folded in a larger?' (¹) That is an ideal of beauty from the Arabian Nights. It is an ideal

Fig. 17. The Venus of Brassempouy

which would not have a universal appeal. Contemporary Euro-peans for example are not enamoured of 'buttocks like cushions' or indeed of fatness of any kind. But it is an image, as we shall see, which would find favour not only in the Arab world.

One of the most important determinants of sexual relationships is physical attraction. This in turn is dependent upon the physical characteristics which a particular society holds are expressions of beauty. Of course few men or women at any time measure up to this ideal standard. But those that are termed 'attractive' come within range of an approximation to the ideal. The factors which govern the conception of the ideal are unique to the particular society or group of societies. (For example Western society, with the possible exception of a few eccentrics, sets no great store by

women who possess elongated labia, whereas the Bushmen of
South-west Africa in fact do so.) Such factors are extremely varied.
They represent the interaction of tradition, occupation, ideology,
superstition, clothing and the conceptions of the erotic upon the
mind of man over periods of time. The result, viewed anthropo-
logically, is an astonishingly variegated pattern with the most
amazing contrasts. Each society sets its own standards within a
particular framework of custom and idea.

The thesis is sometimes advanced that the variation in standards
is more apparent than real, and that underlying the superficial
differences there is a universal 'sexual desirability' which is biological in origin. We shall try to show that the evidence points
very much the other way. Briffault advocated this view of the
universality of sexual desirability. He went even further in sug-
gesting that the 'uncultured races' were indifferent to their own
standards, and thus sought qualities which were repulsive to the
taste of the European.([2]) He supported his thesis with examples of
the following kind: 'Among the Tuareg the beauty of the girls of
good family is promoted from an early age. They are entrusted,
when six or seven years old, to energetic slaves, who compel them
to swallow several times a day large quantities of milk foods and
flour . . . The young aspirants to beauty are, moreover, every
evening rolled in the sand and vigorously massaged in order to
distribute uniformly the acquired fat and suppress all angles and
concavities. Thanks to this regimen and complete idleness they
are, towards the age of eighteen, monstrously beautiful. They are
then unable to rise or discipline themselves without the aid of two
vigorous slaves; and all the warriors vie for their favours . . .'([3])
Or Mungo Park on Nigerian beauty: 'Corpulence and beauty
seem to be terms nearly synonymous. A woman of even moderate
pretensions must be one who cannot walk without a slave under
each arm to support her, and a perfect beauty is a load for a
camel . . .'([4]) From the European standpoint, both the Tuaregs'
and Mungo Park's West Africans' ideal of female beauty is repugnant. But that is a reaction based on a particular set of aesthetic
values, the European, which (at present) puts a premium on the
over-developed breast and the slim body as attributes of feminine
beauty. The latter viewed from the societies in question would be
equally repulsive. We should add that either Mungo Park and

Captain Aymard grossly exaggerated, or the fashion in fatness in these societies has changed radically, for contemporary observers of the Tuareg and of Nigerian peoples do not remark upon the excessive corpulence of the women. [5]

The principle we are dealing with is that there are variations in what constitutes the ideal of beauty in different societies. Underlying these variations is the insistence on perfection in whatever characteristics which may be favoured. Put in another way those individuals who are felt to express the ideal which is current approximate to good physical specimens.

Some examples will illustrate the profound differences which exist between different societies as to what constitutes sexual beauty.

For the Trobrianders it is: 'Vigour, vitality and strength, a well proportioned body, a smooth and properly pigmented, but not too dark skin are the basis of physical beauty . . . In all the phases of village life I have seen admiration drawn and held by a graceful, agile and well balanced person . . . it is a notable fact that their main erotic interest is focused on the human head and face . . . The outline of the face is very important; it should be full and well rounded . . . The forehead must be small and smooth . . . Full cheeks, a chin neither protruding nor too small, a complete absence of hair on the face, but the scalp hair descending well on to the forehead, are all *desiderata* of beauty . . .' [6]

Malinowski goes on to detail the desired qualities of the face. The eyes should be liquid and shining; the mouth full, but on no account should the lips protrude, the nose somewhat full—a flat or aquiline nose is a real disability; ears should be inconspicuous. Curiously, black teeth are regarded as beautiful, but few Trobrianders bother to blacken them artificially. Hair should be grown into a thick, curly mop. On the other hand body hair of any kind must be eliminated.

The male body which provokes the greatest admiration is tall, slim, and straight. The woman's figure must also have this small-bellied, slender appearance. The ideal of colouring is a full brown but not too dark. Breasts are appreciated when firm and well developed, but a man may prefer them to be small in which case he tells his girl not to massage them. Breast massage is an adolescent practice with the object of achieving the ideal. [7]

The Trobriand ideal of beauty does not appear to be very far

removed from the European. It is somewhat different with the
Chuckchee of Siberia who demand great strength from their
women together with accentuated pelvic development. But perhaps the physical form which is at the furthest remove from the
European's and many other people's conception of physical
attractiveness, is that of the Southern Bushmen and Hottentot
people of the Kalahari region in South-west Africa. These people
are famous for an extraordinary accumulation of fat in the region

Fig. 18. Bushman cave drawing showing steatopygia

of the buttocks; this is known as steatopygia. The effect is most
grotesque as the rest of the body is slim, and the hands and feet
quite small. It is rather as if the Victorian bustle had become attached to, and part of, the human frame. The swollen buttocks of the
woman are regarded as being objects of great beauty by the men.
Authorities appear to be divided as to the exact causes and origin of
steatopygia. It does appear apparently in isolated cases amongst
Southern Europeans and other African peoples (e.g. Somali and
Ituri), but nowhere on the scale of these people of the Kalahari
Desert.

It has been suggested that these deposits of fat serve the same
purpose as those possessed by the camel and other animals such as
the fat-tailed sheep; that in fact steatopygia represents an adapta-

tion to the desert environment which supplies nutriment to the system when ordinary supplies are exhausted. This hypothesis is very probably correct, but it would not account for the occurrence of steatopygia in peoples whose environment is very different. But the Bushmen in particular are a strange physical type as they are not only famous for steatopygia but for the elongation of the *labia minora* in their women, and the ostensibly semi-erect state of the penis in the men. [8] Another type of physical beauty is that of the Masai of East Africa. It '. . . calls for a well-built and slim body with lightly rounded forms. In contrast to the greater number of other negroes . . . a Masai beauty should not be fat. Limbs should be just sufficiently rounded not to seem angular. The other signs of beauty are an oval face, white teeth, black gums, as light a facial complexion as possible, protruding buttocks (we cannot, however, speak of steatopygia), strong thighs, a deep navel. Lips should not obtrude either in shape or colour so that small dark lips are considered beautiful . . .' [9]

This type contrasts strongly with those of West African peoples such as the Ibo, Efik, and others who appreciate corpulence in women and are prepared to produce it artificially as we have seen.

For descriptions of the ideal beauty of pre-literate peoples we have to rely on the accounts of anthropologists, travellers and explorers. These are almost always Europeans, and in nearly all cases suffer from an obvious personal bias in favour of the familiar. In the following picture of the now extinct Carib women of the West Indies by an early eighteenth century French Jesuit, Père Labat this is quite apparent: The women are smaller than the men and are plump and by no means bad looking. They have black hair and black eyes. Their mouths are small, and their teeth are white and even. They look more open and smiling than the men, but with all this are very modest . . .' [10] It is clear that Père Labat was emphasising the European-like qualities he observed in the Caribs. He tells us little of how the Carib men viewed their women.

It is not only that accounts may be biased, but there are sometimes gross contradictions between one writer and another in their descriptions of a particular people. On the other hand, the real observer, such as Captain Cook, is unsurpassed in conveying an impression of the people. Here he is writing of the women of Tonga in the Pacific: '... The women are not so much distinguished from the men by their features as by their general form, which is for the most part destitute of that strong fleshy firmness that appears in the latter (men). Though the features of some are so delicate as not only to be a true index of their sex, but to lay claim to a considerable share of beauty and expression, for the bodies and limbs of most of the females are well proportioned, and some absolutely perfect models of a beautiful figure. But the most remarkable distinction in the women is the uncommon smallness and delicacy of their fingers, which may be put in competition with the finest in Europe . . .' [11] That passage may be compared with Spencer and Gillen's picture of the Arunta women of Australia: 'Naturally, in the case of the woman, everything depends upon their age, the younger ones, that is those between fourteen and perhaps twenty, have decidedly well formed figures, and, from their habit of carrying on their heads pitchers containing food and water, they carry themselves often with remarkable grace. As usual, however, in the case of savage tribes the drudgery of food-collecting and child-bearing tells upon them at an early age, and between twenty and twenty-five they begin to lose their graceful carriage; the face wrinkles, the breasts hang pendulous, and, as a general rule, the whole body begins to shrivel up, until, at about the age of thirty, all traces of an earlier well-formed figure and graceful carriage are lost, and the woman develops into what can only be called an old and wrinkled hag . . .' [12]

That picture of the Australian aboriginal woman is quite different from the stereotype which has been invented by the Anglo-Saxon, a stereotype which approximates much more to the reality of the female Hottentot.

The fatness which we have mentioned above as a desirable quality amongst some African peoples is also found amongst the Zapotec Indians of Southern Mexico: '... To be slim in Tehuantepec is a sign of poor health, and women compliment one another with "How fat and luxuriant ('frondosa,' in the sense of a great leafy tree) you look"—their equivalent of our "You are looking very well." There is a tendency towards plumpness, and "luxuriance" is indeed the most fitting adjective for the *tehuanas'* monumental, solid, strong flesh. Men like their women substantial, and a woman of normal weight among us would be considered skinny in Tehuantepec . . . [13]

Verrien Elwin, the anthropologist, gives the following description of a beautiful girl as seen by the Muria of Central India: 'Her legs should not be too long; they should be neither thin nor fat. The toes must not be big or crooked. She should have a slim waist so that when she ties her cloth around it, buttocks and waist will be level. A long stomach is ugly; so are buttocks that stick out behind. The nose may be small but not snub. A big head or ears, or fat cheeks are ugly. When the hair is combed it should lie flat on the head. A girl must not be very tall. Her eyes should not be black . . . The most important thing is that she should dress well and work well . . .' [14] This appears to be an excellent combination of appearance and virtue.

Amongst the Navrongo people of Northern Ghana we have observed a physical type which, while held in great regard by the people, is curiously enough similar to contemporary Anglo-American ideals of female attractiveness. The legs are long and slender, tapering to a compact pelvis which has the merest suggestion of rotundity. The shoulders are boyish, the arms long, the fingers slim. Breasts are gracefully rounded, with prominent nipples. This is a type which is also found amongst the Nuer of the Southern Sudan. It is in marked contrast to the women of the coastal areas in Ghana, such as the Ga and Fanti, where the preference is for a pronounced fleshy, squat figure which lacks the extraordinary grace characteristic of the northern areas.

When more advanced, literate societies are considered there is a significant difference to be noted. They are able to give expression to what *they* consider, not what the observer considers, are the most attractive physical features. An example which bridges the gap between the two, between the articulate and the inarticulate, comes from Ceylon. J. Davy described the typical Cingalese beauty as he was told of her in the year 1821: 'Her hair should be voluminous like the tail of the peacock, long, reaching to the knees, and terminating in graceful curls; her nose should be like the bill of the hawk, and lips bright and red, like coral on the young leaf of the iron-tree. Her neck should be large and round, her chest capacious, her breasts firm and conical, like the yellow cocoanut, and her waist small—almost small enough to be clasped by the hand. Her lips should be wide; her limbs tapering; the soles of her feet without any hollow, and the surface of her body in general, soft, delicate, smooth and rounded, without the asperities of projecting bones and sinews . . .' [15]

This lyrical quality which attempts to turn the mere anatomical into terms of the erotic ideal is very evident in the evocations of the ideal woman found in Oriental literature. The ultimate in the female form finds expression in the two great Hindu epics the *Mahābhārata* and the *Rāmāyana*. This is how Sita is spoken of in the *Ramayana*: 'Of the right size, pointed, smooth, and white are thy teeth; thine eyes are wide and great, unblemished, and with red corners and black pupils; thy secret parts are spread wide and firmly swell, thy thighs are as elephant's trunks; thy two breasts have a fair, firm fullness, and are round, close set to one another, bold firm-swelling, with lifted nipples, graceful, smooth, and like unto wine-palm fruits.' Another heroine of the *Rāmāyana*, Rambhā evokes this: 'The eye and the heart were ravished by her most intimate parts, swelling plumply, adorned with a girdle—that most splendid gift on the altar of love's pleasure. With her moist beauty-marks laid on (forehead and cheeks) with the juice of flowers from the six seasons of the year, she showed like another goddess of happiness and beauty, in loveliness, splendour, brightness, and glory. All wrapped she was in dark garment, like the water-laden cloud, her face like unto the moon, her glorious brows like two bows of the bowman, her thighs like elephant's trunks, her hands slender as young shoots . . .' [16]

The Hindu ideal shows very definite affinities with what is probably, for the Western readers, the most familiar of Oriental erotic poems, the Hebrew *Song of Songs*. 'Thy rounded thighs are like jewels . . . Thy navel is like a rounded goblet wherein no mingled wine is wanting. Thy belly is like a heap of wheat set about with lilies . . . Thy neck is like the tower of ivory . . .'

It is probably only in the literature of the East that we find this completely uninhibited extolling of the female form. At the beginning of this chapter we quoted the Arabian Nights ideal of Egyptian beauty. Here is how the appearance of a princess from 'a land beyond the confines of China' is described in that most extraordinary book:

'I will tell you of her hair, of her cheeks, of her mouth, of her breasts, of her belly, of her croup, of her middle, of her thighs, and of her feet.

'In the name of Allah!

'Her hair is dark as the separation of friends; she let it fall in three rivers to her feet, and I thought I looked upon three nights at the same time.

'Her face is as white as the day lost friends meet again; the moon shone on it; or, maybe it shone upon the moon. Her cheeks are an anemone, parted into two petals; her nose is a sword; there is purple wine running cool below the crystal of her skin.

'Her lips are coloured agate, eloquent with a water which cures all thirst.

'Blessed be Allah who made her breasts twin fruit of ivory, each fitted for the grasp of a lover's hand.

'Her belly has dimples of shadow, as cunningly placed as are the Arabic characters in the life work of a Coptic scribe.

'Her croup; oh, oh, I shiver and I recollect. It is so heavy that it makes her sit down when she would rise, and rise when she would lie down; A poet has said:

"Her sumptuous bosom calls for a less frail
Waist than is common,
Whereas her waist is frailer:
Therefore when she would rise and take regale
Among her women
Her slim white ankles fail her . . .
There is a thing I cannot keep in gaol,
Being but human,
Of which my drawers are gaoled."

'Such is her croup; her thighs are two branches of marble marrying in the air. I wonder that her feet, though beautiful, can bear such beauty.

'As for the middle and fundament: tongue can but say that one is All, and the other absolute; gesture is dumb before them . . .'[17]

A less literal evocation of Chinese beauty is expressed in a Chinese poem referring to a princess who lived in the eighth century B.C.—

'Her fingers were like pale young blades of grass.
Her skin smooth as liquid ointment.
Her neck white as silk.

Her teeth even and alike as melon seeds.
Her brow broad as the cicada's.
Her eyebrows delicate as a silk-moth's antennae.
How lovely her eyes where black and white gleamed side by side:
Stately she was and tall of stature.' [18]

A German anthropologist in the nineteenth century, J. von Langegg, gives the following account of a Japanese ideal of woman. 'To begin with the head: it must not be either too large or too small. Great black eyes surrounded with a fringe of black lashes and overarched by sharply drawn black brows. An oval face, delicately pale with the faintest trace of rosy colour in the cheeks. A straight high bridged nose. A small symmetrical mouth with fresh lips, that sometimes part and show even white teeth. A narrow forehead on which the long black hair grows in a symmetrical arch. A rounded throat and well-developed but not too plump figure with moderately rounded breasts. Slender hips, and small, but not too thin hands and feet.' [19] Clearly a meticulous beauty framed in accordance with Japanese etiquette.

With literate societies it is possible to trace changing conceptions of feminine beauty. This is very clearly brought out with regard to Egypt. In the classical period the ideal for both sexes is the long limbed, slender body. The woman has small perfectly shaped breasts. It is an ideal which finds expression again amongst the Greeks. This is replaced under the Ptolemys by a much more developed female form in which the desired characteristics of breasts and buttocks tend to become exaggerated. A comparison between the paintings in classical times of dancing girls and goddesses, and those of the later period illustrates the transition. Modern Egypt in common with many near-Eastern countries, shares the predilection for a heavy, fat, and fleshy feminine type.

So far we have discussed the ideal type of woman as it appears in different societies. It would seem as if there is a greater emphasis on female than on male beauty in a majority of societies. There are far fewer references in the literature, with some notable exceptions, to the male than to the female. This may be due to the fact that the observers who recorded their impressions, and poets who wrote of their love, were almost all men. On the other hand there is much in favour of Havelock Ellis' hypothesis that, 'Beauty in the human species is, above all, a feminine attribute, making its appeal to men . . .' [20] He goes on to say that perfection of the male body does not arouse sexual enthusiasm in the female. That in fact the most handsome man in civilised societies is not necessarily the most successful with women—in fact he may be extremely ugly. As Stendhal put it '. . . a woman can become very interested in an ugly man without noticing his ugliness, and in the long run his ugliness becomes beauty . . .' [21] Most men know cases where an individual whom they think unbearably repulsive is remarkably successful, to their mystification, with women. But it is not as Ellis points out, that men are only interested in the physical ideal of women that is presented to them; beauty has to be informed with vivacity. The result is that women who fall far short of the current ideal may be extremely attractive to men. Nevertheless there is little doubt that men are profoundly moved erotically by the visual appearance of women—otherwise it would be impossible to explain the widespread incidence of erotic art.

Ellis' hypothesis appears to have been confirmed by the findings of Kinsey and his co-workers. They discovered that whereas in their total sample seventy-two per cent of the men had an erotic response to the observation of women, clothed or unclothed, only fifty-eight per cent of the women responsed in this way to men. The former's response was of a genital nature, but few of the women reacted in this way. [22] The contrast between the sexes was even more marked when the reaction to nude photographs, drawings and paintings was considered: twelve per cent of the women had some response to representations of nude males, whereas fifty-four per cent of the males were sexually aroused by pictures of nude women. [23] Further evidence, apparently confirmatory, is forthcoming from an appraisal of erotic art in many societies which is being undertaken by workers in this field. It appears that while many male artists have represented the nude female form in an erotic way, very few women artists have done so with the male form. In fact out of eight well-known female painters only one depicted a man's body in this manner. [24]

Results similar to those of Kinsey have been obtained in a German survey conducted by Friedeberg published in 1950: eleven per cent of females were erotically stimulated by nude representations of men, and forty-seven per cent of men by female nudes. [25]

In this connection two literary examples are to the point. One is from Thomas Mann's last novel *The Confessions of Felix Krull* where a woman gives her views: 'All beauty is stupid because it simply exists as an object of gratification by the spirit. Let me see you—see you completely—heaven help me, how beautiful you are!! The breast so sweet in its smooth, clear strength, the slim arms, the noble ribs, the narrow hips, and, oh, the Hermes legs—'

"Stop it, Diane, this isn't right. It is I who should be praising you."

'Nonsense! That's just a male convention. We women are lucky that our curves please you. But the divine, the masterpiece of creation, the model of beauty, that's you, you young, very young men with Hermes legs . . .'[26]

There are few passages of this kind in literature. The fact that it is a man writing might possibly vitiate it as evidence of the feminine point of view. If similar passages were to be found in, for example, Jane Austen, George Sand, or other women writers this would be much more conclusive.

Gautier in *Mlle de Maupin* has, towards the end of that fantastic novel of transvestism, a statement in complete contradiction of Mann's views. The heroine who has been masquerading as a man is speaking: '. . . After all these things, truth to tell, man does not tempt me much. For he has not beauty as women—beauty, that splendid vestment which so thoroughly conceals the imperfections of the soul, that divine drapery cast by God over the nakedness of the world, and which in a way, makes it excusable to love the vilest courtesan of the gutter if only she possesses the magnificent regal gift. If I cannot have the virtues of the soul, I want at least the exquisite perfection of form, the satin flesh, the rounded contours, the suave lines, the soft skin, all that charms one in a woman. Since I cannot have love, let me have, at least, voluptuousness, and replace the sister as well as I can by the brother. But all the men I see seem to me hideously ugly. My horse is a hundred times handsomer, and it would be far less repugnant to kiss it than to kiss certain fops who think themselves very attractive . . .'[27]

There are few women writers in any field who have made actual pronouncements on either male or female beauty. One of these is Simone de Beauvoir. In her book *The Second Sex*, she makes this extremely pertinent statement. '. . . And he, (man) asks for still more: that his loved one be beautiful. The ideal of feminine beauty is variable, but certain demands remain constant; for one thing, since woman is destined to be possessed, her body must present the inert and passive qualities of an object. Virile beauty lies in the fitness of the body for action, in strength, agility, flexibility . . .' [28]

The evidence from Western societies suggests that in fact male beauty does not act as a sexual stimulant for women in anything like the way female beauty does for men. Before, however, one can say categorically that this is the case for all mankind, further research needs to be conducted in pre-literate and less advanced societies. But the evidence so far is most impressive. A certain corroboration exists in the form of public entertainment in societies such as our own. Female nudes or near nudes are normal attractions on the stage, and in night-clubs. They obviously are regarded not entirely in an aesthetic light. The portrayal of nude males in similar circumstances has, so far as we know, never been attempted. While of course embarrassment might be caused through genital arousal on the part of the men concerned it also seems to indicate that female spectators would not be particularly attracted to this form of entertainment.

Evidence from some mammalian species seems to show that females do make sexual advances to the male when *in estrus* ('on heat'). But this again is not conclusive for in the majority of animal species it is the male who exhibits beauty of body and presumably is admired by the female. This is particularly noticeable in the courtship of birds. There are dramatic examples in the peacock and birds of paradise. The male is utterly resplendent whereas the female can only be described as dowdy. Charles Darwin suggested that male birds with the brightest feathers are preferred by the females. This has not been entirely substantiated, '. . . but it is nevertheless evident that the bright colours assumed during the mating season serve to attract the attention of potential sexual partners and may therefore be classified as having a sexually facilitative function . . .' [29]

This suggests that the emphasis amongst birds, at any rate, is the reverse of what is common in some human Western societies. That is to say for birds it is *male* beauty which acts as a sexual stimulant rather than female beauty in distinction to ourselves and

several animal species. Experiments demonstrate that with regard
to some species, such as the macaque, the male exhibits preference
for one type of female rather than another. [30] The subject has
been dealt with by Sir Solly Zuckerman in his *The Social Life of
Monkeys and Apes* (London, 1932), R. M. & A. W. Yerkes in their
Social Behaviour in Infra-human Primates (Boston, 1935), and several
other authorities.

If it is not the apparently beautiful in man which attracts women
there must be other hidden qualities which act in this way.
Havelock Ellis maintained that women admire a man's strength
and translate visible energy into energy of pressure. Also,
'. . . women are more strongly affected by visual impressions
which express qualities belonging to the more fundamentally
sexual sense of touch . . .' [31] Male energy is naturally expressed in
sexual terms—a man of great overt, physical power is presumed
to possess great sexual powers. This, of course, is not always the
case; in fact quite the reverse may be true. But, as Ellis points out,
its efficacy as a symbol remains. This type of symbolism, of
strength in terms of a supposed virility, helps to explain the attraction of physical displays of strength for women in our kind of
society. The 'fans' who attend wrestling and boxing matches are
not all drawn there by the exhibition of skill. It would also explain
the occurrence of marriages between sexually attractive, successful
women and outstanding athletes, often with disastrous results.

The remarks of Petronius seem apposite in this connection:
'This the wild Extravagance of some Women to be in love with
Filth, nor can be rais'd to an appetite but by the Charms, forsooth
of some Slave or Lacquy; Some can be pleased with nothing but
the strutting of a Prize-fighter with a Hacht-face, and a Red
Ribbon in his shirt: Or an Actor betray's to prostitute himself on
the Stage, by the Variety of showing his pretty shapes there . . .' [32]

There are some references in anthropological literature to male
beauty which stress the essential virile qualities of the male from the
woman's point of view. There is this North American Indian song:

'My love is tall and graceful as the young pine waving on the hill.
And as swift in his course as the noble stately deer.
His hair is flowing, and dark as the blackbird that floats thro' the air.
His heart it is fearless and great.
And his arm, it is strong in the fight.' [33]

Such descriptions can be coupled with those we mentioned in connection with courting customs where contests of strength and skill are held between suitors. The victor is acclaimed not only for defeating his opponents but for exhibiting those traits which are admired by male and female alike.

The clean, for cleanliness apparently adds to the sexual attraction of the male in a number of societies, upstanding, broad-shouldered and thus presumably virile man is probably the overt ideal of women in our society. But this image does not provoke the type of sexual stimulation in women which is evoked by the image of female physical beauty in men. A consideration of such factors helps to explain the emphasis on feminine beauty rather than on male handsomeness in literature and life. Perhaps if more clinical research were done into the dreams of women in relation to ideal types of the male the pattern might become clearer. [34]

Amongst the advanced societies of the world, two have been pre-eminent for their advocacy in literature and the plastic arts of male beauty. These are the Arab peoples and the Greeks.

The Arabian Nights is not an entirely Arabic compilation—many of the stories being of Persian and Indian origin—but in this particular respect it exemplifies the feeling for male beauty and, at times, its concomitant homosexuality which is a characteristic of many Arab peoples. For example: ' "Ya Allah! look at the boy Sure that is the moon a fortnight old!" Others added: "Who can the delicious child be? We have never seen him before." or this: "Will you not understand, my lord?

> Beauty like yours is not to hoard.
> But to be thrown adrift, a golden joy,
> My lord, my gentle boy.
> Your thighs are heavy and your waist is small:
> I sipped wine from his tongue
> And I thought the world was young
> And I played the very devil for his curls' sake.
> Oh, the camphor of his teeth,
> And the amber of his breath . . .
> They turned him out of heaven for the girls' sake". ' [35]

But it was in classical Greece that the most perfect expression was given to the adulation of the male form. For the Greeks, true beauty in human form could only be expressed in the shape of a boy. With the result, as has been pointed out, that representations of the female approximate to those of boys. [36] There are few full bosomed statues of goddesses. Figures appear to be essentially epicene. It is probably true that, for the Greeks, male beauty immeasurably surpassed that of woman. This is shown again by the fact that in a great range of vase-paintings boys are far more frequently depicted than girls. The acceptance and praise of homosexual love is naturally connected with this attitude towards beauty. There are a great number of instances in which homosexual love is extolled, the most famous occurring in the *Symposium* of Plato. But it is the evidence from everyday life which illustrates how wholehearted was the worship of male youth. For instance, there was the custom of carving the name of one's lover over the doorway, on a wall or on a tree. There are many examples of boys' names being perpetuated in this way. Again, there was the custom of written inscriptions on graves: 'Philodes the Argive is beautiful; this the pillars of Corinth and the tombstones of Megara announce. It is written that he is fair as far as the battle of Amphiaraus. But what need is there of the testimony of stones? Everyone who knows him will admit it.' (*Palatine Anthology*, XII, 129).

Unlike the Arab, the Greek did not have an ambivalent attitude towards male homosexuality—his appreciation was open and unabashed. Aristotle is not ashamed of saying: 'Lovers look at none of the bodily charms of their favourites more than at their eyes, wherein dwells the secret of boyish virtues.' (frag. 81R, Ath., XIII, 564 b). Sometimes it is difficult to distinguish in Greek erotic literature which sex in fact is being apostrophised. One aspect of the Greek attitude is exemplified in a passage from the *Erotes* which is attributed to Lucian: 'Marriage is for men a life-pressing necessity and a precious thing, if it is a happy one; but the love of boys, so far as it counts sacred rights of affection, is in my opinion a result of practical wisdom. Therefore let marriage be for all, but let the love of boys remain alone the privilege of the wise, for a perfect virtue is absolutely unthinkable in women . . .' [37]

Despite this attitude, which is a constant motif in Greek thought, there is a tremendous amount of evidence that the Greeks were deeply aware of the erotic in women. Ambivalence may creep in as when Hesiod warns girls that they should not sway their but-

tocks in order to lure men with 'that part of the body which the
Greeks especially prized in the young man . . .' [38] But notwithstanding this preoccupation with homosexuality, love between
men and women receives supreme dramatic and poetic treatment.
At one level, there were the beauty contests in which girls appeared almost naked, which Athenaeus mentions (XIII, 609 e);
and at another, superb examples of erotic poetry in which the
ideal of feminine beauty is realised in words. This example from
the Greek Anthology typifies this difficult attitude.

> *Her eyes like gold, her neck like marble shows,*
> *Her lips more lovely than the reddest rose,*
> *Soft gleams her breast, her cheeks like crystal bright,*
> *E'en silver Thetis' feet were not more white.*
> *Grey thistle-down her tresses dark may stain;*
> *I heed it not, nor scorn the ripened grain.* [39]

In Homer there are many references to the power of heterosexual love and the beauty of women. There is for instance the
delightful episode of Nausicaa and her maidens in the Odyssey
when Odysseus surprises them at their games by the river:
'Mistress, I throw myself on your mercy. But are you some goddess
or a mortal woman? If you are one of the gods who live in the
sky, it is of Artemis, the daughter of almighty Zeus, that your
beauty, grace and stature most remind me . . . For never have I set
eyes on such perfection in man or woman. I worship as I look.
Only in Delos have I seen the like, a fresh young palm-tree
shooting up by the altar of Apollo . . .' [40]
The frank sensuality of the Greeks that is enhanced by their
conception of physical beauty in either sex is aptly expressed in
another poem from the Greek Anthology:

> *'To Ganymede an eagle came,*
> *A swan to Leda flew,*
> *Zeus took his joy from both the same,*
> *An equal pleasure he knew.*
> *Let some of women's beauty preach,*
> *Of youths let others tell.*
> *I love them both and find that each*
> *Is incomparable.'* [41]

The Greek ideal of feminine beauty is in one sense hermaphroditic—it has characteristics of both sexes. This reflects the Greek
conception of sexual love as being a duality, both homosexual and
heterosexual. It is an expression of the aesthetic which ignores
sexual differences, which is apparently concerned with proportions, rhythm and movement. The desirable woman has the
shoulders of a youth, breasts like apples, (a common simile in
Greek erotic poetry), a slender body, long legs and rounded
buttocks—the voluptuous charm of a boy-girl. A study of 'Apollo
and the Three Graces' in the National Museum at Naples shows
this emphasis on the epicene.

In many ways Rome is the antithesis of Greek civilisation. The
spirit of the former was essentially practical, necessary in a nation
which was primarily concerned with agriculture, commerce and
empire-building. 'Roman sexual life . . . at first fulfilled in simple,
severe, and prosaic married life, then developing into more sophisticated forms of sensuality, and degenerating into sadism, but
always instinctive and always unspiritual.' [42] What type of beauty
fulfilled these sexual demands? Whereas the Greek admiration for
the beautiful found aesthetic expression irrespective of the sex of
the subject, the Roman approach was far more directly sensual.
'The coarse sensual character of the nation made it impossible for
them to see a naked body as anything but a sexual stimulus . . .' [43]

Curiously enough the rather earthy sensuality of the Romans
produced, at times, charming tributes to the beauty of women. In
a book which is famous for its rough and bawdy atmosphere,
The Satyricon, Petronius has this passage: '. . .. 'twas not long ere'
she usher'd her Lady to meet me; a Beauty excelling even the
flattery of painters; words can't express so perfect a Creature;
whatever I should say of her would fall short of what she was.
Her hair spread all o'er her shoulders, and seem'd in easie Curls to
wanton in the Air. Her Forehead oval, and that naturally inclin'd
the Hair to its advantage. The proportion of her Eye-brows was
most correct. Her Eyes eclypst the Glory of the brightest Star.
Her Nose had an easie turn, and Mouth was such Praxiteles
believes Venus had. Then her Chin, her Neck, her Arms, and
Feet, gently girt with Embroider'd Sandals, to whose witness the
Parian marble would serve but as a foil . . .' [44]

Ovid, in the *Amores* (i, 5) expresses a Roman gentleman's

delight at the female form: 'Now when she stood before my eyes, uncovered, I found her body faultless everywhere. What graceful arms I saw and touched! What shoulders! How sweet her breasts, ready for an embrace! Beneath a moulded waist, what a smooth belly! What a rich flank, and what a slender thigh! Why should I count her beauties? She was perfect.'

That passage can be compared with this from Ovid's *Metamorphoses*: 'As soon as Phoebus saw Daphne, he fell in love with her, and wanted to marry her . . . He eyed her hair as it hung carelessly about her neck, and sighed: "What if it were properly arranged?" He looked at her eyes, sparkling bright as stars, he looked at her lips, and wanted to do more than look at them. He praised her fingers, her hands and arms, bare almost to the shoulders. Her hidden charms he imagined lovelier still . . .'[45]

For the Roman woman the ideal man was essentially masculine and virile—a gentlemanly athlete: 'Away, away, these youths who prink like women: moderate elegance becomes a man. Severity, and hair dressed without fashion, and the dust of exercise became you well. Ah, when you bend the neck of your ardent stallion, I love your skilful riding in the ring; or when you hurl your spear with valiant muscles, your valour and your strength attract my gaze; or when you hold the javelin iron-headed—anything that you do delights my eyes.'[46]

Despite what might appear superficially to be an exclusive passion for heterosexual love the Romans were by no means indifferent to the joys of homosexuality. The works of such writers as Tibullus, Catullus, Persius, Martial and Juvenal, reveal an admiration for both forms of sexual enjoyment. Juvenal is perhaps exceptional in that being a misogynist he has a somewhat, as it were, Pauline attitude towards homosexuality—passion is undesirable and women totally untrustworthy, so that it is better to be the victim of a boy than a woman. The bilateral man as the 'Arabian Nights' terms him was not confined to the sphere of literature. He appears in the forms of heroes and emperors. A reading of Gibbon makes it clear that 'unnatural love' is an attribute not only of the great men such as Caesar and Hadrian, but is found in many lesser figures.

The ability to turn from one kind of love to another does not appear to figure prominently in contemporary Western civilisation. So far as we are aware no one has attempted to trace the changing conceptions of homosexuality in European erotic life.

The distinction between Greek and Roman attitudes towards homosexuality can be explained in terms of thought and action. For the Romans sexual love is essentially sensual and coarse. Again, there is no philosophical-aesthetic basis for their pursuit of the love of boys as existed for the Greeks. There is no Roman utterance which can be compared to Plato's *Symposium*. Instead we have the tumultuous obscene farce of Petronius' *Satyricon* in which the characters turn from one kind of love to the other, indifferently. However there was an aesthetic side to the Roman love of boys. Martial apostrophises his love thus: 'So soft the bloom upon your cheek, so doubtful it fades before a sunbeam or a breath. Such is the delicate down on growing quinces that gleam even from a maiden's gentle touch. When I have pressed your lips with a dozen kisess, my tender Dindymus, I grow a beard.' [47] But he can also show the perfect sensualist in action:

> 'For a whole night, I had a wanton mistress:
> her lewd inventions were beyond compare,
> Exhausted, then I asked for something boyish,
> She gave it me before I'd said my say.' [48]

Surely this must be the most charming description of 'unnatural vice' ever written.

One curious fact emerges: that despite the Latin poets' frank avowal of homosexuality *and* ordinary love there is a strange ambivalence present which makes several of them, Martial, Catullus, and Ovid, deny that their own lives were as their poetry suggests. [49]

The difference between the Greek and Roman conceptions of beauty is very apparent when the sculpture of the two peoples is compared. One has only to compare the Apollo Sauroktonus in the Vatican and the Aphrodite Kallipygos in the National Museum at Naples with the column of Antoninus Pius in the Vatican to see this vividly. The Greek examples have a lightness and grace which is wholly idealistic. The Roman god and goddess, particularly the goddess, are down-to-earth deities—the gods and sculpture of a practical people.

What is probably the earliest surviving description of Nordic womanhood is that of the Roman poet Ausonius. He describes a captive German girl:

'She whom Nature adorned with charms no artist can picture,
Tho' he may well do justice to others, with madder and white lead,
But this heavenly blending of colour escapes him—unless he
Paints with a radiant lily, dipped in the essence of roses.
Tho' by the favour of Rome thou wast mistress, thy beauty unchanging
Keeps the north in the blue of thine eyes, in the gold of thine hair.
Twofold thy glory among us, twofold thine arms and adornment:
Latin tongue for thy wits, Swabian charm for thy face.' [50]

Allowance must be made for the exotic appeal that a fair Nordic woman would have in Italy. Nevertheless we have a vivid picture of the colouring, if not of the figure, of this Teutonic beauty. But in general all the varied tribes of pre-Christian Europe must have evolved their own particular ideal of beauty based upon the physical characteristics possessed by each group. For example the Celts would probably have emphasised the dark colouring and black hair which are common traits amongst them; whereas the Saxons would tend to have emphasised blonde features.

This differentiation of ideals in pagan Europe is borne out in the vast literature of Norse sagas, Celtic tales and romances, and commentaries which exist. Briffault has collected a great number of references dealing with sexual attitudes as well as conceptions of love and beauty. [51] The rather crude imaginings had given way, by the twelfth century, to a more aesthetic ideal. In the hands of the Provençal troubadours this ideal becomes highly conventionalised: 'She is a lady whose skin is as white as milk, whiter than the driven snow, of peculiar purity in whiteness. Her cheeks, on which vermilion hues alone appear, are like the rosebud in spring, when it has not yet opened to the full. Her hair, which is nearly always bedecked and adorned with flowers, is invariably of the colour of flax, as soft as silk, and shimmering with a sheen of the finest gold . . .' [52]

This picture is so conventionalised as to be almost meaningless. The troubadour conception of beauty is excessively etherealised, so that it becomes unreal. At times one wonders if such a woman possessed a body at all. The *trouvères* in the North appear to have been less inhibited. Alain of Lille writing in the twelfth century has this to say: 'A golden comb maintained that abundant hair whose brilliance rivalled it, so that the fascinated eye could scarce distinguish the gold of the hair from the gold of the comb. The expanded forehead had the whiteness of milk, and rivalled the lily; her bright eyebrows shone like gold . . . the teeth seemed cut in ivory; her cheeks, like the carnation or the rose . . . Her chin more polished than crystal, showed silver reflections, and her slender neck fitly separated her head from the shoulders. The firm rotundity of her breasts attested the full expansion of youth; her charming arms, advancing towards you, seemed to call for caresses; the regular curve of her flanks justly proportioned, completed her beauty . . .'[53]

This is a creature of flesh and blood, who is alive and can compare with the Greek and Roman idealisations.

The German ideal of the thirteenth century Minnesingers is described by Scherr: 'In those days a woman who wished to be accorded the prize of beauty, must have been of medium height and of a slender and very supple build. Symmetry and a gracious roundness were essentials, especially in the hips; straight legs, small feet with arched insteps, firm white arms and hands, long smooth tapered fingers and throat, and the bosom firm and with sweeping curves, but not too exuberant. The cheeks must bloom like roses wet with dew, out of the delicate pink of the face. The mouth should be small, firmly shut and sweet of breath . . . The charm of the mouth should melt into a round chin with a dimple white as the blossom of the sloe.

'The eyes should be set wide apart and the nose straight and neither too long nor too sharp, nor too blunt. Thin, long, rather straight lines of eyebrow and the colour was expected to vary slightly from that of the hair. The eyes were expected to be clear and "shine into the heart." A popular colour was blue . . .

'Finally the courtly connoisseurs were very insistent on fair hair, with a golden lustre, curling round white temples, veined with a tracery of blue . . .'[54]

That is a woman of more heroic mould than the *trouvère* picture: she has the Germanic reality. With Dante, however, in the same century, we are back again in a world of pure idealisation. Beatrice is not a woman of flesh and blood but the incarnation of spiritual love which spurns possession. She is the idealisation of the troubadours made, as it were, sacred.

It is an interesting commentary on this period that these ideals of feminine beauty could co-exist, with this varied expression in France, Germany and Italy. In England in the fourteenth century, Chaucer is much more akin to the Minnesingers in his ideals of women. He emphasises everyday features as in this description of the carpenter's wife from 'The Miller's Tale.'

> *'She was a pretty creature, fair and tender,*
> *And had a weasel's body, softly slender.*
> *And certainly she had a lecherous eye.*
> *And she had plucked her eyebrows into bows.*
> *Slenderly arched they were, and black as sloes.*
> *Skittish she was and jolly as a colt.*
> *Tall as a mast and upright as a bolt*
> *Out of a bow . . .*
> *She was a daisy, O a lollypop*
> *For any nobleman to take to bed*
> *Or some good man of yeoman stock to wed'.* [55]

The carpenter's wife seems a whole world removed from the unsubstantial Beatrice of the *Vita Nuova*. The changing ideal of feminine beauty is a motif which runs through European history in all periods. The aesthetic is determined by ideas as well as by peculiarities of physique, custom, fashion, and locale. The result is sometimes bewildering, so abrupt are the transitions at times. Evidence for this is found not only in the form of literature, but in the visual arts. For example, a study of drawings of the Early German masters of the late fifteenth and sixteenth century show considerable variations in form and type—the comparison of Lucas Cranach's 'The Lovers' with Hans Grien's 'Witches Sabbath' makes this very clear. [56] On a wider scale, the charming hour-glass figure of the Queen in a Prague Metropolitan Chapter Library manuscript [57] dating from the early fifteenth century can be compared with the portrait of Joan of Aragon, a sixteenth century beauty, by Giulio Romano in the Louvre. Havelock Ellis quotes a description of this woman from a sixteenth century work on aesthetics *De Pulchro et Amore* by Niphus: '. . . She is of medium stature, straight and elegant . . . The straight long neck, white and full, rises gracefully from the shoulders. On the ample bosom, revealing no indication of the bones, arise the rounded breasts, of equal and fitting size, and exhaling the perfume of the peaches they resemble. The rather plump hands, on the back like snow, on the palm like ivory, are exactly the length of the face ... The chest as a whole has the form of a pear, reversed, but a little compressed, and the base attached to the neck in a delightfully well-proportioned manner. The belly, the flanks, and the secret parts are worthy of the chest; the hips are large and rounded, the thighs, the legs, and the arms are in just proportion. The breadth of the shoulders is also in the most perfect relation to the dimensions of the other parts of the body; the feet, of medium length, terminate in beautifully arranged toes ... ' [58]

Niphus was probably one of the first to describe female beauty in this exact, almost clinical, way.

To illustrate the dramatic changes in the artist's conception of the feminine ideal one has only to compare Rubens' (seventeenth century) 'Rape of the Sabine Women' with Botticelli's (fifteenth century) 'Birth of Venus.' In the first the women are great ponderous fleshy creatures with enormous bosoms and trunks; the Botticelli Venus is smooth-hipped with small breasts. The two ideals of the feminine are utterly opposed. Rubens' women are Flemish giantesses—Botticelli's goddess is almost the modern ideal. In the nineteenth century Courbet's ideal in 'Sleep' represents a tentative return to the Rubenesque. Comparisons are endless—the curious muscular semi-hermaphrodites of Michelangelo's 'Night and Day' in the Sistine Chapel, with Cranach's 'Venus', both roughly of the same period, late fifteenth and early sixteenth centuries.

By the nineteenth century the novel as an art form is able to exploit the varying conceptions of the ideal woman. In Flaubert, for example, the beauty of woman is part of the context of love-making: '... With a movement of her shoulder, she slipped from her sleeve; her dress fell away, she wore no corset, her shift lay open wide. She had one of those splendid bosoms on which one would wish to die, stifled by love. As she sat on my knee, her pose was that of a simple, dreamy child, and her lovely profile was cut in the purest lines. The fold of the ravishing curve beneath her arm-pit was the smile of her shoulder ... I saw her bare hard throat, swelling as if with a continual stormy murmur, her bare pearly belly with its deep hollow navel, that quivering elastic belly, so soft that one would plunge one's head into it as into a pillow of warm satin, Her hips were superb, those truly female hips, the lines of which, declining over a rounded thigh, always recall in profile, the subtle and corrupt form of something serpentine, demonic . . .' [59]

Idealisation takes a totally different form with D'Annunzio: 'She was like a statue placed in full view of the rising sun; her perfection did not fear the light. In her bodily form I saw the impress of the eternal type, and at the same moment I recognised the fragility of the flesh, which bore no immunity from human fate. She was like a delicious fruit at the highest point of its maturity, beyond which point corruption sets in . . .' [60]

The nineteenth century conception of woman in her beauty hovers between these two extremes of the full corruptible flesh, voluptuous in its display, and the ethereal. The opposition is there in poetry as well as in the novel. We can consider the antithesis of Wordsworth and Byron in this respect, of Zola and Pater, of Swinburne and Ruskin, of Baudelaire and Lamartine. Some examples will make clear this duality of conception.

Here is Gautier, the sensualist, describing the beauty of woman: '. . . The beautiful body that posed before him combined everything: delicacy and strength, colour and form, the lines of a Greek statue of the finest period of the art with the tone of a Titian. He beheld, tangible and concrete, the vague chimera he had so often endeavoured to stay in its flight . . . The knees were admirably well shaped, the ankles admirably turned and lissom, the legs and thighs modelled in firm and splendid fashion, the belly shone like an agate, the hips were supple and broad, the bosom was fit to call the gods from on high for the sake of kissing it, the arms and shoulders perfect in shape . . .' [61] That passage may be compared with Keats' ethereal evocation in his 'Ode to Psyche':

> 'O latest born and loveliest vision far
> Of all Olympus' faded hierarchy!
> Fairer than Phoebe's sapphire-region'd star,
> Or Vesper, amorous glow-worm of the sky;
> Fairer than these, though temple hast thou none,
> Nor altar heap'd with flowers;
> Nor virgin-choir to make delicious moan
> Upon the midnight hours;'

It is probably true to say that after Zola it was impossible for the novelist to continue with his dream of fair, unattainable women. They had become part of the realism of the everyday: '. . . Bending back thus, she displayed her solid Amazonian waist and firm bosom, where strong muscles moved under the satin texture of the skin. A delicate line, to which the shoulder and the thigh added their slight undulations, ran from one of her elbows to her foot, and Muffet's eyes followed this tender profile, and marked how the outlines of the fair flesh vanished in golden gleams, and how its rounded contours shone like silk in the candle-light. He thought of his old dread of woman, of the Beast of the Scriptures, at once lewd and wild. Nana was all covered with fine hair, a russet down made her body velvety, while the Beast was apparent in the almost equine development of her flanks, in the fleshy exuberances and deep hollows of her body, which lent her sex the mystery and suggestiveness lurking in their shadows . . .' [62]

But for Rossetti the flesh does not exist and we are confronted once more with dreams:

> When do I see thee most, beloved one?
> When in the light the spirits of mine eye.
> Before thy face, their altar, solemnize
> The worship of that Love through the made known?
> Or when in the dusk hours (we two alone),
> Close-kissed and eloquent of still replies
> Thy twilight-hidden glimmering visage lies,
> And my soul only sees thy soul its own? ' [63]

Many factors contribute to this dualism in the male with regard to feminine beauty. On the one hand, the ideal woman who is shorn of any sexual associations represents an attempt to give life to a spiritual vision which has its origin in Dante and some aspects of Provençal poetry. But this, when analysed, is a vision which is incapable of warmth or feeling. Beauty in woman is worshipped as an ethereal, inhuman, impersonal entity. On the other hand, the expression of the warm, living woman whose beauty is an indication of sexual promise—the fulfilment of desire—represents the extreme of sensuality. This is a vision which can be seen in terms of the everyday. Taken together the ethereal and the sensual might be said to be a reflection of the classical dichotomy between the spiritual and the sensual. Philosophy, convention, religion, fashion and ideology are all factors which help to create the conception of the ideal woman.

We can see that in the twentieth century the dichotomy is no longer so apparent: the unattainable and the ethereal has tended to come down to earth. Woman instead of being either a harlot or a saint is now a being of physical charm but possessing mental powers similar to man. This is partly due to the complete change in woman's status from the one century to the other. Equality of the sexes is incompatible with beauty out of reach on a pedestal. This is reflected not only in literature, but in the new mass media of the twentieth century. The ideal woman is in many ways different from her predecessors. Possibly the most significant difference is in the fields of social relationships and clothes both of which provide a freedom of movement in direct contrast with the preceding century.

In contemporary literature there are thousands of examples of this transformation—this marriage of antitheses which turns into a commonsense eroticism.

The heroine of *Brideshead Revisited* is thus described: 'She was thin in those days, flat chested, leggy; she seemed all limbs and neck, bodiless, spidery; thus far she conformed to the fashion, but the hair-cut and the hats of the period, and the blank stare and gape of the period, the clownish dabs of rouge high on the cheek bones, could not reduce her to type . . .' Julia, however, matures: '. . . She was not yet thirty, but was approaching the zenith of her loveliness, all her rich promise abundantly fulfilled. She had lost all that fashionable, spidery look; the head I used to think quattrocento, which had sat a little oddly on her, was now part of herself and not at all Florentine; not connected in any way with painting or the arts or with anything except herself, so that it would be idle to itemise and dissect her beauty, which was her own essence, and could only be known in her and by her authority and in the love I was soon to have for her . . .' [64]

The popular image, however, fed by the films rather than books still seems to retain a hankering for the nineteenth century duality. How otherwise explain the popularity of physical types which are totally dissimilar such as Audrey Hepburn and Jayne Mansfield?

One possible explanation of this might be that the magnificent resplendence of Miss Mansfield's bosom epitomises the maternal consolations which man is always yearning for, while Miss Hepburn represents the girl who has so much of the boy in her that men can meet her on equal terms. Is it possible that there is also an unconscious homosexual feeling present?

While it is, generally speaking, impossible to discover how the image of female beauty coincided with the reality of life in the past, contemporary observation as well as research, suggests that the ideal of beauty represented by the film does not bear much relationship to ordinary women except in the sense that they tend to model themselves on film stars. In a study made of marriage-relationships of the working class in London, it was found that only forty per cent of the men found some physical attraction to remember in relation to their courtships and subsequent marriage; whereas sixty per cent remembered mental traits. For women in relation to men, the respective percentages are thirty per cent and seventy per cent. It appears for the men that general good looks, which could not be described in detail, were the major attraction on the physical side. Information given was of this order: 'She was not bad looking.'; 'She looked a nice type.'; 'She was a good and lovely girl.'; 'Young, fresh, good looking, and so on.'[65]

This hardly suggests that the film image of beauty is very much at work in determining sexual relationships. Where, of course, its influence is greatest is in the creation of a fantasy world for both sexes. In books, cheap romances foster the same type of fantasy: a world is built up entirely removed from reality where men can imagine themselves in the arms of Marilyn Monroe or Jayne Mansfield, and women can be crushed in the virile embraces of a Clark Gable or a Gary Cooper. Such fantasy apparently does not interfere with the formation of more mundane sexual relationships. But, so far as we know, it is not a topic into which research has been conducted.[66]

In the great majority of descriptions we have quoted there have been few references to the actual sexual organs or primary sexual characteristics as indicative of female beauty. Such references as there are are mainly to be found in Oriental literature, and mostly confined to the *mons veneris* rather than the labia or vagina. References to the male organ are even scarcer. It has been suggested by Havelock Ellis and others that the reason for the emphasis on anatomical features other than the genitals is due to the latter's fundamentally unaesthetic appearance. This, together with the possibility of magical and religious dangers, which we have discussed, and physical dangers, has led to a concentration on the secondary sexual characteristics such as the buttocks and the breast. The result, according to Ellis, is that only 'peoples of a low state of culture' regard the sexual organs as objects of attraction. [67]

The argument on magico-religious grounds cannot really be substantiated. It is just as reasonable to assume that because of the widespread incidence of phallic worship, prominence given to the male organ in everyday life would be more than admissible. Again, in many societies, including classical Greece and Rome, it was customary to carry or wear small phallic charms. There is perhaps more relevance concerning the peculiar vulnerability of the sexual organs. Though again it is perfectly possible to achieve protection and yet draw attention to them simultaneously, as indeed occurred in the Middle Ages when mediaeval suits of armour had interesting and peculiar adornments made to fit over the genital area.

With regard to the unaesthetic appearance of the genitalia it does appear as if this is unanswerable. Rémy de Gourmont in his *Natural Philosophy of Love* maintains this thesis to support the view that woman as a whole is more attractive than man as her organs are largely concealed ". . . The superiority of feminine beauty is real, it has a sole cause, the unity of line. What makes a woman beautiful is the invisibility of her genital organs . . . especially if one considers the male at the very hour of desire, at the moment, that is, when they present the most intense and most natural expression of life. In the woman all the movements are interior, or visible only in the undulation of her curves, conserving thus her full aesthetic value, while the man, seeming at once to recede towards the primitive states of animality, appears reduced, putting off the beauty, to the base and simple condition of genital organ . . .' [68]

Ellis caps the argument by saying no Western artist has ever portrayed a penis in erection as part of his portrayal of perfect masculine beauty. [69] This of course is true if we except so-called pornographic art (the wall paintings of Pompeii). But this is a European aesthetic and not one which has universal application.

In other words our refusal to depict the male sexual organ is due
to cultural conditioning rather than an inherent antipathy on the
grounds that the appearance of the erect male organ is intrinsically
distasteful. In this connection the erotic painting and sculptures of
India demonstrate a completely different attitude from the European. The cave paintings of Ellora and the sculpture of Konorak
show both men and women in a state of sexual excitement. [70]

It would appear that in European art, with the exceptions we
have noted, the nude female form is given far more prominence
than the male. This bears out the assertion that the visual-sexual
sense of the female is less acute than the male. Sir Kenneth Clark in
The Nude [71]) has pointed out the opposing conceptions of Venus
which are perpetuated by Botticelli and Rubens—one the ideal of
refined sexuality, the other a symbol of fertility within the reach
of man. It would be difficult to find paintings which conveyed
similar male sexual images.

In the necessarily incomplete survey we have made of the
changing conceptions of beauty in different societies we have
noted some of the characteristics which societies have chosen to
emphasise. A fuller consideration of particular anatomical features
raises other problems.

If we accept that the female breast, for a great number of societies, is the ultimate symbol of sexuality, it is clear that this is due
not only to the aesthetic-sexual aspect—but also to the association
with the essentially feminine functions. Such association may be
unconscious. Casanova's predilection for 'alabaster globes', as he
termed them, was hardly connected in his mind with maternity.
Nevertheless in our view the European and American males'
obsession with the mammary glands is compounded of more than
the directly visual-aesthetic appeal. The same, of course, could be
said of the appeal to the male of female thighs and buttocks—that
their sexually pleasing proportions are also indicative of the child-
bearing capabilities of the woman.

Amongst many pre-literate societies there is an equivalent
emphasis on the breast as a mark of female beauty. Widely separated groups, such as the Hopi Indians of the American south-west,
the Thonga of East Africa, and the people of Wogeo Island off
Northern New Guinea, favour large breasts. There is, however,
considerable variation in the type and form of breast thought to

be desirable. For example, the Azande of Central Africa believe that the extremely long, pendulous breast is supremely desirable. Whereas the East African Masai ideal is the firm upright breast. If the ideal of the bosom is not produced by nature many peoples, including ourselves, call upon artifice to remedy the defect.

One fairly common device, in those societies which admire the pendulous bosom, is the breast band which is tied tightly across the bosom thus forcing the breasts to hang down. This is found in East Africa amongst the Gall, Bahutua, in several West African and South African peoples, as well as in the Loyalty Islands of the Pacific, and in some South American Indian tribes such as the Payagua of Paraguay. For the most extreme form of breast cons-triction, however, we have to turn to Europe. In seventeenth cen-tury Spain, young girls' breasts were covered with leaden plates, with the result that the breasts failed to develop. [72] In the Europe of the nineteenth century similar deformations were produced by wooden platters. According to Ploss and Bartels this practice was common in Würtemberg and Bavaria. They quote the following account concerning the women of Bregenzer Wald: 'They have muscular, well-knit frames, straight shapely legs, wide hips but no bosom. This strange deficiency is not unknown in mountain districts, but is all the more striking as the women are otherwise of quite exuberant build. This may be because of the wooden platters strapped on the girls, even in those more favoured by nature than the others, thus preventing the development of the woman's chief charm . . .' [73]

The Greeks' ideal as that of the Romans' was of a medium sized bosom or as Martial (Epigrams XIV, 134) put it, so that 'there may be something for one hand to encompass and cover.' To achieve this end, and others, they perfected the ancestor of the brassiere or breast-band: '. . . The object of this band, worn as it was round the breast, usually under the chiton (under-garment) and therefore on the bare skin, was to raise the bosom and thereby not only to prevent the unsightly hanging of the breasts, but also to emphasise them or to cover any defect in their beauty . . .' [74]

Some peoples of Southern Russia, such as the Ossetes and Kabardians, sew the pubescent girl into tight leather garments which are untouched until marriage when it is the husband's privilege to cut them off. A leather girdle, if it can be called that, reaches from over the bust to the hips. The resulting constriction of the breasts can be imagined. A Circassian lament describes a girl in this state: 'Nine years are past since this girl was sewn up; since her breasts were compressed. Sorrow in her heart because her breasts are not free? It is time for the knife of the youth to free her from her bondage; but where is that youth, where is he?' (75)

The importance of the female breast as one of the most powerful European sexual symbols is borne out by the extraordinary mutilations practised by the heretical Christian sect of the Skoptzi in the nineteenth century. These people appear to have been mainly of Russian and Rumanian origin. They indulged not only in mutilations of the breast but in varying forms of castration. With regard to the female bosom, the nipples were burnt or cut off, or an incised pattern was made on both breasts. More extremely, the whole or part of both breasts might be amputated. The object appears to have been the extinction of sexual desire in the female as well as that of the visual pleasure leading to desire experienced by the male. (76) The Skoptzi carried matters to an extreme, but their behaviour is merely a development of one aspect of Christian thought in relation to sex. The horror with which many of the Early Fathers regarded the unclothed form of a woman as the embodiment of lustful desire is well known. The preoccupation with legends and stories of abominable tortures suffered by Christian martyrs, so common throughout the Middle Ages, is not perhaps entirely a matter of virtue but has a sexual significance. This can be seen with regard to breast mutilation. Numbers of female martyrs attained their death and heavenly award by having their breasts amputated. The most famous are Saints Agatha, Christian, and Faith. Their fate was current not only in many legends but in pictures and illustrations of the period.

The other secondary female sexual characteristic which has almost as widespread an incidence in terms of sexual symbolism as the breasts, is the pelvic region. This, as was seen in the case of Hottentot steatopygia, can become the over-riding factor in determining feminine beauty. Among most peoples, however, it does not assume this pronounced form. In the Latin countries of Europe, large buttocks and undulations produced by walking are regarded as sexually stimulating by men. Elsewhere in Europe the back view of a woman walking, irrespective of the size of her buttocks, seems to produce the same effect. The same attraction is evinced in the case of Papuan women and in the Arab countries. There seems to be a connection here with the promise of sexual pleasure symbolised by the movement of the buttocks; the larger the buttocks the greater the promised pleasure. The development of the pelvic region is associated with general plumpness and this is regarded as highly desirable in a great number of societies. These range from some North American Indians such as the Hidatsa to the Siberian Chuckchee, East African Thonga, and several Polynesian peoples.

Few peoples lay any stress on a narrow pelvis and hips. One outstanding example is that of the Yakut of Siberia where such women are greatly admired. The European ideal in this respect has been subject to a great deal of variation. The narrow hipped woman with small breasts occurs as a constant aspect of the ethereal and divine but just as frequently the admired type is the pronouncedly voluptuous figure.

Despite the evidence produced by Ellis and de Gourmont we have quoted above there are societies which lay especial emphasis on the primary sexual characteristics. For example a large clitoris is a prized possession of women in Easter Island. Several pre-literate groups such as Marquesas Islanders, the Venda, Dahomeyans of West Africa and the Thonga of East Africa, admire excessive development of the labia majora.

But if the full range of female characteristics which appear to act as sexual stimulants is considered two things stand out: one is that no part of the female anatomy is not regarded somewhere as possessing great sexual allure. The range here is from the ankle or nose to the clitoris. The other is that despite this the majority of human societies appear to have given far more attention to the breasts and buttocks than to other anatomical features. Reasons for this are not far to seek. Both bosom and pelvis are essentially feminine. The first evokes not only pleasure, but ideas of maternity and thus of the ultimate fulfilment which is an unconscious motive in the choice of a mate. There is also the unconscious memory of the infant feeding at the breast which may be a concomitant of the male attitude towards the breast.

There is one curious episode in the changing pattern of the European female ideal. This concerns pregnancy as an attribute of

Fig. 19. *Bathsheba:* engraving by H. Goltzius, 1583

beauty. In many societies not only is the pregnant woman not considered beautiful or attractive, but she may be absolutely forbidden or tabu to man. In Northern Europe prior to the Renaissance quite contrary ideas prevailed. We find that the distended belly and enlarged buttocks is depicted as the ideal. This is noticeable in the work of the Van Eycks—there is the famous group of the Arnolfini family in the National Gallery in London, and in the paintings of such artists as Memlinc, Urs Graf, and Cranach.[77]

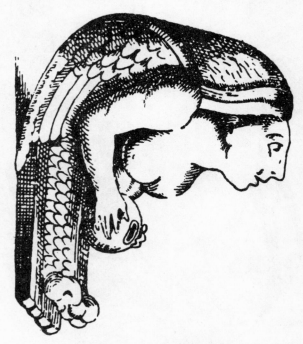

Fig. 20. Female figure in a mediaeval German church

This manifestation can be regarded as an isolated phenomenon as it does not occur in any other period and is contrary to the major European conventions of beauty.

For male beauty, the range of characteristics which are admired is much smaller. There are few particular emphases. The ideal is in general terms that he should convey strength and virility. The period of Greek art when the male figure is idealised is, as we have

Fig. 21. Aldegrever's *Ideal Woman*: sixteenth century woodcut

said, affected by homosexuality; thus the representations tend to be hermaphroditic and so not typical. From the literature of any particular period it seems that beautiful women have taken as lovers the most disparate individuals. This bears out the argument that the visual sense for woman in relation to men has not the same supreme importance it possesses for men in relation to women.

The essential background for beauty in either sex is, ordinarily speaking, one where the individual considered has no deformities, has the ethnic characteristics of his group (for example the albino, though possessing strength, etc., is nowhere considered attractive), is free from disease, and is clean. On the basis of these general essentials, particular ones, which vary from society to society, may occur. Variation here, of course, is enormous. In the case of many groups in North America and Europe pungent or bad breath is considered repulsive but at home the garlic-laden breath of the Southern European is obviously not a disability in these terms. Body odour again is entirely relative in the estimate made of it. In the United States it is held in abhorrence whereas many societies cultivate the natural odour of the body sweat and enhance it by artificial means. Colour and texture of skin and hair may be important aspects of the basis on which beauty is formalised. In some groups unaffected by European influence, the ideal is a dark-skinned person with matted hair. The light-skinned individual cannot hope to fulfil the canons of beauty demanded. Where European influence has affected the development of the ideal, as amongst Negroes in the New World, the individual who approximates most closely to the 'white', although the majority of people are dark, will be considered the ideal. Exception must be made of Brazil where the ideal type appears to represent a compromise between the two extremes of white and black: '. . . Quite significantly, the *morena* (or feminine *moreno*) is the "ideal type" of Bahian femininity. She is in many cases an individual of remarkable beauty. Typically, she has dark brown eyes and dark hair, quite wavy, perhaps even curly, and Caucasian features; her colour is *cafe com leite* (literally, coffee with milk; i.e., like that of one "heavily tanned"), and she has a healthy appearance . . .'[78]

It is upon these bases or essentials that ideals of beauty are built.

The evidence of people's actions in sexual relationships, the literature of many societies, and the millions spent on beauty aids in America and Europe, as well as the thousands of devices used by women all over the world to promote beauty suggests that the physical beauty of women is the most powerful stimulant to the promotion of sexual activity. There is little doubt that there is a sound biological basis to this form of attraction, but the choice of the ideal is dependent upon factors which are inherent in a particular society at any given moment of time. At the one extreme stands the slim-hipped, large-breasted European ideal; at the other

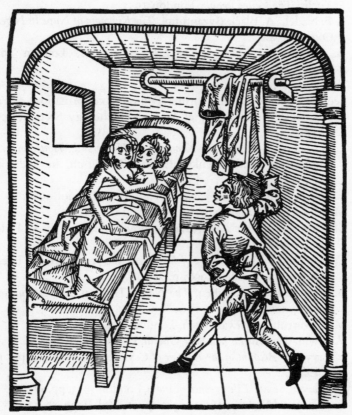

Fig. 22. Illicit love in the Middle Ages: fifteenth century woodcut

the steatopygous beauty of the Hottentot. In between are all the infinite variations of which the human mind is capable. But each one is the result of a particular configuration of ideas and physique.

REFERENCES AND NOTES

1. *The Book of a Thousand Nights and One Night*, translated by E. Powys Mathers from the version of J. C. Mardrus, London 1923, Vol. 3, p. 477.
2. R. Briffault, *The Mothers*, London 1927, Vol. 2, p. 160.
3. C. Aymard, *Les Touaregs*, Paris 1911.
4. Mungo Park, *Travels in the Interior of Africa*, Edinburgh 1860.
5. P. Fuchs, *The Veiled People*, London 1955.

    S. F. Nadel, 'A. Black Byzantium', *The Kingdom of Nupe in Nigeria*, Oxford 1942.
6. B. Malinowski, *The Sexual Life of Savages*, London 1932, pp. 248–50.
7. *ibid. op. cit.*, pp. 250–54.
8. See S. G. Shattock 'On Normal Tumour-like formations of Fat', *Proceedings Royal Society of Medicine*, Pathology Section, 1907, p. 270.

    L. S. Schultze-Jena, '*Zur Kenntnis d. Körpers d. Hottentotten u. Buschmänner*, Jena, Denkscrift., XVII; Forsch. in Südafrika, 1928, V.

    I. Schapera, *The Khoisan Peoples of South Africa*, London 1930.
9. M. Merker, *Der Masai*, Berlin 1904, p. 123.
10. *The Memoirs of Père Labat*, translated and abridged by P. Eaden, London 1931, p. 75.
11. *Captain Cook's Third Voyage of Discovery, the years 1776–80*. Everyman edition, London 1906, p. 287.
12. B. Spencer and F. J. Gillen, *The Native Tribes of Central Australia*, London 1899, p. 46.
13. M. Covarrubias, *Mexico South*, London, N.D., pp. 244–5.
14. V. Elwin, *The Murias and their Ghotul*, Oxford 1947, p. 428.
15. J. Davy, *An Account of the Interior of Ceylon*, London 1821, pp. 110 *et seq.*
16. J. J. Meyer, *Sexual Life in Ancient India*, London 1953, pp. 432–3.
17. *The Thousand Nights and One Night, op. cit.*, Vol. II, pp. 12–13.
18. H. H. Ploss and M. & P. Bartels, *Woman*, ed. E. J. Dingwall, London 1935, Vol. 2, p. 213.
19. *ibid. op. cit.*, Vol. IV, p. 189.
20. Havelock Ellis, *op. cit.*, Vol. IV, p. 189.
21. Stendhal, *Love*, translated by G. and S. Sale, London 1957, p. 48.

22. A. C. Kinsey and others, *Sexual Behaviour in the Human Female*, London 1953, p. 651.

23. Kinsey, *op. cit.*, p. 652.

24. Kinsey, *op. cit.*, pp. 654–8.

25. See footnote in Kinsey *op. cit.*, p. 653.

26. T. Mann, *The Confessions of Felix Krull*, London 1958, p. 157.

27. T. Gautier, *Mademoiselle de Maupin*, translated by F. C. de Sumichrast, Harvard 1906, Vol. II, p. 265.

28. S. de Beauvoir, *The Second Sex*, translated by H. M. Parshley, London 1953, p. 175.

29. Kinsey, *op. cit.*, p. 651.

30. C. S. Ford and F. A. Beach, *Patterns of Sexual Behaviour*, London 1952, p. 90.

31. Ellis, *op. cit.*, p. 191.

32. Petronius Arbiter, *Satyricon*, translated by William Burnaby (1694), London 1933, p. 196.

33. H. R. Schoolcraft, *Archives of Aboriginal Knowledge*, Philadelphia 1851–60, Vol. V, p. 612.

34. Compare in this connection Dr H. Deutsch's *The Psychology of Woman*, London, Vol. I, p. 175.

35. *The Thousand Nights and One Night*, *op. cit.*, Vol. II, pp. 156 and 370–1.

36. H. Licht, *Sexual Life in Ancient Greece*, London 1935, p. 427, *et seq.*

37. Quoted by H. Licht, *op. cit.*, p. 491.

38. Licht, *op. cit.*, p. 27.

39. *The Girdle of Aphrodite*, the Complete Love Poems of the Palatine Anthology, translated by F. A. Wright, London 1923, p. 33.

40. *The Odyssey*, translated by E. V. Rieu, London 1945, p. 106.

41. *The Girdle of Aphrodite*, *op. cit.* p. 45.

42. O. Kiefer, *Sexual Life in Ancient Rome*, London 1938, p. 6.

43. Kiefer, *op. cit.*, p. 148.

44. Petronius Arbiter, *Satyricon*, translated by William Burnaby (1694), London 1933, p. 197.

45. Ovid, *Metamorphoses*, translated by M. M. Innes, London 1955, p. 45.

46. Ovid, *Heroides*, IV, p. 75 *et seq.*

47. Martial, *Epigrams*, X, 42.

48. Martial, *Epigrams*, IX, 67.

49. Kiefer, *op. cit.*, pp. 279–80.

50. Ausonius.

51. R. Briffault, *The Mothers*, London 1927, Vol. III, Ch. 28, pp. 376–467.

52. J. E. Rowbotham, *The Troubadours and Courts of Love*, London 1898, p. 228.

53. J. Houdoy, *La Beauté des Femmes dans la littérature et dans l'art du XIIe au XVIe Siècle*, Lille 1876, p. 119.

54. J. Scherr, *Deutsche Kultur und Sittengeschichte*, 2 Auflage, Leipzig 1858, p. 197.

55. Geoffrey Chaucer, 'The Miller's Tale', *The Canterbury Tales*, translated into Modern English by N. Coghill, London 1957, pp. 112–3.

56. *Drawings of the Early German Masters*, chosen and edited by E. Schilling, London 1936, pp. 40 and 46.

57. *Gothic Drawing*, translated by J. Layton, Prague, N.D., Plate 142.

58. Havelock Ellis, *op. cit.*, pp. 150–1.

59. G. Flaubert, *November*, translated by F. Jellinck, London 1934, pp. 98–9 and 117.

60. G. D'Annunzio, *The Virgins of the Rocks*, translated by A. Hughes, London 1899, pp. 103–4.

61. T. Gautier, *Mademoiselle de Maupin*, translated by F. C. de Sumichrast, Harvard 1906, Vol. II, p. 306.

62. E. Zola, *Nana*, translated by A. Dobkin, N.Y., 1947, pp. 215–16.

63. D. G. Rossetti, *Lovesight*.

64. E. Waugh, *Brideshead Revisited*, London 1945, pp. 158 and 209.

65. E. Slater and M. Woodside, *Patterns of Marriage*, London, 1951, pp. 105–6

66. Slater and Woodside, *op. cit.*, p. 104.

67. Havelock Ellis, *op. cit.*, pp. 156–63.

68. R. de Gourmont, *The Natural Philosophy of Love*, translated by Ezra Pound, N.Y., 1940, pp. 40–41.

69. Ellis, *op. cit.*, p. 162.

70. Mulk Raj Anand, *Kama Kala*, London 1958.

71. Sir Kenneth Clark, *The Nude*, London 1956, pp. 64–5.

72. Comtesse d'Aulnoy, *Travels into Spain*, London 1930, p. 200.

73. H. H. Ploss and M. & P. Bartels, *Woman*, edited by J. Dingwall, London 1935, Vol. I, pp. 446–7.

74. H. Licht, *Sexual Life in Ancient Greece*, London 1935, p. 84.

75. Quoted by Ploss and Bartels, *op. cit.*, p. 447.

76. W. Koch, *Über die Russisch-rumänische Kastrationsskete der Skopzen,* Jena 1921.
77. See Sir Kenneth Clark, *op. cit.,* Ch. VIII.
78. D. Pierson, *Negroes in Brazil,* Chicago 1944, p. 136.

CHAPTER XII

Extra-Marital Sexual Intercourse

THE MARITAL tie once established is regarded in most societies as giving the husband exclusive sexual rights in his wife. There are, however, occasions when this rule is abrogated and these exclusive sexual rights are enjoyed by others. Certain Australian tribes, such as the Arunta, represent in their customs one of the classical types of socially approved extra-marital intercourse.

The basic assumption among these people is that the husband can dispose of his sexual rights if he so wishes. He may thus give consent to his wife having sexual relations with individuals who are in a particular social relationship (*Unawa*) to her. That is to say every man stands in a distinct relationship to a particular group of women. This is the group from which he has to select his wife. After his marriage, he may, with the consent of the husbands concerned, have sexual relations with any of the women of this group. This can be regarded as exemplifying the principle of sexual hospitality which, as we shall see, has a widespread incidence. In the Australian case the limits of the relationship must never be overstepped. Thus a man will never lend his wife to an individual who does not belong to the proper group. As the husband is in

control of the situation—he may give or withhold his consent—
this type of sexual hospitality remains an individual matter within
the framework of custom. That this is the case is seen by the fact
that if an individual does have intercourse with a woman with
whom it is permitted but without the husband's consent, he is
known as a vulva-thief—an offender. [1]

A quite different category of extra-marital intercourse is that
which may be described as being of a public nature. Here there is
no question of individual rights; it is a matter of public concern.
There are two types of this, as it were, communal breaking of the
marriage tie. The first refers to the customs observed at marriage.
Amongst the Kaitish tribe after the girl has been circumcised
'. . . men of the following relationship have access to her in the
order named. *Ipmunna*, that is individuals of the same moiety
of the tribe as her own; mothers' brothers' sons; tribal elder and
younger brothers; and lastly, men whom she might lawfully
marry, but who have no right to her once she becomes the
property of a member of the group to which they belong . . .' [2]
Such sexual access is limited to this particular occasion prior to
marriage.

The second type of public or communal extension of sexual
rights is that which takes place at corroborees; the latter are tribal
meetings of a ritual nature. An important corroboree may last ten
of fourteen days: 'Every day or two three women are told off to
attend at the corroboree ground, and with the exception of men
who stand in relation to them of actual father, brother or sons,
they are for the time being common property to all the men on
the corroboree ground . . .' [3] To illustrate the abrogation of
individual rights, it is the husband himself who approaches his
actual or tribal son-in-law and suggests that he should take his wife
into the bush. What is perhaps even more important is that such
a man, ordinarily speaking, is forbidden to have any dealings of
any kind with a woman in this relationship to him. In other words
intercourse permitted at corroborees appears to be of a ritual
nature. This breaking of the tabu of avoidance by the man, and
reversal of what is normally upheld, is a principle which we shall
see at work in other, totally different societies.

In considering this category of permitted extra-marital activity,
it should be remembered that the aboriginal peoples of Australia

are famous for the extent and intricacy of their scheme of social relationships. This would appear to give added point to the lifting of sexual restraints and the voluntary surrender of the husband's sexual rights at the corroboree. As we hope to make clear, socially sanctioned occasions of sexual licence have a specific function in promoting acceptance of the rules and regulations of ordinary life.

In the Australian pattern, wife lending is not idiosyncratic—the individual cannot choose to whom he will lend his wife. Choice is exercised only in the sense that in the first category quoted a husband may refuse consent. In the others he is dictated to by custom. [4]

An apparent exception to this was the practice of lending women to white men as an act of hospitality. Such acts do not appear to be within the framework of customary wife lending. The white man is outside tribal law. He is not within the system of relationships. To lend your wife to such an individual is not infringing any law. It is a gesture of pure hospitality.

The pattern of ceremonial extra-marital intercourse is somewhat different among the Murngin tribe. They inhabit that area of Australia known as Arnhem Land. As part of what is called the *Gunabibi* ceremony, ceremonial intercourse takes place.

For the Gunabibi, men and women may come from considerable distances: 'When a local man discovers that a certain visitor from a far clan is his tribal brother, he sends his younger brother to inform this person that he may have the local man's wife for ceremonial copulation at the end of the Gunabibi ceremony. He sends presents along with the younger brother. The recipient, either through his own younger brother or through the messenger, offers his own wife in exchange, and also sends presents . . .' [5]

This is the properly and formally constituted way for the Murngin to exchange wives. But there are other ways. Men may agree, without intermediaries, to exchange wives. A couple may make their own arrangements, but for this to be legal the consent of the husband would have to be obtained.

After a meal has been taken in the evening, a dance of the women takes place. The men sit in a half circle round the fire, and the women dance on the other side of the fire in front of them. While this is in progress individual men will get up and walk across to a woman and give her presents of food or red ochre. Such a woman is one with whom an arrangement has been made. Later on presents are exchanged privately between the couple. Part of the gifts received by the woman are given to her husband. The value is not important—it is the ritual of giving which is paramount. There have very probably been secret meetings between the two before the dance; while this is known to everyone it is not thought to be quite proper.

'The position taken in the sexual act differs from the customary one . . . in that the woman sits on the ground on the back of her buttocks. The trunk of the body leans back at an angle from the legs, with the hands on the ground in back of the body to support it. The man puts his legs under hers and his hands around her so that the pudenda meet in closer contact than if he lay on her . . .' [6]

It may very well be that the significance of a different coital position is to mark the occasion as one which is abnormal.

When intercourse has taken place, the husband of the woman takes some of his own sweat and smears it on the arms and legs of the man. This is done so that the man will not get 'sick'.' 'Sickness' may occur possibly because the sexual act at this time, the climax of the Gunabibi, is considered dangerous.

On the last night of the ceremony a woman may copulate with a number of different men. This is generally due to the small number of women who attend the ceremony.

The Murngin pattern demonstrates the obligatory nature of this form of wife-exchange and ritual intercourse. When an individual objects, he or she is told that if they do not participate they will become ill. Murngin opinion is: 'This makes everybody clean. It makes everyone's body good until next dry season . . . It is better that everybody comes with their women and all meet together at a Gunabibi and play with each other, and then nobody will start having sweethearts the rest of the time . . . if a woman says, "I won't go to that corroboree place with you." the man says, "If you don't go with me you are going to be dead." Sometimes we kill that woman by magic, and throw spears at them if they won't do it . . .' [7]

The sanctions against non-co-operation seem to be fairly strong. Spear throwing at a culprit was a fairly common method of punishment for any infraction of tribal law. The remarks that intercourse of this kind made people feel good, and that it pre-

vented liaisons at other times of the year, would seem to reflect
the ancient and respectable hypothesis that the licensed occasion
acts as a safety valve.

Another aspect of such obligatory extra-marital coitus is that
sexual jealousy is apparently at a minimum. Spencer and Gillen,
the great authorities on the Australian Aborigines, state that while
it would be impossible to exclude it on such occasions, nevertheless it is subservient to tribal custom. [8] In other words the emotion
of jealousy is as much subject to conditioning by a culture as the
type of marriage in use. The Marquesans exhibit this type of
conditioning to a great extent. As we have seen these people practised group marriage. In addition sexual hospitality and periods of
licence were common. To exhibit sexual jealousy met with
ridicule, and in a sober condition the Marquesan rarely showed it.
Drunkenness, however, promoted jealousy, and quarrelling and
fighting took place. But, and this is the significant point, next
morning when sober, such individuals were thoroughly ashamed
of themselves for having broken their code of good manners. [9]

The Todas of Southern India are another people among whom
jealousy appears to be somewhat inactive. They are noted, as we
saw, for the extreme freedom of their sexual arrangements. As
Rivers put sit: 'Instead of adultery being regarded as immoral, I
rather suspected, though I could not satisfy myself on the point,
that, according to the Toda idea, immorality attaches rather to the
man who grudges his wife to another. One group of those who
experience difficulty in getting to the next world after death are
the *kasht vainol*, or grudging people, and I believe this term includes
those who would in a more civilised community, be plaintiffs in
the divorce court . . .' [10]

Reasons for the absence of strong manifestations of jealousy can
be sought in the field of compensations provided. The culture
does not merely demand the inhibition of sexual jealousy. There
is a compensatory mechanism at work which grants the privilege
of licence in return for adherence to the social code. If you do not
object to other men cohabiting with your wife, others will not
object to your cohabiting with their wives.

Another people, whose habitat is entirely different from that of
the Australian Aborigines, exhibit a similar pattern of wife-
exchange. These are the Eskimo: 'A strange custom permits a man

to lend his wife to a friend for a whole season or even longer and to exchange wives as a sign of friendship. On certain occasions it is even commanded by a religious law . . .' [11] Wife lending amongst the Eskimo appears to have, in many instances, an extremely practical basis. Men will borrow someone else's wife if for example she has the type of skill he needs on a hunting trip. Or friends on a joint expedition may exchange wives, presumably to enliven the proceedings. [12]

But this type of arrangement did not only depend upon the casual arrangement. There was also the patterned behaviour between individuals who regarded themselves as bond-brothers. If they lived in different villages, whenever a visit was made the host placed his wife at the disposal of his guest. The honour was reciprocated when the host in turn made a visit. [13] This might be regarded as an attenuated form of the very closely defined Australian system where specific rights and duties are laid down. It is, however, in the religious ceremonies of the Eskimo that their behaviour approximates most closely to the Australians.

The Central Eskimo have elaborate annual ceremonies the object of which is to drive away evil spirits. At one stage in the proceedings there '. . . arises a cry of surprise and all eyes are turned toward a hut out of which stalk two gigantic figures. They wear heavy boots; their legs are swelled out to a wonderful thickness with several pairs of breeches; the shoulders of each are covered by a woman's over-jacket and the faces by tattooed marks of seal-skins . . . Silently, with long strides, the *quailertangs* (shamans) approach the assembly, who screaming, press back from them. The pair solemnly lead the men to a suitable spot and set them in a row, and the women in another opposite them. They match the men and women in pairs and these pairs run, pursued by the quailertangs, to the hut of the woman, where they are for the following day and night man and wife. . .' [14]

The functioning of Eskimo extra-marital licence takes place against a background of monogamy, polygamy, and polyandry and a high frequency of divorce. The fluidity of their marital arrangements no doubt helps to explain the comparatively high incidence of wife-lending.

African examples of wife-lending within the group or clan are numerous. The Banyoro of Uganda follow the same model as the

Australian: '. . . The relationship between members of the same clan was of such a character that any man's wife was common to him and the other members of this clan. It was perfectly legitimate for a man to have relations with the wives of the men he called brothers, that is, his clan fellows, and such action was not looked upon as adultery. A man might use his influence with his wife to make her refrain from such action, and might be annoyed if she admitted to her bed a member of the clan with whom he was not on good terms, but he could not accuse her of unfaithfulness for so doing . . .'[15]

A similar practice is reported of the Bahima, Bakunta, and Akamba tribes of East and Central Africa.

Amongst the Masai in East Africa a different pattern was observed: here age-grades took the place of clans. Pre-marital sexual licence was permitted to the young warriors who lived with their sweethearts in 'barracks'. 'At marriage all individuals in an age-grade can demand intercourse with the bride. The groom faces dishonour if he refuses. Throughout the marriage full sexual hospitality can be claimed, and not refused by members of an age-grade . . .'[16]

Something very like the Masai form of interchange of wives is found amongst the Nandi, Chagga and Wataweta of East Africa.

The exchange of wives within the age-grade is characteristic of the Southern Massim of New Guinea. Membership of a Massim age-grade means that you are in a special relationship, *eriam*. 'Each male of the fellowship has marital rights over the wives of his fellow eriam, of which he does not hesitate to avail himself.' [17] Unlike the Arunta or Murngin the husband does not have to give his permission. His friend merely 'informs' him that he has made an assignation with his wife in the bush.

The New Guinea eriam had its more superior counterpart in the Polynesian *areoi* found in Tahiti and Tonga. According to eighteenth century reports membership of an areoi gave the same rights of access to the wives of fellow members.[18] Later reports also speak of feasts which were the occasion for general promiscuous behaviour.[19] It is difficult to assess the veracity of such reports. On the other hand the evidence of W. H. Rivers in connection with Hawaii is much more convincing: '. . . There existed amongst the Hawaiians a definite system of cicisbeism in which the paramours had a recognised status. Of these paramours those who would seem to have had the most definite status were certain relatives, viz., the brothers of the husband and the sisters of the wife. These formed a group within which all the males had marital rights over the females . . . In addition to these *punalua* who had a recognised status owing to their relationship with the married couple, there were often other paramours apparently chosen freely at the will of the husband or wife . . .' [20]

The system of Hawaiian extra-marital arrangements appears to have been both obligatory and permissive. Something very similar to the Hawaiian *punalua* was reported in Tahiti and New Zealand against a marital background of polyandry.

The function of wife-exchange in terms of the clan brotherhood or age-grade can be seen as demonstrating the solidarity of the group to the outside world. There is community of thought, feeling and possession in a great or lesser degree. The lending of one's wife exemplifies this.

Siberian people exhibit another aspect of sexual hospitality. The emphasis among them is less upon mutual than upon individual arrangements. That is to say, groups of individuals do not have mutual rights in each other's wives, but a man may exchange with another, or present his wife to a stranger as he sees fit. This is so for the Chuckchee, Yukaghir, Tungus and one division of the Koryak people. These last are a strange tribe. They are divided into two branches—the Reindeer or Nomadic Koryak and the Sedentary or Maritime. The former are excessively puritanical. Adultery may lead to the murder of the guilty pair by the husband. The women are forced to remove all traces of finery after marriage, go about with a bedraggled air, and dirty themselves deliberately; no doubt in order to destroy their fatal charm for other men. [21] The Maritime group is the complete antithesis. These people are reputedly excessively lascivious and take pride in their wives being embraced by others. [22]

The bestowal of one's wife or daughter on the honoured guest brings up considerations of a different order from those associated with wife-exchange within a group. The practical basis of intra-group activity of this kind is reciprocity. This clearly cannot apply when a stranger is concerned. There does not appear to be any satisfactory hypothesis offered by those authorities who have dealt with this aspect. One view was that the offer of a wife was the extension of a right to the stranger which already existed for everyone else. [23] As we have tried to show, wife-exchange rarely extended to a whole community—it is limited to a group. Westermarck regarded sexual hospitality among what he called 'the lower races' as a symptom of the much wider concept of hospitality in general. He admitted that the attitude towards strangers could take opposing forms—hostility or kindness. But this does not negate his main argument.

The attitude towards the stranger, in our view, is compounded of both hostility and possible benefit. Complete rejection in one sense destroys the stranger's power to harm. The stranger amongst the Pomo Indians of California might be given anything he asked for, but next day he might be killed. [24] The stranger is someone about whom nothing is known. The unknown is almost always equated with the supernatural, and this suggests the possibility of evil. It is very noticeable that amongst peoples at all levels there exist injunctions regarding the treatment of strangers. [25] Lewis Morgan, the pioneer American anthropologist, wrote this regarding the Iroquois Indians of North America: 'If a stranger wanders about your abode, welcome him to your home, be hospitable towards him, speak to him with kind words, and forget not always to mention the Great Spirit.' [26] This is re-echoed in the Laws of Manu: 'The hospitable reception of guests procures wealth, fame, long life and heavenly bliss.' [27] It is the same sentiment that finds expression in Greek, Hebrew and Christian thought.

It is not our purpose to examine the bases of hospitality in general, but merely to point out that sexual hospitality with reference to the stranger is part of a much wider complex of thought, tradition, and sentiment.

If it is accepted that the stranger represents potential danger means must be adopted to ward off or destroy the danger. One of many different methods is in the course of ordinary hospitality to extend the courtesy to one's bed. A most valued possession—a wife or daughter is given temporarily to the stranger. He may be a god, malignant or good; a sorcerer or a benign spirit; he may be harmless but such a gift can only produce good. A further extension might equate the offer of a wife or daughter with sacrifice.

We suggest that the context wherein the stranger is offered

sexual hospitality is of this order—fear, magic, awe, and the incomprehensible.

The Maritime Koryak of Siberia, mentioned above, carry the matter to extravagant lengths. Apparently they used to pester Tsarist officials, especially postmen, to sleep with their wives, and 'overwhelmed him on his return with presents because a son had been born from the transient alliance . . .' [28] Connected with the idea of the powers of the stranger is the possibility that he can endow such offspring with his godlike qualities. This feeling is summed up by Marco Polo when he writes of the inhabitants of Caindu in Eastern Tibet: 'No man considers himself wronged if a foreigner, or any other man, dishonour his wife, or daughter, or sister, or any woman of his family, but on the contrary he deems such intercourse a piece of good fortune. And they say that it brings the favour of their gods and idols, and great increase of temporal prosperity. For this reason they bestow their wives on foreigners and other people . . .' [29]

This attitude might help to explain the extraordinary willingness with which many savage peoples offered their womenfolk to the first Europeans they encountered. There are accounts from all over the world: these are generally couched in terms deploring the sexual depravity and lasciviousness of the 'natives'. [30] On the other hand a number of societies at first contact with the European immediately hid their women as they thought the strangers would steal them. For example, the Veddas of Ceylon, a tribe noted for their puritanism in sexual matters and rejection of divorce, refused to allow their women to be seen in case they were abducted. [31]

Sexual hospitality was also practised by more advanced peoples: '. . . In old Arabia the husband was so indifferent to his wife's fidelity that he might send her to cohabit with another man to get himself a goodly seed; or might send her to a guest, as the Asir did up to the time of the Wahhabites (W. L. Burckhardt, Travels in Arabia ii, 378) (London 1829), and as the people of Dhahatān must have once done according to Ibn Al-Magawir's account (ca. A. H. 639); or going on a journey might find a friend to supply his place, as the Yām did in the time of Burckhardt (op cit 11, 386); or might enter into a partnership of conjugal rights with another man, in return for his service as a shepherd . . .' [32]

The ancient Arabian custom appears essentially practical.

Robertson Smith, from whom that quotation is taken, interpreted this practice as deriving from a still more ancient state of poly-andry . . . [33] This would agree with the sexual hospitality found amongst such peoples as the Toda and Marquesas Islanders. Burckhardt, the Arabian explorer, found the custom still existed in the early nineteenth century in the Yemen: 'Custom requires that the stranger should pass the night with his host's wife, what-ever may be her age or condition. Should he render himself agree-able to the lady, he is honourably and hospitably treated; if not, the lower part of his 'abba' or cloak is cut off and he is driven away in disgrace . . .' [34] The obligation might prove quite a burden to the stranger in the Yemen.

In ancient India the precept of Manu that the guest must be honoured in all things finds poetic expression in the Mahābhārata. The story of Sudarçana and Oghavati tells of their marriage. Sudarçana vows that he will overcome death. He tells his wife; "Unto a guest thou must nowise do anything that might displease him. Whatever it be whereby a guest would be gladdened, be it even the giving of thyself—thou must never harbour hesitation or scruple . . ." Oghavati answers: "For me there is nought that I would not do without question at thy bidding." While Sudarçana is out of the house fetching firewood Death follows him seeking an opportunity. Meanwhile a Brahman arrives at the house. "I would have thee, O thou of the lovely face, show me hospitality today, if indeed the law laid down for the estate of father of the house is unto thee a guiding rule." Oghavati invites him in and asks: "What is thy business? What shall I give thee?" "It is with thee I have business, O lovely one. Do thou carry it out without hesitation or thought. If unto thee the law laid down for the estate of the father of the house is a rule of conduct, then show me an act of love, O princess, by giving thyself to me." Oghavati tries to get out of the situation by offering anything except herself. But the Brahman is insistent and ravishes her. Sudarçana comes back and calls out for his wife. But Oghavati is too ashamed to answer—"I am only what another man has left over." The Brahman answers the husband. "This wife of thine, O bent one, offered me every kind of offer for guests, but I wished for her myself. In this wise did the lovely-faced one come to me. Whatever else is fitting her, do thou do it." Death overhearing says to himself: "If he is untrue now to his pledge, I shall slay him." Sudarçana smiles and replies: "Luck to thee in the pleasures of love, O first among Brahmans. For to me this now is the greatest joy. The first law of the father of the house is, indeed to honour the guest that is come. The wise say there is no higher law and merit than this . . . I, indeed, have taken this vow: "My life and my wife, and whatever else I have I must give my guests." ' He calls the gods to witness his vow. As he does so the Brahman reveals that he is a god. He praises the virtue of the couple and tells the husband that his virtue has conquered Death. [35]

The tale emphasises the point that while fidelity is to be expected in wives, the laws of hospitality are superior to this—to the guest all must be given. This was a necessary injunction in ancient India where people were not at all given to hospitality of any kind. [36]

There are other references in the Mahabharata of the same kind. Sanatsujāta speaks of the six marks of true friendship one of which is the giving to a friend of son and wife. Krishna is willing to give his wife and son to his friend Arjuna. Karna is willing to give his wives and children to the man who can show where Arjuna is to be found in a battle. [37] Clearly the extension of this favour to a friend is not a matter of obligation, but merely to show the depths of your feeling for him by giving him what is dearest to you.

Hospitality itself protects the individual against the evil which the stranger may bring, and at the same time it reinforces the bonds that bind the community together. For it demonstrates the necessity of establishing proper relationships between people. Rules of hospitality developed in a historical past when the traveller was entirely dependent upon those he met for sustenance—there were no neutral sources to which he could turn. This, of course, did not only influence the behaviour of the host for good. The guest frequently found himself at the mercy of his host. One example may help to make this clear. The traveller in eighteenth century Jamaica had no inns or hotels on which to rely. He either was *persona grata* with the planters and could thus stay in their 'great houses', or he could not travel. Thus adverse critics of slavery found it difficult, if not impossible, to get about the island.

In Europe, sexual hospitality for the stranger occurred in a number of societies. The pagan tribes appear to have had a marital system which was compounded of monogamy, polyandry, and polygyny in much the same way as the Lepchas of Sikkim and the Tibetan peoples. Caesar in *De Bello Gallico* (VI 19, 3) wrote of the Ancient Britons: 'In their domestic life they practise a form of community of wives, ten or twelve men combining in groups, especially brothers with brothers, and fathers with sons . . .' This seems to be the classical pattern of fraternal polyandry which we have spoken of elsewhere.

Ancient Ireland provides a number of examples of chiefs and kings who had more than one wife. [38] The stereotype of the hero in folk stories appears to be happily married to two women simultaneously: 'Genuine popular tradition implies a society in which a multiplicity of such rewards (a damsel as a wife) causes no difficulty . . .' [39] Polyandry also occurred: a Queen of Connaught married three brothers. [40] It is in this context that we find the practice of sexual hospitality.

It is possible that the Celtic background was similar to that which promotes clan brotherhood and age-sets amongst so-called savage peoples. The typical situation is the arrival of a hero and his friends at the court of a king.

In the case of Cuchulain, at the court of the King of Ulster, the Celtic legend of The Feast of Bricriu gives this account: 'There-upon Mève went out by the high door of the palace into the court, thrice fifty warders in her train, with three vats of cold water for the three valiant heroes in front of the hosts, in order to alleviate their thirst (*lit*. heat). Choice was straightway given to them whether a house a-piece should be allotted them or one house among the three. "To each a house apart." quoth Cuchulain. Thereafter such as they preferred of the one hundred and fifty girls are brought into the house, fitted up with beds of surpassing magnificence. Findabair (the Queen's daughter) in preference to any other was brought by Cuchulain into the house where he himself was . . . They slept there that night. The women were apportioned among them. Findabair, with a train of fifty damsels, was brought into the stead of Cuchulain. Sav the Eloquent (Sadb Sulbair), another daughter of Achill and of Mève, with fifty maids in attendance, was ushered into the presence of Conall Cernach. Conchend, daughter of Ceit mac Māgach, with fifty damsels along with her, was brought into the presence of Loirgaie the

Triumphant. Moreover, Mève (the Queen) herself was wont to resort to the stead of Cuchulain . . .' (41)

There are numerous examples of similar gestures of hospitality. King Aed Mac Ainmerch's son on his travels through Ireland is given the bed of a different chieftain each night. (42) The envoys of the King of Connaught negotiating for a sacred bull with Dare Mac Fiachna tell him as an inducement that the King's wife will sleep with him. (43) You did not have to be of royal blood to have the privilege extended you of a woman of the household for the night. Pilgrims might be enjoined by their host each to take a woman for the night. (44)

By the Dark Ages a somewhat different concept seems to have emerged. The woman is now given as a reward for the services of the hero or knight—services either to herself, or to her parents, or husband. The gift is temporary—there appears to be little thought of marriage on either side. The reward is the temporary possession of the woman's body. The early French poem *Li chevalier as deus espées* recounts how the lord of Chateau du Port tells the knight Gawain that he may have his daughter if he defeats his enemy. Gawain does so and claims his reward. After supper the girl is brought to him stark naked. Gawain enjoys himself and leaves her next day. (45) 'Having accomplished an exploit and won the lady attached to it as a prize, the knight promptly rides off and leaves her . . .' (46) The rewards could be made *en masse* as when in the 'Chanson de Doon Nanteuil' the knights are promised that 'they will be free to take their choice of the most beautiful ladies in the court . . .' (47)

The early mediaeval period in Europe is characterised by very similar customs. The ordinary reward for valiant knightly service begins to disappear, but the visitor is still entertained by a woman provided by his host. The hostess, if a widow or unmarried, might find herself obliged to offer herself to her guest. (48) On the other hand she might provide a substitute—a relative or a serving woman. (49)

By the late Middle Ages sexual hospitality has almost entirely disappeared. It is possible that it lingered on in remote parts of the Continent, but there is no authentic record of its existence. It was reported, however, from rural Ireland during the seventeenth century. The guest of an Ulster chief 'was at the door with sixteen women all naked except their loose mantles; whereof eight or ten were very faire and two seemed very nymphs. (50)

The dying out of the custom can be attributed to a number of factors. The changing pattern of feudal society led to the disappearance of the knight-errant. It also led to the development of moral ideas associated not with the nobility but with the rising bourgeoisie. The power and influence of the Church, as well as the rise of the public inn and the protective power of the State, all

Fig. 23. A mediaeval love-feast

played their part in eliminating the function of sexual hospitality in Europe.

It is possible that those peasant customs associated with night-courting and trial marriage, which were discussed in the Chapter on Courtship, may in part be derived from traditions of sexual hospitality. There is, however, so far as we are aware, no direct link which can be traced between the two. On the other hand wife-lending or wife-exchange has persisted amongst friends and asso-

Fig. 24. A seventeenth century engraving of a Bacchanalian festival

ciates in Western societies up to the present day. There are reports from time to time in the national press of couples who have made an arrangement whereby they exchange wives temporarily. Such arrangements are essentially unpatterned in the sense they are not institutionalised in the way sexual hospitality has been in the past. Reasons for such understandings between married couples are simple. A search for variety or some economic motivation.

As we saw in the case of the Australian Aborigines, the marital tie may be broken in a socially accepted way for reasons outside the control of the individual. There can either be public or com-

munal participation, or secret, individual acts of coitus. A division
can be made in the practices which fall into these two categories.
In one section would be intercourse with gods, priests and devils,
as well as religious prostitution; in the other, religious-sexual
festivals. The function of such extra-marital intercourse varies a
great deal.

We have shown how ritual defloration by a priest or other
person, is an important part of marriage ceremonies in a number
of societies. Amongst some peoples ritual intercourse may be
extended to the post-marital stage. The function is somewhat
different. Defloration by someone other than the bridegroom (a
priest or friend) removes the danger from the initial coital act;
it is in the nature of a spiritual act. When a married woman has
'divine' intercourse with a god, priest or stranger, it may be in
order to become fertile. Examples of this are found in India. In
eighteenth century India the Abbé Dubois tells us: '... There are
few temples where the presiding deity does not claim the power
of curing barrenness in women. And there are some whose renown
in this respect is unrivalled, such, for example, as that of Tirupati in
the Carnatic, to which women flock in crowds to obtain children
from the god Venkateswara (Vishnu) ...' They are advised by the
priests to pass the night in the temple, and 'the great Venkateswara,
touched by their devotion, will perhaps visit them in the spirit and
accomplish that which until then has been denied to them through
human power. I must draw a curtain over the sequel of this deceit-
ful suggestion. The reader already guesses at it. The following
morning these detestable hypocrites, pretending complete ignorance of what has passed, make due enquiries into all the details; and
after having congratulated the women upon the reception they
met with from the gods, receive the gifts ... Fully convinced that
the god has deigned to have intercourse with them, the poor
creatures return home enchanted, flattering themselves that they
will soon procure for their husbands the honour of paternity ... (51)

Even if the impersonation were known to the women it is very
probable that they would refuse to admit it to themselves. Such
attitudes are common wherever, for a variety of purposes, men
impersonate supernatural beings. It hardly affects the efficacy of
belief. Individuals who impersonate gods believe that the divine
has entered into them—they are in fact vehicles of the gods. Both

priests and congregation at the Katcina ceremonies of the Zuni Indians are aware of the human beings behind the terrifying masks and costumes, but this does not disturb their faith in the proceedings.

It should perhaps be remembered that Dubois was a Catholic priest and so would be somewhat opposed to such sexual irregularities!

Another aspect is brought out by Dubois which emphasises that fertility could be obtained if copulation with strangers took place within the sacred precincts of the temple: 'There are temples in certain isolated places, too, where most disgusting debauchery is the only service agreeable to the presiding deity. There children are promised to women, who, laying aside all shame, grant their favours to all persons indiscriminately. At such places a feast is celebrated every year in the month of January, at which both sexes, the scum of the country-side meet. Barren women, in the hope they will cease to be so, visit them after binding themselves by a vow to grant their favours to a fixed number of libertines. Others, who have entirely lost all sense of decency, go there in order to testify their reverence for the deity of the place by prostituting themselves, openly without shame, even at the very gates of the temple . . .' [52]

In contrast to this, as it were, public invocation of fertility from the god the Tallensi of Northern Ghana have a much more utilitarian but essentially formal approach to the problem: 'A man who is sterile or impotent may allow his wife to conceive by another man. The proper way to do this is for him to inform the elders of his lineage first. With their blessing and consent he may give his wife permission to find a lover wherever she wishes . . . let her walk about to get a belly; if she meets a Mossi man or a Hausa man (i.e., any passer-by) let her copulate—is the traditional formula with which he sets her free to be promiscuous, if she chooses, in order to become pregnant. Sensible men and women prefer a more reputable procedure, however. Either the husband asks a friend or kinsman not of his own clan, to deputise for him sexually, or he lets the wife choose one of her own distant clan-brothers as a lover. This man is then formally deputed . . . to be the woman's lover by being presented to the lineage elders, who sacrifice a fowl on his behalf to the lineage ancestors, with an explanation of the circumstances and pleas for a blessing on the affair. The arrangement, though formal, is strictly private, for no man willingly admits to sterility or sexual incapacity, and when, as inevitably happens, it leaks out, public opinion is sympathetic rather than contemptuous . . .' [53]

Here there is no hoped for godlike intervention but merely a practical solution to a possibly infrequent problem. It is, of course, an example of licensed extra-marital intercourse. Again it illustrates the strength of that which is *socially approved*. The Tallensi attitude towards adultery is that it is a grave sin, an affront to the husband's ancestors, and may bring sickness and death to the husband and children of the marriage. 'The woman has committed something not far short of sacrilege, for she has flouted the rights of her husband's lineage over her reproductive powers.' [54] What is even more interesting is that the wife continues her 'affair' with her official lover throughout her pregnancy and the liaison only comes to and end with the birth of the child. The husband treats the child as he would his own, that is he is tender and affectionate towards it. The lover treats it as any other child not his own: 'No kinship tie is recognised between the physiological father and the child he was deputed to beget.' [55]

Perhaps our current polemicists concerned with the moral implications of A.I.D. might have something to learn from a study of Tallensi behaviour when presented with the problem of the childless couple. It is not entirely facetious to imagine a situation where a committee chosen from amongst the most eminent in the land, presided over by the Archbishop of Canterbury, would with due ceremony formally grant permission to such a couple to seek a suitable 'lover'. This being done the 'lover' would then be presented to the committee, be approved, and finally blessings would be invoked and nature would take its course.

The belief that divine interest or intervention will facilitate fertility in women is not entirely absent from Christianity. Many saints have curiously acquired the reputation for the promotion of fertility. Curiously because sainthood is almost always synonymous with continence or celibacy. Phallic emblems were frequently placed in churches in the Middle Ages with this object in view. A similar practice persisted up to the eighteenth century in Southern Italy. At Isernia near Naples on the 17th September, the feast of

St. Cosmo and Damian (the patron saints of doctors, chemists, and barbers) a relic of the big toe of St. Cosmo was exhibited. Votive offerings in the form of wax penises were bought by women who made offerings to the church. The pilgrims remained overnight in the village. It is said that many pregnancies resulted from the efforts of the Saints on the women's behalf. [56]

The holy man could bring general blessings as well as fertility to a married woman. In other words the children of such temporary unions would be endowed with the spiritual qualities of the father. The union itself might produce spiritual benefits for husband and wife. For example, although there are no instructions in the Koran to this effect, some Muslim communities in Morocco formerly welcomed the public copulation of a saint with a woman; '. . . her companions, who surrounded her, uttered exclamations of joy, felicitated her on her good fortune, and the husband himself received complimentary visits on this occasion . . .' [57]

A similar attitude is found in classical India where the Mahābhārata has many accounts of the felicitation with which the sexual attentions of Brahmins towards women and wives are viewed. Sexual intercourse of this kind, as was seen in the story of the Brahmin quoted above, does great honour to the family concerned. This priestly power is demonstrated in a totally dissimilar people, the Eskimo of Greenland. The Angakut (prophet-priest) of the Eskimo is entreated by husbands to copulate with their wives, Some even paid the Angakut to do so. The belief was that the children of this priestly union would be bound to be most virtuous. [58]

The association between 'divine' defloration and later intercourse is made clear by the Roman custom, to which we have referred, of seating the virgin bride on a gigantic phallus of the god Mutunus or Tutunus. [59] This again was to ensure fertility. The belief that conception will never take place unless the woman, apart from ritual defloration, has had intercourse with the god or his intermediary may underlie some aspects of another phase of socially approved extra-marital matings.

The sacred character of intercourse with gods through their representatives extends, as we have suggested, to the stranger. This is apparently the assumption on which many of the manifestations of temporary religious prostitution are based.

'The Babylonians have one most shameful custom. Every woman born in the country must once in her life go and sit down in the precinct of Venus, and there consort with a stranger. Many of the wealthier sort, who are too proud to mix with the others, drive in covered carriages to the precinct, followed by a goodly train of attendants, and there take their station. But the larger number seat themselves within the holy enclosure with wreaths of string about their heads—and here there is always a great crowd, some coming, and others going; lines of cord mark out paths in all directions among the women, and the strangers pass along them to make their choice. A woman who has once taken her seat is not allowed to return home until one of the strangers throws a silver coin into her lap, and takes her with him beyond the holy ground. When he throws the coin he says these words—"The goddess Mylitta prosper thee". (Venus is called Mylitta by the Assyrians). The silver coin may be of any size; it cannot be refused, for that is forbidden by the law, since once thrown it is sacred. The woman goes with the first man who throws her money, and rejects no one. When she has gone with him, and so satisfied the goddess she returns home, and from that time forth no gift however great will prevail with her. Such of the women as are tall and beautiful are soon released, but others who are ugly have to stay a long time before they can fulfil the law. Some have waited three or four years in the precinct. A custom very much like this is found also in certain parts of the island of Cyprus . . .' [60]

Herodotus emphasises the essentially temporary nature of the prostitution even though the woman according to her charms might have to wait a considerable time until the obligation was discharged. This is also mentioned in the Old Testament where the gods of the Babylonians are castigated: 'The women also with cords about them, sit in the ways, burning olive stones. And when any of them, drawn away by some passenger, lieth with him, she upbraideth her neighbour, that she was not thought worthy as herself, nor her cord broken.' (Baruch, VI, 42–43).

The custom in Cyprus has been described by Justin: '. . . it was a custom among the Cypreans to send their daughters on stated days before their marriage, to the seashore, to prostitute themselves, and thus procure money for their marriage portions, and to pay at the same time, offerings to Venus for the preservation of their chastity in time to come . . .' [61]

The Cypriot practice brings in the element of material gain for a specific purpose, but it does not overshadow the religious element —the appeal to Venus to safeguard their future chastity. The women are virgins in this case. But it appears that in all the cases which are recorded (Syria, Cyprus, Babylon, Lydia, Egypt, Armenia, etc.) of this type of prostitution, both virgins and married women were involved. Thus at Baalbek or Heliopolis, which Constantine destroyed, 'those who dignify licentious pleasure with a distinguishing title of honour, had permitted their wives and daughters to commit shameless fornication . . .' [62]

The religious significance is again shown in the custom of Byblos in Syria where the annual ritual of the death of Adonis demanded that women should shave their heads. Failure to do so meant they had, on a particular day, to prostitute themselves to strangers. The money earned in this way was given to the temple of the Mother Goddess. [63] The sacrifice of hair was equivalent to the surrender of chastity as it symbolised the woman's fecundity. [64] Briffault compares this to the practice of nuns shaving their heads on taking their final vows—they are dedicated to Christ. [65]

The ancient Jews had a very similar custom to those deplored in the book of Baruch: 'For the spirit of whoredoms hath caused them to err, And they have gone a-whoring from under their God. They sacrifice upon the tops of mountains, And burn incense upon the hills, Under oaks and poplars and elms, Because the shadow thereof is good: Therefore your daughters shall commit whoredom, And your spouses shall commit adultery' (Hosea, IV, 12–13). The Israelites had succumbed to the idolatrous temptations of their neighbours.

The incidence of this type of sacred prostitution appears to have been very largely confined to the Mediterranean area. The advent of Christianity and the rise of Islam destroyed the greater part of the worship of those deities that demanded this type of behaviour. But there was an interesting exception which apparently persisted until the nineteenth century. The city of Tanta, about half way between Cairo and Alexandria celebrated the Feast of Ahmed al-Bedawi in a way very similar to the customs described above. Tremendous crowds of people from all over Egypt were attracted. Several hundred women in specially erected tents acted as sacred prostitutes. Respectably married women, and young girls, had vowed to the saint to attend the festival and to offer themselves to the first comer. [66] This pleasant blending of Islam and the ancient Mediterranean practice demonstrates that the function of religious prostitution of this type is not necessarily associated with fertility and vegetation cults.

A rather different type of religious prostitution was found in the same area and elsewhere as those we have been discussing. In this type, women were dedicated to the service of the god or goddess. They served the deity by offering their bodies for gain to anyone. The classical examples are India—the Devadasi, and Carthage and Corinth. [67] It has also been reported from West Africa among the Ewe.

In our tentative and elementary exposition of one type of religious prostitution it has not been our purpose to discuss the various hypotheses which have been put forward to account for religious prostitution as a whole. Our aim was to try and show that the type described has a specific function, namely to promote fertility, and to sanctify the woman and her husband. [68] This is the view advocated by A. Van Gennep in his Les Rites de Passage (Paris, 1911, p. 242 et seq.).

Communal or individual sexual rites and orgiastic festivals are another form of permitted extra-marital matings. In many instances such rites are connected with cults of fertility in the widest sense—that is with the growth of crops and general prosperity. Their incidence is far greater than that of religious prostitution, being found in societies from the simplest to the most advanced level. The principle at work is that human copulation, by the process of 'imitative magic, encourages the growth of the crop'. The Pipele Indians of Central America abstained from coitus for four days before the ritual planting of seed. On the night of this event specially appointed couples copulated at the precise moment that the seed was planted. Although not necessarily an example of sexual licence, the behaviour of the Pipele illustrates in a dramatic way the supposed connection between human coitus and the fertility of the ground. [69]

Agricultural festivals of this kind are common in Central and South America as well as amongst the Plains Indians of North America. The choice of time is either spring or the harvest. It has been reported amongst the Indian peoples of Chile [70] Nicaragua and Peru. These last held a feast each year when the alligator pears ripened. A long period beforehand was spent in fasting and abstinence. On the day of the festival everyone congregated together stark naked. A race was organised and every man that caught a woman copulated with her. [71] In Brazil the Bororo and Choroti Indians permit indiscriminate public intercourse after major ritual dances. [72] The old people amongst the Arapaho Indians of North America encouraged the young men to copulate as much as possible at such feasts. [73]

The same pattern of licence in association with an agricultural event is observable in many Polynesian and Melanesian societies. For example in Mailu near New Guinea: 'The dancing which takes place with increased intensity during the few days of the feast, seems to be associated with opportunities for short-lived intrigues, and occasionally there even seem to be features of licentiousness, groups absconding together . . .' [74]

African societies exhibit a similar tendency. The yam festivals in Ghana amongst the Ashanti were, in the early nineteenth century, marked by an extravagance of speech and behaviour. Bowdich, a famous explorer, wrote: 'The Yam custom is like a Saturnalia; the grossest liberty prevails, and each sex abandons itself to its passions . . .' [75] But it is in India that such festivals became a marked feature of the ritual life of the diverse peoples of that sub-continent. A typical example is that of the Holi Festival in Northern India: 'The Holi . . . takes place on the full moon of the month Phalgun (February-March), when it becomes a spring fertility rite. The fire is lighted on the night of the full moon . . . Some articles, miscalled "offerings", are thrown into the fire, and the villagers walk round it in the direction of the sun . . . On the second day the people throw dust, dirt or red-coloured water at each other. Foul abuse and indecencies of act and word are used . . . The general intention of this complex of observance is probably to mark the coming of spring and to promote the fertility of men, animals and crops . . .' [76]

A French traveller in the middle years of the nineteenth century described the same festival in this way: '. . . the most licentious debauchery and disorder reign throughout every class of society. It is a regular Saturnalia. Indian persons of the greatest respectability, without regard to rank or age, are not ashamed to take part in the orgies which mark this season of the year . . .' [77] An interesting feature of Holi was the procession of decorated carts on which were represented scenes from the amorous life of the gods. Some of the images were mechanically operated so that clumsy but effective imitations of coitus were possible. Dubois relates a similar occurrence: 'At Mogur . . . there is a small temple dedicated to Tipamma, a female divinity, in whose honour a great festival is celebrated every year. The goddess, placed in a beautifully ornamented palanquin, is carried in procession through the streets. In front of her there is another divinity, a male. These two idols which are entirely nude, are placed in immodest postures, and by help of a piece of mechanism a disgusting movement is imparted to them as long as the procession continues. This disgusting spectacle, which is worthy of the depraved persons who look upon it, excites transports of mirth, manifested by shouts and bursts of laughter . . .' [78]

Spring and harvest festivals of the same type as the Holi have existed all over India.

Consideration of the agricultural festivals of the Mediterranean world presents a more complex picture. There is a large group of such festivals which were originally primarily agricultural, such as the Eleusinian mysteries. There are others which can be described as Dionysiac; the chief characteristic here is their female homosexual character—the rites being barred to men. Lastly there is the type of Saturnalia characterised by the inversion of roles, and originally the death of the lord or king of the rites. One aspect is common to all—the orgiastic element in which copulation or tribadism (psuedo-copulation between women) takes place, and marital ties are set aside. We are not concerned to examine the wider implications of such rites but merely to assess their significance in the context of the temporary setting aside of marital ties. [79] It is clear from the descriptions which have come down to us that the sexual element in the rites was pronounced.

The mystic rites of the worship of Dionysius in the Hellenic and pre-Hellenic world can serve as the typical example of religious festivals which permitted and encouraged sexual licence. The association with the powers of nature and vegetation symbolised by the union of the sexes or of tribadistic union are very evident.

'The Maenad frenzy was probably more than a mere frantic ebullition of pent-up religious emotion; we may conjecture at least that in Thrace as in Greece it subserved the ends of a certain nature-magic and was intended to invoke fructifying powers of the earth . . .' [80] Nilsson distinguishes two elements in the Dionysiac ritual: '. . . the cult of Dionysius is composed of two elements: one is the trieteric orgia, in which the god is dismembered and eaten in the shape of an animal, and the other is the conception of the newborn child in the winnowing fan and of the death of the god. Here he is clearly the spirit of vegetation, and as such must be born and die annually . . .' [81]

Whipping often formed part of the ritual: '. . . Therefore Lykourgos pursued and struck the Maenads with ox-thongs, the women at Alea in Arcadia were scourged in the festival of Dionysius; and there is reason to believe that the modern Bacchanalian mummers at Bizye were at one time accustomed to be whipped in the course of the miracle play . . .' [82] For the animal symbolising Dionysius a human victim might be substituted. [83] There is the story told by Plutarch (*Narr. Amat*, 2) of the beautiful boy Aktaion who is torn from his home by Maenads and killed. The phallus figures prominently. Plutarch mentions this: 'The festival of the Dionysius was in old times celebrated in a popular and cheerful manner; a wine-jar was carried round and a vine-branch; then someone brought a goat, another a basket full of figs; and over all the phallus . . .' (*De Cupiditate divitiarum*, 527 d).

The sexual element comes entirely to the forefront when we consider the festivals of the Cyprian Aphrodite. Again there is the original connection with fertility and vegetation. The, admittedly, biased accounts given by Clement of Alexander (*Protrepticon*, p. 13) and Arnobius (*Adversus Gentes*, 5, 19) demonstrate that the goddess was worshipped in an appropriately sexual way in which no regard was paid to marital vows of chastity. The annual festival at Palaipaphos outside Paphos was renowned for its erotic rites. Associated with this festival was a custom similar to that described by Herodotus in connection with the Babylonian Mylitta.

Curiously enough the orgiastic character is marked in the worship of Artemis: 'Dances are very common in her cult. The Laconian virgins danced in her honour at Caryae and in the festival of the Titheridia at Sparta; dances are mentioned as taking place

at the temple of Artemis Limnatis at the foot of Taygetos, and at
that in Ellis, and in the colonies of South Italy and Sicily. These
dances were of an orgiastic and at times indecent character; sometimes the dancers wore masks; they seem ill-suited to the virgin
goddess . . . ' (84)

The same sensual element emphasising the orgiastic is found in a
number of Roman rites associated with a variety of deities. Many
were in fact of Greek origin such as the Bacchic rites and worship

Fig. 25. *The Triumph of Priapus*

of Cybele. The official Roman attitude was to deprecate the excesses they engendered, but despite this they appeared to be extremely popular. Dionysius of Halicarnassus in his 'Roman Antiquities' shows something of this depreciation in describing the
virtues of Romulus, one of the traditional founders of Rome:
'He (Romulus) established temples, sacred precincts and altars . . .
in all of which he followed the best customs in use amongst the
Greeks. But he rejected all the traditional myths concerning the
gods that contain blasphemies . . . looking upon these as wicked,
useless, and indecent . . . And one will find among them (the
Romans) even though their manners are now corrupted, no
ecstatic transports, no Corybantic frenzies, no begging under the
colour of religion, no bacchanals or secret mysteries, no all night
vigils of men and women together in the temples, nor any other
mummery of this kind . . . And, the thing which I myself have
marvelled at most,—notwithstanding the influx into Rome of

innumerable nations which are under every necessity of worshipping their ancestral gods . . . yet the city has never adopted any of
these foreign practices . . . but, even tho' she has, in pursuance of
oracles, introduced certain rites from abroad, she celebrates them
in accordance with her own traditions, after banishing all fabulous
clap-trap. The rites of the Idaean goddess (Cybele) are a case in
point; for the praetors perform sacrifices and celebrate games in
her honour every year according to the Roman custom, but the

A sixteenth century engraving by Galviati

priest and priestess of the goddess are Phrygians, and it is they who
carry her image in procession . . . But by a law and decree of the
Senate no native Roman walks in procession . . . or worships the
goddess with the excesses of the Phrygians . . .' (Bk. II, XVIII and
XIX.) Dionysius sounds like an official government spokesman
deploring the inevitable. In fact we know from other sources that
the very excesses he deplores were enjoyed by many Romans.
Livy, for example, describes the secret society, to which apparently
a great part of the population belonged, which developed around
the Bacchanalia: '. . . As to the Bacchanalia, I am assured that you
have learned that they have long been celebrated all over Italy and
even now within the City in many places, and that you learned
this not only from rumour, but also from their din and cries at
night . . . but I feel sure you do not know what this thing is: some
believe that it is a form of worship of the gods, others that it is an
allowable pastime and play . . . that it concerns only a few. As

regards their number, if I shall say that there are many thousands of them, it cannot be but that you are terrified ... a great part of them are women, and they are the source of this mischief; then there are men very like the women, debauched and debauchers, fanatical, with senses dulled by wakefulness, wine, noise, and shouts at night. The conspiracy thus far has no strength, but it has an immense source of strength in that they grow more numerous day by day ...' (*Ab urbe* XXXIX, 15). Livy goes on to relate how the 'conspiracy was smashed', people were arrested, and a senatorial decree was issued 'that there should be no Bacchanalia in Rome or Italy'. The proviso was added that they could take place if the custom was sworn to be of venerable antiquity and no more than one hundred people attended.

Livy, tells us about the actual character of the Bacchanalian rites: 'There were initiatory rites which at first were imparted to a few, then began to be gradually known among men and women. To the religious element in them were added the delights of wine and feasts, that the minds of a larger number might be attracted. When wine had inflamed their minds, and night and the mingling of males with females, youth with age, had destroyed every sentiment of modesty, all varieties of corruption first began to be practised, since each one had at hand the pleasure answering to that which his nature was more inclined. There was not one form of vice alone, the promiscuous matings of free men and women, but perjured witnesses ...' (*Ab urbe* XXXIX, VIII)

These Bacchic rites appear to have been originally introduced into Italy at the end of the Second Punic War. They did in fact lead to the most gross behaviour imaginable, and were regarded as a public danger. The senatorial decree Livy speaks of is still preserved on a bronze tablet (The *Senatus Consultum de Bacchanalibus*). [85]

Another cult, that of Isis, was introduced into Italy in Sulla's time. It appears that it was given only lukewarm official recognition. There are references in Juvenal, Ovid (*Ars Amatoria* I, 76) and Propertius (ii, 33, 1) to sexual ceremonies in which there were tribadistic practices. But it is the worship of the Bona Dea that has caused acute controversy as to whether the rites associated with it were such as would not disgrace an Anglican convent, or were of the most depraved order. Plutarch in his Lives of the Caesars (9), gives the impression that all was purity and chastity. The goddess demanded that men should be excluded from the celebrations: 'The Romans have a goddess whom they call the Good One, as the Greeks call her the Woman's Goddess. The Phrygians say she belongs to Phrygia and was the mother of their King, Midas. The Romans think she was a dryad who lived with Faunus. The Greeks again say that she was that one of the mothers of Bacchus who must not be named. Accordingly, when they celebrate her festival, the women erect tents roofed with vine twigs, and in accordance with the legend, a holy snake lies beside the goddess. It is unlawful for any man to come to the festival, or even to enter the house. The women remain quite alone and are said to perform many rites like those of the Orphic mysteries. When the time of the festival comes, the consul or praetor, in whose house it is held, leaves the house with all the other men in the household. His wife takes over the house and arranges the ceremonies. The greatest of them takes place at night, and are interspersed with gaiety and music . . .' (Plutarch, *Caesar*, 9).

A totally different picture is given by Juvenal in his Sixth Satire: 'Who knows not now my friend, the secret rites of the Good Goddess; when the dance excites the boiling blood; when to distraction wound, by wine, and musick's stimulating sound, The Meanads of Priapus, with wild air, Howl horrible, and toss their flowing hair! Then, how the wine at every pore o'erflows! How the eye sparkles! how the bosom glows! How the cheek burns; and as the passion rise, How the strong feelings burst in eager cries! Saufeia now springs forth and tries a fall with the town prostitutes, and throws them all; But yields, herself, to Medullina, known for parts, and powers, superior to her own. Maids, mistresses alike the contest share, And 'tis not always birth that triumphs there. Nothing is feigned in this accursed game: Tis genuine all, and such as would inflame The frozen age of Priam, and inspire, The ruptur'd, bedrid Nestor with desire. Stung with their mimick feats, a hollow groan of lust breaks forth; the sex, the sex, is shown! And one loud yell re-echoes through the den, "Now, now, 'tis lawful now admit the men." There's none arrived. "Not yet! then scour the street, And bring us quickly, here, the first you meet." "There's none abroad." "Then fetch our slaves." "They're gone." "Then hire a waterman." "There's none." "Not one!" [86]

The obvious reference to tribadistic practices as a prelude to more normal intercourse serve to emphasise the essentially feminine element in the worship of the Bona Dea. Even if Juvenal was guilty of great exaggeration, it is clear that there was a strong orgiastic element in the cult of the good goddess. The truth would seem to lie between the two extremes of Plutarch and Juvenal—they were contemporaries. Respectable people would conduct the rites with decorum. Others would use them as an opportunity for licence.

Phallic worship was extremely common in Rome itself and Italy generally. It was a matter of the everyday. Model phalli were used as charms and trinkets in the form of amulets, brooches, and even sweetmeats. There are numerous references to them in the literature. (Juvenal ii, 95; Petronius *Satyricon*, 60; Pliny, *Nat. Hist.* XXVIII, 4).

Festivals in honour of Priapus or Liber were very popular. Augustine, who of course was a hostile critic, described the behaviour which accompanied these feasts: 'Varro says among other things that the rites of Liber were celebrated at the crossroads in Italy so immodestly and licentiously that the male genitals were worshipped in honour of the god—and this not with any modest secrecy, but with open and exulting depravity. That shameful part of the body was, during the festival of Liber, placed with great pomp on waggons and carried about to the crossroads in the country, and at last into the city. In the town of Lanuvium a whole month was dedicated to Liber. During it, all the citizens used the most disgraceful words until the phallus had been carried across the market place and put to rest again. It was necessary that the most honourable of the matrons should publicly place a wreath on that disgraceful effigy. The god Liber had to be propitiated to ensure the future of the crops, and the evil eye had to be repelled from the fields by compelling a married woman to do in public that which not even a harlot might do under the eyes of married women in the theatre . . .' (*De civitate Dei*, VII, 21).

Augustine's account stresses two important elements of Priapic worship which appear in other socio-religious activities amongst the Romans. One is the emphasis on obscene jesting: this was apparently a normal accompaniment of harvest festivals.[87] It appears to have been associated with phallic worship in Egypt and

West Africa. [88] And the other is the half-concealed attempt to belittle social status in the obligation for a respectable matron to wreathe the phallus. This denigration of status is presented in a developed form, with complete reversal of roles, in the Saturnalia.

The Saturnalia was supposed to represent the state of affairs which existed in the legendary time of Saturn. Its most well-known feature was the reversal of roles. On the first day of the festival masters became servants, and servants masters, there was disorder,

Fig. 26. An eighteenth century conception of the worship of Liber

feasting and merry making. It became the prototype for a whole succession of festivals in mediaeval Europe. One of the most interesting characteristics of the Saturnalia was the election of a king or lord of the festival. The king could do no wrong for the period of his rule— he could taste all the pleasures with impunity. At the end of his rule (a month) he is put to death. [89] This clearly is closely connected with the whole complexus of vegetation rites and regicide which is dealt with by Frazer in *The Golden Bough*. There is little doubt that the Roman Saturnalia was accompanied by indiscriminate sexual intercourse between men and women, whether married or not.

The provenance of the Saturnalia type of festival extends from Europe into Western Asia. The mediaeval Feast of Fools had many of the elements of the Graeco-Roman prototype. It has been very fully described by E. K. Chambers.[90] It was generally held at Christmas time and, in France, was in many ways a religious festival. On December 26th the clergy of a cathedral met to elect a Pope of Fools, a Bishop of Innocents, and an Abbot of Ninnies: 'It was then the joyous reign of this Pope or this Bishop or this Abbot of Folly which constituted the Festival of Fools and dominated its whimsical phases, the grotesque and sometimes impious masquerades, the merry and often disgusting scenes, the furious orgies, the dances, the games, the profane songs, the impudent parodies of the catholic liturgy . . .'[91] In different parts of France, there was variety of detail. For example at Beauvais on January 14th, the Flight into Egypt, complete with ass, was mimed. The pseudo-virgin and her mount were brought into the chancel of St. Stephen's Church and a parody of the Mass was performed. Refreshments were served throughout the service to both congregation and ass. The proceedings ended with a great procession in the evening to a specially erected theatre opposite the church. The congregation was then edified with a number of obscene performances. It is probable that the behaviour on the stage was reflected in the audience.[92]

The Hebrew Feast of Purim can be regarded as another example of the Saturnalia. In the Book of Esther the Jews are enjoined: 'That they should receive the fourteenth and fifteenth of the month Adar (roughly March) for holy days, and always at the return of the year should celebrate them with solemn honour: Because on those days the Jews revenged themselves of their enemies, and their mourning and sorrow were turned into mirth and joy, and that there should be days of feasting and gladness, in which they should send one to another portions of meats, and should give gifts to the poor.' 'And since that time these days are called Purim, that is of lots: because Pur, that is the lot, was cast into the urn.' (Esther, IX 21–22; 26). The festival celebrates the victory of Esther and Mordecai over the wickedness of Haman. However it may have been celebrated in ancient times, by the seventeenth century in Europe, Jews are being exhorted to drink until they cannot tell the difference between 'Cursed be Haman' and 'Blessed be Mordecai.' In fact it became a regular Bacchanal. People ate and drank until they were stupefied, exchanged clothes in direct contravention of the prohibition in Deuteronomy (XXII, 5) fought, and misbehaved sexually. [93]

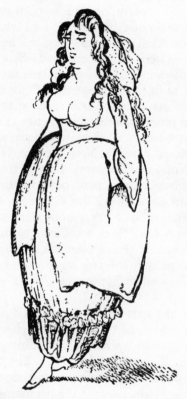

Fig. 27. An eighteenth century caricature of a London prostitute

The specifically sexual element appears in the mediaeval Russian festivals of St. John the Baptist held in June. The Chronicle of Nestor relates how at these feasts every man was allowed to carry off the woman of his choice. [94] Apparently in the nineteenth century remnants of these rites still persisted in parts of European Russia. [95] There are, however, few other instances of the persistence into modern times of communal festivals of this kind.

Rites, such as we have described, originating in the Mediterranean world were modified in the mediaeval period. Remnants
lingered on until the late eighteenth century. But the orgiastic
feast in the post-mediaeval age tends to become a matter of private
endeavour rather than one of communal participation.

The conflict in the contemporary European mind with regard
to sexual intercourse outside of marriage, and what are considered
sexual offences is reflected in differing national legislation on these
topics. In Britain adultery is not a criminal offence. In the United
States, however, the vast majority of States exact either a fine or
imprisonment, or both for such activity. Only in Nevada, New
Mexico, and Louisiana does the law agree with that of Britain.
Again, fornication is not an indictable offence in Britain; whereas
in the United States only the laws of Arizona, California, Dela-
ware, Iowa, Louisiana, Nevada, New Mexico, New York, Okla-
homa, South Dakota, and Vermont do not treat it as a crime.
There is almost general agreement between the two countries
regarding the crime of sodomy. But a resident in the District of
Columbia, New Hampshire, or Vermont is free to indulge in this
type of sexual behaviour. [96] It is difficult to discover why this
anomaly exists. Britain in recent years has seen a much more permissive and liberal attitude towards homosexuality. There is little
doubt that the Wolfenden Report has done a great deal in this
respect.

Wife-exchange, the various types of sexual hospitality, intercourse with gods, priests, or strangers, and religiously sanctioned
promiscuity are all means by which the ordinary marital ties can
be set aside in a socially approved manner. The temporary abandonment of such ties serves a variety of functions. In the case of
the Eskimo, which we discussed at the beginning of the chapter,
wife-exchange may be a matter of convenience or of religious
injunction. Hospitality demands certain duties. To give up, even
temporarily, a prized possession (one's wife) is to incur favour
from the gods as well as the community.

In a general sense such customs can be said to act at distinct
levels: at one level it appears as if the abandonment of the marital
tie has a cathartic effect—individuals are reinvigorated for normal
life. This is very forcibly demonstrated by the Saturnalia in its
different forms. The flouting and disregard for what is normally

held to be sacrosanct has a tonic effect on the human being en-meshed in social bonds of his own making. There is a release of tension which enables the duties and obligations incumbent upon man in society to be taken up again.

At another level, if we look at the quasi-sacred intercourse with priests and strangers, this seems to be sought after for practical reasons. Fertility in a marriage is essential if that marriage is to make its contribution to society as a family. That we recognise this in our own society is seen in the controversy over artificial in-semination. Children satisfy both a biological and a social need of man. Thus the 'divine' intercourse is used as a means of assuring that (a) the event will take place, or (b) that a 'divine' child will be born who will be a paragon. The Tallensi example showed the perfect blend of the religious and practical in the appointment of an 'official' lover.

The cathartic and the practical exist at two different levels, but the sanctioned breaking of the marital tie may affect both.

If this hypothesis is accepted then the form which is utilised to achieve the purpose is dependent upon factors which exist within a particular culture.

REFERENCES AND NOTES

1. B. Spencer and F. J. Gillen, *The Native Tribes of Central Australia*, London 1899, pp. 106-7.
2. *Ibid.* q. 107.
3. B. Spencer and F. J. Gillen, *op. cit.*, p. 97.
4. We have discussed the 'Pirrauru' relationship amongst the Dieri tribe in Ch. 7.
5. Lloyd Warner, *A Black Civilisation*, revised ed. N.Y. 1958, p. 306.
6. Lloyd Warner, *op. cit.*, p. 307.
7. Lloyd Warner, *op. cit.*, pp. 307-8.
8. Spencer and Gillen, *op. cit.*, p. 99.
9. R. Linton, *The Study of Man*, N.Y. 1937, p. 137.
   Also 'Marquesan Culture' in A. Kardiner's *The Individual and his Society*, N.Y. 1946, pp. 174-5.
10. W. H. R. Rivers, *The Todas*, London and N.Y. 1906, pp. 529-30.
11. F. Boas, 'The Central Eskimo' in *6th Annual Report of Bureau of Ethnology* (1884-5), Washington 1888, p. 579.

12. J. Murdoch, 'Ethnological Results of the Point Barrow Expedition', *9th Annual Report of the Bureau of Ethnology*, p. 413.
    W. E. Passey, *Journal of a Second Voyage for the Discovery of a N.W. Passage* . . . , London 1824, p. 529.

13. E. W. Nelson, 'The Eskimo about Bering Strait', *18th Report of the Bureau of Ethnology*, p. 412 *et seq.*

14. F. Boas, *op. cit.*, p. 605.

15. J. Roscoe, *The Bakitara or Banyoro* in 1st Pt. of Report of the Mackie Ethnological Expedition to Central Africa, Cambridge 1923, p. 239.

16. A. C. Hollis, *The Masai*, Oxford 1908, pp. 261 *et seq.*

17. C. S. Seligman, *The Melanesians of British New Guinea*, Cambridge 1910, p. 470 *et seq.*

18. J. R. Forster, *Observations . . . during a Voyage round the World*, London 1778, p. 412.

19. G. L. de Rienzi, *Océanie*, 3 Vols., Paris 1836–7, Vol. II, p. 320.

20. W. H. R. Rivers, *History of Melanesian Society*, Cambridge 1914, Vol. I, pp. 386 *et seq.*

21. S. P. Krasheninnikoff, *The History of Kamschatka*, London 1764, p. 223 *et seq.*

22. A. Erman, *Travels in Siberia*, London 1848, Vol. II, p. 530.

23. Lord Avebury, *Origin of Civilisation*, London 1912, p. 107.

24. S. Powers, *Tribes of California*, Washington 1877, p. 153.

25. The reader who wishes to pursue the topic of the significance of the stranger should consult *The Golden Bough* (J. G. Frazer), London 1900, Vol. I, pp. 298 *et seq.*

26. L. Morgan, *League of the Iroquois*, Rochester, N.Y. 1851, p. 172.

27. *Laws of Manu*, *Sacred Books of the East*, translated by G. Buhler, Oxford 1886, Vol. XXV, p. 106.

28. A. Erman, *op. cit.*, Vol. II, p. 630.

29. Marco Polo, *The Book of Ser Marco Polo, etc.*, translated and edited by Sir Henry Yule, 3rd ed. 2 Vols., London 1903, Vol. II, pp. 53 *et seq.*

30. See for example G. A. Farini, *Huit mois au Kalahari*, Paris 1887.
    Compare the attitude of the Easter Islanders to Captain Cook with their reaction to La Pérouse in G. Forster *Voyage round the World*, London 1777, Vol. I, p. 577, and J. F. Galoup *Voyage de la P. autour de monde*, Paris 1797, pp. 97 and 108 *et seq.*

31. M. Moszkowski, *Bei den letzen Weddas*, *Globus*, Brunswick 1908, XCIV, p. 135.

32. W. Robertson Smith, *Kinship and Marriage in Early Arabia*, New Edition London 1903, pp. 139–40.

33. W. H. Robertson Smith, *op. cit.*, footnote pp. 40–1.

34. J. L. Burckhardt, *Notes on the Bedouins and Wahábys*, London 1830, Vol. I, pp. 179 *et seq.*

35. The story of Oghavati and Surdarçana is taken from the *Mahā-bhārata*, xiii, 2, 34 ff.

36. J. J. Meyer, *Sexual Life in Ancient India*, London 1953, 2nd ed., p. 517.

37. J. L. Meyer, *op. cit.*, pp. 517–18.

38. H. d'Arbois de Jubainville, *La Civilisation des Celtes et celle de l'epopee homerique*, Paris 1899, pp. 292 *et seq.*

39. G. Schoepperle, *Tristan and Isolt*, London 1913, Vol. I, p. 257.

40. K. Meyer, *The Edinburgh Gaelic Manuscript*, The Celtic Magazine, Inverness 1877, XII, p. 211.

41. *The Feast of Bricriu*, edited and translated by G. Henderson, London 1899, pp. 69 and 81.

42. H. Zimmer, *Keltische Beiträge*, Zeitschrift für deutsches Alterthum und deutsche Litteratur, Berlin 1889, Vol. XXXIII, p. 284.

43. *Táin bó Cualnge*, translated by H. d'Arbois de Jubainville, Paris 1907, p. 36.

44. H. Zimmer, *op. cit.*, p. 167.

45. *Li chevalier as deus éspées*, edited by W. Forster, Halle 1877, VV. 4804 *et seq.*, 5086.

46. G. Schoepperle, *op. cit.*, Vol. I, p. 162.

47. P. Mayer, 'La chanson de Doon Nanteuil', Fragments inédits, *Romania*, Vol. XIII, p. 22.

48. *Le Livre du chevalier de la Tour Landry*, Paris 1854, p. 268.

49. E. Meray, *La vie au temps des trouvères*, Paris 1873, pp. 76 *et seq.* and G. Schoepperle, *op. cit.*, Vol. I, pp. 254 *et seq.*

50. Fynes Moryson, *Itinerary*, Fol. 181, *Travels*, London 1617.

51. Abbé J. A. Dubois, *Hindu Manners, Customs and Ceremonies*, 3rd ed., reprinted 1947, pp. 593–4.

52. Dubois, *op. cit.*, p. 596.

53. M. Fortes, *The Web of Kinship*, Oxford 1949, p. 23.

54. Fortes, *op. cit.*, p. 117.

55. Fortes, *op. cit.*, p. 24.

56. R. Payne Knight, *Remains of the Worship of Priapus*, London 1786, pp. 5 *et seq.*

57. L. de Chenier, *The Present State of the Empire of Morocco*, translated London 1788, Vol. I, p. 187.

58. H. Egede, *Description of Greenland*, translated London 1774, p. 140.

59. Lactantius, *Diuinae Institutiones*, i, 20, 36.

60. *Herodotus*, Bk. 1, Ch. 199.

61. Justin, *Historiae Philippicae*, XVIII.

62. Eusebius, *Vita Constantini*, II 58 in J. P. Migne *Patrologiae*, Series Graeca, Paris 1857–66, Vol. XX, p. 1124.

63. Lucien, *De Syria dea*, 6.

64. J. G. Frazer, *Golden Bough*, London 1922, Vol. I, pp. 30–1.

65. R. Briffault, *The Mothers*, London 1927, Vol. III, p. 220.

66. S. I. Curtiss, *Primitive Semitic Religion To-day*, London 1902, pp. 154 *et seq.*

67. Dubois, *op. cit.*, pp. 584–6.
Corpus inscriptionium semiticarum, Paris 1881.

68. The matter may be pursued in E. Westermarck, *History of Human Marriage*, London 1921, Vol. I, Ch. VI, and J. G. Frazer, *Adonis, Attis, and Osiris*, London 1919, Vol. I, Chs. I–IV.

69. H. Bancroft, *The Native Races of the Pacific States of N. America*, N.Y. 1875–6, Vol. II, pp. 719 *et seq.*

70. R. E. Latcham, *Ethnology of the Araucanos*, J.R.A.I., XXXIX, p. 354.

71. P. J. de Arriaga, *Extirpacion de la idolatria del Piru* (Original 1621), Lima 1920, pp. 35 *et seq.*

72. V. Eric and P. Radin, *Contribution to the Study of the Bororo Indians*, J.R.A.I., XXXVI, p. 390.

73. A. L. Kroeber, *The Arapaho*, Bulletin of the Amer. Museum of Natural History, XVIII, p. 15.

74. B. Malinowski, *Natives of Mailu*, in Trans. Royal Soc. South Australia, Adelaide 1915, XXXIX, pp. 562 and 564.

75. T. E. Bowdich, *Mission from Cape Coast Castle to Ashantee*, London 1819, p. 226.

76. W. Crooke, *Religion and Folklore of Northern India*, 2nd ed., Oxford 1926, pp. 342–3.

77. R. Rousselet, *India and its Native Princes*, translation. London 1876, p. 173.

78. Dubois, *op. cit.*, p. 595.

79. The general significance of these rites has been dealt with exhaustively in J. G. Frazer, *The Scapegoat*, London 1919, Ch. VII, and *Adonis, Attis, and Osiris*, London 1919, 2 Vols.

L. R. Farnell, *Cults of the Greek States*, Oxford 1896.

J. E. Harrison, *Proleogomena to the Study of Greek Religion*, Cambridge 1908.

80. L. R. Farnell, *Cults of the Greek States*, Oxford 1896, Vol. V, p. 102.

81. M. P. Nilsson, *The Minoan Mycenaean Religion*, 2nd ed., University of Lund 1950, p. 567.

82. Farnell, *op. cit.*, p. 163.

83. Farnell, *op. cit.*, p. 164.

84. Nilsson, *op. cit.*, p. 503.

85. J. Allen, *Remnants of Early Latin*, London, N.D., pp. 28–31.

86. Juvenal *6th Satire*, 464–90, translated by W. G. Gifford, London 1817, Vol. I, pp. 239–40.

87. Horace, *Epistolae*, ii, 1. 148.

88. *Herodotus*, ii, 1. 148.

A. B. Ellis, *The Ewe-speaking Peoples of the Slave Coast*, London 1890, p. 44.

89. J. G. Frazer, *The Scapegoat*, London 1919, pp. 207–309.

90. E. K. Chambers, *The Mediaeval Stage*, Oxford 1903, Part I, pp. 317 et seq., and 336 et seq.

91. F. Cortet, *Essai sur les Fêtes réligieuses*, Paris 1867, pp. 53–6.

92. F. Cortet, *op. cit.*, p. 56.

93. J. G. Frazer, *The Scapegoat*, *op. cit.*, pp. 363–4.

94. L. Leger, *Chronique dite de Nestor*, Paris 1884, p. 10.

95. T. Volkor, *Rites et usages nuptiaux ex Ukraine*, L'Anthropologie, Vols. II–III, Paris 1891–2.

96. M. L. Ernst and D. Loth, *Sexual Behaviour and the Kinsey Report*, London 1949, pp. 129–32

POSTSCRIPT

WE have attempted to survey some aspects of the sexual activity of man in society. The field of enquiry is vast and we have only emphasised those aspects which appeared to be of significance in relation to our main theme. That theme is implicit in the preceding pages. Man is endowed with certain biological equipment which provides the basis for his sexual behaviour. Obviously without continued generation society cannot persist. The problem which confronts man is to secure the ordered sequence of events by which children are born in a socially approved way, and to satisfy his sexual needs. How the problem is solved depends upon the whole configuration of cultural factors which occur in a particular society at a particular time. In other words there is not one solution—there are an infinite number. The culture may permit the dominance of the sexually uninhibited woman as in the Marquesas Islands, or it may demand the austere sexual standards of the aboriginal Veddas of Ceylon. Neither solution is more correct than the other. They are merely different ways of solving the same problem.

For the individual in our own type of society a consideration of alternative methods of solution can be salutary. Not that we should adopt customs and practices evolved in another cultural context, but it may enable us to view our own institutions with a mind less full of righteousness. We have now reached the stage where more and more individuals are claiming the right to create their families in their own time and not nature's. Birth control has established sexual love in marriage on a different basis. Are we now prepared to extend the right of sexual love to the unmarried? Are adolescents to continue their explorations of sex in the clandestine and furtive manner characteristic of this phase of sexual life? We are now beginning to recognise the distinction between the reproductive principle in marriage and the enjoyment of sexual pleasure. Will society sanction the expression of adolescent sexuality? It is possible that a consideration of the sexual behaviour of societies other than our own might help towards a solution of such problems.

ACKNOWLEDGMENTS

I. Schapera, *Married Life in an African Tribe*, Faber and Faber, 1940.

J. Peristiany, *The Social Institutions of the Kipsigis*, Routledge, 1939.

B. Malinowski, *The Sexual Life of Savages*, Routledge, 1932.

V. Elwin, *The Murias and their Ghotul*, O.U.P., 1947.

E. E. Evans-Pritchard, *Kinship and Marriage among the Nuer*, O.U.P., 1951.

G. Gorer, *Himalayan Village*, Michael Joseph, 1938.

INDEX

2

INDEX OF SIMPLE SOCIETIES
referred to in the text

431